All The King's Armies

All The King's Armies

A Military History of the English Civil War 1642–1651

STUART REID

British Library Cataloguing in Publication Data:
A catalogue record for this book is available
from the British Library

ISBN 1–86227–028–7

First published in the UK in 1998 by
Spellmount Limited
The Old Rectory
Staplehurst
Kent TN12 0AZ

1 3 5 7 9 8 6 4 2

Typeset by Palimpsest Book Production Limited
Polmont, Stirlingshire
Printed in Great Britain by
T.J. International Ltd
Padstow, Cornwall

Contents

List of Maps

List of Plates

1 William Barriffe: as the author of *The Young Artilleryman*, Barriffe was one of the more influential figures in shaping infantry tactics during the English Civil War.

2 Cuirassier equipment as depicted in John Cruso's *Militarie Instructions for the Cavallrie* – and cribbed from an earlier work by Wallhausen. A number of individuals and Lifeguard units were equipped as cuirassiers.

3 Sir Thomas, afterwards Lord, Fairfax, Lord General of Parliament's forces.

4 Marston Moor: the Cromwell Monument, marking the approximate area in which he defeated Goring's cavalry in the closing stages of the battle. The Allied front line was probably drawn up along the road in front of the Monument, while the Royalist front line was in the distant hedgerow.

5 Streeter's famous engraving of the Battle of Naseby.

6 Although the musket-rest was little used in the Civil War this illustration from Jacob de Geyhn's *Exercise of Arms* (1607) provides a good picture of a musketeer's equipment.

7 The Swedish Brigade

8 William Cavendish

9 Marston Moor: the Allied position. The front line was almost certainly drawn up along the road in the foreground and the second line on the low ridge behind. The third line was hidden in the dead ground between this ridge and the higher one crowned by 'Cromwell's Plump', seen in the distance.

10 Cavalry fight as depicted in Cruso's *Militarie Instructions for the Cavallrie*.

All pictures are from the author's collection.

To all who go about the manor of Kentwell

Preface

In the year of our Lord 1639 there began an unparalleled conflict in the three kingdoms of Britain. It is popularly known as the *English* Civil War, but it began first in Scotland, then spread to Ireland and by the time it ended a little over twenty years later, men had died on battlefields as far apart as Caithness and Cornwall, and from Flanders to Virginia.

This book is primarily a military history of the three periods of Civil War fought in England between 1642 and 1651 As such it has two principal objectives. The first and perhaps rather obvious one is to chronicle the military operations and to highlight those actions, battles and campaigns which had a more or less decisive effect upon the course of the war and its ultimate outcome.

Inevitably decisions have had to be made as to which battles and incidents *were* important or at the very least merited some examination and which, regrettably, should be omitted or passed over with barely a mention. This is by no means as straightforward a task as it might at first appear for there is always a tendency among historians to follow the available material and give undue prominence to events which are well documented irrespective of their actual significance. An excellent case in point might be the action at Chalgrove Field in June 1643, and it is hard to escape a strong suspicion that Sir Ralph (later Lord) Hopton's high reputation owes much more to his very readable memoirs than to his military achievements. On the other hand, while the battle of Marston Moor is well documented, the campaign in Northumberland and the major battle outside Sunderland which preceded it are all but forgotten.

At the same time it has also been necessary in writing this study to adopt a flexible approach to the chronology of events. The war was fought on a number of fronts, and rather than switch from one to another at periodic intervals, it was thought best to follow each campaign from its outset to its end and only to switch at natural break-points. Thus it has been found helpful to treat the war on the central front and the war in the north as two entirely separate conflicts and, for example, to follow the fortunes of the King's army in 1644 from Cheriton to the Second Battle of Newbury without interruption.

The second objective of this study is to examine the evolution of military doctrine during the war, and to illustrate the way in which military operations were influenced by the availability of arms and

ix

ammunition as much as by normal strategic and tactical considerations. An obvious case in point is the increasing reliance on firearms by both sides which extended to many regiments abandoning pikes altogether before the process was partially reversed in the New Model Army created by Parliament in 1645.

I make no apology for paying scant regard in these pages to the political and religious aspects of the war. This is a study of how the war was fought on the battlefields, and I am pleased to leave discussion of its other aspects to those better qualified than myself.

In closing it is customary to thank those who have assisted in some manner. They are of course a numerous band, but particular thanks are due to David Ryan, Dr Les Prince, Keith Roberts, John Tincey, John Barratt and all the other participants in the very lively discussion group centred on Partizan Press.

Introduction

The Beginning of the Wars

As this is a military rather than a social, religious or political history of the English Civil War, it is sufficient for the present purpose to appreciate that the war was essentially a conflict between the forces of absolutism, as represented by the King himself and his Archbishop of Canterbury on the one hand, and the rising power of Parliament and the Protestant middle classes on the other.

In 1603 King James VI of Scotland had the great good fortune to succeed Queen Elizabeth to the English throne as well. Grateful for the opportunity to escape from the endless round of plots, coups and bloody murder, which passed for court life in 16th-century Scotland, he hurried southwards with quite indecent haste to assume his inheritance. His new English court was probably just as much inclined to intrigue as his old Scottish one, but at least James now no longer had to contend with pitched battles fought within the confines of the palace itself, and armed gangs unceremoniously bursting into his bedchamber variously intent on intimidation, kidnapping, or even assassination.

As a monarch who had been forced to spend the greater part of his life in constant terror of its violent termination, James naturally warmed to the doctrine of the Divine Right of Kings, and was gratified to find that his new English subjects appeared willing at least to pay lip service to the concept. Nevertheless he remained astute enough not to push his luck, and the doctrine remained no more than a useful philosophical idea rather than a political reality until the accession of his son, Charles I in 1625.

Unfortunately, Charles not only genuinely believed that he was by God anointed and consequently possessed of something akin to a Protestant equivalent of Papal infallibility, but he also attempted, initially with some success, to put the doctrine into practice by dismissing his less than co-operative Parliament in 1629 and ruling as an absolute monarch for the next eleven years. During this time his most pressing need was to raise sufficient revenue to meet his growing expenditures. Although the courts upheld his royal prerogative to do so without the authority of Parliament the imposition of additional taxes and in particular the extension of 'Ship-money' to inland as well as coastal areas, proved particularly unpopular. Ultimately however it was to be his ecclesiastical policies that were his undoing.

· ENGLAND · IN THE · CIVIL WAR ·

From absolutism in secular matters to absolutism in religious matters is but a short step. Both Scotland and England were preeminently Protestant, and for the past hundred years they had also in effect been engaged in a low-level cold war with the Catholic states of Europe. Consequently Charles' unyielding determination that his subjects should accept a more rigidly hierarchical structure in the Church of England, his marriage to a French Catholic princess in 1625, and his subsequent pursuit of a Spanish alliance all served to raise uncomfortable suspicions in some quarters that a return to Rome might perhaps be his ultimate aim.

Very broadly speaking the Civil War was also to be in some degree a struggle between town and country in as much as Protestantism and its associated secular politics were most strongly rooted in the industrialised and commercial centres, while rural areas were still dominated for the most part by a conservative squirearchy. The reasons for this are quite simple and again illustrate the degree to which politics and religion were inextricably linked. In the first place of course, the local squire was able to exert a considerable degree of direct pressure upon his tenantry, particularly if an estate had been held by his family long enough for a tradition of service to become firmly established. Even where it had not, the squire could still exert a more subtle pressure through the medium of the church.

In the 17th century the minister of a rural parish did much more than simply preach the word of God, for his pulpit also provided a platform from which the news of the day could be disseminated to a largely illiterate population. Naturally the 'slant' placed upon that news almost invariably reflected the viewpoint of the King and his bishops as well as that of the local landowner who had nominated the minister in the first place. It was possible for contrary views to be heard at markets, but inevitably such contacts were normally too transient to have much real effect upon local opinion.

In towns and other commercial/industrial centres it was a very different matter, since the obligations which a squire could impose on his rural tenants did not apply. Indeed many municipalities seem to have gone out of their way to oppose the local landowners as a matter of principle. It was also relatively easy for an individual to exercise some degree of choice as to where and in what manner he worshipped. Moreover not only were levels of literacy higher in towns but there was obviously a far greater level of opportunity for the exchange of political as well as religious ideas both within the community and with the wider world beyond.[1]

This is of course something of an over-simplification, but it can actually be seen quite clearly in Lancashire. There the impoverished agricultural Hundreds of Lonsdale, Leyland, West Derby and in particular the Fylde country of Amounderness Hundred were strongly Catholic and for the King, while the weaving and clothworking communities in the Blackburn and Salford Hundreds, centred on Bolton, Blackburn and Manchester, were both strongly Protestant and pro-Parliamentarian. Although some Catholics made strenuous efforts to avoid any kind of involvement in the struggle, contemporaries were in no doubt that religion was a major factor in deciding political allegiance in this area. Bolton indeed was so militantly Protestant as to be popularly known as the 'Geneva of the North', and in 1644 hundreds of soldiers and civilians were massacred when the town was stormed by Catholic troops.

Lancashire might well be somewhat untypical in hosting two such dramatically disparate communities in such close proximity to each other, but if the colours are a little too sharply drawn to be truly representative, they do serve to provide a microcosm of what the war was all about. On the one side was the arbitrary rule of the old order as represented by the Earl of Derby and his Catholic tenantry, and on the other the rising power and confidence of the commercial and industrial middle classes and their militantly Protestant workforce.

Although the King's religious reforms were swallowed uneasily in England, his attempt to impose similar reforms on the far more radically Protestant Scottish church precipitated disaster. Charles had originally paid very little attention to his Scottish kingdom. His father had crossed the border with few obvious regrets, and he himself did not even deign to visit Edinburgh for his coronation until 1633 – eight years after his accession to the throne! Then, having rather belatedly woken up to the fact that he possessed a northern kingdom, he ordered a broad range of measures aimed at bringing the government of both church and state into conformity with English practice. In itself this was bad enough, but in order to finance the reforms Charles also announced his intention of recovering former church lands from the families who had held them since the Reformation. Understandably both these high-handed moves so alarmed the Scots that a formidable combination of otherwise disparate opposition groups came into being, and formalised their rejection of the planned reforms by signing the famous National Covenant of 1638. Oliver Cromwell was afterwards to declare that the Civil War did not begin as a religious conflict, but in reality, just as there was but a small step from political to religious absolutism in the 17th century, so now Charles discovered to his cost that once men began to defy his religious authority as self-proclaimed head of the church, they were all the readier to carry their dispute over into secular matters and defy his authority as head of state as well.

A challenge to Royal authority of the National Covenant's magnitude could not be ignored, and like any self-respecting 17th-century monarch, the King felt compelled to meet it with military force. The problem was that he had no regular military forces at his immediate disposal. He was forced to rely upon unenthusiastic levies drawn from the Trained Bands, and in 1639 his planned invasion of Scotland ground to an ignominious halt without even crossing the border. A second attempt in the following year only invited a Scottish counter-invasion, defeat in battle and the capture of Newcastle upon Tyne for the first time in hundreds of years of cross-border conflict.

The protracted Scots crisis, often referred to as the Bishops' Wars, and the humiliating concessions which followed it only served to reveal the extent of the King's vulnerability. This point was underlined by his being forced to call a Parliament, the so-called 'Long Parliament', in order to raise the money needed to keep the victorious Scots north of the river Tees. Even here Charles miscalculated, for this Parliament, like the 'Short Parliament' which preceded the war, proved to be militantly unco-operative. It was far more interested in asserting what it regarded as its legitimate rights and privileges, and in opposing the King's religious policies, than in voting for taxes to aid the Crown in quashing the very similar rights being defended by the Scots.

Hostilities were officially brought to a close by the Treaty of Ripon signed on 26 October 1640, but savouring their triumph the Scots held on to Newcastle until the following August, thus giving the new Parliament time to consolidate its position. A visit to Edinburgh by the King late in 1641, ostensibly to attend to the fine print of a peace settlement, was marked in the very best Scottish tradition by a bungled coup against the leading Covenanters. Betrayed at the last minute the 'Incident' as it was quaintly referred to was no sooner smoothed over than the King's early morning round of golf on 28 October 1641 was interrupted by news of a bloody rebellion in Ireland.

There was a small standing army in Ireland which Charles had at one time hoped to employ against the Scots in 1639 and in 1640, and notwithstanding the contrary advice of his advisers on the spot, he had also proposed to reinforce that army with fresh levies drawn from amongst the Catholic 'Old Irish'. Predictably this particular plan never reached fruition,[2] but the King's apparent willingness to employ the army outside Ireland raised suspicions at Westminster that he might also be prepared to contemplate employing it against his dissident English subjects. Whether or not such a move was actually contemplated is immaterial, for when the army's commander, the Earl of Strafford, was so incautious as to utter certain remarks which might conceivably bear that interpretation, he was promptly impeached by Parliament and then executed six months later.

Apart from hardening the King in his growing determination to grant no further concessions to the opposition, this execution only served to underline Parliament's paranoid hostility towards the 'Old Irish'.

Unfortunately it did so just at the very time when the failure of the Scots War was demonstrating to the Irish that a rebellion had every chance of succeeding against a militarily impotent Crown.

The importance of the Irish rebellion cannot be over-emphasised, for whilst the Scots War had been a surprisingly civilised affair, the Irish one was accompanied by widespread ethnic cleansing of the worst kind. The true scale of the massacres and the number of Protestant refugees harried out into the snow or killed over the winter of 1641-2 was certainly exaggerated by contemporary propagandists. Nevertheless there is no doubting that most people on the mainland genuinely believed at the time that tens of thousands of Protestants were being barbarously murdered by their Catholic neighbours – and they responded accordingly.

Ever since King Henry VIII had broken with Rome because he would not accept that the Pope's authority transcended his own, English (and Irish) Catholics had been feared and distrusted. This suspicion sprang not from simple doctrinal differences, but rather from the much more urgent fear that English Catholics considered their first loyalty was to the Papacy rather than to the Crown. Worse still they might conceive themselves to have more in common with foreigners who shared their faith, than with their Protestant neighbours. Consequently the violent outbreak of an overtly Catholic rebellion in Ireland in 1641 raised very real fears that English Catholics might also rise in support of their Irish co-religionists. These fears in turn had a strong influence on patterns of support for King or Parliament in the wider conflict which followed.

The Irish crisis demanded an army to suppress the rebellion and the raising of it led to the final breach between King and Parliament. The question was the outwardly simple one of who should control this army. The King considered, perhaps with some considerable justice and at any rate the overwhelming weight of precedent, that all military forces should come under the authority of the Crown. On the other hand, Parliament was by this time only too alive to the possibility that he might be tempted to turn the regiments upon his unruly English subjects before succouring the Irish Protestants.

These suspicions were dramatically borne out in the first week of January 1642. His enthusiasm for conspiracy undimmed by the failures of an abortive 'Army Plot' and the Scottish 'Incident' little more than two months earlier, Charles attempted to have five leading members of Parliament arrested. Denied legal sanction for the move, he tried to effect their seizure by invading the House of Commons with an armed gang. Duly warned, his prey escaped him, but the wheel had turned full circle. King James VI had abandoned Scotland in order to escape such dramatic interventions in government. Now his son had become a leading exponent of the technique and so precipitated a full-scale civil war.

With Parliament and the London mob united against him, the King fled from London on 10 January 1642 and eventually made his way to York. For the moment Ireland and the suffering Protestants were forgotten and both sides rallied their forces.

NOTES

1. This also applied to the Royal Navy whose personnel were largely drawn from the urban commercial and working classes – a ship was in a very real sense an industrial undertaking. It is hardly surprising therefore that despite the money lavished upon it by the King, the Navy should have declared for Parliament on 2 July 1642.
2. One regiment was sent to garrison Carlisle in 1640 but none of the expeditionary forces ever sailed.

CHAPTER I

All the King's Horses and all the King's Men:
The Soldiers

Before proceeding further it is necessary to pause for a moment and look at the nature of the forces being raised by King and Parliament. In the years leading up to the Civil War the military forces of the Crown comprised little more than the Sovereign's personal bodyguards and a handful of chronically underpaid gunners and garrison soldiers whose principal job seems to have been to prevent anyone from walking off with the cannon and stores left in their charge. Consequently England still relied, as it had in Elizabethan times, upon the county militias both for its own defence and also for operations farther afield, such as the wars with Scotland in 1639 and 1640.

Whilst it was in theory possible to call up every able-bodied man, the terms Militia and Trained Bands were to all intents and purposes synonymous. The latter, sometimes also known as the Freeholders' Bands, were, as their alternative title indicates, supposedly composed of men who actually owned or leased land: 'none of the meaner sort, nor servants; but only such as be of the Gentrie, Freeholders, and good Farmers, or their sonnes, that are like to be resident.' Far from being a rustic peasant rabble, they were to be men of some substance who had a stake in the country and a consequent interest in preserving it from foreign invasion or domestic insurrection. Nevertheless, while the Lieutenant or his deputy might be greatly encouraged (and perhaps astonished as well) by the appearance of a local magnate at a muster, attended by his sons and tenants in all the awful panoply of war, it was generally considered no great matter if only his servants and hired substitutes turned up instead. Notwithstanding which William Barriffe complained of how 'Porters, Colliars, Water-bearers, & Broom men, are thrust into the rooms of men of better quality, as though they themselves were too good to do the King and their Country service.'[1]

Not surprisingly this militia has often been dismissed as ineffectual where it was not actually moribund, and indeed it is suggested that the best use which the King could make of it in 1642 was simply to disarm it in order to equip his own volunteer regiments.[2] Nevertheless the initial reliance by both sides upon voluntary recruiting rather than calling out the Bands did not reflect their supposed inefficiency – after all the volun-

1

teers who replaced them could scarcely be expected to be any better trained or equipped – but was rather an acknowledgement that neither side possessed sufficient authority to cause the Bands to be mustered and to march wheresoever they were required. It was simply much easier to ask for volunteers. In any case, once the territorial limits of the opposing factions did become well established, considerable use was in fact made of the Bands by both sides although, with some notable exceptions, they tended to stay in their home areas.

As to the marching regiments, they were initially recruited by beat of drum and by the exertions of the local gentry, which is a polite way of saying that some men volunteered without compulsion and others came forward because their landlord or employer told them to. Naturally enough there was a limit to the number of men who could be raised in this manner, especially once the initial enthusiasm evaporated, and both sides soon resorted to more formal methods of conscription, including, in its most direct form, demands that the parish constables produce a certain number of able-bodied and decently clothed men on a certain date. It is little wonder therefore that desertion should have been so rife later in the war or that the common soldiers so readily changed sides when taken prisoner.

THE OFFICERS

The absence of a standing army before the Civil War has fostered the notion that it was an affair conducted by amateurs. By comparison with the previous civil war in the 15th century this may very well have been so, but in fact even at the outset there was no shortage of technical expertise on either side. The Dutch and Spaniards had been at each other's throats in the Low Countries for over seventy years, and since 1618 an even greater conflict had been raging in Germany. Both wars, or rather series of wars, provided ample employment opportunities for younger sons and other adventurous souls. For the most part the English ones seem to have learned their trade in Protestant Holland, a choice readily explained by the close cultural, trading and sometimes family links which existed between south-east England and the Low Countries. While some Scots also fought for the Dutch, most of them went farther afield, serving in both the French and most notably in the Swedish armies. Nor was foreign service confined to the Protestant powers. Scots and Englishmen were also to be found in the Imperial and Spanish armies and a few, such as Sir Arthur Aston, even went as far as Poland and Muscovy.

All in all, there was a considerable body of experience available to the opposing commanders. Indeed the King's General for much of the war was Patrick Ruthven (Lord Forth in the Scottish peerage and later Earl of Brentford in the English), who spent thirty years in the Swedish service before coming home in 1638. On the other side the Earl of Essex, though perhaps not able to boast as much experience, had commanded a regiment in the Dutch service and fought under Sir Horace Vere in the Palatinate.

Over sixty officers in the Parliamentarian army at Edgehill were professional soldiers, as were at least thirty on the King's side including Sir Arthur Aston, Sir Jacob Astley, Charles Gerard, Richard Fielding, and Sir Nicholas Byron and his nephews. Indeed only one of the King's infantry brigades was not commanded by a professional soldier. In Scotland the recruitment of professional soldiers was handled quite systematically. Even before the armies began to be raised Scots officers serving abroad were invited to return home and paid retainers until employment could be found for them. In the main, Scottish regiments and companies were entrusted to local magnates but they were backed up by professional soldiers at every level. Wherever possible lieutenant colonels, majors, lieutenants and even sergeants were chosen from amongst the large pool of veterans.

The vast majority of the officers on both sides however had no military experience beyond what some of them might have picked up at Trained Band musters. Some inevitably learned the hard way or died trying, others turned to drill-books. It is a little appreciated fact that the invention of printing revolutionised warfare by making theoretical and practical texts readily available to potential officers.

At a company and even regimental level there were a bewildering selection of drill-books, theoretical texts and even military memoirs upon which the newly commissioned officer could draw. Some, such as John Bingham's *Taktics of Aelian,* a comparative study of classical texts and the more modern doctrines of Mauritz von Nassau, probably went over the heads of most, but there were also more accessible titles. In addition to the very basic *Directions for Musters* produced in 1638 to give Trained Band officers a grounding in infantry drill, there was William Barriffe's very much more comprehensive (and influential) *Militarie Discipline: or the Young Artillery-man.* This went through six editions between 1635 and 1661 and despite its slightly misleading title, it may fairly be considered to have been the standard work on infantry. As to the cavalry there seems to have been broad agreement that the most important treatise was John Cruso's *Militarie Instructions for the Cavallrie,* first published in 1632 and sufficiently well thought of to be reprinted at Cambridge in 1644.

By and large however, most of these works, whose initial target audience was Trained Band officers and the members of volunteer military societies, are pitched at a fairly low tactical level. Both *Directions for Musters* and Cruso's *Militarie Instructions* are aimed primarily at the officers of companies and troops. Barriffe goes a stage further and also deals with battalion-sized formations, but the handling of brigades and higher formations was very largely a matter of practical experience, and it was there that the professionals made their mark.

THE INFANTRY

The basic tactical unit was what might best be referred to as a battalion, although the term was not much used at the time. In theory infantrymen were organised in regiments commanded by colonels, each subdivided into a number of companies commanded by captains. Ideally there should have been ten companies each with its own colour or flag and numbering at least 100 men[3], but in practice a regiment could comprise anything from three to thirteen or fourteen companies, and would be counted lucky if they all mustered as many as thirty soldiers apiece. This was particularly true of Royalist formations. The King's Lifeguard, exceptionally, may have had as many as thirteen companies at the outset, but seven companies, and sometimes fewer appears to have been the rule since commanders preferred to maintain the numbers of soldiers in each company at a reasonable level even if this meant disbanding weak ones and drafting their personnel into the stronger ones. Consequently intelligence reports on both sides tended to estimate the strength of enemy formations from the number of colours on display.

As a further complication, the fact that most units comprised two quite distinct types of soldier – pikemen and musketeers – meant that a regiment's constituent companies did not line up one beside the other, but were broken up before going into action, and their personnel formed into combined divisions of the respective arms. It is a commonly held belief, in part fostered by that famous row at Edgehill, that there were two quite distinct tactical doctrines – the Dutch and the Swedish – employed by the Civil War armies. In reality both the authors, Mauritz von Nassau and Gustaf Adolf respectively, were in their graves long before the war began, and the distinctions between them had long since been blurred by practical experience. This is most strikingly revealed in the case of the Scottish army. Given the considerable body of officers trained in the Swedish service, it would be reasonable to suppose that Swedish doctrines were employed, yet there is not one single example of Scots regiments adopting the infantry formation known as the 'Swedish Brigade'. Instead they were invariably drawn up in the battalion formations common to all of the armies fighting in Germany and the Low Countries by that time. Ordinarily the pike division was deployed in the centre of the battalion with the musketeers forming on either flank. The optimum size for such a formation – usually drawn up six deep – seems to have been about 300-500 men. Very large regiments, recruited well up to their theoretical strength, could and did form two battalions, but conversely it was much commoner to find two or more very weak regiments combining to form a single battalion rather than each standing alone.

At the outset of the Civil War the ideal was regarded as one pikeman for every two musketeers, and the regiments raised to go to Ireland at the beginning of 1642 were not only organised in that ratio, but also mustered a company of firelocks, presumably to act as skirmishers in the bogs and woods. Frequently enough in the early days a shortage of muskets dictated a more equal division. For example, on 18 February 1643 a muster discovered that out of 513 soldiers serving in the King's Lifeguard of Foot – which certainly ought to have been properly equipped – no fewer than 322 men were completely unarmed. By 23 April some firearms and a total of 212 pikes had been issued which would certainly suggest an equality of pike and shot. Nevertheless this situation did not last, particularly after the Royalists captured the Bristol firearms manufactories in 1643, and the proportion of pikemen declined dramatically. By March 1644 both the King's and Queen's Lifeguards were being issued with 'Two parts Musquetts with Bandaliers, and the rest Pikes', while an increasing number of units were being armed with muskets alone.

It was a similar story in the Parliamentarian ranks. Although most of the 1642 regiments were properly equipped, at least two, Lord Saye and Sele's, and Lord Wharton's, had to make do with three musketeers to two pikemen and one for one respectively. Like their Royalist counterparts however, Parliamentarian officers soon began fielding much greater numbers of musketeers, and when Essex's army was re-equipped after having been disarmed in the Lostwithiel disaster in 1644, the 6,000 remaining foot were issued with 5,000 muskets and only 1,000 pikes.

However disposed, when infantrymen fought each other in the open field, the two opposing battalions would normally march towards each other, occasionally exchanging fire before coming to a halt at a distance of twenty or thirty yards in order to let the musketeers concentrate on winning the firefight. Sooner or later however, one of the battalions might feel sufficiently confident to advance into physical contact with the other. In practice this could be a protracted and indecisive business, but the Royalists, perhaps because they were chronically short of ammunition, seem to have been prone to firing only a single volley before falling on with swords, pikes and the butt-ends of muskets.

While it seems to have been by no means uncommon for pikemen to throw down their pikes and fall on with swords, deliberate encounters between two opposing stands of pikemen were generally conducted at 'push of pike'. This was by no means as dangerous as it might at first appear, and hostile commentators such as Daniel Lupton claimed that it was virtually impossible for a pikeman to run someone through, even if he was only wearing a buffcoat. The real object of the exercise seems to have been to push the opposition back sufficiently violently to cause them to lose their footing, or better still to break and run. Nevertheless both sides needed to enter into the spirit of the occasion and, if one side was less than enthusiastic, the push might only be a token one with the reluctant party throwing down its pikes and giving way almost at once.

If neither side was too keen on the idea they might even be reduced to an ineffective 'foyning' or fencing, standing off at a pike's length and going through the motions of jabbing at each other while they waited for something to turn up. After the initial clash the infantry battle at Edgehill in 1642 seems to have settled down into an affair of this kind:

> When the Royalist army was advanced within musket shot of the enemy [wrote the future King James] the foot on both sides began to give fire, the King's coming on and the Rebells continuing only to keep their ground, so that they came so near one another that some of the battalions were at push of pike, particularly the regiment of the Guards . . . The foot thus being engaged in such warm and close service, it were reasonable to suppose that one side should run and be disordered; but it happened otherwise, for each as if by mutual consent retired some few paces, and then struck down their colours, continuing to fire at each other even until night, a thing so extraordinary as nothing less than so many witnesses as were present could make it credible.[4]

In the smaller battles it seems to have been the practice for all the pikemen of the army to be gathered together in one reasonably large body or stand rather than scattered along the line in penny-packets. This stand would then be kept in reserve until the decisive moment. A good example of this is provided by Adwalton Moor in 1643. Initially the battle began as a firefight along the line of a hedge and ditch separating the Marquis of Newcastle's Royalist musketeers and Lord Fairfax's men. Although in overall terms the Parliamentarians were outnumbered, they seem to have had rather more musketeers than the Royalists, and after a time they began to drive them back. Fairfax appeared to be on the point of victory but then Colonel Posthumous Kirton, the commander of Newcastle's own regiment, led the massed Royalist pikemen in a charge against the Parliamentarian left:

> At last the pikes of my Lord's army having no employment all the day were drawn against the enemy's left wing, and particularly those of my Lord's own regiment . . . who fell so furiously upon the enemy, that they forsook their hedges, and fell to their heels.[5]

While such examples were suitably dramatic affairs, they worked through sheer intimidation and were not as a rule typical. The pikeman's primary role was not to kill other infantrymen but to defend the flanking musketeers against hostile cavalry. William Barriffe illustrates a surprising variety of formations which could be adopted for this purpose, including hollow squares similar in conception if not necessarily in appearance to those employed at Waterloo. On the other hand, although they doubtless formed diverting exercises to be practised by the various pre-war military clubs, most of the squares appear rather too complicated for a real battlefield – indeed Barriffe freely admits as much and there is little contemporary evidence of such formations being adopted in action. On the contrary, all too often the usual reaction of infantrymen was simply to run away from cavalrymen and Barriffe recommends arming musketeers with half-pikes in order to fend off cavalry:

> Whole pikes alone are too weak, because the Horseman carries fiery weapons, & can kill the Pike-man at a distance, they neither being able to defend themselves, nor offend their enemies. Secondly, musquettiers with Rests, are not able in open Campania, to withstand the able and resolute Horse-men, which will break them through & through. Thirdly, both conjoyned in one body, are too weak in open and even Countries to withstand the Horse: for if your Pikes be flanked with Musquettiers (according to the usual manner) then the Horse-men kill the Pikes at a distance (as aforesaid) and rout and plunder the Musquettiers on the flanks, they having little possibility of aid from their Pike-men, when the Horse are entred pell-mell amongst the Musquettiers, knocking and treading them down. [6]

While the bayonet eventually proved to be a much better idea than encumbering the poor musketeer with a half-pike in addition to all his other kit, the important point to note here is that Barriffe clearly implies that hollow squares were seldom if ever employed during the Civil War. Instead they maintained their normal battalion formation, and what normally happened is revealed by Richard Elton, a Parliamentarian officer who like Barriffe had once been a member of the Society of the Artillery Garden:

> In my opinion the best way of opposing the Horse charge is that which we learned of our ever honoured Captain, Major Henry Tillier in the Military Garden; which was Files closing to the midst to their closest order, insomuch that there was not above half a foot intervall of ground between File and File, the pikes Porting, and after closing their ranks forward so close, that they locked themselves one within another, and then charged on. Which in my judgement is so secure a way from routing, that it is impossible for any body of Horse to enter therein.[7]

Despite the fact that he was often employed both to deliver the decisive blow in the infantry battle and to defend the musketeer against the cavalryman, the pikeman's relative importance declined quite dramatically during the war. Next to the cavalryman, the grimly armoured pikeman is perhaps one of the more enduring images of the Civil War soldier, yet both he and his armour were rapidly becoming an anachronism on battlefields dominated by musketeers. The fully equipped pikeman is well illustrated by the Dutch artist, Jacob de Geyhn. However, as far as the Civil War soldier is concerned, De Geyhn's prints are extremely misleading on one very important point. His pikeman wears a corselet, comprising back and breast plates, covering the torso, a pair of tassets protecting the thighs, a gorget or steel collar at the throat, and an iron headpiece, commonly referred to as a 'pikeman's pot', doubtless because it served just as well for cooking as it did for protection. Just how much armour was actually worn during the Civil War is a moot point. The Earl of Clarendon famously remarked of the King's army at Edgehill:

> . . . the foot (all but three or four hundred who marched without any weapon but a cudgel) were armed with muskets, and bags for their powder, and pikes; but in the whole body there was not one pikeman had a corselet, and very few musketeers who had swords.[8]

Nor was Parliament's army much better. Initially at least two of the Earl of Essex's London-based regiments may have been provided with corselets, and at least one other may have received armour after Edgehill, but no armour appears to have been purchased or issued after the early part of 1643.[9] Indeed, although the pike itself was considered by military theorists to be the more honourable weapon, its comparative ineffectiveness soon created a tendency towards the entirely understandable view that 'real' soldiers carried muskets. As for the tactics employed by the musketeers, it is necessary first to appreciate the limitations of their weapons and how those limitations were overcome.

The musket most commonly used during the Civil War was the matchlock – fired as its name implies by touching off the priming charge with a piece of burning slow-match. It was cheap, robust and usually reasonably reliable. There were, however, a number of drawbacks to the weapon. In the first place, practice was necessary to gauge the correct setting of the match in the lock, and if firing was delayed for any reason, the match required constant adjustment as it burned down. In wet weather it was virtually useless. The flash pan cover had to be opened manually before firing, and the priming charge might easily, therefore, become soaked, although the biggest problem was that once the slow-match became damp it refused to burn hotly enough to ignite the powder.

Besides the matchlock, increasing quantities of the more expensive firelock came into use during the war. The firelock took a number of forms, such as snaphaunces, and wheel-locks, but the commonest was what is generally now known as a flintlock. This was a much handier weapon, though rather less soldier-proof than the matchlock. Generally speaking firelocks were given in the first instance to sentries, artillery guards and General officers' lifeguards, since they had to be ready to use their weapons at all times and would otherwise burn up immense quantities of slow-match. However they were also issued to small special service or ranger companies, themselves referred to as Firelocks, in much the same manner that some later sharpshooters became termed Riflemen.

Notwithstanding the firelock's apparent advantages, the matchlock remained the commonest form of firearm throughout the period, largely because it was cheap and comparatively robust. Moreover, although an individual soldier might find it highly advantageous to be armed with a firelock, there was little real difference in their battle performance since the limitations of the matchlock were sufficiently well recognised for tactical doctrines and unit drills to be devised which minimised their effect.

Depending on his level of training, a musketeer could reasonably be expected to have reloaded well within a minute of having fired. This did not, however, mean that during that time his regiment stood helpless in the face of an attack. The depth of the formation adopted reflected the loading time. Regiments were normally drawn up six men deep and in a firefight discharged their muskets one rank at a time. The front rank, having fired, fell away to the rear to reload, followed in succession by the other five until, by the time all six had fired, the original front rank was back in place to begin the cycle anew. Thus it was possible for a regiment to fire off some kind of volley, not every thirty or sixty seconds, but every ten seconds.

Nevertheless it was also possible for massed volleys or *salvees* to be delivered by three ranks at once, but for obvious reasons this was only resorted to in certain circumstances; either to precede a headlong assault – something which increasingly became a Royalist trademark – or else to receive one, particularly by cavalry.

THE CAVALRY

Cavalrymen were organised first and foremost into troops, which like infantry companies were led by a captain and generally mustered anything between thirty and a hundred men. Although many operated as independent formations, it was normal for them to be brigaded together to form regiments ideally comprising about six troops. The Royalists certainly appear to have aimed at such an establishment with three of the troops commanded by field officers; colonel, lieutenant colonel and major, and three or sometimes four captains commanding the others. For example at Cropredy Bridge on 29 June 1644 Lord Wilmot's Brigade comprised four regiments, the Lord General's and Prince Maurice's, each mustering seven troops, Colonel Thomas Howard's with eight and Colonel Gerard Croker's with only two. Parliamentarian units were similarly organised save that their establishment included a colonel and major, but no lieutenant colonel.

John Cruso, in his magisterial *Militarie Instructions for the Cavallrie* divided that arm into two classes, heavy cavalry which comprised lancers and cuirassiers, and light cavalry which comprised harque-busiers, carbines and dragooners. Both of the former wore three-quarter armour, while the latter were much more lightly mounted and equipped. While Cruso's book certainly appears to have been used by the Parliamentarians at least as an unofficial manual – it was reprinted at Cambridge in 1644 – there was inevitably perhaps some considerable divergence from his ideal. There were, for example, no lancers. Although they had appeared in comparatively large numbers at Trained Band musters as recently as 1637, the anonymous 'J.B.' who contributed a supplement on cavalry to the 1661 edition of Barriffe dismissed lancers with the comment that they were not used at all.[10] Fully equipped cuirassiers were nearly as scarce, and most Civil War cavalrymen proba-bly looked like harquebusiers or carbines. In theory the two should have been distinguished by the first wearing a corselet while the latter relied upon his buff-coat alone, but in practice no such distinction was possible and many a harquebusier rode forth protected only by a buff-coat.

It may seem odd that armoured harquebusiers should have been regarded as light cavalry, but appreciation of this point is necessary to understand why the Royalist horse should at first have been so very much superior to their Parliamentarian opponents. According to Cruso and the other contemporary authorities, the cuirassier was regarded as the heavy, battle-winning cavalryman. His function, in brutally simple terms, was to ride down the opposition by locking up knee to knee and charging 'in full career'. Harquebusiers on the other hand, as light cavalry, were expected to guard the flanks and rear of the cuirassier formations. Consequently they were primarily armed with carbines and pistols and expected to use them rather than emulating their heavier comrades by charging home.

Conventionally the initial superiority of the Royalist horse is attrib-uted to Prince Rupert's introduction of Swedish tactical doctrines which supposedly emphasised the use of shock tactics rather than firepower, but the truth of the matter is that they were being employed as cuirassiers, or at least as heavy rather than light cavalry. The Cavalier horse might not have been equipped as cuirassiers, but just as a lack of corselets did not prevent either side from fielding pikemen, a similar shortage of cuirassier arms did not deter the Royalists from fielding heavy cavalry trained to charge home. Parliamentarian officers took rather longer to appreciate that the outward appearance of a trooper need not dictate his role, and at the outset their troops of harquebusiers and carbines tried (with a marked lack of success) to shoot it out instead of charging, but they did come around to it at least by 1644 and Cromwell's famous Ironsides were certainly cuirassiers in all but name.[11]

Dragoons were neither fish nor fowl in that they were expected to ride to the battlefield and dismount to fight. Consequently some units were organised in the same manner as infantry regiments, while others adopted a cavalry-based organisation. At the outset of the war they represented a considerable proportion of the cavalry arm on both sides amounting to between a quarter and a third of those taking part in the Edgehill campaign. However regimental-sized battle-groups were soon recognised to be too unwieldy, and the practice grew up of attaching a small troop of dragooners to some of the larger regiments of horse. Such a troop could provide some local fire-support as and when required, and more prosaically could also act as sentries for the regiment's quarters and horse-lines. Although at the outset they were intended to serve simply as mounted infantry rather than troopers, having once got on horseback they grew increasingly reluctant to get off again, and while the expedient of attaching a troop of dragooners to a cavalry regiment may have had its advantages, in the long run it served only to blur the distinction between the two.

This gradual alteration in role, which ended with their almost complete assimilation into the horse, was also reflected in their equipment. 'J.B.' writing in 1661 declared that:

> The other Arming of the Cavalry used in these Modern times, known by the Name of Dragoones, (being only Foot mounted) is a Sword (all) and some Musquets, and some Pikes, both having Leather Thongs fixed to them, whereby they may be the easier carried; his lighted Match and Bridle in his Left hand, having his Right hand at Liberty for the better ordering of his Pike or Musket in their March, as occasion shall require. Yet in these English Wars, it was observed that the Dragoones seldom used any Pikes, and of late times most Snap-haunce Locks; [12]

ARTILLERY

The artillery, by its nature, had a far from rigid hierarchy, but broadly speaking the General of the Artillery (an administrative post) supervised five different groups; gunners, fireworkers, conductors, pioneers, and a variety of craftsmen, storekeepers and workmen. The first obviously looked after the guns, while the fireworkers attended to the slightly more esoteric skills of firing mortars and preparing a variety of explosive and incendiary devices. Conductors were transport officers, so named because they were responsible for 'conducting' the train from place to place, and the Pioneers did all the dirty work. Parliamentarian artillery trains also had their own integral security force in the form of a company or two of Firelocks, but both the Scots and Royalist armies made do with ad hoc detachments (normally armed with matchlocks) drawn from ordinary infantry units.

In the 17th century the Train of Artillery was not only responsible for the firing of a variety of cannon, but also encompassed a number of now quite separate supporting services. The Train supplied small arms ammunition of all types to both infantry and cavalry units, 'new and fixt' muskets, snaphaunce muskets, pikes, half-pikes, lances, swine feathers, pistols and holsters, armour, swords and sword-belts, the various tools which the gunners themselves required, and the more mundane bits and pieces which the army needed to function as a community; spades, mattocks, duck boards, axes, horse-shoes, nails, rope, hides, tar and so on and so forth.[13]

It was however the cannon which were the Train's primary responsibility. Generally speaking only the main field armies could afford to encumber themselves with more than a handful of light guns. This was not because the actual cannon were in short supply, since a single moderately well equipped warship generally mounted as many if not more guns than the average army. The real impediment to assembling a large train was the difficulty in moving and supporting it. Each gun required a team of horses – or occasionally oxen – to pull it, while yet more horses (and carts) were needed to transport the powder and ball, and they in turn called for farriers and other craftsmen to keep them all on the road.

On 16 May 1643 a warrant was issued for the assembling of a small train of artillery to accompany Prince Maurice into the West Country. It comprised only one brass cannon (a 12-pounder) and a brass mortar piece, with 50 and 24 rounds of ammunition respectively, yet it required two wagons, ten carts and sixty-seven draught horses to transport the ammunition and tools. Not surprisingly the personnel assigned to this train included a carpenter, a wheelwright and a blacksmith.

Although there were some light pieces, most guns were emplaced in static positions on the battlefield and rarely if ever influenced the outcome. The true value of artillery at this period still lay in siege work, but while a single gun could sometimes make all the difference, it is surprising how often supposedly fragile mediaeval walls proved sufficient to hold attackers at bay; the siege of Newcastle upon Tyne in 1644 being a particularly striking example. Castles perching upon rocky outcrops were particularly difficult to deal with, although Stirling Castle surrendered fairly rapidly in 1651 when a mortar dropped bombs into the middle of it and thoroughly demoralised the garrison.

Despite these limitations the train was an essential part of any well conducted army, but as Lord Percy gloomily observed it was an expensive sponge which could never be filled.

NOTES

1. Barriffe *Militarie Discipline* (1661) p42
2. Clarendon *History of the Rebellion . . .* Vol.II p347
3. In theory the colonel's own company should have been 200 strong, the lieutenant colonel's 150 strong, and the major's 120, but it is most unlikely that any regiments achieved their full establishment before the Protectorate.
4. Young *Edgehill* p276
5. *Memoirs of the Duke of Newcastle* p25
6. Barriffe, p147. Sometimes however the musketeers could still give a good account of themselves, as James II ruefully recalled at the battle of the Dunes in 1658: 'Tis very observable that when we had broken into this battalion, and were gott amongst them, not so much as one single man of them asked for quarter, or threw down his arms, but every one defended himself to the last; so that we ran as great a danger by the butt end of their muskets as by the volley which they had given us. And one of them had infallibly knocked mee off my horse, if I had not prevented him when he was just ready to have discharged his blow by a stroke I gave with my sword over the face, which laid him along the ground.'
7. Elton, *Complete Body of the Art Military* Vol.II p3
8. Clarendon Vol.II p347
9. Peachy & Turton *Old Robin's Foot* pp45, 47. Warrants exist for the issue of 500 corselets to Essex's and Wharton's regiments in August 1642 (WO 55/1754) but there are no corresponding receipts to indicate whether the corselets were actually forthcoming.
10. Barriffe – Appendix p22. 'We find that the Lances (which have been much in use formerly, both in this Kingdom and Forreign parts) are now generally laid aside, and not used at all in our late Civil Wars, only some few that Duke Hamilton had when he invaded England in the year 1648, but their lances were but Half-pikes, and their Defensive Armes very mean, so that they were of no great use to them then;'
11. John Vernon's *Young Horseman* published in that year is a useful indicator of the change in tactics although he appears to have been serving in the Earl of Essex's army rather than alongside Cromwell in the Eastern Association forces.
12. Barriffe – Appendix p22
13. Roy, I. *Royalist Ordnance Papers* p233

CHAPTER II

Over by Christmas:
The Edgehill Campaign 1642

The King's military preparations got off to an uninspiring start. On his arrival in Yorkshire the local Trained Bands were called out and although they accompanied him on an abortive attempt to secure the great magazine at Hull on 29 April, it was also clear that they would not be willing to march beyond the county boundary. If he was to raise a proper army he needed to look elsewhere.

In June therefore the King began issuing both *Commissions of Array*, empowering the authorities in each county to muster and arm troops, and also military commissions directing named individuals to raise regiments. Although some units were raised in Yorkshire it soon became clear that a more central location should be chosen for the mustering point. To that end therefore he left York and formally set up his standard at Nottingham on 22 August 1642. By this symbolic act he announced that he was taking the field not as Charles Stuart, but as King of England and that all who stood against him were rebels. Unfortunately it soon became apparent that the choice of Nottingham was less than inspired.

Parliament too was busily enlisting volunteers. Backed by City money and ready access to both existing magazines and the continental arms markets, it planned to raise no fewer than twenty regiments of foot for an army to be led by Robert Devereaux, Earl of Essex. The call met with an enthusiastic response and on 18 August two of those regiments were ordered to Warwickshire. Having been joined on the road by a third regiment, they successfully brushed aside a Royalist detachment at Southam on the 22nd[1] and afterwards occupied Coventry, leaving Sir Jacob Astley to pessimistically declare; 'He could give no assurance that the King would not be taken out of his bed if the rebels made a brisk attempt to that purpose.'[2]

On 7 September more regiments left London and Essex opened his headquarters at Northampton on the 10th. In the face of this growing threat the King was persuaded to move westwards either to Shrewsbury or Chester where he could pick up the numerous levies expected out of Wales and the North West. Accompanied by just five regiments of foot and a bare 500 horse he evacuated Nottingham on the 13th and marching by way of Derby, Uttoxeter, Stafford and Wellington, he established himself at Shrewsbury on the 20th while his nephew, Prince Rupert took up an advanced position at Bridgenorth with the cavalry. It took a few days for Essex to learn of this move and consequently he did not leave Northampton until the 19th, with the intention of occupying Worcester. In so doing he precipitated the first serious clash of the campaign.

In July the Oxford colleges had pledged their silver plate to the King, but making the offer and actually delivering it were two entirely different matters. A cavalier officer, Sir John Byron was therefore ordered to Oxford with 150 horse and dragoons and instructions to secure as much of it as possible.[3] Given that the Midlands were already infested with Parliamentarian detachments and recruiting parties this was a risky business, but any delay could mean that the plate might be seized by the Parliamentarians instead – Oliver Cromwell had already prevented a similar donation by the Cambridge colleges. In the event the first phase of the operation went smoothly enough. Byron and his newly raised regiment were convoyed south as far as Leicester by Prince Rupert and apart from a minor skirmish at Brackley they arrived unmolested on 28 August. Naturally it took some time to gather in the plate and assemble a pack-train and as the days passed Byron's situation grew ever more perilous. This was particularly so after Rupert's withdrawal from Leicester on 5 September. Returning to Nottingham was no longer possible, so instead spurred on by the news that Essex was establishing himself at Northampton, Byron evacuated Oxford on the 10th and headed westwards.

Slowed down by the heavily laden pack-train he took ten days to cover the sixty-odd miles from Oxford to Worcester and having thrown himself into the dubious shelter of the city's crumbling walls on the 20th, he decided to dig in there and wait for help. As the King was also on the move he may in any case have been uncertain as to where to go next. At any rate Rupert, alerted to his plight moved south and two days later was at Bewdley, but by that time the Parliamentarians were also closing in fast.

At dawn on the morning of the 22nd a detachment of about 1000 of Essex's horse and dragoons[4] led by Colonel John Brown made a half-hearted attempt to force the city's Sidbury Gate. The guard refused to be intimidated but although Brown made off before Byron could mount a sortie, he had no intention of giving up. Hauling off to the south he crossed the Severn at Upton and then headed back up the west bank to take up an ambush position just south of the river Teme at Powick shortly before dawn on the 23rd. Worcester itself lay on the east bank and Brown correctly foresaw that when Essex arrived Byron would try to make a run for it up the west bank. As soon as the convoy broke cover Brown planned to move forward and snap it up in open country and so although the dragoons took up a covering position on a low ridge, overlooking the Teme he kept his cavalry mounted and ready to move at a moment's notice.

For a time nothing happened, but later that afternoon a number of Parliamentarian sympathisers hurried out of the city to advise him that Byron was preparing to leave. As the Royalists can have been only too well aware that Brown was waiting for them this could only mean that Essex was approaching. Sure enough confirmation of this came at 4pm and Brown decided to make his move.

Oddly enough there appears to have been a surprising lack of enthusiasm on the part of some of his troop commanders. The MP Captain Nathaniel Fiennes for one is said to have urged caution, but Brown had his heart set on capturing the convoy and while he mounted up his dragoons Colonel Edwin Sandys led the rest of the cavalry across the narrow pack bridge and into the equally narrow lane beyond. Unfortunately what neither Brown nor Sandys realised was that in the meantime Prince Rupert had arrived and in order to cover Byron's withdrawal was taking up a blocking position in Wick Field, just to the north of the bridge. The hedges lining the lane were consequently stuffed full of Royalist dragoons who very properly saluted Sandys with a volley delivered at point blank range. Sandys naturally responded by spurring forward in order to get clear of the lane and into Wick Field, but there he received a second unwelcome shock, for the field was full of Royalist cavalrymen frantically catching and mounting their horses.[5]

Not expecting a Parliamentarian move so late in the day, the cavaliers had literally been caught napping. All or most of them had dismounted and were sleeping under the trees and now a desperate race developed as both sides deployed into a hasty battle-line. Having been forewarned by the noise of the ambush, the Royalists had a crucial few moments' advantage and Rupert charged first, sword in hand. Only one of the Parliamentarian troops, commanded by Fiennes, seems to have put up much of a fight. Sandys himself went down and his whole command was sent tumbling back down the lane. As soon as the ambush was tripped Brown had dismounted his dragoons again and now he checked the Royalist pursuit at the bridge, but the fugitives themselves kept going, recrossed the Severn at Upton and running into Essex's own Lifeguard troop at Pershore carried them away in the general rout.

It is difficult to assess the casualties suffered by either side in this affair and all that can be said is that the Royalists reckoned to have taken about 50 or 60 prisoners. They also put it about that they had killed and wounded as many more, but given the brief duration of both fighting and pursuit, this claim is probably more optimistic than accurate. Naturally enough their own losses were light although a surprising number of officers seem to have managed to get themselves wounded as a result of going into action without waiting to buckle on their armour. On one thing at least both sides were agreed; Sandys' Regiment was destroyed as a military unit and although the fight was otherwise of no real military significance it had enhanced Royalist morale and left the Parliamentarian cavalry with a decided inferiority complex.

Balked of his prey, Essex occupied Worcester on the 24th and then waited for the rest of his forces to catch up. His army had still not been fully concentrated when he took it out of Northampton and it was not until two weeks later that the last of them trudged in. On 7 October Cholmley's Regiment was pushed up the valley as far as Bridgenorth but this was evidently considered a little too exposed, for by the 11th Essex had established a proper set of forward positions in the area of Bewdley and Kidderminster. Despite his brief to seek out the King, Essex seems to have been reluctant to act aggressively and instead his dispositions indicate that he was anticipating a Royal advance down the Valley.

Unfortunately, if one excepts the vicarious employment of spies this tripwire was the extent of Essex's intelligence gathering. If the King did what was expected of him the detachments at Kidderminster and Bewdley would give adequate warning of the direction and strength of the offensive and perhaps even delay it while Essex brought his main force out of Worcester to meet the Royalists on ground of his own choosing. The King, however, failed to oblige. While a march down the Valley was certainly the obvious approach, the professional soldiers advising the King successfully argued for a thrust straight at London. Essex would certainly try to intercept such a move, but it was better that the inevitable encounter should take place in the Midlands where the countryside was generally open, rather than in the Severn Valley where the numerous enclosed fields would hamper the employment of the Royalists' best asset – their cavalry.[6]

In order to cover this movement Rupert marched on 10 October to Shifnal and then from there to Wolverhampton and down to Stourbridge on the 14th. In the face of this advance Lord Wharton obligingly fell back from Kidderminster and confirmed to Essex that the King was indeed coming down the Valley. In reality the King had actually marched out of Shrewsbury with all his foot on the 12th and by the 19th when Essex at last realised what was happening the Royalists were at Kenilworth with the road to London wide open before them. There was no question of course of their making a dash for the capital while Essex's army remained in being, but the threat was sufficient to bring the unfortunate general marching eastwards and worse still marching blind.

It was at this point that the evil effects of the Powick Bridge debacle first became apparent. Essex ought to have had his cavalry out observing the Royalists but instead he kept them close at hand and lacking proper intelligence the two armies blundered into each other by accident. Contact was established not through aggressive patrolling but through the chance encounter of two parties of Quartermasters seeking billets at Wormleighton in Warwickshire on the 22nd. The Royalists were evidently taken just as unawares but they won the fight which followed and on further investigation found Essex moving into quarters around the small market town of Kineton.

At midnight orders were given for the Royalists to concentrate later that morning on Edgehill, a three mile long ridge lying astride the Kineton to Banbury road. They were also as it happened forming up between Essex and London. Bad weather on the march had been forcing both armies to disperse each night in search of shelter and consequently they were slow to concentrate. Rupert seems to have been on the ridge by daybreak but it was after two before the King's army was fully concentrated[7] and some of Essex's regiments were still arriving as the battle ended.

Edgehill proper is rather too steep and commanding to invite an attack and so the Royalists descended about as far as the 350 foot contour line which represents the point at which the slope rather abruptly begins to level out and fall away rather more gently towards the north-west and the village of Kineton. Most of the ground was taken up with an open expanse of unenclosed ridges and furrows known as Red Horse Field, which offered no impediment to a textbook deployment and thanks to the preparation of a map by the Walloon engineer Bernard de Gomme[8] it is a relatively straightforward matter to reconstruct the Royalist dispositions.

The cavalry deployment at first glance appears quite straightforward although a close examination throws up some interesting questions. In the first place de Gomme omits any mention of the Royalist dragoons, but it is clear from other sources that four regiments were present – and not three as is usually assumed – under the overall command of an experienced professional soldier named Sir Arthur Aston. According to the Duke of York, Aston (who had just been commissioned as Major General of Dragoons) took post on the right[9] and a number of sources also testify to the presence there of Colonel James Usher's Regiment, commanded by Lieutenant Colonel Henry Washington. The second regiment in his little brigade is unidentified but there is no reason to doubt that it was Sir Edmund Duncombe's since both regiments on the left *can* be identified. Colonel Edward Grey's Regiment was certainly there and Bulstrode[10] refers to the dragoons on that flank being commanded by Lieutenant Colonel George Lisle and Lieutenant Colonel John Innes. The latter is known to have commanded Prince Rupert's Dragoons and Lisle, therefore, presumably fought under Grey who also appears from the Duke of York's account to have served as acting brigade commander. While both Washington and Grey were to be employed in clearing the hedges to their immediate front the role played by Rupert's and Duncombe's dragoons is less certain although Belayse asserted that; 'before every body of foot were placed two pieces of cannon, and before them the dragoons and 1,200 commanded musqueteers as Enfants Perdu.'[11] If true this would suggest that in addition to covering the flanks the dragoons formed a rudimentary skirmish line ahead of the infantry brigades.

There is no evidence that any of these regiments were particularly strong and as the Royalists are generally credited with having around 1,000 dragooners it can be assumed that both Aston's and Grey's brigades mustered 500 men apiece.

As to the Horse, de Gomme's representation of their deployment appears at first glance to be quite straightforward with both wings being drawn up in 'checquer', that is with three regiments in the front line and two more in the rear covering the gaps between.

On the extreme left of the front line stood three squadrons of Lord Wilmot's Regiment, and then Lord Grandison's and Lord Caernarvon's regiments with two squadrons apiece. In the second line were Sir Thomas Aston's and Lord Digby's regiments, each forming only a single squadron. With the exception of Lord Wilmot's Regiment the number of cornets depicted by de Gomme corresponds to the number of troops known to have been mustered with each regiment and the additional cornet in Wilmot's outermost squadron may represent the troop commanded by 'Blind Harry' Hastings, whose whereabouts are otherwise unknown. Assuming this to be the case it would seem likely that the first line, commanded by Wilmot himself, numbered about 850-900 officers and men, with a further 300 or so in support.

Turning to the right wing however there at first appears to be an odd discrepancy both as to the number of cornets depicted by de Gomme and in the apparent strength of Sir John Byron's Regiment. On the extreme right of the front line stood the King's Lifeguard comprising a single squadron said by Sir Philip Warwick to have been 300 strong. Its proper place should have been with the King himself, but stung by unkind jibes from the rest of the cavalry they insisted on taking part in the attack.

The Lifeguard aside there were, as on the left, three regiments in the front line; the Prince of Wales' Regiment, Prince Rupert's and Prince Maurice's Regiments. All three were formed in two squadrons and all three according to de Gomme's plan mustered four troops apiece. Maurice's Regiment certainly had only four troops but the other two were rather stronger with Rupert's mustering six troops and the Prince of Wales' perhaps as many as eight. Conversely however, Sir John Byron's Regiment in the second line is depicted with six troops organised in two squadrons. As he had mustered no more than 200 horse and dragoons at

Worcester only a month before this looks rather unlikely.[12] It is rather more probable therefore that the two squadrons which de Gomme shows under Sir John Byron's command is actually an ad hoc brigade comprising his own embryonic cavalry regiment and the reserve troops of the Prince of Wales' and Prince Rupert's regiments.

Assuming that one third of both regiments went into the reserve, as was certainly a common practice, then the front line ought to have numbered close on 900 officers and men, while Byron's two reserve squadrons may have mustered anything from 300-500 men depending on just how strong his own regiment was. Both wings of horse were therefore of a similar size except for the addition of the 300 Lifeguards on the right.[13]

The equally neat looking deployment of the infantry forming the centre masks a furious row over their deployment. Like the cavalry they were initially drawn up in 'checquer' with three brigades in the front line and two in the second.

From right to left stood Colonel Charles Gerard's brigade, comprising his own, Sir Lewis Dyve's and Sir Ralph Dutton's regiments. In the centre of the front line Colonel Richard Fielding's brigade was made up from Sir Thomas Lunsford's, Colonel Richard Bolle's, Sir Edward Fitton's and Sir Edward Stradling's regiments, but apparently not his own one which may have been part of a small force covering Banbury. Finally, on the left Colonel Henry Wentworth's brigade comprising Sir Gilbert Gerard's, Sir Thomas Salusbury's and Lord Molyneux's regiments. Covering the substantial gaps between these brigades were the two standing in the second line; on the right, Sir John Belasyse's brigade which again consisted of his own, Sir William Pennyman's and Thomas Blagge's regiments, and on the left; Sir Nicholas Byron's brigade comprising the King's Lifeguard of Foot (de Gomme depicts the Royal standard with the right hand division of this brigade), the Lord General's and Sir John Beaumont's regiments. On the basis of a pay warrant dated 16 November 1642, just three weeks after the battle it has been estimated that the strength of these brigades was probably in the region of 1800 or 1900 men apiece.[14]

The operational deployment of these brigades proved to be controversial. The King's Lord General, the Earl of Lindsey intended to array them in the conventional Dutch or German manner, that is with two battalions up and one back. Each of these battalions would have been drawn up with a stand of pikes in the centre and musketeers on each wing. Instead a furious row broke out when the Field Marshall[15] Patrick Ruthven insisted on employing a quite different formation known as the Swedish Brigade.

This was essentially a diamond formation comprising four battalions. The point battalion was drawn up with its stand of pikemen forward and the musketeers behind. To the right and left rear of this battalion were two more, deployed with their pikes towards the centre of the formation and the musketeers on the outside. The fourth or reserve battalion was deployed like the first and standing directly behind it.

There is no doubting that this was a complicated formation which required the constituent regiments to be broken up and their personnel redistributed throughout the brigade. At first sight therefore it seems to have been asking too much of the inexperienced Royalist infantry and it has been suggested that the adoption of the 'Swedish' brigade contributed to their poor performance in the battle. However the decision was not blindly based upon dogma but upon a very sensible appreciation of just how poorly equipped those infantrymen really were.

It is clear from de Gomme's map and from the surviving records of arms and ammunition issued in the months after the battle that at this early stage of the war most regiments could only muster equal numbers of musketeers and pikemen – and some perhaps more pikemen – rather than the two musketeers for each pikeman required to form German style battalions. This shortage of musketeers was obviously going to place the Royalists at a significant disadvantage in a firefight so Ruthven decided to form them up in the old 'Swedish' brigade which was in fact an assault formation quite literally spearheaded by pikemen.

As to the King's artillery little needs to be said. A pair of light guns were attached to each infantry brigade and six heavier ones appear to have been emplaced just to the north of Radway, some 300 metres behind Gerard's brigade.

Sadly no-one in the Parliamentarian ranks drew a plan like de Gomme's to record the disposition's of Essex's army standing before Kineton. According to the official account Essex had eleven regiments of foot, forty-two troops of horse and 700 dragoons (in two regiments) amounting in all to some 10,000 men. As to their dispositions the account goes on to report that the infantry formed three brigades in the centre, that three regiments of horse; Lord Fielding's, the Lord General's and Sir William Balfour's were posted on the right and that Sir James Ramsay commanded twenty-four troops of horse on the left.[16]

Unfortunately it was not quite so simple as that and if we take as our fixed point the Parliamentarian left wing we find Sir James Ramsay at the head of his twenty-four troops posted behind and perhaps in amongst a series of hedged enclosures by the Kineton Road. While elements of at least three regiments – his own, Sir William Waller's and Colonel Arthur Goodwin's – can be identified, the wording of the official account suggests that his command included a substantial number of independent troops. Although nothing is known of their actual deployment it would be reasonable to suppose that they were paired off into squadrons and were deployed in two lines.

21

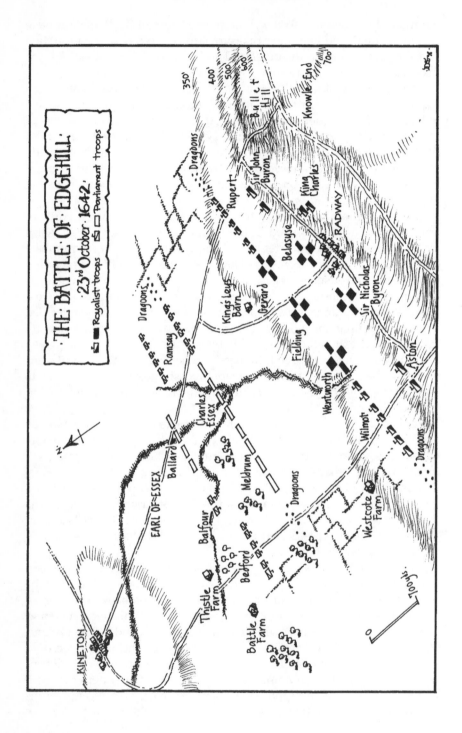

THE·BATTLE·OF·EDGEHILL·
·23rd October· 1642·
■ Royalist troops ▢ Parliament troops

Having deducted those twenty-four troops on the left, eighteen others remain to be accounted for, but here we run into some difficulty. At first sight all of them should have belonged to the three regiments named as standing on the right, but on closer examination it appears that some of them may have been elsewhere. While there is no doubting that Fielding's Regiment was on the right and swept away by Wilmot's charge, some Royalist accounts, most notably Rupert's and the Duke of York's state that most of the cavalry on this wing was posted behind the foot. However notwithstanding the support of Colonel John Brown's and Colonel James Wardlawe's dragoons it is scarcely credible that Fielding's Regiment mustering about 300 men should have been expected to face Wilmot's 1,000 odd cavaliers.

The likeliest explanation is that since this wing was 'in the air' Essex ordered his General of the Horse, the Earl of Bedford to refuse the flank by drawing up his three regiments level with the second line rather than the first. It is just possible that the right hand regiment of the brigade – probably Balfour's – may have been standing behind some of the front line infantry, but it seems likelier that what the Royalists saw was a fourth, ad hoc regiment made up of the three oversized cuirassier troops raised by Essex, Bedford and Balfour. After deducting these three troops Bedford ought therefore to have had fifteen, not six troops of horse mustering between 750 and 900 men on the right wing; still outnumbered by Wilmot perhaps but by no means decisively.

Essex's infantry present fewer problems although there were evidently twelve regiments present rather than the eleven referred to in the official account. They were organised in three brigades and as all or most of the regiments were at or pretty near full strength it is quite possible that each regiment was in turn divided into two battalions.

At any rate Sir John Meldrum's brigade, comprising his own, Lord Robartes, Sir William Constable's and Sir William Fairfax's regiments stood on the right. On the left was Colonel Charles Essex's brigade which in addition to his own regiment included Lord Wharton's, Lord Mandeville's and Sir Henry Cholmley's regiments. The third or reserve brigade forming the second line proper consisted of the Earl of Essex's, Lord Brooke's, Denzill Holles' and Thomas Ballard's regiments and was commanded by Ballard.

As all 700 Parliamentarian dragoons were with Bedford and Fielding on the right, some 600 musketeers were drawn out of this brigade – 400 from Holles' Regiment and 200 from Ballard's own regiment – to line the hedges on the left and interlace Ramsay's squadrons.

Thanks to the incompetence of du Bois, the General of the Artillery, most of Essex's guns were still on the road from Worcester and he only had seven rather light pieces at Edgehill.

The battle began at about three o'clock in the afternoon with a cannonade which predictably enough did little damage to either party, and then, as Bulstrode famously records:

> Just before we began our March, Prince *Rupert* passed from one wing to the other, giving positive Orders to the Horse, to march as close as was possible, keeping their Ranks with Sword in Hand, to receive the Enemy's Shot, without firing either Carbin or Pistol, till we broke in amongst the Enemy, and then to make use of our Fire-Arms as need should require; which Order was punctually observed.[17]

First the advance was preceded by the dragoons, who were sent forward to clear the hedgerows to their immediate front. On the right this task was by all accounts performed by Lieutenant Colonel Washington at the head of Usher's Dragoons, and on the left by Colonel Grey. Once the hedges were cleared a more general advance took place and in the face of it Ramsay's command literally melted away.

> . . . the Royalists march'd up with all the gallantry and resolution imaginable, especially the right wing led by Prince Rupert; tho while they advanced, the Enemy's cannon continually played upon them, as did the small divisions of their Foot which were placed in the intervals betwixt their squadrons, neither of which did in the least discompose them so much as to mend their pace. Thus they continued moving, till they came up close to the Enemy's Cavalry, which after having spent their first fire, immediately turn'd their backs, the Royalists pursuing them with great eagerness.[18]

And well they might, particularly as Charles Essex's infantry brigade also turned tail and ran and everyone seems to have trampled over Holles' Regiment in the second line. Unfortunately Sir John Byron's little brigade which formed the reserve went after the fugitives too and the whole mob excitedly galloped off towards Kineton and the Parliamentarian baggage train.

On the other flank it was a very similar story. Wilmot's charge evidently swept away Bedford's men, both horse and dragoons, and Sir William Fairfax's Foot as well. Once again nearly all of the cavaliers joined in the chase, but Caernarvon's Lieutenant Colonel, Sir Charles Lucas began rallying a few troops for a second charge.

This early success must have been vastly encouraging to the Royalist infantry advancing across Red Horse Field, but they were about to discover that the battle was far from over. Although Charles Essex's brigade had run away, Thomas Ballard brought what was left of the reserve brigade up from the second line and took post beside Meldrum just in time to receive the attack. Had Byron's reserve brigade remained

24

under control Rupert might have been able to prevent or at least retard this move, but he could only rally three of the twenty troops on that wing and instead the Royalist advance was brought to a complete halt.

There is ample testimony that the Royalists brought all or most of their brigades to push of pike, but unable to make any impression on the Parliamentarian regiments, they broke contact again and fell back to engage in a long range firefight. There seems little reason to doubt that superior firepower was responsible since not only did Meldrum's and Ballard's brigades have more musketeers, but they were deployed in such a way as to make better use of them than their Royalist opponents. At this point Sir William Balfour made a dramatic intervention.

Just how many Parliamentarian cavalry were left at this stage is rather problematic. Ramsay and his whole command had gone, and judging by the notable silence as to his deeds, so was Bedford. Most modern accounts follow Brigadier Young in assuming that only Fielding's Regiment was swept away by Wilmot's charge and that Balfour counter-attacked with his own and Essex's regiments. However notwithstanding the Duke of York's claim that Wilmot only faced some dragoons it is clear from Parliamentarian accounts that the only units which can be identified with any certainty as remaining on the field afterwards are the cuirassiers of Essex's Lifeguard, under Sir Philip Stapleton and Sir William Balfour's own cuirassier troop, although it would be reasonable to suppose that Bedford's cuirassier troop might also have been at hand.

At any rate Balfour now took the opportunity to move them forward and according to the official account he

> ... broke a Regiment of Foot that had green Colours, beat them to their Cannon, where they threw down their Arms, and ran away; he laid his hand upon the Cannon, and called for Nails to nail them up, especially the two biggest, which were Demy-Cannon; but finding none, he cut the ropes belonging to them, and his Troopers killed the Canoneers; then he pursued the Fliers half a Mile upon Execution; and after returned to Sir *Philip Stapleton*, who in the meantime was Charging of the Red Regiment, where the King's Standard was, and had Charged it home to push of Pike with his single Troop; and they then, together with some of the Foot of our Rear, utterly broke it.[19]

It was not quite so glorious as that and the sequence of events is rather compressed. Balfour certainly broke Colonel Richard Fielding's brigade (the regiment with green colours was evidently Sir Thomas Lunsford's[20]) for he was captured along with two of his regimental commanders, Lunsford and Stradling. Stapleton also attacked at pretty much the same time, but was less successful. Ludlow, who was serving in his troop recalled that it 'charged them with some loss from their pikes, tho very little from their shot; but not being able to break them, we retired to our former station.'[21] As Stapleton fell back, Lindsey called on Belasyse's brigade for assistance[22] but no sooner had it come up than Balfour returned and while the Royalists were hotly engaged in fighting the Parliamentarians to their front, Balfour and Stapleton put in a second charge and caught Byron's brigade in flank. This time it broke. Lindsey was badly wounded and captured (he died three days later) and a number of colours taken from all three regiments, including the Banner Royal, seized by Ensign Arthur Young of Constable's Foot.

What happened to Belasyse's brigade is less clear. Joshua Moone's account suggests that they were also hit by Stapleton's men and subsequently rallied on Wentworth's brigade, but at any rate they and the remnants of Byron's brigade fell back to the foot of the hill and the battle petered out into a half-hearted firefight. With both Gerard's and Wentworth's brigades still holding their ground on the right and left wings respectively the exhausted Parliamentarians were understandably reluctant to press their advantage.

Nor were the Royalists any better off. Sir Charles Lucas had managed to mount a second charge on the left but it seems to have gotten bogged down cutting up the fugitives from Charles Essex's brigade and its only solid achievement was the recovery of the Banner Royal by Captain John Smith. Both Rupert and Wilmot eventually turned up with a miscellaneous collection of horse and dragoons, but when they were urged to put in a last charge against Balfour's cuirassiers Wilmot summed up the prevailing mood by wearily declaring; 'we have got the day, and let us live to enjoy the fruit thereof.'

NOTES

1. The Royalist Sir Richard Bulstrode (in Young, P. *Edgehill 1642* p264-5) says that the cavaliers retired without offering to charge the enemy, although the Parliamentarians were in open country and without cavalry support.
2. Clarendon, Edward Hyde, Earl of, *The History of the Rebellion . . .* (1826) Vol.III p194
3. Byron only commanded a regiment of Horse at Edgehill, but contemporary accounts certainly refer to his having dragoons at Oxford and a recruiting poster which he had printed there also calls for volunteers to enlist as dragooners.
4. Brown's force comprised his own regiment of dragoons; about 350 strong, Colonel Edwin Sandys regiment of horse; about 250, and six other unregimented troops which probably averaged about 60 officers and men apiece. SEE Turton, Alan; *The Chief Strength of the Army: Essex's Horse (1642-1645)*
5. Young *Edgehill* p171 identifies fourteen troops of horse under Rupert although he only refers to eight in his later *The English Civil War*. The eight were probably Rupert's own troop commanded by Richard Crane, Prince Maurice's, the Prince of Wales' commanded by Lieutenant Thomas Daniel, Lord Wilmot's, Lord Digby's, Sir Lewis Dyve's, Sir Thomas Byron's, and Sir

William Pennyman's. In addition he was evidently joined on the march by a number of other troops including the Earl of Northampton's and Lord John Stuart's. Young also lists Captain John Frescheville, Sir Charles Lucas, Captain Henry Hastings and Lord Crawford though no source is given. Another possibility is Captain Francis Bertie's troop which like Stuart's belonged to Lord Grandison's Regiment and had certainly been serving alongside Stuart earlier in the campaign. As to the dragoons, there were four units with the Royalist army at this time. Of these, one, Byron's was in Worcester and another, Duncombe's was probably with the foot at Shrewsbury. Consequently the ten troops of dragoons presumably belonged to Usher's and Grey's Regiments. Northampton's Troop, according to Bulstrode, was 100 strong and indeed later formed the nucleus of a regiment, if an average of 50 officers and men apiece are allowed for the others then Rupert may have had something in the region of about 700 horse, though probably a little less as some were detached to assist Byron and did not take part in the charge across Wick Field. The dragooners may have accounted for another 500 men but this seems rather high.

6. Clarendon op.cit. p349
7. Royalist Official Account – in Young *Edgehill* p261-2
8. Or so he is generally known. Rupert however refers to him as de Gomez.
9. Young, p275
10. Ibid. p269
11. Ibid p289
12. Oddly enough Byron's Dragoons disappear from history after the evacuation of Worcester. It is always possible that he turned them all into troopers of horse, but there remains an intriguing possibility that they were hived off to become Prince Rupert's Dragoons, whose origins are otherwise unknown.
13. In calculating the strength of each wing I have largely relied upon the figures in Young's *Edgehill*, with the proviso that there were not three but four dragoon regiments, and that the organisation of the Royalist cavalry on the right wing was rather different than he supposed.
14. Young p89-90 and 180-1. Although Young adds Fielding's Regiment to his brigade and accordingly estimates it to be considerably stronger than the other four, the regiment does not appear in de Gomme's list. While Fielding himself was present, two of the other brigade commanders had no regiments of their own so it does not follow that his own must have been present. It is possible that Sir Nicholas Byron's brigade was stronger than the others for while de Gomme depicts four of them with fourteen colours apiece, Byron's brigade has sixteen.
15. At this period a Field Marshall was an experienced staff officers who quite literally had the job of marshalling the regiments in their battle positions.
16. Young p306-7
17. Ibid p269-70
18. Ibid (Duke of York's account) p276-7
19. Ibid. p309-10
20. Or so it may be inferred from the fact that both Stradling's and Fitton's regiments had blue colours while Bolle's had white.
21. Young p312
22. Ibid. p290. After being over-ruled on the deployment of the foot, Lindsey had flounced off in a fit of pique to fight at the head of his own regiment, but the unfolding crisis evidently recalled him to his duty.

CHAPTER III

The King's Road:
Stalemate on the Central Front

What was left of both armies remained on or near the battlefield all night, unwilling to admit they were beaten, and yet at the same time too battered and exhausted to finish the business. In total about 1,000 men had been killed and twice that number wounded, mostly amongst the infantry, and on the whole the Royalists seem to have been in pretty poor condition next morning. Their infantry had certainly been hard hit, and although the cavalry lost very few casualties in their grand fox chase, they too appear to have been afflicted by that apathetic reaction which so often follows the excitement of battle.

When it was suggested that the battle might be resumed, some of the cavalry officers (comparatively few of whom were professionals) gloomily replied that 'the bodies which were in view were rather an assembly of all the horse of the army than regiments or troops under their officers, and so they knew not how to draw them out, or to depend upon them'.[1]

The Parliamentarians were in little better condition. One of their three infantry brigades had been pretty comprehensively scattered, and all but a handful of the cavalry chased off the field. On the other hand, John Hampden had come up at the end of the battle with two fresh regiments of foot, Lord Willoughby's regiment of horse, and a few stray troops such as Oliver Cromwell's, which had either turned up late to the Kineton rendezvous or else contrived to miss the battle completely. Unlike the Royalists they at first had sufficient fight left in them to draw up in order of battle outside Kineton, but as they lacked the cavalry to support a renewed assault, and the Royalists lacked the stomach for one, both sides eventually retired late in the evening.

For the Royalists this meant a return to their former quarters near Edgecote, but as the King still lay astride the direct route to London, Essex elected to abandon his artillery and retire northwards toWarwick Castle. Understandably encouraged by this failure of nerve, Prince Rupert managed to get his cavalry moving again, and although Caernarvon's Regiment failed to come up to the rendezvous in time, he still managed to launch a successful attack on Essex's baggage train on 25 October. Just as encouragingly, Banbury surrendered on the 27th and the

28

three regiments which had been blockading the castle were able to rejoin the main army. Next day Rupert seized Broughton House, and then rather startled some of the King's advisors with a proposal to move directly on London with a flying column and take Westminster and the Parliament house before Essex could return. Had his plan been accepted he would have ' . . . march'd with ye Horse and Dragoons, and 3000 foot to follow after as fast as they could.'[2] Although Ruthven, who had been appointed General in Lindsey's stead, was prepared to back him, nothing came of the proposal. This was just as well since, unbeknown to the Royalists, a second army group was being hastily assembled under the Earl of Warwick to defend London in Essex's absence. Instead a more cautious advance southwards secured an undefended Oxford next day, and on 4 November the King's army entered Reading.

This was all very well, but in the process contact with Essex's forces had been broken, apart from a skirmish at Aylesbury on 3 November which resulted in the final destruction of Grantham's Regiment.[3] While the advance on London was proceeding at a rather more leisurely pace than Rupert had wanted, the King was evidently suffering from the pleasant delusion that merely setting foot in the capital was going to be sufficient to secure victory and the submission of Parliament. In the meantime Essex was winning the race. By 5 November he was at St Albans, and two days later, with the Royalists still no closer than Windsor, he re-entered London to be greeted like a conquering hero. Despite his failure to defeat the King's army, it was in Parliament's interest to represent Essex in the best possible light at that juncture, but in truth there was much to be satisfied about. The Earl of Warwick had raised seven fresh regiments in and around London, and although they may not have been fully recruited up to their authorised establishment, they were still a formidable reinforcement. Moreover should these levies not be sufficient, Parliament could also call upon the 6,000 men of the London Trained Bands to help defend the city.

By the time the Royalists eventually hove into view, London was well covered with strong detachments at Kingston, where Sir James Ramsay held the bridge over the Thames, Acton and Brentford. Parliament therefore felt secure enough to send a delegation to the King at Colnbrooke on 11 November, proposing talks, but uneasy at the growing concentration of hostile troops, Charles wanted submission rather than negotiation, and in order to strengthen his hand he approved Prince Rupert's proposal to attack Brentford at dawn next morning.

The town was held by two infantry regiments, Lord Brooke's and Denzill Holles', both veterans of Edgehill where they had stood and fought in Ballard's brigade. Rupert for his part had at least four cavalry regiments under his command, his own, the Prince of Wales', Lord Grandison's and Sir Thomas Aston's. Although he had requested infantry support, a thick fog encouraged him to attack at once without waiting for it, but predictably enough he was beaten off in short order. Then up came Ruthven at the head of Wentworth's brigade which had been strengthened since Edgehill by the addition of Earl Rivers' Regiment.[4] After a stiff fight they stormed the barricades and as John Gwynne, then a volunteer in Salusbury's Foot, relates they carried the town just before Hampden's and Robartes' regiments could come up to support the garrison.

> ... we marched up to the enemy, engaged them by Sir Richard Winn's house, and the Thames side, beat them from one Brainford to the other, and from thence to the open field, with a resolute and expeditious fighting, that after once firing suddenly to advance up to push of pikes and the butt end of muskets, which proved so fatal to Holles his butchers and dyers that day, that abundance of them were killed and taken prisoners, besides those drowned in their attempt to escape by leaping into the river.[5]

Some of Brooke's men may have got away, but Holles' 'butchers and dyers' were roughly handled indeed and driven into the river where a number were drowned, including Lieutenant Colonel James Quarles and Captain Richard Lacey. According to Clarendon the Royalists took over 500 prisoners and eleven colours[6] which if true must have accounted for more than half the garrison.[7]

Not content with this the Royalists followed up their success when Colonel Thomas Blagge occupied Sion House and sank some barges taking supplies upstream. Satisfying though the morning's events might have seemed from a purely military point of view, they also in a very real sense played into the hands of the extremists in the Parliamentarian camp. Rumours that the Cavaliers intended to plunder the City from end to end were already current. Now the assault on Brentford and the 'massacre' of Holles' Londoners were portrayed as having been carried out in violation of a cease-fire. This might have been rather stretching things, but with righteousness on their side the London Trained Bands mustered that afternoon on Chelsea Fields.

By the next morning Essex was no doubt highly gratified to find himself at the head of 24,000 men barring the London road on the common at Turnham Green. A further 3,000 men still lay under Sir James Ramsay at Kingston, but once a pontoon bridge had been thrown over the Thames at Putney, Essex ordered Ramsay to evacuate the town and take up a fresh position on the Surrey side of London Bridge. His reasoning, as usual, is obscure. The Brentford disaster may have convinced him that Ramsay was too exposed and so vulnerable to a similar coup-de-main, but by abandoning Kingston Bridge without a fight, he was also leaving the way open for the King to cross the Thames and strike at the capital from the south rather than mounting a bloody frontal attack on the Turnham Green position.

As it was the two armies spent 13 November watching each other rather uneasily. Not only were the King's forces badly outnumbered, but they also lacked the firepower to mount such an assault. That night under cover of darkness, Ruthven retired to Hounslow, covered by a rearguard under Rupert and Astley. In theory it would still have been possible for them to strike southwards and cross the bridge at Kingston, but instead the King surrendered the initiative and retired westwards first to Reading and then north to Oxford. A Royalist detachment led by Lord Wilmot[8] successfully stormed Marlborough on 5 December, but four days later the King formally closed the campaign by dispersing his army into winter quarters.

The largest concentration was at Reading, where Sir Arthur Aston commanded six regiments of foot and two small cavalry regiments, but Wallingford, Abingdon, Faringdon, Winchester, Burford, Brill, Banbury, Woodstock, Eynsham and Islip all maintained at least one regiment. Secure within this ring Oxford, which was to become the Royalist capital for the next four years, was comparatively lightly held with only four regiments of foot and the Lifeguard of Horse.[9]

Although both armies had gone into winter quarters, hostilities did not end. Instead the war became an affair of outposts with Winchester falling to Sir William Waller on 13 December and Goodwin launching an unsuccessful attack on Sir Gilbert Gerard's garrison at Brill on 27 January. Against this background of largely inconsequential bickering, the King's generals strove to strengthen the army for a fresh campaign in the spring. A number of Edgehill veterans, such as Thomas Tyldesley and Gervase Holles, returned home before Christmas to recruit fresh regiments, but unfortunately most of them promptly became embroiled in local conflicts. Consequently Wales was looked upon with good reason to be the King's most important recruiting area, since there was an almost complete absence of pro-Parliamentarian activity in the Principality. Indeed most of the reinforcements which joined the army after Edgehill had come from Wales, but they had to run the gauntlet of the Parliamentarian garrisons left by Essex in the lower Severn valley.

The Earl of Stamford's Regiment garrisoning Hereford was particularly troublesome, but the abandonment of Worcester had made his position untenable. In early December, just as the King's army was taking up its winter quarters, he fell back to Gloucester, turned his regiment over to Lieutenant Colonel Edward Massey, and took himself off to the more congenial West Country. This enabled the Marquis of Hertford, who had been recruiting in South Wales to bring 2,000 horse and foot into Oxford on 9 January and at his suggestion an operation was then mounted to take Cirencester.

There had been an earlier and unsuccessful attempt to take the town on 7 January, but now Rupert was recalled from a sweep which he was undertaking through Warwickshire and Northamptonshire, and at a rendezvous at Northleach on 1 February he was joined by reinforcements drawn out of the Oxford garrison. This gave him some 4,000 men made up from elements of six regiments of horse, four regiments of dragoons and a body of commanded musketeers from the Oxford garrison, all supported by six guns and a mortar[10] This was more than sufficient for the task in hand and next day, after some hard fighting, he took the town and 1,100 prisoners.[11]

Useful though it was, the capture of Cirencester was only the first step in creating a broad military corridor similar to the network of friendly garrisons and way-stations which formed the famous Spanish Road linking Italy with Flanders. The King's Road was obviously a much more modest affair, but it was no less vital to the Royalist war effort since it not only carried recruits, but also iron cannon from Dudley, roundshot from Stourbridge, swords and pikeheads from the numerous small ironworks scattered up and down the valley, and more mundane but no less important commodities such as salt from Droitwich. Unfortunately the Road was never secure. In theory the local commissioners of array should have raised sufficient garrison soldiers as well as providing billets and supplies for the convoys passing through. In reality the level of Parliamentarian activity all too often demanded the diversion of regular units from the very army they were supposed to be supporting.

On 11 February a Western Association was formed, formally linking the Parliamentarian authorities in Somerset, Gloucestershire, Worcestershire, Shropshire, Wiltshire and the city of Bristol. At first the Parliamentarians held little sway in Shropshire and the upper part of the valley, but in neighbouring Staffordshire Sir John Gell proved troublesome. Lichfield was taken on 4 March, and Stafford might have followed had not the Earl of Northampton appeared on the scene with his own and the Prince of Wales' regiments of horse and some commanded foot from Oxford. Near Stafford he was joined by Blind Harry Hastings[12] at the head of a rather scratch cavalry brigade, and with the aid of these reinforcements he planned to retake Lichfield.

Sir John Gell had other ideas, and arranged to join forces with the Cheshire Parliamentarians led by Sir William Brereton at Hopton Heath on 19 March. The intention was to launch a preemptive strike against Northampton's forces in Stafford, but Brereton was late in coming up to the rendezvous, and as soon as Northampton learned of Gell's arrival, he called his forces together and hastened out to launch a preemptive strike of his own.

Gell was occupying a good defensive position on a ridge about three miles north-east of the town with his left flank anchored on the stone wall surrounding Ingestre Park. Another park wall in the centre of his position provided cover for his foot and guns, while the cavalry were posted on the right on a piece of open moorland. Here they were joined by Brereton's horse, but the Cheshire foot still had not arrived on the scene when Northampton put in his first assault. Keeping well clear of the Parliamentarian infantry and guns esconced behind the park walls, Northampton masked Gell's left with his dragoons, and after shooting up a big plump or stand of Parliamentarian pikemen with his big demi-cannon, he charged at the head of his horse.

This first charge succeeded in routing most of the Parliamentarian cavalry, and Northampton must have kept his men well in hand for he then mounted a second one against the few horsemen who remained. This one was less successful, for they were badly shot up by Gell's foot, and although they briefly overran the Parliamentarian gun-line, Northampton himself was unhorsed and killed. A third charge, this time led by Sir Thomas Byron at the head of the Prince of Wales' Regiment, finally drove off the last of the enemy cavalry and overran the gun-line for the second time, but then he too was wounded. Hastings now succeeded to the command of the by now scattered Royalists, but although he was unable to organise a final charge to finish off the battered Parliamentarians, Gell decided that he had had enough and retreated under cover of darkness, leaving behind about 500 casualties and all eight of his guns.

Although the Royalists had won the day largely thanks to Brereton's tardy arrival on the scene, it was decided in Oxford to send Prince Rupert to recapture Lichfield and open up another military corridor linking Oxford with the north. In the meantime however, a more urgent crisis was developing in the lower Severn valley. Lord Herbert had succeeded in raising some 1,200 foot and 200 horse in South Wales, and with these it was planned to besiege Gloucester and deal with Massey once and for all. To that end also Colonel Richard Lawdey, the Governor of Hereford, joined him with another 600 men, and was entrusted with overall command of the foot while Herbert's brother, Lord John Somerset, took the cavalry.

Undismayed by this concentration, Massey sallied out and killed Lawdey in an ambush at Coleford, in the Forest of Dean, before retiring into Gloucester again.[13] Pushing on, the Royalists surrounded the city but they were unable to prevent Massey from sending boats downriver and getting word to Sir William Waller, who had been appointed commander of the Western Association forces on 21 March.

Responding with characteristic energy, Waller stormed Malmesbury on the 23rd, picked up Massey's boats at Framilode, and used them to ship his army across the Severn. Then marching past Huntley, he deployed his army behind the Welsh. In the meantime Lord Herbert had prudently taken himself off to Oxford, leaving Brett in sole charge. The Royalist cavalry were also absent, having for some reason withdrawn to Tetbury, and as Brett was fully occupied in repulsing another sortie by Massey, he was unaware of Waller's approach until the Parliamentarian guns opened up on his rear. At this point Massey very properly renewed his assault and, under pressure from two sides, the Welsh gave up the fight and surrendered at Highnam. Waller afterwards modestly reported the capture of 150 officers and gentlemen, and 1,444 common soldiers, and better still Tewkesbury was captured without a fight shortly afterwards. The King's Road was cut, and with Rupert already earmarked to go north, his younger brother Prince Maurice was ordered to open it once more.

At Evesham the Prince learned that Tewkesbury had been abandoned on the mere rumour of Waller's approach, but nothing daunted he called up Sir William Vavasour from Worcester and arranged to meet with Somerset's cavalry (now commanded by Lord Grandison) outside the town. One gallant rush should have taken town and garrison both, but as it happened Grandison hesitated and Nathaniel Fiennes received just enough warning to make his escape before the Royalists closed in.

In the meantime Waller, thinking that he was safe enough on the Welsh side of the Severn, proceeded to mount a destructive raid into Monmouth, taking the county town, Chepstow and Ross-on-Wye in quick succession. The loss of these towns was extremely damaging to the Royalists, but while Waller was thus preoccupied, Maurice got his 2,000 men over the river on 9 April, some by an extemporised bridge of boats at Tewkesbury, and the rest across at Upton. He then attempted to cut Waller off from his base at Gloucester by sending a detachment under Sir Richard Cave to retake Monmouth, but quick-footed as ever the Parliamentarian general passed his infantry, guns and baggage across to the now unguarded east bank and then broke through Maurice's picket line in the Forest of Dean with his cavalry. Once all were safely reunited at Gloucester, he allowed them a few hours' rest while Massey marched north to retake Tewkesbury. As usual it was abandoned by its garrison without a fight, and Waller moved up there himself on the evening of 12 April.

Thus far he had easily outmanoeuvred Maurice, and now to inconvenience him further a company of Massey's Foot was sent to break the bridge at Upton on the 13th. As chance would have it Maurice turned up in the nick of time, mounted an immediate assault and drove off the Parliamentarians before they could cut the bridge. So far so good, but Waller himself was coming on fast with his cavalry and some guns, so Maurice deployed his men in Ripple Field some three and a half miles north of Tewkesbury.

Waller's advance guard promptly put in a hasty attack but was just as smartly beaten off. Without further ado Waller then decided to pull back to Tewkesbury since, not only were his 1,500 men outnumbered, but the hedged enclosures which lay between Ripple Field and the village were no place to fight a cavalry action. Unfortunately just as he began his withdrawal Maurice put in his own charge, and despite a delaying action by Sir Arthur Hesilrige's Troop[14] and Massey's Bluecoats, the whole lot were tumbled back down the Tewkesbury road in considerable confusion. In all Waller lost about eighty killed[15] while the Royalists only admitted to losing two. Afterwards the Royalists fell back to Evesham feeling justifiably pleased with themselves. Maurice might not have been Waller's equal as a general, but his sense of timing had been perfect.

In the north meanwhile Prince Rupert had been doing equally well. Leaving Oxford on 29 March at the head of 1,200 horse and dragoons, 700 foot and four guns, he stormed and sacked Birmingham on 3 April, and then took Lichfield on the 21st after a ten-day siege and the explosion of a gunpowder mine under the walls of the cathedral close.[16] Afterwards he might very well have gone on to deal with Brereton in Cheshire, but profiting from the absence of the Princes, Essex suddenly went on to the offensive.

On 13 April he left his headquarters at Windsor and two days later, before the surprised Royalists could react, he sat down before Reading with 16,000 infantry[17] and 3,000 horse. The town itself was a considerable prize since it lay astride the main road from London to the west and shut off the passage of the Thames. Opening that road was justification enough for attacking the town, but the timing of the attack also caught the Royalists in a very awkward situation since it held a substantial part of their field army.

The governor, Sir Arthur Aston, had some 3,000 infantry, belonging to Henry Lunsford's, Richard Bolle's, Richard Fielding's, Sir Thomas Salusbury's, Sir Edward Fitton's and John Belasyse's regiments, together with his own regiment of horse, but only four guns. This was the single largest concentration of Royalist infantry outside Oxford and not surprisingly it took some time for Ruthven to scrape together a relief force.

At this time the town was wholly situated on the south side of the Thames, and at a sufficient distance from it to require a complete circuit of earthworks. Opinions differed as to the effectiveness of these fortifications with the Parliamentarians claiming that they were formidable and the Royalists insisting that they were 'too mean to stand a siege, being intended for winter quarters, not a garrison.'[18] It was also poorly provisioned and the King and his Council of War had already discussed its evacuation. In the event they had decided to hold on to it, but it was to be a costly mistake.

There is disappointingly little information available on the siege and much of it is contradictory, but Essex certainly established his headquarters at Southcott House, just below the town and had his guns emplaced and in action by 16 April. Aston had returned a suitably dramatic reply to the customary summons, but on the 19th he was struck on the head by a roof-tile and played no further part in the proceedings. Command then passed to Richard Fielding, and on the 25th he asked for terms.

In the meantime Ruthven had been moving heaven and earth to put a relief force together, stripping every man he dared from Oxford and the surrounding garrisons, recalling the two Princes and even the newly established garrison of Cirencester, which was evacuated on the 22nd. Alerted to the fact that Fielding was about to surrender, he marched from Oxford on the 23rd and arrived before the siege lines on the morning of the 25th. He was still on the wrong side of the river, but nothing daunted he drew out a body of 1,000 musketeers and attempted to force a passage across Caversham Bridge. Unfortunately the wooden bridge was so narrow that they could only march five or six abreast in the teeth of a murderous fire:

> ... for the enemy raised a breast-work and a battery against the bridge-end, and the commanded party, or forlorn-hope of the King's army, desperately attempted to force over the bridge against the cannons mouth, which cut them off as fast as they came.[19]

The only real hope of success was for Fielding to mount a sally at the same time and had he chosen to do so, things may have turned out differently, since it is unlikely that Essex could have concentrated sufficient men to prevent a breakout. In the event however Fielding, perhaps a little too punctiliously, considered that he was already prevented from doing so by the terms of the capitulation. Unable to establish a bridgehead, Ruthven was forced to give up the attempt, and two days later Fielding handed over the town and marched his garrison out with the honours of war.

Predictably enough the King was far from impressed. Fielding was promptly court-martialled and sentenced to death. While he has generally been condemned on all sides for surrendering too prematurely and failing to support Ruthven's relief attempt, in reality he almost certainly made the right decision. The poorly fortified town was likely to fall in any case within a few days, and it was Fielding's first duty therefore to preserve the small army trapped within it. Even if Ruthven had succeeded in forcing a passage across Caversham Bridge and linking up with Fielding, there was no question of the outnumbered Royalists fighting a general action with a single narrow bridge at their backs. At best Ruthven might have covered the evacuation of the town. He could not save it. On the other hand Fielding had already secured a promise that he could take his men back to the Royalist lines, and if he broke the cease-fire Essex would have been perfectly within his rights to insist on their becoming prisoners of war instead. It was perhaps a more measured appreciation of this fact which won him a reprieve, although he lost both his regiment and his brigade.

In any case the loss of Reading itself probably made little real difference. It was a rare success for Essex, but in the course of the siege, his army had become infected by typhus and the surviving pay warrants indicate that his regiments were hit hard by the epidemic.[20] Indeed it would not be going too far to say that the Parliamentarian army was immobilised as a result. This had serious consequences, but at least the Royalists were no better off. Arguably they were probably in worse condition. On 1 May a large entrenched camp was established on some rising ground between Culham and Abingdon, and some 5-6,000 infantry in fifteen regiments – effectively the king's entire marching army – were quartered there in improvised hutments. Unfortunately the regiments which came from Reading were infected by the same typhus raging in the Parliamentarian army and it soon spread throughout the camp.

Just as debilitating was a chronic shortage of ammunition. An inventory carried out on 8 May revealed that only fifty-seven barrels of powder were held in the army's principal magazine at Oxford[21], barely enough for a single day's fighting. Happily relief was at hand. As early as 22 February Queen Mary[22] had arrived at Bridlington on the Yorkshire coast with a substantial quantity of arms and ammunition purchased in Holland. The landing of this vital materiel was covered by the local Royalist forces commanded by the Marquis of Newcastle, and all of it was safely carried to York. Unfortunately there most of it remained, for Newcastle was preoccupied with fighting the Yorkshire Parliamentarians led by Lord Fairfax. This struggle will be more closely examined in a later chapter, but a combination of Lord Goring's victory at Seacroft Moor on 30 March and Rupert's capture of Lichfield less than a month later, persuaded Newcastle to risk running a powder convoy through to Oxford. Colonel Thomas Pinchbeck was accordingly sent off with 1,000 men and 136 barrels of powder, arriving safely in Oxford on 16 May.

He arrived just in time, for a crisis and an opportunity had simultaneously arisen in the west. The natural consequence of the withdrawal of so many troops to take part in the abortive relief of Reading was to leave the King's Road inadequately guarded. When Maurice returned to Oxford he had left Sir Richard Cave in charge at Hereford, with instructions to organise the defence of the Road. At first he seemed to make some progress by obtaining the agreement of the commissioners of array for Hereford, Monmouth and Glamorgan to the formation of an Association for mutual defence. Then it all turned sour. Only 300 foot came to a muster at Hereford on 15 April, and to make matters worse Cave and his cavalry were also called to Oxford by Maurice on the 22nd. Cave's nominal superior, Lord Herbert, told him to stay put and went off to Oxford himself in an attempt to have the orders rescinded, but in the meantime profiting from the Royalists' disarray, Waller lunged forward and arrived before Hereford on the 24th. The already demoralised and nearly mutinous garrison was quite unable to put up any kind of defence, and when Waller blew in one of the gates on the 25th, Cave ordered the horse to break out and head for Oxford, let his foot disperse, and then surrendered. Almost at a stroke the King's Road had once again been cut.

Had Waller been stronger the situation might have been very bleak indeed, but judging he had insufficient men to leave a garrison in the city, he prudently returned to Gloucester on 18 May. Encouraged by his success, he next contemplated a similar attack on Worcester, then held by some 1,500 men under Colonel Samuel Sandys. Learning of Waller's approach on the evening of 28 May, Sandys mustered his men and was waiting when Sir William turned up at daybreak next morning with about 3,000 men and eight guns.

Hoping to take the city without a fight, Waller sent his trumpeter to the Sidbury Gate to demand a surrender. Sandys refused to be intimidated and stoutly told him 'he was not at Hereford'. Offended by his bluntness, the trumpeter stood his ground and accused him of being uncivil, where-upon Sandys became even more uncivil, told him to be off and stamped back to his own quarters. The trumpeter, who was evidently a pompous fool, still refused to leave without a more politely worded reply, and when Sandys returned to demand why he he was still hanging about, he turned insulting. Not surprisingly at this point the Royalists lost patience and shot him.[23]

Correctly taking this to signify that Sandys refused to surrender, Waller opened fire with his guns at about 6am, and then launched a couple of assaults. The suburbs and outworks were cleared by 10am, but attacks on both the Sidbury and St Martin's gates were repulsed in short order. Sandys then riposted by launching a sortie through the St Martin's gate, and having lost two officers and sixteen men to no advantage Waller decided that enough was enough, and next morning retired first to Tewksbury and then on the 31st back to Gloucester.

He had in fact good reason for this abrupt departure. On 16 May the Earl of Stamford had been soundly beaten by the Cornish Royalists under Sir Ralph Hopton at Stratton. Seeking to exploit this victory the King resolved to send the Marquis of Hertford and Prince Maurice into the West Country and join with Hopton in an offensive against Bristol. They left Oxford at the head of 1,500 cavalry and 1,000 foot[24] on the 19th and rendezvoused with Hopton at Chard in Somerset on 4 June. Waller quickly realised that the threat from the west was of more immediate importance than operations in the Severn valley and, turning over the command at Gloucester to Edward Massey, he marched for Bristol and an unhappy encounter with an old comrade-in-arms.

NOTES

1. Clarendon Vol.II p355
2. Young (Rupert diary) p286
3. Turton & Peachy, *Old Robin's Foot* p7
4. This brigade must have been a rather cosy organisation for two of the regiments, Gerard's and Molyneux's, came from Lancashire; Rivers' came from Cheshire, and Salusbury's from North Wales. All of them had been raised under the authority of the Earl of Derby and a number of the officers in the Lancashire regiments were related to one another.
5. Gwynne *Military Memoirs* (1822) p24
6. Clarendon Vol.III pp327-8
7. Brooke's Regiment mustered some 480 men in mid-November. Holles had 1,100 men at Edgehill, but as they were comprehensively ridden over by just about everyone with a horse on that flank of the battlefield, it is unlikely there were more than 500 of them at Brentford. Both regiments disappeared from Essex's order of battle that winter and the survivors were drafted into other units.
8. Wilmot's command included a brigade of dragoons comprising Usher's (commanded as usual by Henry Washington), Grey's and a small unit raised by Lord Wentworth, three regiments of foot, Pennyman's, Blagge's and Rivers', and at least two regiments of horse, Digby's and Grandison's. It would be natural if Wilmot's own regiment was also present and at least one account mentions Captain Daniel O'Neale of Prince Rupert's Horse. SEE Young pp182-3
9. BM Harl 6851 transcribed in Young *Edgehill* pp184-5
10. Young *Edgehill* pp186-188. The full list was: the Prince of Wales', Rupert's, Maurice's, Byron's, Caernarvon's and Colonel Slaughter's Horse, Usher's, Duncombe's, Wentworth's and Rupert's Dragoons*, and detachments drawn from the King's Lifeguard, Dutton's, Charles Gerard's and Sir William Pennyman's Foot.
    * not in Young's list although Lieutenant Colonel John Innes was certainly present.
11. The exact composition of the Parliamentarian garrison is uncertain although it certainly included Colonel Arthur Forbes' regiment – a Gloucestershire Trained Band unit.
12. So nicknamed because he had only one eye. He later became more formally known as Lord Loughborough.
13. According to Clarendon (Vol.III p465) this left the Royalists without any experienced commanders, but in fact Lawdey was replaced by Sir Jerome Brett, a professional soldier who had commanded a regiment in 1640. Herbert had a nasty habit of disappearing at awkward moments such as this.
14. This was an ordinary troop of harquebusiers. The famous cuirassier regiment was not raised until his return to London after the Ripple debacle.
15. Inevitably most of the casualties were suffered by Massey's company, and he afterwards blamed Waller for abandoning them.
16. Oddly enough one of the Royalist casualties in the initial assault was Colonel James Usher, who had been conspicuous by his absence from Edgehill and Cirencester. After his death Henry Washington took over his regiment.

17. The infantry had recently been reorganised, and since February seven regiments were disbanded and their personnel drafted into other units.
18. Clarendon Vol.V p120. He also adds that the garrison had only forty barrels of powder.
19. Gwynne pp31-2
20. Turton and Peachy pp9, 58
21. Roy, Ian*The Royalist Ordnance Papers* Vol.2 pp477-8
22. More properly named Henrietta Maria she appears to have been popularly known by this Anglicised designation. The Royalist field word at Naseby was *Queen Mary*
23. Bund, W. *The Civil War in Worcestershire* pp93-6
24. They also took a 12-pounder, two light Minions and a brass mortar. Roy p233-4

CHAPTER IV

Cornishmen and True:
The Western Front 1642–1643

Fighting broke out in the west even before the King raised his standard at Nottingham on 22 August 1642. At the end of July the Marquis of Hertford turned up in Bath with the King's commission as Lieutenant General of the six western counties of Cornwall, Devon, Dorset, Somerset, Hampshire and Wiltshire. Charged with distributing commissions of array to the King's supporters in those counties, he chose to proclaim the fact not in hostile Bristol but in the rather safer atmosphere of Wells. Unfortunately his call to arms met with a muted response, and while the local Trained Band was persuaded to muster under Sir Edward Rodney, they made it plain that they had absolutely no intention of fighting anybody. This was unhelpful to say the least, but on the other hand Lieutenant Colonel Henry Lunsford succeeded in raising some 240 volunteers for a marching regiment to be commanded by his brother Sir Thomas. Three troops of horse were also raised, two for Lord Grandison's Regiment and the third commanded by Sir Ralph Hopton.[1]

Meanwhile Sir Alexander Popham was having rather better success in raising volunteers and Trained Bands for the service of Parliament. On 1 August 1,200 men were mustered at Shepton Mallet, and although Hopton turned up as well hoping to disrupt the proceedings, he hastily withdrew after counting heads. This reluctance to initiate hostilities did not last long. Just three days later the first shots were fired in a minor skirmish at Marshall's Elm on 4 August. Although the Cavaliers claimed a famous victory, their celebrations were cut short next day when

Popham moved forward with his whole force and compelled them to retreat to Sherborne.

Thereafter there was something of a lull, but the Earl of Bedford was sent down from London to take charge, and with 7,000 men at his back, he turned up before Sherborne on 2 September. Not surprisingly the Royalists hastily threw themselves into the castle, but then finding Bedford more cautious than his numbers warranted, they reoccupied the town with some 300 foot. A rather half-hearted siege, or rather blockade, then followed, but Bedford pulled out on the 6th and fell back to Yeovil.

The following afternoon Hertford sent Hopton after them with 100 horse, sixty dragoons and 200 foot. It was intended to be no more than a reconnaissance in force, but Hopton nearly came to grief just as he was preparing to withdraw from his observation post on the curiously named Babylon Hill. Intent on watching Yeovil Bridge, the Cavaliers failed to see a party of Parliamentarians coming out of the town until it was almost too late. Sending off his foot at once, Hopton tried to cover their retreat with his cavalry. Two of his troops led by Captain Edward Stowell:

. . . charg'd verie gallantly and routed the enemy, but withall (his troops consisting of new horse, and the Enemy being more in number) was rowted himselfe; and Capt. Moreton, being a little too neere him was likewise broaken with the same shocke, and the trueth is in verie short tyme, all the horse on both sides were in a confusion: At the same tyme a troope of the Enemyes horse charg'd up in the hollow-way on the right hand, where (Sir Tho: Lunsford having forgotten to put a party of muskettiers as before) they found no opposicion till they came among the voluntiers upon the topp of the Hill, where by a very extra-ordinary accident, Sir James Colborne with a fowling gunne shott at the Captain in the head of the troope, and at the same instant Mr. John Stowell charg'd him single (by which of their hands it was, it is not certaine) but the Captain was slayne, and the troope (being raw fellows) immedyately rowted. In this extreame confusion Sir Ralph Hopton was enforced to make good the retreate with a few officers and Gentlemen that rallyed to him . . .[2]

Despite seeing the Royalists off the premises, Bedford made no attempt to exploit his little victory. On the contrary, displaying his usual lack of resolution, he promptly decamped to Dorchester. Heartily glad to find him gone, the Cavaliers hung on at Sherborne until news came through on the 18th that Portsmouth had been taken by Sir William Waller. This unhappy news seems to have finally convinced Hertford that he was engaged in a hopeless task, so he abandoned Sherborne and headed north with all his forces to Minehead. The intention was then to ferry them across the Bristol Channel and march to join the King, but when they arrived in the little port it was to find only two ships there. These were sufficient to carry Sir Thomas Lunsford's Regiment and the guns, but the cavalry had to be left behind. With Bedford closing in, there was little alternative but for Hopton to bid goodbye to Hertford and the Lunsford brothers and retire westwards into Cornwall.

Bedford made no attempt to pursue him, and instead rejoined Essex to play a less than glorious part in the Battle of Edgehill.[3] This was rather unfortunate, for Hopton's arrival in Cornwall altered the balance of power there in the King's favour. Encouraged by the arrival of his cavalry, the local Royalists managed to bring over 3,000 men to a muster on Moilesbarrow Down on 4 October. For the most part they belonged to the Trained Bands, and although they enabled Hopton to occupy Launceston and secure the line of the Tamar, they also displayed the Bands' traditional reluctance to cross the border into neighbouring Devon. Consequently five of the Cornish leaders engaged to raise and maintain volunteer regiments, and with this little army at his back Hopton turned ambitious and cast his eyes on Plymouth.

As a first step they moved forward and occupied Mount Edgecumbe House and Millbrook, thus securing the Cornish side of the sound, and then forced a Parliamentarian detachment to retire from Plympton. This detachment had a curious history. At the beginning of October Lord Forbes' regiment of Scots mercenaries, who had been carrying out a series of piratical raids on rebel-held territory in Ireland, put into Plymouth and were promptly hired to defend it. Thus fortuitously garrisoned, the town was secured pending the arrival of Bedford's replacement, Lord Robartes, and three newly raised regiments. Two amphibious raids by the garrison on the outpost at Millbrook were beaten off, but on the night of 6 December Colonel William Ruthven, the mercenaries' commander launched an altogether more successful raid on Modbury.

Hopton had arrived there earlier that day in an attempt to raise the Devon Royalists, but the gathering 'was rather like a great fair'[4], and he could scarcely find enough armed men to mount sentries. Inevitably Ruthven (who had also been appointed commander-in-chief of the western forces) mounted a raid which scattered the assembled Royalists, captured the High Sheriff and very nearly snapped up Hopton as well. Then, taking no chances, instead of returning directly to Plymouth, he marched hard for Dartmouth and shipped both his men and the prisoners back by sea.

Without the Devon men there was no hope for the present of taking Plymouth, yet Hopton needed to secure a proper base where he could shelter and supply his army through the winter. An alternative had to be found, and so he turned his attention to Exeter instead. At first all went well. The city was summoned on 30 December, and Topsham was seized in order to prevent supplies or reinforcements coming up the Exe estuary. Unfortunately for the Royalists, while they were thus occupied in sealing off the seaward approaches to Exeter, Colonel Ruthven mounted a large body of musketeers on every nag he could find, and threw himself into the landward side of the city. This unexpected stroke did far more than simply dash the Royalists' hopes of taking Exeter, for as Hopton admitted:

> Their expectation of ammunition, subsistence and increase from the County utterly failed, so as the army was enforced in that bitter season of the year (encumbered with all sorts of wants, and with the disorder and general mutiny of the Foot) to retreat towards Cornwall.[5]

Baffled, the Cavaliers fell back by Crediton and Okehampton. Ruthven, indefatigable as ever, soon got on their track and, notwithstanding a creditable rearguard action at Bridstowe, he chased them all the way back into Cornwall and mounted an unsuccessful attack on Saltash. Even this minor reverse worked to his advantage for, while the Cavaliers' attention was fixed on the town, he managed to pass a body of men across the Tamar at Newbridge. Hopton was now in a most unenviable position. Ruthven had forestalled him at every turn and was now mounting an invasion of Cornwall. What was more, additional Parliamentarian troops were known to be on the way, commanded by the Earl of Stamford who had hitherto been making a nuisance of himself in the Severn valley. Once he joined forces with Ruthven the two of them would be well nigh unstoppable.

At this point Hopton had an undeserved stroke of luck. Three Parliamentarian ships were driven by bad weather to seek shelter in Falmouth. Naturally enough they were promptly seized by the Royalists, and the powder found on board (together with an equally welcome supply of hard cash) encouraged them to fight one last battle. At a muster held at Boconnoc on 18 January Hopton's *de facto* position as commander of the Cornish army was formally confirmed[6] and the decision was taken to counter-attack.

Accordingly they marched next morning from Boconnoc, and at about noon came up with Ruthven's army on some rising ground known as Braddock Down, just outside Liskeard. The Parliamentarians had rather more cavalry than the Royalists, but fewer infantry. Moreover all of Ruthven's foot were a mixture of raw country levies and Trained Bands; his Scots mercenaries had been left behind to hold Plymouth. Nevertheless his position was strong enough to give Hopton pause to think, and he drew up his army on another low hill, leaving a shallow valley between them.

For about two hours both commanders maintained their positions. Understandably enough neither general felt too keen about descending into the valley and fighting uphill. Ruthven might have done well to avoid battle altogether and wait for Stamford, but he had done well enough against Hopton thus far and he was no doubt confident of beating him again before the Earl arrived to steal his thunder. For his part Hopton was equally keen to anticipate Stamford's arrival and so, firing two cannon as a signal, he sent the Cornish surging forward. Both horse and foot crossed the valley and advanced so resolutely that Ruthven's men were seized with a sudden panic. The Parliamentarian foot fired just one ragged volley, and then broke and ran before the Royalists could come up with them. To add to Ruthven's chagrin, as they streamed back through Liskeard in great disorder, the townspeople suddenly rediscovered their loyalty to King Charles and rose up against them. Afterwards the Cornish claimed to have lost just two men and, while it is likely that most of Ruthven's men ran away too quickly to be killed, some 1,250 of them surrendered along with five good guns and all his baggage.

Otherwise Ruthven got clean away, for the Cavaliers rested at Liskeard on the 20th, but once they had sobered up, Hopton divided his forces. One column directed upon Launceston sent Stamford into headlong retreat, while he himself marched on Saltash. Ruthven was busily digging in there, but the town was peremptorily stormed on the 23rd. This time Hopton claimed to have taken another 140 prisoners, but Ruthven and most of his men were taken off in small boats. Buoyed up by their altered fortunes the Royalists then proceeded to overstretch themselves again by making a second attempt to blockade Plymouth.

Once again they were hampered by the customary refusal of the Cornish Trained Bands to cross the Tamar. There was no alternative but to divide the army into a number of relatively small detachments and quite inevitably, on 21 February, Ruthven sallied out and fell upon Sir Nicholas Slanning's post at Modbury. The Cavaliers at first put up a creditable resistance, but as soon as it grew dark, they fell back to Plympton leaving behind 100 dead, 150 prisoners and five guns. To make matters worse it was learned that Stamford was pulling an army together at Kingsbridge, so next day Hopton mustered his forces on Roborough Down and then retired to Tavistock.

On the 28th he, Ruthven and Stamford agreed a local cease-fire. Bitter experience had shown that neither side was strong enough to invade the territory of the other, so it seemed sensible to call a halt to unnecessary raiding during what remained of the winter. What was perhaps more surprising was that the cease-fire actually held for the stipulated forty days and nights. Naturally enough both sides made good use of this time to rest and refit their forces, but the truce ended at midnight on 22 April, and a few hours later hostilities resumed with an unnecessary disaster for the Royalists.

At the time Stamford was lying at Exeter recovering from an attack of gout. In his absence the Parliamentarian field army was commanded by Major General James Chudleigh. Soon after midnight he set off from Lifton with 1,500 musketeers, 200 pikemen and five troops of horse with the intention of attacking Launceston. Warned of his approach Hopton took up a defensive position on Beacon Hill with Sir Bevill Grenville's Regiment, and was joined there by Godolphin's just before Chudleigh turned up at about 9am. Finding the hedges at the foot of the hill stuffed full of Royalist musketeers made Chudleigh hesitate, but an hour later he launched his attack and cleared the hedges. However further progress was arrested by the arrival of Lord Mohun's Regiment and some horse and dragoons led by Sir John Berkeley.

Thereafter the battle settled down into an inconclusive firefight, while both sides waited for further reinforcements to come up. The next to appear were Colonels Slanning and Trevannion, but Chudleigh was joined at the same by Sir John Merrick's Foot (a regular regiment sent down by Essex), and a detachment of Northcote's Regiment. Nevertheless, with his whole army now concentrated, Hopton felt confident enough to launch a full-blown counter-attack. By this time it was starting to get dark and the attack threw Chudleigh's men into confusion. A hasty retreat then followed, covered by Merrick's regulars, but as the Royalists took neither guns, colours nor any appreciable number of prisoners, it may be concluded that the victory was by no means as complete as they thought.

At any rate Hopton now decided to follow up the supposed victory by mounting a dawn assault on what he fondly imagined to be the shattered remnants of Chudleigh's army at Okehampton, on the morning of the 26th. This entailed a night march, but the Royalists blithely set off and walked straight into an ambush on Sourton Down.

Hopton himself admitted afterwards that he and some of the other Royalist commanders were 'carelessly entertaining themselves in the head of the dragoons'[7] when they abruptly discovered a body of cavalry a mere carbine shot away. It was all too obvious that they were within carbine range, for they greeted the Royalists with a volley which inflicted few casualties but naturally inspired a fearful panic. As it happened there were only 100 Parliamentarians but none of the Royalists were disposed to hang around counting heads. Following up his initial success, Chudleigh plunged into the disordered Royalist ranks. Hopton's dragoons turned and ran, carrying away their own cavalry who had halted uncertainly behind them. They in turn rode over the infantry until Grenville and Mohun made a desperate stand by the guns. Hopton himself, mounted on a faster horse, got as far as the rearguard, but then finding that no one was actually pursuing him, he turned around and brought up Sir Nicholas Slanning's Regiment to reinforce Grenville.

At this point there was a pause as Chudleigh, not wishing to push his luck, drew off and summoned up 1,000 foot from Okehampton. During the lull the Cavaliers manned an old ditch and planted swine feathers (pointed stakes) in front of their guns. Eventually they saw the distinctive glow of slow-match as Chudleigh's infantry came up and fired two cannon-shot into them. This unseasonable welcome halted the Parliamentarians in their tracks. They may not have been too keen about fighting in the dark – which can hold all manner of terrors for those unused to it – and the prospect of assaulting a force of unknown size dug in with artillery was too much for them.

Nothing daunted, Chudleigh himself essayed another cavalry charge but found his way blocked by the swine feathers. Baffled by this unexpected obstacle and thoroughly disgusted by the craven behaviour of his foot, he then decided to call it a night and returned to Okehampton under the cover of a sudden rainstorm which thoroughly drenched both armies. The Royalists had survived the night, but there was no disguising the reality of their defeat and they fell back in to Bridstowe in considerable disorder. In the process they also managed to lose Hopton's personal baggage and with it correspondence detailing Royalist plans to advance into Somerset in order to open up communications with the King's Oxford Army.

Stamford, whose gout had been miraculously cured by the victory on Sourton Down, was determined to prevent this, and ordering his forces to concentrate at Torrington, he crossed the Cornish border on 15 May. Knowing that Hopton would be certain to launch an immediate counterattack, Stamford took up a strong position on a 200-foot ridge at Stratton and waited for him. The Parliamentarian forces appear to have comprised some 5,400 foot, 200 horse and thirteen small guns. Hopton on the other hand, distracted by Ruthven's still active garrison in Plymouth and by a diversionary raid on Bodmin, could muster only 2,400 foot and 500 horse. Nevertheless a council of war concluded that 'notwithstanding the great visible disadvantage, that they must either force the Enemies' Camp, while the most part of their Horse and dragoons were from them, or unavoidably perish.'[8]

Thus far the fighting in the west had been extremely volatile and characterised by sudden assaults and even more precipitate retreats, but the battle of Stratton was altogether different. The Royalists moved forward to their start-line under cover of darkness, and at dawn commenced a brisk firefight with the Parliamentarian musketeers lining the hedges at the foot of the hill.

For some reason the Cornish Royalists do not appear to have deployed their infantry in conventional brigade or battalion formations, but rather seem to have favoured forming a front line of musketeers behind which stands of pikemen waited until called forward to effect a breakthrough, or to mount a counter-attack, as the case might be. This can be seen quite clearly at Stratton, for while the musketeers were thus engaged, Hopton formed his pikemen into four assault columns each about 600 strong. The first, under his personal command, was to attack on the right against the southern end of Stamford's position, two more under Grenville and Slanning were to attack in the centre, while the fourth led by Godolphin formed the left wing. In reserve were some 500 horse under Colonel John Digby.

At about 5am all four columns rolled forward but were unable to clear the hedge-line and the battle degenerated once more into a desultory firefight. Hopton stubbornly refused to pull off, and this phase of the battle lasted for about ten hours. By about 3pm, however, the Cornish musketeers were running short of ammunition and Chudleigh decided, possibly independently of Stamford, that the moment had come for a counter-attack. Placing himself at the head of a stand of pikemen, he swept down the hill and ran full tilt into Sir Bevill Grenville's pikemen. So sharp was the shock of the onset that Grenville and most of his front rank were knocked off their feet.[9] Naturally enough Chudleigh's men were also a little disordered as a result and unable to withstand a very prompt counter-attack launched by Sir John Berkeley. Not only were the Parliamentarians thrown back in their turn, but Chudleigh too may have been knocked off his feet for he was amongst the prisoners.

While the Parliamentarians were thus distracted the Royalist flanking columns renewed their assault and this time managed to push their way on to the upper slopes of the ridge. Stamford's left abruptly gave way, and with his infantry reserves already committed to Chudleigh's ill-fated counter-attack and most of his cavalry off raiding Bodmin, he was unable to prevent his line being rolled up. Regiment by regiment his army was broken, but he bravely remained on the field until, according to Colonel John Weare, he had but twenty men standing by him. Then, having fired off his guns one last time, he and Weare fled to Exeter, leaving behind 300 dead, 1,700 prisoners, the thirteen guns and most precious of all, seventy barrels of powder – enough to fight another battle.

Hopton now proceeded to occupy Launceston where he received the happy news that the Marquis of Hertford and Prince Maurice were marching to join him with a substantial force of horse and foot. He had already received warning that such a move was imminent, and so he made a dash for Chard in Somerset and there rendezvoused with Hertford and Maurice on 4 June. Once combined, their forces mustered a very respectable 2,000 horse, 4,000 foot, a regiment of dragoons and a useful train of artillery. Clarendon implies that the army's command structure was less than satisfactory for:

> . . . how small soever the Marquis's party was in number, it was supplied with all the general officers of a royal army, a general, a

lieutenant-general, general of Horse, general of the ordnance, major-general of Horse, and another of Foot . . .[10]

It was no doubt intended that they would recruit an army large enough to justify their employment. In the meantime, although Hertford still held the King's commission as notional General of the Western Counties, his Lieutenant General, Prince Maurice, was the one who actually exercised that command. The Earl of Caernarvon was General of the Horse, with Sir James Hamilton as Major General under him. The Earl of Marlborough was General of the Ordnance, and Sir Ralph Hopton served as Field Marshall. As was customary the important strategic decisions were taken by a Council of War comprising all the senior officers of the army.

As to those strategic decisions, thus far the campaign in the west had been of only local significance, but now the Cornish army was required for something far more important. As we have seen in the previous chapter, the Royalists' overriding concern at this time was the security of the King's Road. Bitter experience had shown that it could not be kept open by locally raised forces, and that it was equally dangerous to divert troops from the main Oxford army for that purpose. Now Maurice was once again charged with taking Bristol and securing the lower end of the Severn valley.

Instead of marching directly upon the city, he first set about securing his position by taking Taunton Dene – which surrendered under the threat of being stormed – and then Bridgewater and Wells. At the latter place the Royalists received the disturbing but not unexpected news that Sir William Waller was concentrating his own army from the Severn valley and what remained of the Western forces at Bath. Notwithstanding the fact that Stamford's foot had been well beaten at Stratton, Waller probably mustered about the same number of infantry as Maurice. As for the cavalry, Stamford's 1,200 horse and dragoons were still available for service. In addition Waller also had his own veteran regiments of horse and dragoons, Colonel Robert Burghill's regulars and a newly raised regiment of cuirassiers commanded by Sir Arthur Hesilrige.[11]

Some sort of reconnaissance in force was obviously called for, so Maurice took Caernarvon's Regiment out on the 10th to have a look at them. As frequently happens in this sort of affair, he ventured too close and was promptly attacked by some horse and dragoons. Caernarvon's men evidently did not put up much of a fight for they were promptly beaten back into Chewton Mendip where Maurice was wounded and captured. The rest of the Royalist army was moving into its quarters when the unhappy news came through and a rather odd argument ensued. Some officers of Maurice's own regiment held that they were under his direct orders to take up their quarters, and that should they attempt to rescue him they could be court-martialled for disobedience! Captain Richard Atkyns however announced himself willing to take the risk and set off at the head of his squadron.

Happily he almost at once ran into the Earl of Caernarvon who professed himself heartily glad to see the Captain and readily gave him orders to attempt a rescue. Thus reassured, Atkyns pushed on and ran into some dragoons, but providentially or so he says, a thick mist suddenly descended and under cover of it the dragoons mounted up and fell back. If this was true they cannot have fallen back far for Atkyns and Caernarvon then encountered two squadrons of Waller's Regiment, flanked by dragoons lining some hedges. Nothing daunted Atkyns promptly charged the left-hand squadron commanded by Captain Edward Kightley:

> The dragoons on both sides, seeing us so mixed with their men that they could not fire at us, but they might kill their own men as well as ours; took horse and away they run also. In this charge I gave one Captain Kitely quarter twice, and at last he was killed: the Lord Arundel of Wardour also, took a dragoon's colours, as if it were hereditary to the family to do so; but all of us overran the Prince, being a prisoner in that party; for he was on foot, and had a great hurt upon his head, and I suppose not known to be the Prince. My groom coming after us, espied the Prince, and all being in confusion, he alighted from his horse, and gave him to the Prince, which carried him off: and though this was a very great success, yet we were in as great danger as ever; for now we were in disorder and had spent our shot; and had not time to charge again; [ie; to reload] and my Lieutenant and Cornet, with above half the Party, followed the chase of those that ran, within half a mile of their army; that when I came to rally, I found I had not 30 men; we then had three fresh troops to charge, which were in our rear, but by reason of their marching through a wainshard before they could be put in order: I told those of my party, that if we did not put a good face upon it, and charge them presently, before they were in order, we were all dead men or prisoners; which they apprehending, we charged them,; and they made as it were a lane for us, being as willing to be gone as we ourselves.[12]

Having suffered 'two shrewd cuts' on the head, and then having been ridden over by his own men, rather slowed Maurice down, and it was not until 2 July that his outriders reached Bradford-on-Avon, about five miles south-east of Bath. Waller was already waiting for them, covering Bath in a strong position on Claverton Down, so the decision was taken to swing farther east in an attempt to outflank him. This turned out to be a surprisingly delicate operation for Maurice was clearly determined not to take any unnecessary risks. As a first step Hopton was sent with a detachment of Cornish foot to dislodge a covering party from Monkton Farleigh. This was accomplished without much difficulty, and the Parliamentarians were then driven back through Batheaston and on to the southern slopes of Lansdown Hill, a long steep-sided ridge running north-west from Bath. At the same time Maurice successfully crossed the Avon only to find Waller retiring into Bath. That evening the Royalists decided to continue their turning movement in the hope of seizing Lansdown Hill and thus interposing their forces between Waller and Bristol.

Unfortunately Waller was equally alive to this possibility, and next morning the Cavaliers were dismayed to find his whole army occupying Lansdown. Judging the position to be too strong to force, they then drew off to Marshfield, some six miles north of the city. There they were well placed both to act against Waller's communications with Bristol and to receive supplies and reinforcements from Oxford. Waller however had no intention of being turned out of Bath without a fight and began digging in on top of the ridge.

Early on the morning of 5 July this fact was discovered by a party of Royalist horse led by Major George Lower, but he allowed himself to be driven off so vigorously that the Cavaliers turned out expecting a full-scale attack. Some desultory skirmishing then followed. Preceded by dismounted dragoons, the Royalists pushed forward and eventually established themselves on Freezing Hill, immediately to the north of Waller's opposition astride the Bath Road where it crosses Lansdown. At this point it was decided to call it a day, since too much ammunition was being expended to little purpose and the decision was taken to return to Marshfield.

Had Waller been content to let them go, things might well have turned out differently, but at about 3pm Colonel Robert Burghill moved forward with some 300 horse and a large body of dragooners. At first he met with some success, and the Royalist withdrawal became disorderly. Maurice had earlier ordered Hopton to provide detachments of musketeers to interline the cavalry squadrons, but far from strengthening the horse they only got in the way. Relations between the Cornish foot and the Oxford horse were already bad enough[13], and the necessary happy cooperation between the two was consequently non-existent. Unable to coordinate any counter-attacks, the cavalry fell back, and some even ran as far as Oxford, abandoning the musketeers to their own devices. They for their part very bloody-mindedly held on to their positions amongst the hedgerows and momentarily brought the Parliamentarian advance to a standstill.

Granted this brief respite Caernarvon at last managed to fight back. First the Marquis of Hertford's own Lifeguard troop, commanded by Lord Arundell of Trerice, put in a charge, and in the melee Robert

Burghill was badly wounded. Caernarvon then tried to second this success by leading forward his own regiment and, although he succeeded in driving the Parliamentarians into the valley separating Freezing Hill from Lansdown, he in his turn was wounded when Waller committed reinforcements of his own. Nevertheless the Parliamentarians were unable to clear the valley bottom and soon retired back up the hill.

So far so good. The Royalists might now have retired to Marshfield in safety, but finding that his Cornish infantry had worked themselves up into something approaching hysteria, Hopton decided to give them their heads and, without bothering to consult Prince Maurice, he ordered a frontal assault on the Lansdown position.

Not surprisingly this hasty attack quickly came to grief. Hopton began by employing his favourite tactic of pushing a column of pikemen straight up the Bath Road, while:

> . . . sending out as they went strong parties of musketeers on each hand to second one another, to endeavour under the cover of the enclosed grounds to gain the flank of the enemy on the top of the Hill, which at last they did . . .[14]

As the Royalist pikemen went up the road they marched into a blizzard of fire from both entrenched guns and Parliamentarian musketeers alike which at first stopped them dead in their tracks. The attack might have stalled altogether were it not for Sir Bevill Grenville who rallied the pikemen, placed some musketeers on one flank – where they very prudently established themselves behind a stone wall – and got some horse to cover his right. Again pushing up the road, littered by now with dead and wounded men, Grenville gained the brow of the hill before being halted by a succession of cavalry charges – three according to Hopton. The last of them seems to have been most successful for Grenville, and many of his men were cut down and in the end the Cornish pikemen may only have held because Grenville's fifteen year-old son was hoisted into his father's saddle.[15]

In the meantime relief was at hand in the shape of some cavalry led by Sir Robert Walsh and Richard Atkyns:

> As I went up the hill, which was very steep and hollow, I met several dead and wounded officers brought off; besides several running away, that I had much ado to get up by them. When I came to the top of the hill, I saw Sir Bevil Grinvill's stand of pikes, which certainly preserved our army from a total rout, with the loss of his most precious life: they stood as upon the eaves of an house for steepness, but as unmoveable as a rock; on which side of this stand of pikes our horse were, I could not discover; for the air was so darkened by the smoke of the powder,

that for a quarter of an hour together (I dare say) there was no light seen, but what the fire of the volleys of shot gave; and 'twas the greatest storm that ever I saw[16]

Unable to dislodge Grenville's men and threatened by the Royalist musketeers working their way up on either flank, Waller meanwhile pulled back to what Atkyns describes as a very large sheep-cote surrounded by a stone wall. From there it proved impossible to dislodge him and both sides settled down to shoot it out until nightfall. During the night the Royalist commanders decided upon a withdrawal for their losses had been terrible and they were almost out of ammunition. In preparation for this their guns were sent away, but at about one in the morning some suspicious activity inspired them to send forward a scout who made the happy discovery that Waller was gone. As a Royalist Colonel named Slingsby afterwards remarked: 'we were glad they were gone for if they had not I know who had within an hour . . .'[17]

The Royalists may have been left in possession of the field, but to all intents and purposes it was they and not Waller who had lost the battle – a quite unnecessary one brought on by Hopton's insubordination. At daylight they began retiring to Marshfield and might have taken up their old quarters there had not Hopton been badly injured when a precious ammunition cart blew up. Waller's army was in much better shape and, having called up reinforcements from Bristol, he quickly got on their trail and hustled them straight through Marshfield. They then halted at Chippenham for two days, but with Waller now pressing hard on their retreat, they set off again and reached Devizes on the night of 9 July. Maurice tried to make a stand on Roundway Down next day, but finding the army had neither the stomach nor the ammunition for another battle, he pulled it back into the town. That night a Council of War agreed that the foot would stand a siege there while Hertford, Maurice and the horse broke out and rode for Oxford to bring relief.

NOTES

1. The two troops which Sir John Digby and Sir Francis Hawley raised for Grandison's Regiment never succeeded in joining it. All three troops were eventually expanded into full regiments.
2. Hopton, Sir Ralph *Bellum Civile* (1902) pp15-16
3. Oddly enough Bedford's own troop may have taken part in the routing of Lunsford's Regiment at Edgehill.
4. Hopton p25
5. *ibid.* p27
6. Up until this point the army had theoretically been commanded jointly by Lord Mohun, Sir Ralph Hopton, Sir John Berkeley and Colonel William Ashburnham.
7. Hopton p38

8. *ibid.* p42
9. None of them it will be noticed were actually skewered, thus bearing out Daniel Lupton's remarks upon the subject.
10. Clarendon Vol.IV p109
11. Hesilrige had returned to London after his own troop of harquebusiers was cut up at Ripple in April. His new regiment, which he equipped as cuirassiers, appears to have been a mixture of new recruits and troops transferred from other regiments.
12. Atkyns *Vindication* pp14-15
13. Atkyns p12: '. . . the Cornish foot could not well brook our horse (especially when we were drawn up upon corn) but they would many times let fly at us: these were the very best foot I ever saw, for marching and fighting; but so mutinous withal, that nothing but an alarm could keep them from falling foul upon their officers'. This 'God damn all Gentlemen' attitude was echoed by Hopton p47: 'There [at Taunton] began the disorder of the horse visibly to break in upon all the prosperity of the public proceedings . . . [the generals] were yet never able to repress the extravagant disorder of the horse to the ruin and discomposure of all.'
14. Hopton p54
15. Some doubt has been cast on this legend as the letter describing the incident may be a 19th century forgery, but nevertheless it does reflect a long-standing tradition.
16. Atkyns p19
17. Footnote. Hopton p96

CHAPTER V
High Tide:
The Central Front 1643

After taking Reading at the end of April, Essex was immobilised by a typhus epidemic, but on 10 June he got his army moving again and shifted his headquarters to Thame in Buckinghamshire. There he ought to have been well-placed to threaten Oxford, but evidently considered that his army was still too weakened by disease to execute that threat. For their part the Royalists too were hampered not only by the same epidemic, and a continuing shortage of ammunition, but also by the need to divert troops to keep the King's Road open. As a result their response to this dangerous move was pretty well confined to launching heavy raids against Essex's outlying quarters.

In the first of these Prince Rupert led 1,000 horse, 350 dragoons and a detachment of 500 musketeers on a sweep through Chinnor on the night of 17-18 June, and Sir John Hurry[1] led a similar one through West Wycombe a week later. Neither affair was of any real importance, although the former led to the death of John Hampden in an unsuccessful attempt to stop Rupert at Chalgrove Field on the 18th. However the stalemate was about to be dramatically broken.

Prince Maurice's union with the Cornish foot had been facilitated by an ammunition convoy which Colonel Thomas Pinchbeck ran into Oxford on 15 May. He had managed to slip safely through the Midlands in the wake of the Royalist victory at Hopton Heath and Rupert's capture of Lichfield, but by the end of May Lord Grey of Groby had assembled some 5-6,000 Parliamentarian troops in the Nottingham area. It was clear therefore that if the Queen was to bring the rest of the great magazine down from York, she was quite literally going to have to fight her way through to Oxford.

The march of this convoy is one of the most neglected campaigns of the war, yet it was also in its way one of the most crucial and one of the best planned and executed. The Queen set off from York on 4 June with something under 3,000 men. The core of this little army was the wreckage of Lord Derby's forces who had been driven out of Lancashire in April. At least four of Derby's former regiments can be identified; Thomas Tyldesley's horse and foot, and two other cavalry regiments commanded by Lord Molyneux and Thomas Dalton. Other Lancashire men helped form the nucleus of the Queen's Lifeguards of horse and foot, though the former was also substantially made up of French volunteers. In addition Newcastle provided two of his own infantry regiments commanded by William Eure and Conyers Darcy.

The first stage of the march, to the Royalist garrison at Newark, was accomplished without difficulty, but the next stage was going to be much more dangerous. Lieutenant General Charles Cavendish now assumed responsibility for the operation and added Sir Thomas Blackwell's Foot and a cavalry brigade of his own to the escort. Leaving Newark on the 21st he headed west in order to avoid a head-on clash with Groby's forces. In this he was successful for the noble lord displayed a remarkable lack of initiative, but it meant that the convoy was still on the wrong side of the Trent.

A bridge was needed and Cavendish found it at Burton on 2 July. The Parliamentarian garrison in the town was hopelessly outnumbered, but knowing the importance of the bridge, they refused to surrender. Consequently Cavendish was forced to mount an assault over a nearby ford while Tyldesley earned himself a knighthood by leading a desperate cavalry charge straight across the thirty-six-arched bridge. Having safely passed the convoy over the river, Cavendish's responsibility was at an end, and rather against his inclinations he returned with his cavalry to Newark. The final stage of the march was to be covered by the Oxford Army itself. In anticipation Prince Rupert had been occupying a forward position at Buckingham since 1 July, and on the 11th he met with the 'She-

Generalissima' at Stratford on Avon before convoying her to a symbolic meeting with the King himself on Edgehill two days later.

Consequently when Maurice and Hertford, having broken out of Devizes, arrived in Oxford on the morning of 11 July they found both the King and Prince Rupert absent. Worse still none of the remaining foot there could be spared to go to the aid of the beleaguered Western Army. It was not just men which were lacking. Immediately after Lansdown Maurice had dispatched the Earl of Crawford to Oxford in order to fetch a fresh supply of ammunition. On the 9th fifteen barrels of powder together with match and musket-balls were delivered to him from the magazine, and with 500 cavalry to guard it (his own Scots mercenaries and Colonel James Long's Regiment) it should have been safe enough. Unfortunately he was ambushed by a party of Waller's horse under Major Dowett and lost five of the six wagons and tumbrils.[2]

Now Maurice had to haggle for a fresh supply of powder and shot. At first Lord Percy would only release ten barrels of powder and a pair of brass 6-pounders, but a little later he was persuaded to part with a further ten barrels and some additional artillery ammunition.[3] More encouragingly, although no infantry were available, he learned that Lord Wilmot's brigade was already earmarked for service in the west. As it was now no longer a question of reinforcing but rescuing the Western Army, this move was delayed and a rendezvous appointed at Marlborough on the 12th. There Maurice assembled not only Wilmot's brigade, but Sir John Byron's as well, and a third commanded by Crawford. Notwithstanding the absence of any infantry, the relief of Devizes was to be no dashing cavalry raid for the ammunition was carried in a train of no fewer than thirty-seven carts.

The same day Waller was offering terms to Hopton. Having lost all their ammunition at Lansdown the Royalists were fortunate enough to find two barrels of powder when they entered Devizes. This little supply, together with a quantity of improvised match, had enabled them to hold out thus far, but it is questionable whether they could have stopped the Parliamentarians had they tried to storm the barricades instead of wasting eight hours in futile negotiations. Finding Hopton obstinate, Waller resolved to do just that, but his preparatory bombardment was halted next morning by the news that a large body of Royalist cavalry was approaching from the east.

Responding swiftly he pulled his army together and marched it up on to Roundway Down. There he occupied what seemed a strong position in the shallow down astride the Marlborough Road, flanked on the south by Bagdon Hill (now Roundway Hill) and on the north by King's Play Hill. In his centre were five regiments of foot totalling about 1,800 men and seven guns. His six regiments of horse totalling another 2,000 men were formed on the flanks. Nothing is said as to the deployment of his regiment of dragoons. They may have been posted in support of the cavalry but their natural habitat was hedgerows, not open downland and it is more likely that they were left behind to mask Devizes. Waller could certainly have been forgiven for assuming that he could spare them, for his horse and foot outnumbered the approaching Cavaliers by more than two to one.

For their part they could only muster some 1,800 men – all of them cavalry – drawn up in conventional fashion with two brigades forward and one in reserve. Nine regiments can be identified; Wilmot's brigade appears to have included his own, Sir John Digby's and Prince Maurice's Regiments. Byron's on the other hand had only two rather weak regiments commanded by Thomas Morgan and Henry Sandys besides his own. Consequently it was probably beefed up by the addition of Lord Digby's Regiment which had itself been displaced from Wilmot's Brigade by Prince Maurice's Regiment. Crawford's mercenaries and Long's regiment formed the reserve and may also have been tasked with the protection of the ammunition train.[4]

Although the Royalists had announced their arrival to their friends in Devizes by loosing off two cannon-shots, it is unlikely that this was a signal for the foot to break out of the town and effect a rendezvous. What Waller would have made of such an opportunity does not bear thinking about. In any case the Royalists lacked the ammunition for a battle, and beyond acknowledging the signal with a cannon-shot of their own, Hopton's foot very prudently remained in the town.

Nevertheless Maurice and Wilmot were obviously none too keen on attacking Waller head on, and instead both armies commenced by sending out forlorn hopes. The Royalist one commanded by Major Paul Smith of Wilmot's, set about their opponents so vigorously that they drove them back into Waller's left wing, throwing it into some disorder. Wilmot thereupon seized what could only be a fleeting opportunity and either on his own initiative or at Prince Maurice's urging, he suddenly led his whole brigade forward against them.

Richard Atkyns, who was in temporary command of Maurice's Regiment, commented that the decision to charge was taken so suddenly that he hardly had time to buckle on his helmet. Moreover, when the Cavaliers moved forward, they were still in open order and this, together with the fact that they were deployed only three deep, meant that they considerably overlapped Hesilrige's regiments. Indeed Atkyns records that:

> All the horse on the left hand of Prince Maurice his regiment, had none to charge; we charging at the utmost man of their right wing [sic] . . . for though they were above twice our numbers, they being six deep, in close order and we but three deep, and open (by reason of our sudden charge) we were without them at both ends.[5]

56

Byron quickly followed suit by charging Waller's right with equal determination. Although they had the advantage of the slope, the
Parliamentarians on both wings stood fast and blazed away with
carbines and pistols. The Royalists on the other hand came straight in,
and after a stiff fight which Byron intriguingly describes as 'pushing', he
drove them back on their own reserves and then tumbled the whole lot
down the sharp slope overlooking Devizes.[6]

As his cavalry were swept away Waller formed all his infantry into a
large hollow square. Crawford meanwhile may have been employed in
masking this square, but there could have been no question of mounting
a serious attack on it until Wilmot and Byron returned from their pursuit
of the Parliamentarian cavalry. A number of uncoordinated attacks were
indeed mounted but made little impression. Then, rather late in the day,
the Cornish foot eventually came out of Devizes, and in the face of this
threat, Waller tried to march off. Naturally the Parliamentarian formation
soon started to become ragged, and seeing this Byron managed to put in
a good charge which scattered them completely. Waller and a few other
mounted officers managed to escape in the confusion but all his infantry
and guns were lost.

Immediately after the battle Wilmot, whose senior commission
entitled him to claim the credit for what was probably Maurice's victory,[7]
returned with his cavalry to Oxford. There it was quickly realised that the
astonishing victory had presented the Royalists with an opportunity to
clear the King's Road once and for all just at the very moment when the
safe arrival of the Queen's convoy provided them with the resources
which they would need to accomplish it.

The primary objectives were Bristol and Gloucester. Maurice was
already moving forward with the Western Army to seize Bath, and
Rupert very quickly got a substantial part of the Oxford Army moving in
the same direction. On the 15th the three infantry brigades quartered at
Culham, two cavalry brigades under Sir Arthur Aston and Charles
Gerard, and nine companies of dragoons led by Colonel Washington
were ordered to a concentration area at Fyfield. Two demi-cannon accompanied the Oxford contingent of this force, and on the 17th they were
followed by the train proper. This included another six guns, two
culverins, two 12-pounders, two 6-pounders, and a mortar. In addition to
large quantities of artillery and entrenching stores the train also carried
no fewer than eighteen barrels of coarse-grained powder for the guns and
forty-two barrels of finer powder for musketeers.[8]

Bristol had originally been sited on a strong position on what was
effectively an island between the Frome and the Avon, but latterly its
suburbs had spilled out beyond these natural boundaries. More seriously
it was overlooked on the west and north by a range of hills along which
it was necessary to extend the line of defences, not for the direct protec-

tion of the city but in order to deny the heights to any attacker. Essentially the defensive line was little more than a low earthen rampart and ditch linking a series of self-contained strongpoints. Afterwards de Gomme reckoned the walls to be no more than five or six feet high and the ditch sometimes shallower, except at the forts where it was generally eight or nine feet deep. Moreover although the governor, Colonel Nathaniel Fiennes, had no fewer than ninety-seven guns and a mortar piece scattered along the line, he only had some 1,500 foot and 300 horse besides an unknown number of armed citizens to cover the five-mile circuit.

On the 23rd Prince Rupert conducted his reconnaissance and then summoned the city next day while his troops were moving into position. Fiennes very properly refused to surrender, and a Council of War agreed to storm the city at daybreak on the 26th. Although Maurice and the Western officers were in favour of digging in and conducting a proper siege, this was undoubtedly the correct decision. Except in their own sector, on the south bank of the Avon, the ground was generally too hard for digging, and while Fiennes might have been able to sit out a siege, he had far too few men to resist a general assault. Recognising this Rupert planned to increase his difficulties by directing each of the six infantry brigades to attack independently at a number of points scattered all the way round the perimeter.

The operation was to be synchronised by the firing of the two demi-cannon, but in the event the Western Army decided unilaterally to go in early under cover of darkness. At about 3am Maurice's three brigades commanded by Basset, Slanning and Buck,[9] moved forward and attacked on a fairly narrow front on either side of the city's Temple Gate. Unfortunately the comparative softness of the ground had allowed Fiennes to dig the ditch out to a good depth, and although the storming columns were well provided with carts and fascines, they were unable to bridge it and effect a lodgement on the walls. After only half an hour they were beaten back with heavy losses, particularly among the officers – two of the three brigade commanders being killed and the third, Bassett, wounded.

Elsewhere Rupert's army also found it tough going at first. Lord Grandison's brigade launched an unsuccessful attack on the Stokes Croft gate on the north side, but after failing to blow it in with a petard, they then moved uphill to attack the Prior's Hill Fort instead. Their intention may have been to assist Colonel John Belasyse who was attacking the Colston's Mount Fort in the adjacent sector, but in the event both forts proved too strong. Lord Grandison was fatally wounded and, notwithstanding Rupert's personal encouragement, Belasyse's men could not get over the ditch. In the end however Rupert's calculation that an all-out assault would overstretch the garrison was proved correct.

Colonel Henry Wentworth had been tasked with putting in an attack on the Windmill Hill Fort on the western sector with his own brigade and Washington's Dragoons. In the event his men were funnelled in some disorder into a re-entrant lying between that work and the adjacent Brandon Hill Fort. There they quite fortuitously found themselves in dead ground and grenaded their way over the curtain. At this point they should have been counter-attacked by Fiennes' cavalry reserve, but there was a fatal delay and the Royalists were given time to throw down part of the earthen rampart and begin passing troops through. By the time Fiennes' cavalry finally moved, some 300 Royalist infantry were in and the attack broke up when several Royalist officers ran at the horses brandishing fire-pikes.[10] By about 4am Wentworth's men had pushed on to take a barn[11], or strongpoint, known as the Essex Work, and there he very prudently called a halt until Belasyse's brigade and Aston's cavalry came through the breach to reinforce him. Although the outer perimeter had been pierced, Fiennes still held the older mediaeval one, and it took two more hours of often vicious street fighting before the arrival of Grandison's brigade finally enabled the Royalists to break through the Frome Gate and into the city proper.

Fiennes marched out next day to face a Parliamentarian court-martial which very nearly placed him in front of a firing squad, and Sir Ralph Hopton was appointed governor in his place. Costly though it had been, the capture of Bristol was of crucial importance, for quite apart from the threat which it had posed to the King's Road, it gave the Cavaliers a major port, the nucleus of a small fleet and manufactories which would eventually be capable of turning out 300 muskets a week. From now on the Cavalier regiments would no longer be short of firearms, and by the war's end many of them would have abandoned pikes entirely.

Maurice and Caernarvon exploited the victory by leading the rather battered Western Army off on a great sweep through Dorset and Devon which successively captured Dorchester, Weymouth and Portland almost without a fight. Exeter surrendered after a siege on 4 September, and Dartmouth fell on 6 October. By the end of the year Plymouth and Lyme would be the only garrisons of any importance still holding out for Parliament, and Royalist blockade runners would be bringing large quantities of arms and ammunition into the western ports.

For his part Rupert was to move north and lay siege to Gloucester, but first a certain reorganisation was necessary. Only two of the brigades which had stormed Bristol were available for this service; Grandison's, now known as the Lord General's, and Wentworth's. Belasyse's old brigade was broken up, part being left in garrison at Bristol while the remainder marched in a new one commanded by Sir Ralph Dutton.[12] Some four or five miles north of Cirencester he met with the King and

Patrick Ruthven, bringing another infantry brigade[13] and fifty barrels of powder. Yet more troops were summoned from garrisons all along the King's Road and on 10 August the Royalist army appeared before Gloucester.

The governor, Colonel Edward Massey, had only some 1,300 foot[14] and 200 horse, but the perimeter which he had to defend was considerably shorter than Fiennes' position at Bristol. Left to himself Rupert might have tried an escalade, but the King and Ruthven opted for a regular siege – given the abysmal performance of the Bristol veterans at Newbury six weeks later they may well have been right. Unfortunately, despite the steady arrival of reinforcements, all that the Royalists managed to achieve was an unsustainable expenditure of ammunition.

Meanwhile on 4 August Essex had received explicit orders to relieve Gloucester. His own typhus-ravaged forces were quite inadequate for the task; he had only 5,000 foot in twelve regiments and about 3,000 horse,[15] but five regiments were promised from the London Trained Bands besides another three regular units. On 29 August long-awaited supplies of fresh clothing began to be issued to his ragged regiments, and the following day the reinforcements arrived in the concentration area at Brackley Heath just outside Aylesbury. The move could be delayed no longer, so on 1 September the army moved to Bicester and then on the 2nd to Hook Norton.

Throughout the siege Wilmot had been keeping Essex's forces under observation and, noting the concentration and unmistakable preparations for a move, he sent off a warning. This in turn led to a hasty order for the Oxford magazines to prepare a train of ten field guns to supplement the existing siege train. The order was sent off on the 2nd but it was not until the 5th that the train left Oxford, probably in order to avoid running into Essex.[16] In the meantime Rupert took out all the cavalry and 1,000 commanded musketeers led by Lieutenant Colonel George Lisle.[17] On the 4th he ran into Essex at Stow in the Wold, and there fought a series of delaying actions in order to cover the rest of the Royalist army as it cleared the siege lines. This was successfully accomplished and next morning they drew off to a concentration area at Painswick.

Alerted to this fact by the smoke rising from their burning huts, Essex proceeded cautiously and only entered Gloucester on the 8th. Although the garrison, down to their last three barrels of powder, were heartily glad to see him, he was now faced with the problem of returning safely to the Thames valley. There was no thought of actively seeking out and engaging the King's forces – quite the reverse. On the 10th he feinted northwards to Tewksbury, and the Royalists obligingly moved up from Sudely to Pershore, still as they thought blocking the direct route to London. Then, on the night of the 14th, Essex slipped out of Tewksbury and headed south to Cirencester where he had the great good fortune to surprise two Royalist cavalry regiments[18] and forty wagon-loads of food and other supplies.

It was some hours before the main Royalist army was alerted to this move and set off in pursuit amidst a shower of recriminations. By the 16th Rupert was at Farringdon with 3,000 horse, and on the 17th Essex lay at Swindon while the King was some ten miles behind at Alvescote. In the prevailing wet and muddy conditions this should have been as good as a whole day's advantage, but on the 18th Rupert's cavalry caught Essex's men strung out across Aldbourne Chase. Whether he could have made more of the opportunity than he did is open to question, but at least he managed to hustle Essex southwards, forcing him to cross the Kennet at Hungerford and make for Newbury.

Nevertheless the Parliamentarians woke next morning only nine miles short of their objective, while the Royalist army still lay sixteen miles away at Wantage. Even allowing for the appalling state of the roads, they should have reached Newbury well ahead of the Cavaliers, but perhaps because they thought themselves safe on the south bank of the river they moved too slowly. Essex's quartermasters had no sooner ridden into the town on the afternoon of the 19th than they were kicked out again by Rupert's cavalry. By a tremendous effort the King's army had succeeded in winning the race.

A more resolute commander might have pushed on to dispute possession of the town, but Essex called a halt on Enborne Heath, two miles to the west and made no attempt to interfere with the Royalist concentration just to the south of it.

Most of the major battles of the Civil War were fought in open fields or heathlands which offered no impediment to the scientific deployment of armies, but Newbury was different. The battlefield was pretty effectively bounded on the north by the river Kennet and the heavily enclosed watermeadows which lined its banks. This low-lying ground then slowly rises towards the south eventually to form a broad open plateau known as Wash Common. The increase in height is by no means even, and two short spurs jut forward to the north of the plateau proper. The significance of these would not have been apparent when the common itself was hastily reconnoitred on the evening of the 19th, but the western spur was to play a crucial part in the battle.

In the early hours of the morning both armies prepared for battle. Essex's fifteen regular infantry regiments were divided into four brigades commanded from left to right by Robartes, Skippon, Barclay and Holbourne. The cavalry were divided into two wings; under Colonel John Middleton on the left and Sir Philip Stapleton on the right. As the ground in front of Middleton was cut up by hedges he was also given a strong body of musketeers (referred to by Skippon as a 'forlorn hope')

61

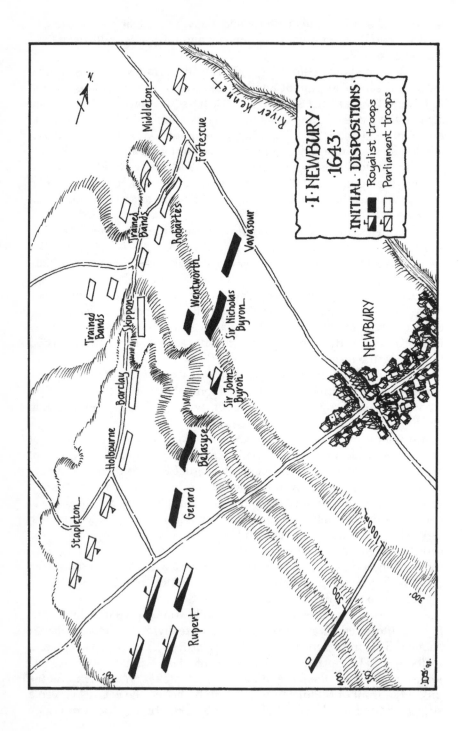

under Major Richard Fortescue of Bulstrode's. The five London Trained Band regiments formed a reserve behind the centre.

Thus deployed Essex advanced eastwards and succeeded in getting up on to the plateau before the Royalist cavalry pickets could be reinforced. There he deployed two of his infantry brigades along the hedge separating Bigg's Hill Lane from the open ground of Wash Common proper. Skippon's brigade occupied the western spur covering the junction with Skinner's Green Lane, where the London Trained Bands were posted, and Robartes drew up on the long slope down to the river, with Fortescue astride the Enborne-Newbury road.

Although some details are unclear, the Royalist army forming up along the Andover Road had been partially reorganised while it lay at Sudely. Now it comprised five cavalry brigades and four infantry brigades. The former were commanded by Rupert, Wilmot, Caernarvon, Charles Gerard and Sir John Byron. Most of the cavalry were deployed on to the open ground of Wash Common, but Byron was posted in the lower ground to the north of it with two of his regiments.

As to the infantry; what remained of the Culham Camp regiments which had stormed Bristol had evidently been reorganised into two brigades under John Belasyse and Sir Gilbert Gerard, and both were standing on Wash Common.[19] All the Oxford regiments formed a third brigade led by Sir Nicholas Byron, which together with the Bristol musketeers (now commanded by Henry Wentworth) was posted on the slope down towards Newbury. A fourth brigade commanded by Sir William Vavasour comprised the Welsh and Marcher regiments summoned to the siege of Gloucester[20] and was deployed astride the Enborne-Newbury road facing Robartes and Fortescue.

At about 7am the Royalists began moving off from their start-line on the Andover Road. The battle which followed can conveniently be discussed in terms of three virtually independent sectors. In the northern sector Vavasour's Brigade advanced to contact with Robartes' Brigade and Fortescue's musketeers. Initially there was a sharp little encounter which cost Robartes his own Lieutenant Colonel, but Skippon quickly stabilised the situation by sending the Blue Auxiliaries from the reserve. Thereafter fighting on this sector subsided into a static firefight. This rather worked to the Royalists' advantage for Vavasour was probably outnumbered, but the hedgerows provided him with a good defensive position and prevented Middleton's cavalry from accomplishing anything. Indeed it is difficult to understand what Middleton was doing on this flank at all for he would have been much better employed up on Wash Common.

As it was, Stapleton very quickly found himself in difficulties. Although Wash Common was good open cavalry country, there was little room to deploy to the south of Holbourne's infantry brigade. Stapleton had only managed to get one of his brigades clear of Bigg's Hill Lane when he was charged by one of the Royalist brigades. Firing into the Cavaliers at close range, the Parliamentarians succeeded in driving them back on the main body still standing by the Andover Road. This useful little victory allowed the other two brigades to deploy on to the common, and coming back from his charge Stapleton was able to rally on them.

A second Royalist attack was similarly beaten off, but then Rupert came forward with at least three brigades and in a series of actions managed to drive Stapleton's men back off the common and into Bigg's Hill Lane where they apparently remained for the rest of the day. It should now have been up to Gerard's and Belasyse's infantry brigades to clear Essex's men out of the hedgerows and tumble them down the hill, but neither officer was able to bring them forward. Indeed, apart from a reference by John Gwynn to their running away from some of Essex's cavalry (which must have been early on), they played little or no part in the battle. It may well be significant that both brigades were composed of the Culham Camp regiments which had seen some hard service both at Reading and in the bloody storming of Bristol. They may simply have had enough.

In the centre it was a very different matter as Sir John Byron recounts:

. . . about 5 in the morning I had orders to march towards a little hill full of enclosures which the enemy had possessed himself of and had brought up two small field pieces and was bringing up more, whereby they would have secured their march on Reading (the highway was lying hard by) and withall so annoyed our army which was drawn up in the bottom, where the King himself was, that it would have been impossible to have kept the ground. The hill, as I have mentioned, was full of enclosures and extremely difficult for horse service, so that my orders were only with my own and Sir Thos. Aston's regiment to draw behind the commanded foot led by Henry Wentworth and Col. George Lisle, and to be ready to second them, in case the enemy horse should advance towards them: the rest of my brigade[21] was by Prince Rupert commanded to the Heath where most of the other horse and foot were drawn.

Wentworth and Lisle quickly realised they were outnumbered, so Sir Nicholas Byron was ordered to bring up his brigade. A furious battle then ensued in which the Royalists suffered heavily. Lieutenant Colonel Edward Villiers of Charles Gerard's Regiment was wounded, and at one point no fewer than eleven of the twelve ensigns went down[22] and so, despite the unsuitability of the ground, they called for cavalry support.

Sir John then came up with his two regiments but was delayed for a time while a gap was torn in one of the hedgerows. As soon as he could get his own troop through, he put in a charge but was quickly beaten off. Nevertheless this gave time for Sir Thomas Aston to deploy his regiment, and a second charge forced the Parliamentarians back to the far side of the enclosure. There they made a stand and forced Byron off for a second time before retiring into Bigg's Hill Lane. Byron then caught some of the stragglers with a third charge, but by that time Skippon had brought up the Red and Blue regiments of the London Trained Bands and the Red Auxiliaries from the reserve and he prudently drew back.

Thanks to his nephew's intervention, Sir Nicholas Byron's infantry gained a toehold on the eastern side of the lane. However, as neither Belasyse nor Gerard had advanced to contact, Essex's own regiment was able to launch a local counter-attack against the left flank of Sir Nicholas's Brigade. This succeeded in pushing them off the hill again, and although Rupert afterwards put in a number of ineffectual cavalry charges against the Parliamentarian regiments at the north end of Wash Common, the battle thereafter degenerated into a series of firefights.

By nightfall fighting had petered out entirely. Rupert and Sir John Byron were in favour of holding on and resuming the battle next day. The battle had been hard, but there was no reason to suppose that Essex's men were any less exhausted and indeed, after their initial advance stalled, the Parliamentarians had done little more than hold their ground. Another day's fighting they argued would be decisive, but Lord Percy disabused them of this happy notion by reporting that only ten barrels of powder remained out of the ninety with which they had begun the battle. What was more it was all coarse grained powder for the cannon; the long day's hedge-fighting had completely exhausted the infantry's supply.[23]

Sir John was afterwards scathing about this 'foolish and knavish suggestion'. The Civil War might indeed have been won at Newbury had the Royalist army not run out of ammunition, but for want of powder there was no alternative but to evacuate their positions at midnight and let Essex through to Reading. He was not allowed to get there unmolested, for Rupert attacked his rearguard near Aldermaston and managed to hustle him straight through Reading. The town was subsequently reoccupied by the Royalists on 3 October but it was a poor consolation prize. The summer's campaigning had begun with its loss, and generally speaking, the Royalists were now in a much stronger position, having captured Bristol and to some extent secured the King's Road. Nevertheless the recapture of Reading symbolised that little had changed. Neither side was strong enough to win the war without outside help.

NOTES

1. A professional soldier hailing from Aberdeen Hurry was an engaging villain who had been in the service of Parliament until defecting with intelligence of the pay convoy which was Rupert's primary objective on the night of the

17th. Although the Royalists failed to find it, Hurry was knighted on his return to Oxford.

2. Roy, I. *Ordnance Papers* p253. Atkyns *Vindication* p22. This setback was nearly compounded when Maurice and Crawford blundered into each other in the dark and almost came to blows.

3. Roy *op.cit.* pp253-4

4. Atkyns p23 See also the list of regiments in Appendix III (p35) though the analysis here is the present author's.

5. Atkyns *op cit.* His reference to charging the 'utmost man of their right wing' is confusing and has led some historians to place Wilmot's brigade on the Royalist left. He must however have been speaking of the right flank of the Parliamentarian *left* wing, for not only does he state that the charge was launched to exploit the confusion on that wing caused by Major Smith's action, but Sir John Byron explicitly states that Waller 'advanced with his own brigade of horse with two pieces of cannon before, and two great bodies of foot on the left flank of it.' It might also be worth remarking that it would be most unusual to find 17th century generals placing their own regiments on the left of their armies without very good cause.

6. In H.C.B. Rogers *Battles & Generals of the Civil War* p88

7. Atkyns p26 'Prince Maurice . . . intended to send the Trophies and Letters to the King by me, but upon comparison of commissions, 'twas found that the Lord Wilmot was commander in chief for that expedition . . .'

8. Roy pp255-9 According to de Gomme the infantry comprised no fewer than 14 'very weak' regiments:

Grandison's Brigade:	Lord General's Regiment (Lt.Col. Herbert Lunsford)
	Lord Rivers' (Lt.Col. John Boys)
	Lord Molyneux's (Lt.Col. Roger Nowell)
	Sir Gilbert Gerard's
	Sir Ralph Dutton's
	Colonel John Owen's
Wentworth's Brigade:	Sir Jacob Astley's Regiment (Major Toby Bowes)
	Sir Edward Fitton's
	Colonel Richard Herbert's (Major Edward Williams)
Belasyse's Brigade:	Colonel John Belasyse's Regiment
	Sir Edward Stradling's (Lt.Col. John Stradling)
	Colonel Henry Lunsford's
	Colonel Charles Lloyd's (Lt.Col. Edward Tyrwhitt)

One other regiment from Culham, Colonel Richard Bolles' is not included in this list although it certainly took part in the subsequent siege of Gloucester and I Newbury.

9. According to de Gomme they were made up as follows:

Buck's Brigade:	Marquis of Hertford's Regiment
	Prince Maurice's
	Colonel Brutus Buck's
Slanning's Brigade:	Sir Nicholas Slanning's Regiment
	Lord Mohun's
	Colonel John Trevannion's
Bassett's Brigade:	(late) Sir Beville Grenville's Regiment
	Colonel William Godolphin's

10. Fire-pikes were intended to serve the same function as colours in night operations, that is as markers and rallying points – hence their being carried by officers.

11. A 'barn' in military engineering terminology was a casemated and loopholed strongpoint.

12. The exact composition of Dutton's brigade is uncertain. He presumably brought his own regiment from Grandison's Brigade and it probably included Lloyd's and Stradling's men from what had been Belasyse's one.

13. Referred to in Ordnance papers as Darcy's Tercio it comprised at least five regiments; Conyers Darcy's, William Eure's, Sir Thomas Blackwell's, Sir Thomas Tyldesley's and Sir Henry Vaughan's.

14. His own and Colonel Nicholas Devereaux's regiments.

15. Peachy, S & Turton, A. *Old Robin's Foot* pp10-11, 58. Turton, A. *The Chief Strength of The Army*

Horse:	**Foot:**	
Lord General's Regiment	Lord General's Regiment	(726)
Sir William Balfour's	Thomas Tyrell's	(450)
Hans Behre's	Francis Martin's	(250)
John Meldrum's	Lord Robartes'	(365)
John Middleton's	Sir William Constable's	(365)
John Dalbier's	Philip Skippon's	(516)
James Sheffield's	Harry Barclay's	(496)
Arthur Goodwin's (Gilbert Blare)	John Holmstead's	(416)
Sir James Ramsay's	James Holbourne's	(290)
	George Langham's	(431)
Total 2,800+	Henry Bulstrode's	(376)
	Francis Thompson's	(351)
	Total	5032

Numbers above are based on regimental and troop musters chiefly dating from July 1643. Although all of Essex's foot are accounted for – with the proviso that on 31 July he reported he had only 3,000 fit to march with another 3,000 sick – it is possible that the horse are slightly underestimated. The horse also included the three cuirassier troops; Stapleton's, Balfour's and Bedford's which had fought at Edgehill.

Additional Forces for relief of Gloucester:

Colonel Richard Norton's Horse	London Brigade *(5,000)*:
Colonel Edmund Harvey's Horse	Colonel Randall Mainwaring's Foot
	Red Regiment (London Trained Bands)
Sir William Brooks' Foot	Blue Regiment (ditto)
Sir William Springate's Foot	Red Auxiliaries (ditto)
	Blue Auxiliaries(ditto)
	Orange Auxiliaries (ditto)

16. Roy pp283-5. A Saker, five 6-pounders and four 3-pounders were sent, together with spare harness and other stores needed to prepare the siege train for marching, but only fifty barrels of powder were sent instead of the sixty ordered.

17. This unit was made up of various parties sent up from the regiments left behind at Bristol; principally belonging to Belasyse's, Maurice's and Prince Rupert's. The latter regiment had originally been Henry Lunsford's but was taken over by Rupert after Lunsford was killed.

18. Sir Nicholas Crispe's and Colonel Richard Spencer's. John Gwyn describes them as 'Kentish men, and new raised regiments' (p36). The former was certainly officered by Londoners and Spencer did indeed come from Orpington in Kent – whether he actually raised his men there is rather doubtful.

19. Byron refers to the Parliamentarian guns on 'Round Hill' being able to annoy 'our army which was drawn up in the bottom, where the King himself was'

but this must have been very early in the day for later in his account (H.C.B. Rogers *Battles and Generals* pp105-7) he expresses his dismay at the failure of the main body on the heath – i.e. Wash Common. John Gwynn, then serving in either Belasyse's or Gerard's brigade, also mentions that his regiment was on the heath.

20. **Byron's Brigade:**
King's Lifeguard
Charles Gerard's Regiment
Thomas Pinchbeck's
Lord Percy's
Sir Thomas Blackwell's
Sir Thomas Tyldesley's
Colonel William Eure's
Colonel Conyers Darcy's
Sir Henry Vaughan's

Vavasour's Brigade (incomplete listing):
Sir William Vavasour's Regiment
Prince Charles' Regiment (Michael Woodhouse)
Colonel Samuel Sandys'
Colonel Richard Herbert's
(Lieutenant Colonel Arthur Blayney's)

21. Sir Thomas Morgan's and Colonel Henry Sandys' Regiments – Morgan was to be killed during the battle.

22. Or so Byron says – but twelve ensigns are too many for a single regiment so he must either be referring to the brigade as a whole, which is unlikely, or else Villiers was commanding a composite battalion made up of the Oxford garrison detachments which had joined the army during the siege of Gloucester.

23. Roy. pp291-2, 491. At some point during the day the King himself had sent to Oxford for a further fifty barrels but the messenger did not arrive until between 7 and 8pm. Although the ordnance officers rose to the occasion and a convoy of thirteen carts and wagons was sent off at 3am on the 21st it obviously would not arrive in time.

CHAPTER VI

Coals from Newcastle: The Northern War 1642–1643

Until the fateful winter of 1643 the Civil War in the north was for the Royalists at least fought entirely independently of operations on the Central Front. Some of the first fighting may have taken place outside Hull when the King personally demanded its surrender on 29 April 1642, but thereafter all was quiet until his departure for the south.

Before leaving York he took care to leave the north in safe hands. On 20 June 1642 he appointed William Cavendish the Earl (and later Marquis) of Newcastle to be Lieutenant General of the five northern counties; Cumberland, Westmoreland, Northumberland, the Bishopric of Durham and the City and County of Newcastle upon Tyne. His principal duty however was to raise an army for the protection of the Queen who was expected to land in the Tyne on or about 28 September with the arms she was presently purchasing in Holland. The Earl therefore moved swiftly. While there was a strong puritan tradition in Newcastle upon Tyne he quickly overawed the local Parliamentarian supporters by the brutally direct expedient of exercising his newly raised regiment in the city's streets. At the same time a Durham Trained Band regiment led by Sir Thomas Riddell was thrust into Tynemouth Castle and a Dutch engineer Hendrick Van Peer set to remodelling its defences.

Quite apart from providing a landing place for the Queen, control of the Tyne was vital to the Royalist war effort since it was, with the exception of Chester, the only considerable port not in Parliamentarian hands. Moreover while Chester was merely a gateway to Ireland, the Tyne was the only port through which arms could be imported from the continent.[1] Prince Rupert himself had landed at Tynemouth Castle late in August, and shortly afterwards the first of a number of Danish ships loaded with arms and ammunition got into the river.

In order to prevent this traffic the Royal Navy, which went over to Parliament in early July, blockaded the Tyne but, although it successfully stifled the large peacetime traffic through the river, it was never able to seal it off completely. There were suggestions that patrols could sometimes find it worth their while to look the other way and from time to time over the next two years blockade runners would ship coal across to the continent and bring ammunition back. Dunkirk privateers also sheltered in the river occasionally. Even as late as April 1644, when the river was blockaded by land as well as by sea, the City Chamberlain's accounts record four ships clearing the Tyne in that month; one of them a collier bound for Hamburg. In some respects the Navy's blockade actually worked to the Royalists' advantage. London had long been dependent upon 'sea coal' for domestic heating, and shutting off the trade caused real hardship and consequent unrest.[2] What was more many of the Tyneside pitmen who were thrown out of work by that slump in the coal trade were recruited into Newcastle's regiments.

Apart from an easily suppressed mutiny in one of the Durham Trained Band regiments, Newcastle faced no real opposition in the area of his command, but in neighbouring Yorkshire it was a different matter. When the King left York at the outset of what would be the Edgehill campaign, he appointed Henry Clifford, Earl of Cumberland as Lieutenant General of the county and confided the care of the city to a professional soldier named Sir Thomas Glenham. Despite having some of the Trained Bands at their disposal, their position was far from secure since the more enthusiastic Royalists had marched off with the King. On the other hand, Ferdinando, Lord Fairfax had been commissioned by Parliament to execute the Militia Ordinance and was busily engaged in levying troops in the cloth manufacturing towns of the West Riding. Sir John Hotham the governor of Hull was also levying troops for the service of Parliament in both the East and North Ridings. These included the local Trained Bands, and it is ironic to note that after Newcastle had moved into the area, he demanded that those very same Trained Bands should turn out again for the King's service. One of the Trained Band officers named Sir Hugh Cholmley occupied Scarborough, and although he proved reluctant to acknowledge the authority of either Fairfax or Hotham, he cheerfully cooperated with the latter in extending Parliamentarian control over the North Riding.

Their activities so alarmed Cumberland that on 26 September he and the other Yorkshire Commissioners of Array despatched an urgent appeal to Newcastle, requesting him to march to their assistance. Initially the Earl appeared reluctant to respond since his primary task was to secure the Queen's landing place. Moreover, taking the view that he had no legal authority to march his embryonic army outwith the limits defined in his commission, he eventually replied to the Yorkshire Commissioners by setting out a list of conditions or 'propositions'; that his army should be paid, provisioned and billeted 'by the country'. He also warned that 'since this army was levied a purpose to guard her Majesty's person' he reserved the right to march it away at any time for that service.[3]

Any doubts which the Commissioners may have entertained about these terms were quickly brushed aside when Hotham's son (also named Sir John) ignored a local cease-fire and seized Cawood Castle, just ten miles south of York on 10 October. Lord Fairfax also took the field on 21 October but seemed content to engage in inconsequential skirmishing, and Newcastle therefore held out for a promise of hard cash before warning the Queen to delay sailing. Consequently he did not begin marching southwards until late November, by which time he had assembled a marching army of some 4,000 foot and 2,000 horse and dragoons.

On 1 December his advance guard, comprising Colonel Thomas Howard's Dragoons and a Durham regiment of foot led by Sir William Lambton, ran into young Sir John Hotham at Piercebridge. Hotham may only have had four companies of foot and three troops of horse, but he had little alternative but to fight if he was not to abandon the regiments in process of being raised in Richmondshire and Cleveland. Predictably enough however the vital bridge over the Tees was carried in a rush, although Howard was shot dead in the process and Hotham seems to have escaped without much loss.

Apart from this minor skirmish no attempt was made to impede Newcastle's march. Within a day or two he reached York and immediately set about dealing with Fairfax. While Hotham had been busy in the north Lord Fairfax and his son, Sir Thomas, had at last made their move and occupied Tadcaster, just ten miles from the city. While Fairfax's 1,500 men were probably insufficient to mount an attack on York itself, they still presented an undeniable threat. However, the arrival of Newcastle's army completely altered the local balance of power, and Fairfax may already have been contemplating a withdrawal when the Earl appeared outside the town early on the morning of 6 December.

In the 17th century Tadcaster stood on the west bank of the river Wharfe which at that point was pretty well unfordable. The only crossing available to the attackers was a stone bridge covered by a small earthwork fort, but nevertheless when the Parliamentarians convened a hasty council of war; 'the town was judged untenable, and that we should draw out to an advantageous piece of ground by the town; but before we could all march out, the enemy advanced so fast that we were necessitated to leave some foot in a slight work above the bridge to secure our retreat;'[4]

Their haste was justified for Newcastle had no intention of simply launching a frontal assault. His Lieutenant General, Mountjoy Blount, Earl of Newport, had been ordered to swing northwards with the bulk of the horse and dragoons in order to cross the river at Wetherby and come in on Fairfax's rear. Unfortunately, according to a Royalist officer named Sir Henry Slingsby, he allowed his march to be retarded by two light cannon and moved far too slowly. Newcastle meanwhile launched what were intended to be a series of holding attacks throughout the day, but although he successfully pinned down the Parliamentarians in the town, Newport's failure to make an appearance ensured that none of the attacks were developed. By about four o'clock in the afternoon the light began to fail, and at that point Newcastle called it a day and ordered Newport to fall back on Wetherby.

Heartily relieved the Fairfaxes decamped under cover of darkness. Their logical line of retreat would have been westwards towards their base in the Pennine clothing towns, but the presence of Newport's cavalry at Wetherby forced them to make for Selby instead. There Newcastle was content to leave them while he occupied Pontefract Castle and sent a detachment commanded by Sir William Saville to take Bradford. His attack on 18 December failed, but the threat to the Parliamentarian base brought Sir Thomas Fairfax hastening back to take command of the local militia.

Meanwhile Newcastle had sent Sir John Henderson, one of the many Scots mercenaries serving in his army, to occupy Newark. The town not only covered an important crossing of the Trent, but would come to serve as a vital staging post between Newcastle's forces and the main Royalist army based on Oxford. Otherwise, short of ammunition, he seemed content to retire into winter quarters, but on 23 January Sir Thomas Fairfax stormed Leeds. This in turn led to the Royalists evacuating Wakefield and temporarily abandoning Pontefract as well. Matters were regarded as sufficiently serious to justify recalling some of the troops sent to Newark, but a full-scale counter-attack had to be delayed pending the arrival of fresh supplies of ammunition from Newcastle upon Tyne.

The convoy was overdue. There had been difficulties over finding a sufficient escort for it, and while the Durham Trained Bands were willing enough to look after it as it passed through the Bishopric, they flatly refused to cross into Yorkshire. All that could be spared for the purpose was a newly raised regiment of 400 foot commanded by Colonel Guilford Slingsby,[5] but he was defeated (and in the process fatally wounded) by Cholmley at Guisborough on 16 January. Recognising that the operation was going to be more difficult than he had first anticipated, Newcastle then despatched a cavalry brigade under another of his Scots mercenaries, James King. An experienced officer from the Swedish service, King had just been appointed Lieutenant General in place of Newport, and proceeded to demonstrate his fitness for the job by routing Cholmley in a sharp little action at Yarm near Stockton on 1 February.

No longer immobilised for want of ammunition, Newcastle once again took the field. This time his objective was to cover the long-delayed landing of the Queen, not in the Tyne as had originally been planned, but at some point on the Yorkshire coast. Given the presence of the Parliamentarian garrisons in Scarborough and Hull, this was far from being a satisfactory situation, but there was no alternative if he was to keep his army in Yorkshire. In the event, despite some unpleasantness on the part of the Royal Navy, it all went smoothly enough. The Queen landed safely at Bridlington on 22 February and sent a messenger to summon Newcastle who was then lying at Pocklington. He and General King duly turned up two days later, just in time to cover the unloading of Captain John Strachan's three transports, and by 7 March the Queen and her precious cargo were safely lodged in York. Although most of the munitions were destined for Oxford, a part at least was turned over to Newcastle's army, and Sir Henry Slingsby records that Sir Marmaduke Langdale's regiment, raised in the East Riding, was equipped with the Queen's arms.

Better was to come. Little more than two weeks later Cholmley changed sides and handed over Scarborough. Then Lord Fairfax began with some reason to suspect the reliability of the Hothams and, anticipating that Hull might also be delivered into Royalist hands, he decided that his position at Selby was untenable and resolved on a retreat to Leeds. In order to mask this movement, he ordered his son Sir Thomas to take up a covering position at Tadcaster. Unfortunately, although he occupied the town without a fight on the 30th, this movement was interpreted as the beginnings of a possible raid on York. General King promptly sent off 500 horse under Lord Goring and then followed after him with all the foot he could muster.

Having word of their coming, Sir Thomas prudently broke down the bridge and marched off as fast as he could, but Goring's men scrambled across the river and were soon on his track. For the most part the Leeds Road was surrounded by enclosed fields, but periodically these gave way to open expanses of common grazing land. The first of them was Bramham Moor, and there Fairfax halted his three troops of horse to cover the retreat of his infantry. While it is unclear just how large Sir Thomas's force was at this point, his own account of the action quite explicitly states that none of them were armed with pikes. His regulars were all musketeers, but it seems that the greater part of his men were poorly armed rustic levies.

At any rate his stand in the hedgerows should have given them the time they needed to get safely across the moor, but instead they hung about waiting for him. There was no alternative therefore but to march them straight across the open moor in two divisions while he and his cavalry brought up the rear. Goring's three regiments[6] made no attempt to close at this time, but during the next stage of the retreat through an area of hedged enclosures lying between Bramham Moor and Seacroft Moor, the Parliamentarian foot began to straggle badly. It was a warm day and many of them began breaking into houses in search of drink. Predictably enough when they passed out of the cultivated area and on to Seacroft Moor it all fell apart.

> Ye Enemy got, another way, as soon as we, upon ye Moor. But wn we had almost passed this plaine also, they seeing us in some disorder, charged us both in Flanke & Reer. The Countrymen presently cast downe their Armes & fled; & ye Foot soone after, wch, for want of pikes were not able to stand their horse. Some were slaine, & many taken prisoners. Few of our Horse stood ye Charge. Some Officers wth me made our Retreat, wth much difficulty, in wch Sr Henry Foulis had a sleight hurt. My Cornet was taken prisoner, yet got to Leeds about 2 hours after my Father & ye Forces wth him were arrived thither safe.[7]

Goring afterwards reckoned to have killed upwards of 200 and to have taken 800 more. The only consolation for the Parliamentarians was that Lord Fairfax reached Leeds unmolested but, with the Queen safe at York, General King now advised Newcastle to retain the initiative by invading the West Riding. Accordingly the Royalists marched to Leeds, but finding it too strongly held, after a few days they turned south, placed a strong garrison in Wakefield and proceeded to take Rotherham on 4 May and Sheffield two days later. Both towns were to be extremely important to the Royalists for they were already famous for their ironworks and sword-cutlers. At this point however the offensive seems to have run out of steam and it was Sir Thomas Fairfax who next took the initiative by attacking Wakefield in the early hours of Sunday 21 May.

Oddly enough the operation was undertaken with no better object in mind than the capture of prisoners who could be exchanged for the Parliamentarians taken at Seacroft Moor. This rather casual decision probably accounts for the fact that the raid was launched on the basis of quite inadequate intelligence. Believing the garrison to be only some 800-900 strong, Sir Thomas appointed a midnight rendezvous at Howley Hall where he assembled 1,000 foot and 500 horse and dragoons.

Wakefield occupied a hilltop site centred on the church and market place. Both were approached by the four principal streets; Kirkgate, Westgate, Northgate and Warrengate. Defensive works appear to have consisted of little more than barricades at the end of these streets, and as he approached the town, Fairfax divided his force in two. One division commanded by his cousin, Sir William Fairfax, was to attack down Northgate while he and Major General John Gifford assaulted up Warrengate.

The first inkling the Parliamentarians had that all was not as it appeared came when Fairfax discovered that the hedges lining the approaches to the town were stuffed with Royalist musketeers. Not only had the Cavaliers been alerted to his approach by the survivors of a skirmish at Stanley Hall, but as the resistance stiffened, it began to dawn on Fairfax that the garrison was much stronger than he had been led to believe. Nevertheless it was resolved to press on with the attack, and Gifford succeeded in rushing the barricade at the end of Warrengate. As soon as it was opened Fairfax charged straight through at the head of his own troop of horse, closely followed by two more troops under Captain John Bright and Lieutenant John Alured.

Whilst it might at first seem odd to employ cavalry in street fighting – particularly as in this instance they had to make their way up a fairly steep hill – there was in fact a very good reason for doing so. In defending a town it was obviously necessary to deploy a substantial part of the garrison along the perimeter or at least in strongpoints at the entrances to the town as was the case at Wakefield. The remainder of the garrison would then be drawn up as a quick reaction force in the market place which was invariably located at the centre of the town's road network. Consequently, as soon as a gate could be opened or a breach made in the walls, it was imperative that the attacking force should press on at once to seize the market place as quickly as possible, since that was the surest method of paralysing the defence. Conversely of course, should the defender succeed in retaining control of the market place and the streets radiating outwards from it, he would then be enabled not only to launch his quick reaction force in a counter-attack, but could also draw troops off from other less threatened sectors and pass them through the market place to the point of danger. Far from being foolhardy as some historians have suggested, by charging straight up Warrengate Fairfax was doing exactly the right thing.

Predictably enough, as he advanced up the street, he was in fact counter-attacked by some Royalist cavalry led by Goring himself. In a confused fight both sides unsurprisingly came adrift and Fairfax became separated for a time from his men. Meanwhile Gifford pushed up the hill with his infantry to find Sir William Lambton's Foot and a couple of troops of horse still drawn up in the market-place. Enterprisingly he ordered his trumpeter to nip across and offer them Quarter, but naturally they refused, so he fired a captured gun into them at point-blank range. This was then followed up with a cavalry charge which tumbled the Durham men down the length of Westgate and out of the town.

After that it was just a matter of rounding up the prisoners, and by daylight the full extent of the Parliamentarian victory became apparent, for there had actually been no fewer than six regiments of foot and seven troops of horse numbering about 3,000 men in the town[8]. About half of them (including Lord Goring) were captured together with twenty-seven colours, three horse cornets, four guns and a substantial part of Newcastle's reserve ammunition. Oddly enough no mention is made of any other casualties inflicted on the Royalists, although at least two officers, Captain Edward Row and Captain William Lambton, were certainly killed[9] and at least two others wounded.[10] Fairfax for his part admitted to losing no more than seven killed including an ensign of foot and a quartermaster of horse although 'many of our men were shot and wounded.'

Sir Thomas made no attempt to hold Wakefield, but immediately retired instead to Leeds, although he could not resist giving out that the only reason for doing so was that he had insufficient men to guard both town and prisoners. Indeed if anything the very success of the operation left the Fairfaxes apprehensive that they might have gone too far. On 23 May Lord Fairfax wrote urgently to Parliament requesting ammunition – for his communications with the magazine at Hull were now cut – money and reinforcements.

The Royalist response however was slow in coming because Newcastle's first priority remained the safety of the Queen and the supplies which she had brought from Holland. One convoy had already been sent off safely but the rest could no longer be delayed, and a conference was held at Pontefract Castle at the beginning of June where the options were discussed.

Now ye Queen was preparing to march to ye King, & his excellence with his army convey'd her to Pomphret, where his excellency caus'd a councell of warr to be caus'd, yt advice might be taken wch were ye most useful service in ye army, whether to march up with ye Queen & so joyne wth ye King, or else wth ye army to stay, & only give order for some regiments to wait upon her majesty. If he march'd up, his army would give a gallant addition to ye Kings, but yn he left ye country in my Ld Fairfax his power, & it might be he should have him march in ye rear of him, joyne in ye parliaments forces. If he stay'd he might send some forces with ye Queen, & yet be able to lay siege to my Ld Fairfax in Leeds, or fight him in ye field. Well, this latter was resolved on, of sending some forces only wth ye Queen, & himself to stay, & to try ye mastery wth my Ld Fairfax.[11]

Accordingly the Queen marched off to Newark, and Newcastle set about recruiting more men before invading the West Riding towards the end of the month. His principal objective was Lord Fairfax's headquarters at Bradford, but the campaign got off to a good start when Howley Hall was stormed on 22 June and 245 men of Sir John Saville's Regiment were captured. Thereafter bad weather delayed Newcastle's march for nearly a week, but on the morning of 30 June he and his men set off for Bradford.

As chance would have it, the day before the Fairfaxes had come to the unpalatable conclusion that their position there was untenable. Rather than stand and await Newcastle's advance they therefore resolved to launch a preemptive attack next morning. Although the original intention had been to set off at four o'clock, the Parliamentarians did not get under way until nearly eight and then, having marched but four miles, their forlorn hope encountered the Royalist advance guard amongst some hedged enclosures at the village of Adwalton.

At first both sides were brought to a stand but the Royalists gradually gained the upper hand and forced the Parliamentarians back far enough to allow the main body of Newcastle's army to turn off the Bradford Road and deploy along a 'great ditch and high bank' separating the arable land around the village from the east side of Adwalton Moor. Their right flank seems to have remained resting on the road, but the left found itself entangled amongst some coal pits. As Lord Fairfax's army came up it conformed by facing them on the open moor, again with one flank resting on the Bradford Road and their back to a rising ground known as Wyket Hill.

The two armies were markedly different in size and the best account of the Parliamentarian one comes from Thomas Stockdale, who describes it as:

> . . . consisting of 1200 commanded men of the garrison of Leeds, seven companies of Bradford, 500 men of Halifax, Pomfret, Saddleworth, Almonbury, twelve companies of foot brought out of Lancashire, and of horse we had ten troops of our own and three from Lancashire. We had four pieces of brass ordnance with us and a great part of our powder and match, and many club-men followed us, who are fit to do execution upon a flying enemy, and with this strength, not being full 4,000 men horse and foot armed.[12]

As to their deployment the forlorn hope which opened the battle was commanded by Captain Mildmay and comprised a mixed bag of horse foot and dragoons which probably did not amount to more than some 300 men.[13] They presumably fell back to join the Leeds companies forming the left wing commanded by Major General Gifford. The deployment of the remainder of the Parliamentarian troops is a touch uncertain. Stockdale asserts that the main body commanded by Lord Fairfax included the two Lancashire regiments commanded by Colonel Ralph Assheton and Colonel Richard Holland, and the 500 men from Halifax 'and the moors', while the rear – or right wing as it became – comprised the Bradford companies led by Lieutenant Colonel William Forbes. The cavalry, he says, were commanded by Sir Thomas Fairfax. On the other hand Sir Thomas himself declared afterwards that in the battle he had 1,000 foot and five troops of horse on the right and that Gifford had the same on the left.[14]

Taken together this would suggest that the Parliamentarians drew up with five troops of horse on each flank and six battalions of infantry in their front line – Gifford's and Sir William Fairfax's on the left, Assheton's and Holland's in the centre, Forbes' and the Halifax companies on the right.[15] Behind them, and forming a rather dubious reserve, were the 'club-men'[16], and the three Lancashire troops.

The composition of the Royalist army is impossible to establish. Indeed it is difficult enough to ascertain just how strong it was. What appears to be Newcastle's own account merely says that they were outnumbered by the Parliamentarian foot, and his Duchess slightly more helpfully states the Royalists had 'not above half so many musketeers as the enemy had; their chiefest strength consisting in horse.'[17] As all of Fairfax's regulars seem to have been musketeers this would suggest that the Cavaliers had something in the region of about 5,000 infantry and perhaps as many as 3-4,000 horse.

At any rate the Parliamentarian predominance in musketeers enabled them to drive the Royalists back from the ditch and bank, but there they stopped for having once got themselves behind its cover they were understandably reluctant to climb over it. Nor did the Royalist cavalry fare any better. Those on the right wing, commanded by General King, seem to have been unable to deploy and get into the fight, while on the left wing their horse were not only hampered by the coal pits but, as Sir Thomas Fairfax relates, once the Parliamentarians seized control of the bank it proved impossible then to pass out on to the moor:

Ten or 12 Troops of Horse charged us in ye Right Wing. We kept ye Enclosure, placing or Musketteers in ye hedges in ye moor, wch was good Advantage to us who had so few Horse. There was a Gate, or open place to ye Moor, where 5 or 6 might enter a breast. Here they strove to enter, and we to defend; But after some Dispute, those yt entred ye passe found sharpe entertainmt; & those yt were not yet entred, as hott welcome from ye Musketteers yt flanked ym in the hedges. All in ye end were forced to retreat, with ye loss of one Coll: Howard, who commanded them.[18]

The cavaliers soon rallied and led by Colonel George Heron, who had just succeeded Thomas Howard as brigade commander, they came forward again. The fight this time was rather stiffer, but Heron too was killed and this time Fairfax pursued the Royalists back as far as their gun-line before being halted by a stand of pikes. This was the critical point of the battle and Fairfax even asserts that Newcastle ordered a withdrawal. Had the Parliamentarian foot actually crossed the bank and ditch they might have won a famous victory, but instead it was the Royalists who seized the initiative and counter-attacked.

Thus far their pikemen had played no part in the battle, save on the left where they stopped Sir Thomas, but now the pikes of the Marquis of Newcastle's own regiment, led by Colonel Posthumous Kirton, surged forward on the right[19] and an astonishing collapse took place. Neither Gifford nor Lord Fairfax made any real attempt to stem the rout although to be fair there was probably little that they could have done for the only reserve was the undisciplined mass of club-men and the three troops of Lancashire horse.

What probably happened was that when Kirton's charge scattered either Gifford's or Sir William Fairfax's regiments the ditch and bank prevented Holland's and Assheton's regiments from swinging around and instead, with their left flank exposed and more Royalist pikemen coming forward, they quite naturally dropped away towards the southern side of the moor.

There Sir Thomas Fairfax claimed to have been unaware of the unfolding disaster until he suddenly received orders to retreat. However this is unlikely, for not only did the Royalist guns suddenly switch their fire away from the Parliamentarian infantry and begin dropping rounds amongst his cavalry, but the Cavalier horse came forward again. This time, as the Duchess of Newcastle relates, they finally got across the ditch and bank:

> Hereupon my Lord's horse got over the hedge, not in a body (for they could not) but dispersedly two on a breast; and as soon as some considerable number was gotten over, and drawn up, they charged the enemy and routed them.[20]

The absence of any resistance to the Royalist crossing clearly indicates that the Parliamentarian left was already in trouble. As the centre collapsed Fairfax's musketeers must also have peeled away from the hedgerows, permitting the Cavaliers to get over unhindered. Fairfax's own failure to charge the Royalists in those vulnerable few moments while they formed up on the moor also points to him having his hands full. Consequently the order to withdraw probably came as more of a relief than a surprise, and he escaped southwards to Halifax with his own men and the two Lancashire regiments as well.

His father was less fortunate, for as Newcastle's own account cheerfully relates, the Royalists chased him two miles down the Bradford Road. In the process they claimed to have killed 500 – a pardonable exaggeration in the circumstances – and taken 1,400 prisoners. As to their own losses they admitted only to losing the two Colonels, Heron and Howard and 'not above twenty common soldiers slain', although a number of officers including Colonel William Throckmorton and Colonel Francis Carnaby were wounded.[21]

Having halted at Bolling Hall, just to the south of Bradford, the Royalists were still digging in their guns that night when Sir Thomas Fairfax managed to throw himself into the town. The two Lancashire regiments had flatly refused to follow him and he had left 200 foot to garrison Halifax, but the rest of his men had stuck by him. This was just as well because his timorous father was in no state to conduct a gallant defence. For some time Sir John Hotham had been engaged in negotiations to change sides, and although the plot had just been uncovered (Sir John and his son were subsequently executed), this was excuse enough for Lord Fairfax to march at once for Leeds, leaving Sir Thomas and 800 men to hold Bradford.

The town was quite untenable, and although Fairfax says nothing of the reasons for his being ordered to hold the town, it is hard to escape the impression that it was no more than a delaying action designed to give his father time to get clear. Terms for the town's surrender were discussed, but the following night it was Sir Thomas's turn to break out of the town. Unfortunately it all went wrong. The foot led by a Colonel Rogers blundered into some Royalist dragoons and only about eighty managed to break through. Fairfax and his party got farther, but at daybreak they ran into a Royalist cavalry regiment and in a running fight nearly all of them were killed or captured.[22] Only Fairfax, Gifford, Sir Henry Foulis and three troopers eventually made it to Leeds and there discovered his Lordship on the point of fleeing to Hull.

Within two hours they were all off again, leaving Leeds to be seized by the Royalist prisoners held there. Newcastle sent word alerting the various Royalist garrisons between Leeds and Hull, but the fugitives got the length of Selby before being intercepted by three troops of horse from Cawood. Once again Lord Fairfax ran for it, escaping across the ferry while Sir Thomas fought a brisk little rearguard action in the streets. At one point he was shot in the left wrist, but once the Royalists had been chased out of the town, he and his remaining men fled eastwards towards Barton-on-Humber. By now they were absolutely exhausted and continually harassed by Royalist detachments, but when they reached Barton a ship picked them up and ferried them across to Hull. There for the moment they were safe, but their army was destroyed and, should he choose to, Newcastle was free to march south.

NOTES

1. Hartlepool was also in Royalist hands but it was too small and too easily blockaded to be of real use.
2. Commons Journals 3 p171. In July 1643 an Alderman Adams appeared before the Commons to report: 'he was commanded to recommend unto the House the great and pressing Necessities of Coals; which will so pinch the Poor, that the Consequences thereof will be full of Horror and Danger.' It is possible that there may also have been a knock-on effect in diverting wood and charcoal supplies away from the Wealden ironworks which were supplying weapons for the Parliamentarian armies
3. Firth, ed. *Memoirs of the Duke of Newcastle* pp189-91
4. Fairfax, Sir Thos. *Short Memoriall*
5. Firth *Memoirs* p192
6. The three regiments are nowhere identified, but they were presumably the same ones which he afterwards had with him at Wakefield, viz: Colonel Francis Carnaby's, Sir Edmund Duncombe's and Lord Widdrington's.
7. Fairfax, Sir Thos *Short Memoriall* Yorkshire Archaeological Journal Vol.8 pp211-12
8. The composition of the Royalist garrison cannot be ascertained with any certainty. While Lord Fairfax's official report estimated them to comprise six regiments of foot and seven troops of horse, Lambton's is unfortunately the only one mentioned by name. However by comparing the names of officers listed in the report as having been taken prisoner with the 1661 *List of Indigent Officers*, it is possible more or less tentatively to identify the regiments involved as follows – probable prisoners appear in italics.

Colonel Cuthbert Conyers' Foot	Sir Edmund Duncombe's Horse
Captain (Michael) Pemberton	*Lieut.Col. Richard MacMoyler*
Sir William Lambton's Foot	Sir William Widdrington's Horse
Ensign Lambton	*Lieutenant (William) Nicholson*
Sir Marmaduke Langdale's Foot	*Lieutenant Thomas*
Lieutenant Monckton	Colonel Francis Carnaby's Horse
Ensign (Robert) Squire	*Major (Thomas) Carnaby*
Sir Francis Mackworth's Foot	
Major (George) Carr	
Sir George Wentworth's Foot	
Lieut.Col. Sir Thomas Bland	
Lieutenant (Thomas) Wheatley	
Sir William Widdrington's Foot	
Captain (John) Carr	

Oddly enough the composition of the Parliamentarian army is even more obscure. Fairfax had 1,000 foot divided into two bodies which it would be tempting to identify as the regiments of Sir William Fairfax and John Gifford. However this interpretation is almost certainly far too neat, and although none of the other signatories to the official report – with the exception of Sir Thomas Fairfax – are known to have commanded regiments it is probable that the two or three regular regiments were supported as usual by a number of irregular militia. The horse appear to have comprised a number of independent troops.

9. *The Royal Martyrs*

10. Fairfax reported that a Major Carnaby and a Captain Nuttall were left behind wounded in Wakefield 'upon their Ingagements to be true prisoners'.

11. Parson, D. *The Diary of Sir Henry Slingsby* p95

12. HMC Portland Mss Vol.i p717

13. Stockdale *ibid.* lists Captains Mildmay, Askwith, (Thomas) Morgan, Farrer, Salmon and Mudd.

14. *Short Memoriall* p213

15. Forbes actually appears to have been Lieutenant Colonel to Sir William Constable. The commander of the Halifax companies is unknown, although the subsequent breakout from Bradford was led by a Colonel Rogers, and a Colonel Maulverer was reported captured there.

16. The 'club-men' who feature so prominently in reports of provincial operations were so named not because they were armed only with clubs or cudgels, but because they belonged to local associations or clubs!

17. Firth, ed. *Memoirs of the Duke of Newcastle* pp24, 215. The calculation is complicated by the fact that we simply do not know the average ratio of musketeers to pikemen in Newcastle's regiments. There is a widespread belief that they could only muster equal numbers of both. However there is absolutely no evidence to support this curious assumption. On the contrary, unlike the Oxford Army, Newcastle's men were receiving arms shipments from the continent, and there is no reason therefore why they should not have been achieving ratios of 2:3 or even 1:2 pikes to muskets.

18. *Short Memoriall* p213.

19. Firth, *Memoirs* p25 Fairfax *op.cit.* p214 refers to him as 'Coll: Skirton, a wild & desperate man'. Evidently a professional soldier, both he and his brother Theodore had served in the 1640 army. The regiment was actually a double one (see next chapter – note 14) and the 1663 *List of Indigent Officers* also evidences a second Colonel, Sir Arthur Basset. Peter Newman in *Royalist Officers in England and Wales* and in *The Battle of Marston Moor* (Chichester 1981) misidentifies him with Sir Arthur Bassett of Umberleigh, Co. Devon. The Basset in question actually appears to have been related to Newcastle through his first wife Elizabeth the daughter and heir of William Basset of Blore, Co. Stafford. Instead Newman claims that the commander of Newcastle's Regiment was Sir William Lambton. However this identification is based simply on the quite erroneous assertion that Lambton was the only Northern infantry colonel to be killed at Marston Moor and the even more extraordinary claim that the alleged 'Lambs' nickname was derived from his arms rather than their wearing white coats. In any case not only was Lambton's Regiment raised in Durham rather than Northumberland as Newcastle's was, but both Sir Thomas Fairfax and the Duchess of Newcastle clearly distinguish between the Marquis's regiment and Sir William Lambton's.

20. *ibid.*

21. *ibid.* p216

22. One of the prisoners was Fairfax's wife who had been mounted behind one of his troopers. Newcastle subsequently released her.

CHAPTER VII

The Newarkers:
The War in Lincolnshire 1643

Between Newcastle's Northern Army and the King's Oxford Army lay a vital but sometimes rather lonely garrison at Newark, where the Great North Road crosses the Trent. Sir John Digby of Mansfield Woodhouse managed to occupy it with a Trained Band regiment and a volunteer troop of horse at the beginning of December 1642, and Newcastle had sent Sir John Henderson to assist him shortly before Christmas. Both Nottingham and Lincoln by this time were in Parliamentarian hands and at first sight it seems odd that they had not seized Newark as well, particularly as it also provided a crossing point on the roads linking the two garrisons. The fact that it lay on the Nottinghamshire border may have meant there was some uncertainty over who was responsible. However the real problem was that during this critical period the county authorities had their hands full with much weightier matters than thrusting garrisons into every village and town for miles around.

On 15 December a Parliamentary ordinance had set up a Midland Association covering Leicester, Derby, Nottingham, Northampton, Buckingham, Bedford, Rutland and Huntingdon. Within these counties a central committee was established to levy forces to be commanded by Lord Grey of Groby. Five days later another ordinance launched the famous Eastern Association initially comprising the counties of Essex, Suffolk, Norfolk, Cambridge and Hereford. However it naturally took some time for the central committees to organise themselves, and indeed Lord Grey of Wark was unable to mobilise troops in the Eastern Association until the following March. Newark certainly ought to have been the responsibility of the Midland Association, but Henderson slipped in before anyone realised what was happening.

Getting him out again was clearly going to be a problem – apart from anything else the Association needed to raise an army first – and he was pretty well left alone until the end of February 1643. This was just as well for it gave him time to consolidate his position and provide a base for the local Royalists. With their aid he not only fortified the town in a rather rudimentary manner, but also established a chain of outposts covering the south-western approaches from Nottingham and Leicester.

When the attack eventually came the Midland Association's real

military commander, Major General Thomas Ballard, swung around
these outposts to approach Newark from the more accessible eastern side.
Henderson had word of his coming, and on the night of 23 February he
sallied out with ten troops of horse to beat up Ballard's advance guard at
Beckingham, just five miles outside the town. However, finding the
Parliamentarians alerted, he retired without fighting and prepared to
stand a siege. Despite his proximity to the town Ballard delayed his
advance until the 27th, presumably because he was waiting for the arrival
of a Lincolnshire contingent under young Sir John Hotham and Lord
Willoughby of Parham, although it soon became apparent that he was
less than enthusiastic about the operation.

At this early stage in the war the defences which Henderson had
thrown up were by no means formidable. The river Trent certainly
provided adequate protection along the long north-west side of the town,
but the landward perimeter was covered only by a low earthwork bank
and ditch, without proper bastions or outworks. As one commentator
remembered: 'Most pitiful works they were, very low and thin, and with
a dry ditch which most men might easily leap on the east and south.'[1] It
was however this very weakness that encouraged the Parliamentarians to
mount an immediate escalade instead of sitting down to conduct a
regular siege.

On the 28th Ballard formally summoned the town, and on receiving
the expected refusal, proceeded with the attack. Although the precise
composition of his force is unclear, the Royalist estimate of 6,000 men
must be too high. He certainly had three brigades of infantry and ten
guns, but as the Lincolns only mustered 1,500 men at Ancaster Heath in
April, it would be surprising if he had more than 2-3,000 foot and an
unknown number of horse and dragoons. Henderson was still outnumbered as he only had ten troops of horse and a couple of regiments of
infantry, and could probably muster rather fewer than 1,500 men all told.[2]

Ballard was a professional soldier who had done well at Edgehill, but
his attack on Newark was poorly coordinated. After a preliminary
bombardment, all three brigades moved forward at about noon. The
Lincolns were afterwards criticised for retiring almost at once, but the
Midland brigade[3] advanced to within pistol-shot of the works.
Unfortunately, having got into the cover of a ditch, they stayed there. All
they then achieved was to shoot off all their ammunition to no purpose,
and Lieutenant Colonel Hutchinson afterwards complained that Ballard
failed to support them or organise a replenishment.

Then at about 3pm a more general assault was launched in the same
sector. Henderson was ready for it, and although at least some of the
Parliamentarians got over the ditch and bank, he managed to hold them.
Ballard himself was slightly wounded and while his injury was evidently
not serious enough to deflect criticism of his leadership it knocked the

stuffing out of him. He ordered a retreat and Major Mollanus afterwards complained to Sir John Gell that they were betrayed: '... for that they had entered the town and mastered the works, and then commanded back by the same Ballard . . .' Their retreat was hastened by Henderson who sallied out and chased them back in great disorder to a hedge, capturing three guns in the process. According to the official Royalist account only one of Henderson's men was killed which is quite possible although the estimate of 200 Parliamentarians killed and sixty captured sounds very much more optimistic than credible. Next day 'all the captains' urged a second assault but Ballard insisted on a retreat which shortly afterwards cost him his job.[4]

In the aftermath of this debacle the Midlanders and the Lincolns parted. Newcastle on the other hand found himself able to spare a cavalry brigade led by Charles Cavendish. With its assistance Henderson was able to storm Grantham on 23 March, although he very sensibly declined to overstretch his forces by placing a garrison of his own in the town. Then on 11 April he defeated Hotham and Willoughby at Ancaster Heath, and followed up this success by temporarily occupying Stamford and Peterborough. Hotham might have fared better had he been supported by the Eastern Association's forces mustering at Cambridge, but Lord Grey of Wark had marched most of them off to join the Earl of Essex's army besieging Reading on the 7th. All that remained were a few regiments commanded by Colonel Oliver Cromwell, and his primary responsibility was the defence of the Eastern Association's northern border. Basing his own regiment of horse at Huntingdon, Cromwell watched the crossings of the Ouse while a garrison comprising a detachment of dragoons and Sir Miles Hobart's Regiment of foot was placed in Wisbech.

Nevertheless when Henderson and Cavendish pulled their forces back in order to cover the passage of Pinchbeck's ammunition convoy, Cromwell began to be slightly more aggressive. On or about 22 April he occupied Peterborough and then joined with Hobart in a successful attack on Crowland. Possession of both towns enabled him to advance the Association frontier to the river Nene, but otherwise he remained reluctant to stray farther afield. This proved to be particularly unfortunate when Essex sent him instructions to join with the Lincolns and Lord Grey of Groby in intercepting Pinchbeck. Groby however was reluctant to stray far from Leicester since he feared an attack by Blind Harry Hastings[5], and by the time Cromwell joined with Sir John Hotham and Lord Willoughby at Sleaford on 9 May it was too late.

Nevertheless, feeling that they ought perhaps to try to achieve something, they moved off towards Newark, although as they had neither infantry nor guns it seems rather unlikely that they considered a serious attack on the town. In the event they were never given the chance. Having marched into Grantham on the 11th they were still there two days later when Cavendish and Henderson turned up like the Devil at prayers. This was a carefully planned operation in which Cavendish dropped down from Gainsborough to meet Henderson at dead of night just outside Grantham. Their combined forces comprised twenty-one troops of horse and three or four companies of dragoons amounting to about 1,200 men[6], and in the early hours of the morning of the 13th they destroyed three of Willoughby's troops in their quarters at Belton. Curiously the Parliamentarians seem to have been paralysed by this sudden attack, for both Willoughby and Cromwell remained inactive until the Royalists renewed their advance late in the evening.

The fight on low lying ground by the river Witham was a curiously half-hearted affair in which the dragoons on either side skirmished for about an hour. The Royalists must have been outnumbered for they proved reluctant to attack, and eventually in Cromwell's words 'we agreed to charge them'. This they did at a good round trot and routed the Royalists standing opposite them. Unfortunately the agreement to charge must have been confined to Cromwell and his captains for the Lincolns stayed where they were as passive spectators. The consequence was that, although the Royalists then withdrew[7], the Parliamentarians for their part fell back on Lincoln.

The Lincolns' failure to support Cromwell can have hardly have endeared them to him and led to the failure of another projected rendezvous at Nottingham on 24 May. This time the intention was to march north to join with Lord Fairfax who had particularly requested the assistance of Colonel Cromwell and his regiments. However, after hanging about for over a week, they advised Fairfax that in their view Newcastle's army had been so weakened by the defeat at Wakefield that their help was unnecessary. Not surprisingly his Lordship was infuriated rather than encouraged by this news, but in reality Groby and the others had probably made the right decision. Two days after they wrote to Fairfax the Queen left York on her march to Oxford and reached Newark on 16 June.

She remained there until the 21st before heading west under the protection of Cavendish, but any chance of intercepting her was frustrated when tensions between the three commanders at Nottingham all but turned into open warfare. Hotham and Cromwell quarrelled violently, and an exasperated Essex despatched Sir John Meldrum to take command of the combined force. As Cromwell had reported that Hotham was in communication with the enemy, Meldrum promptly arrested him, only to have him escape and ride off back to Lincoln with some of his forces. He was subsequently re-arrested at Hull before he could effect a handover of both that fortress and Lincoln as well. Unfortunately by the time the crisis was over it was too late and the Queen had safely passed through the danger zone.

Worse still, profiting by the royal diversion and by this falling out amongst the Parliamentarian commanders, the Newarkers sallied forth in mid-July to capture Stamford again and launch an unsuccessful attack on Peterborough. However, while they were thus employed, Lord Willoughby rallied the Lincolns. Hotham's attempted defection had at best rattled them, and there may well have been justifiable doubts about the reliability of some of his men. By way of restoring their battered confidence Willoughby was therefore forced to display some unwonted initiative by seizing Gainsborough on 16 July.[8] Since the town served as an important link between Newcastle's forces in Yorkshire and the Newark garrison, as well as a base for the Lincolnshire Cavaliers, it was by any reckoning an important military objective. Unfortunately Willoughby's reluctant coup came at a particularly inconvenient time for Meldrum and Cromwell.

The Earl of Essex had just summoned them to a rendezvous at Stony Stratford. With his own army depleted by typhus he desperately needed reinforcements if he was to exert effective pressure on the Oxford Army. Following the destruction of Waller's forces at Roundway, it was closing in on Bristol. Just how effective this pressure might have been is open to question in view of the timing, but in any case Meldrum's assistance would have been invaluable when Essex subsequently marched to the relief of Gloucester.

Unfortunately Essex was never to receive those reinforcements. Instead Cromwell marched off to recapture Stamford which he accomplished on or about the 19th, and then became involved in a short siege of nearby Burghley House. At first, having only some cavalry and dragoons, he was unable to effect anything, but after two infantry regiments came up the Cavaliers surrendered on the 24th. With his line of communications to Peterborough now secure he then marched north again and rejoined Meldrum at Grantham on Wednesday the 26th. Gainsborough was already being blockaded by Cavendish's brigade, and it was imperative that supplies and reinforcements should be passed into the town as soon as possible. Pressing on, Meldrum next met with Captain Edward Ayscoghe, the commander of Willoughby's cavalry at North Scarle, just ten miles from Gainsborough on the evening of the 27th.

When he resumed his march at 2am on the 28th he had something in the region of 1,200 men, all of them mounted. The advance guard comprised three or four troops of dragoons, then came Ayscoghe's eight troops of Lincolns. Meldrum himself had three troops from Nottingham and two more from Northampton, and finally in the rear came Colonel Cromwell with six or seven troops of his Eastern Association horse.[9]

About a mile outside Gainsborough they ran into Cavendish's forlorn hope, comprising about 100 horse. The Parliamentarian dragoons tried to beat them back without dismounting but were promptly charged and quite roughly handled before the rest of the Parliamentarians could come up to their assistance. Gainsborough lies on a damp stretch of flat ground beside the Trent but overlooking it is a very steep hill rising to about 100 feet above the river. As the Parliamentarians reached the town-end and made contact with Willoughby the Royalists withdrew up on to the top of the hill.

The Lincoln horse then tried to follow and, notwithstanding the fact that they had to pick their way up by way of some tracks and found their progress contested by the Royalist forlorn, they eventually made it. By the time all of Meldrum's men were up, Cavendish had arrayed his forces to meet them with what appeared to be three regiments in front and his own large regiment of six or seven troops in reserve. As far as can be ascertained two of the front line regiments were probably Lord Henry Cavendish's and Sir William Pelham's, while the third was a composite formation made up of two small regiments commanded by Colonel Edward Heron and Colonel Sigismund Beaton.

The Parliamentarian deployment was hindered by a large rabbit warren, but when the Royalists came forward they charged them any old how. Cromwell was on the right wing and in his letter to the committee at Huntingdon he described what happened next:

When we all recovered the top of the hill, we saw a great Body of the enemy's horse facing us, at about a musket-shot or less distance; and a good Reserve of a full regiment of horse behind it. We endeavoured to put our men into as good order as we could. The enemy in the mean time advancing towards us, to take us at disadvantage; but in such order as we were, we charged their great body, I having the right wing; we came up horse to horse; where we disputed it with our swords and pistols a pretty time; all keeping close order, so that one could not break the other. At last they a little shrinking, our men perceiving it, pressed in upon them, and immediately routed this whole body; some flying on one side and others on the other of the enemy's Reserve; and our men, pursuing them, had chase and execution about five or six miles.

I perceiving this body which was the Reserve standing still unbroken, kept back my Major (Edward) Whalley, from the chase; and with my own troop and the other of my regiment, in all being three troops, we got into a body. In this reserve stood General Cavendish; who one while faced me, another while faced four of the Lincoln troops, which was all of ours that stood upon the place, the rest being engaged in the chase. At last the General charges the Lincolners, and routed them. Immediately I fell on his rear with my three troops; which did so astonish him that he gave over the chase, and would fain have delivered himself from me. But I pressing on forced them down a hill, having good execution of them; and below the Hill, drove the General with some of his soldiers into a quagmire; where my Captain-Lieutenant slew him with a thrust under his short ribs. The rest of the body was wholly routed, not one man staying upon the place.[10]

It was indeed a famous victory. In addition to Cavendish, and his Lieutenant Colonel, Thomas Markham, Colonels Heron and Beaton were killed.[11] The jubilant Parliamentarians began passing ammunition into the town, but then discovered that the battle was far from over. Word came in – presumably from some of the cavalrymen who had been following up the retreating Cavaliers – that a small force of Royalists was standing unbroken within a mile of the town. These were estimated to comprise six troops of horse, about 300 foot and two guns. It was naturally supposed that this detachment was a remnant of Cavendish's force, so Meldrum borrowed 400 foot from Willoughby[12] and climbing the hill once more he pushed north in search of them. When the Parliamentarians reached the ground where Cavendish had originally drawn up they encountered two troops of Royalist cavalry. Cromwell promptly charged them and drove them down into the village of Lea. So far so good, but when he gave over the chase and rejoined Meldrum on top of the hill, it suddenly became apparent that the men they were seeking were the advance guard of a much larger force.

Cromwell's letter of 30 July vividly conveys their dismay: '. . . when we came with our Horse to the top of that Hill, we saw in the bottom a whole regiment of Foot, and after that another and another, – and as some counted, about Fifty Colours of Foot. Which was indeed my Lord Newcastle's Army:'[13] The official account tallies with this and adds the intriguing detail that the second regiment to appear was 'my Lord Newcastle's own Regiment, consisting of nineteen colours.'[14] Exactly what happened next is a little unclear, but Meldrum seems to have sent Cromwell back to warn Willoughby of this unwelcome development. It was agreed at once that the foot should be withdrawn into the town, but when Cromwell ascended the hill for the fourth time that day he found them already engaged:

Colonel Cromwell was sent to command the Foot to retire, and to draw-off the Horse. By the time he came to them, the Enemy was marching up the hill. The Foot did retire disorderly into Town, which was not much above a quarter of a mile from them; upon whom the Horse also did retire in some disorder about half a mile – until they came to the end of a field where a passage was; by the endeavour of Colonel Cromwell, Major Whalley and Captain Ayscoghe, a body was drawn up. With these we faced the Enemy; stayed their pursuit; and opposed them with about four troops of Colonel Cromwell's and four Lincoln Troops; the Enemy's body in the mean time increasing very much from the Army. But such was the goodness of God, giving courage and valour to our men and officers, that whilst Major Whalley and Captain Ayscoghe, sometimes the one with four Troops faced the Enemy, sometimes the other . . . they with this handful forced the enemy so, and daring them to their teeth in at least eight or nine several removes, – the Enemy following at their heels; and they, though their horses were exceedingly tired, retreating in order, near carbine-shot of the Enemy, who thus followed them, firing upon them; Colonel Cromwell gathering up the main body and facing them behind those two lesser bodies, – that despite of the Enemy, we brought-off our Horse in this order, without the loss of two men.[15]

Having successfully broken contact Meldrum, Cromwell and Ayscoghe retired through Lincoln and sent off appeals on all hands for reinforcements. Willoughby meanwhile soon discovered that Gainsborough was quite indefensible – the hill where the fighting had taken place completely dominates the town – and the day after the battle he asked for terms. Newcastle agreed to let him march out on the 31st, but only the officers were permitted to carry their arms and all their colours had to be surrendered. Afterwards he made for Lincoln, but hearing that Newcastle was marching towards him, he hastily evacuated the town and retired to Boston, from where he wrote to a disgusted Cromwell on 5 August:

Since the business at Gainsborough, the hearts of our men have been so deaded that we have lost most of them by running away, so that were forced to leave Lincoln upon a sudden; and if I had not done it, then I should have been left alone in it.[16]

Even as he was writing the crisis had passed. In theory the recapture of Gainsborough had opened the way for Newcastle to march southwards and join with the King, but now that the moment had arrived, it became clear that he was unwilling to relinquish his independent command. By way of an alternative the King was willing to countenance an advance 'over the Washes into Norfolk and Suffolk, and the associated counties'[17], but the Earl appears to have been more relieved than disappointed when a resurgence of Parliamentarian activity in Yorkshire led to the projected invasion being aborted.

Undismayed by the defeat at Adwalton Moor the Fairfaxes had been reassembling their shattered army. It was not unlike the Spanish ones of the Peninsular War – frequently beaten and scattered but always doggedly refusing to give up and taking advantage of every opportunity to embarrass the enemy. Now based on Hull they had succeeded in raising over 2,000 foot and 700 horse. Newcastle had been quartering his regiments in the East Riding in anticipation of laying siege to the fortress when the news came of the crisis in Lincolnshire. Initially he had sent off General King with some horse and dragoons to reinforce Cavendish, before thinking better of it and following with most of his army.

In his absence the Fairfaxes sallied out and made an attempt to beat up the garrison of Stamford Bridge. Although the Royalists fled before the Parliamentarians arrived the results were all that could have been hoped for. The Yorkshire Cavaliers sent urgently to Newcastle for help and no doubt glad of the excuse, he appointed Sir William Widdrington to command the Royalist forces in Lincolnshire, and retraced his steps northwards. On 25 August Sir Thomas Fairfax was forced to evacuate Beverley and fall back within the fortifications of Hull. The siege of the town began a week later, and on 13 September the Parliamentarians cut the sluices in order to flood the surrounding countryside. This move very effectively prevented the Royalists from making regular approaches to the town and turned the exercise into a mere blockade. In theory as the town, like Plymouth, could easily be re-supplied by sea it should also have been a futile exercise. Unfortunately this was not at first the case, for the town was too small to accommodate both its ordinary garrison and the Fairfaxes' field army – which is why Sir Thomas's men were quartered at Beverley – especially since the flooding prevented their gathering forage for the cavalry.

Farther south the defeat at Gainsborough and the subsequent abandonment of Lincoln resulted in a dramatic increase in the Eastern Association's forces and an equally radical shift in its military priorities. Hitherto the primary purpose of the Association had been the levying of troops to reinforce the main Parliamentarian army led by the Earl of Essex. Although he clearly interpreted his defensive remit very aggressively Colonel Cromwell's operations in Lincolnshire were very much subsidiary to this aim. Now, alarmed by the Royalist successes in the north, Parliament issued a series of ordinances placing the administration of the Association on a firmer footing and ordering the levying of a further 10,000 foot and dragoons. On 8 August Edward Montague, Earl of Manchester, was appointed Major General in command of those forces, and on the 16th a further ordinance empowered the county committees to impress up to 20,000 men for the service of Parliament.

It was one thing of course to order that these troops should be raised and quite another to see them actually mustered in regiments. The process took time and was sufficiently unpopular to provoke a pro-Royalist uprising around King's Lynn. This broke out on 23 August, and although Manchester was quick to lay siege to the town, he was hampered by a shortage of supplies and the reluctance of the local Trained Bands to assist him. There were understandable worries that the rebellion might have been timed to coincide with a Royalist offensive, but to the Association's relief the town surrendered on 15 September.

Throughout the siege Cromwell and Willoughby had commanded a covering force based on Boston, but now, freed of that responsibility, they rode north and instead assisted in the breakout of Fairfax's cavalry from Hull on the 26th.[18] With this valuable reinforcement they rejoined Manchester at East Kirkby on 10 October. There the combined Parliamentarian army mustered some 6,000 foot and dragoons and 1,500 horse. With this mighty array it was planned to lay siege to nearby Bolingbroke Castle. While the presence of the Royalist garrison was no doubt an inconvenience to the Parliamentarians at Boston, this seems an odd proceeding given that a Royalist field army was already on the move.

At Lincoln Widdrington and Henderson had scraped together some 1,500 horse and 700 dragoons – many of the latter being hastily mounted infantrymen. Exactly what they intended to do with them is less than clear. The accepted version of events is that they were under orders from Newcastle to go to the aid of the garrison at Bolingbroke, but it is questionable whether they could actually have achieved much beyond evacuating it. At any rate their approach was detected by a cavalry screen, and on the 11th a council of war was convened at Bolingbroke to decide whether to fight or to fall back. Notwithstanding their overwhelming superiority in infantry, Cromwell was apparently in favour of the latter course since he reckoned his horses were tired. Manchester quite rightly overruled him.

The Royalists by this time were coming on fast and both armies met head-on at Winceby, facing each other across a shallow valley which offered no impediment to their deployment. Manchester posted his dragoons, commanded by Colonel Bartholomew Vermuyden, on the forward slope of his position and behind them a brigade comprising his own and Colonel Cromwell's regiments. Sir Thomas Fairfax's Yorkshire brigade formed a reserve but the infantry, commanded by Sir Miles Hobart, were still sorting themselves out at Bolingbroke, three miles to the rear. The Royalists to some extent conformed to this deployment, throwing out their own dragoons to face Vermuyden and backing them up with three divisions of horse and a reserve.[19] Sir William Saville commanded the division on the left while Henderson led the right-hand division.

Quite inexplicably, having deployed his cavalry, Manchester then left the field and returned to Bolingbroke, announcing that he was going to hurry the infantry along! Shortly afterwards the battle began in his absence when the Royalist dragoons advanced into the valley floor. Vermuyden moved forward to meet them, and as soon as the firefight began the rest of the Cavaliers set off. Cromwell in turn then led his brigade forward, but as they threaded through the gaps in Vermuyden's dragoons they were shot up by the Royalists. The second volley was delivered at point-blank range and Cromwell himself had his horse shot from under him. A general *melee* then followed, but although the Parliamentarians claimed to have driven the Royalists back on their supports, it actually looks as though they were stopped in their tracks. At any rate Cromwell himself was attacked before he could remount which would hardly be the case if his brigade had advanced beyond him.[20] Whatever the truth of the matter there is no doubt that most of Widdrington's reserve division was committed at an early stage in the fighting.

On the Parliamentarian side Sir Thomas Fairfax's brigade remained unengaged. There was clearly little point in his bringing them forward to stand at the back of the fight, and a hedge out to his left inhibited a flanking movement in that direction. Consequently he led his brigade around the right before putting in a very effective charge. Sir William Saville's brigade broke and ran before they made contact and he went on to roll up the remaining supports as well. In a few moments the outcome of the battle was decided. Widdrington afterwards reckoned to have got most of the cavalry away, but the dragoons and mounted foot were abandoned and forced to surrender.

On the same day an equally dramatic battle was fought under the walls of Hull. That morning Sir John Meldrum led a sortie against the Royalists siege works on the west side of the town. Initially he was successful in obtaining a lodgement in the fort covering the Anlaby Road, but a Royalist counter attack swept the Parliamentarians out again. Undaunted Meldrum and Lord Fairfax rallied their men for a second attempt and this time captured the fort. Unable or unwilling to dislodge them the demoralised Royalists, who had spent weeks ankle-deep in mud, broke up the siege that night and retired to York.

In the wake of this double success Meldrum was able to take both Lincoln and Gainsborough and to contain the Newarkers. With his army no longer immobilised before Hull, Newcastle (who had just been elevated in the peerage to the rank of Marquis) ought to at least have been able to save Gainsborough, but instead he spent the remaining weeks of 1643 in a futile little campaign in Derbyshire.

NOTES

1. RCHM *Newark on Trent: the Civil War Siegeworks* p29
2. *ibid* pp54-7. Sir John Digby's regiment had numbered only 400 men when he drew it into the town in December and it is unlikely that Gervase Holles had time to recruit many more. Henderson arrived with a commission to recruit 1,000 musketeers but confessed on 5 January that he was too busy to raise them. Instead he offered to 'levie 5 comp: of Scots Lanciers amounting to 300'.

It is unlikely that he ever had much more than a troop though they may well have been Scots for only one officer appears under him in the *List of Indigent Officers* and he could have been serving in *any* of the garrison regiments. Besides Henderson's own troop there were elements of two others commanded by Sir Gervase Eyre and Sir Charles Dallison. Henderson also appears to have commanded a small regiment of dragoons but it is unclear whether they were included in the total of ten troops.

3. The brigade appears to have comprised detachments from Sir John Gell's Derbyshire Foot under Major John Mollanus, and Colonel Francis Pierrepoint's Nottinghamshire Foot under Lieutenant Colonel John Hutchinson.

4. RCHM p61. Ballard may simply have been easily discouraged but his conduct on this occasion also cost him a spell of imprisonment, after which he went abroad and died at Rouen in 1645.

5. Ironically enough when the convoy left Newark on 8 May it was escorted by Hastings.

6. As Henderson had about ten troops in Newark (see note 2 above), it seems likely that Cavendish provided eleven belonging to his own, Lord Henry Cavendish's and Sir William Pelham's regiments. The dragoons were probably Henderson's.

7. Cromwell claimed to have inflicted 100 casualties and to have taken forty five more, but while the number of prisoners may be believed it is likely that the Royalists ran away too quickly to be killed in such numbers.

8. The Royalist commander, Robert Pierrepoint the Earl of Kingston, was particularly unlucky. Willoughby sent him off to Hull but the pinnace carrying him down the Trent was intercepted by some of Newcastle's men commanded by General King 'who being desirous to rescue the Earl of Kingston, and making some shots with their regiment pieces to stop the pinnace, unfortunately slew him and one of his servants.'

9. Edward Ayscoghe, John Broxholme & Oliver Cromwell to Speaker Lenthall 29 July 1643 'Official Account' in *English Civil War Times* 51 p31. 'John Broxholme' is almost certainly an error for John Meldrum, the third of the Parliamentarian commanders.

10. Oliver Cromwell 31 July 1643, in *ibid* p33. There are various accounts of how Cavendish met his fate in the boggy land (now allotments) just south of Lea. Although he was certainly brought down by James Berry at least one report claimed that he was finished off with a brace of bullets after refusing quarter.

11. *Royal Martyrs*. Cavendish's Regiment was subsequently taken over by Samuel Tuke and known as The Duke of York's Regiment.

12. In his letter of 30 July (*English Civil War Times* 51 p32) Cromwell refers to them as being musketeers.

13. *ibid*. Formidable though this sounds – and no doubt looked – if we assume an average of about fifty men to each colour, Newcastle may have had as few as 2,500 foot. If on the other hand his own double regiment was better recruited than the others the total might conceivably rise to around 3,500.

14. *Official Account*. The Duchess (Firth p84) states that 'Amongst the rest of his army, my Lord had chosen for his own regiment of foot, 3000 of such valiant, stout and faithful men (whereof many were bred in the moorish grounds of the northern parts) that they were ready to die at my Lord's feet . . .' With nineteen colours Newcastle's regiment was clearly much larger than usual. With his own, a Colonel's, Lieutenant Colonels', two Majors' and fourteen Captains' companies. The colours also sound as though they were distinctive. Included amongst the Allied trophies acquired at Marston Moor a year later

were eleven colours described as 'red with white crosses'. These are almost certainly Newcastle's. It seems to have been the practice in the Royalist army at least for regiments commanded by General officers to have red colours and eleven colours are in any case too many for an ordinary sized unit. The reference to white crosses is unclear. It may simply mean that the several companies were distinguished by varying numbers of white crosses on a red field. However the other trophies recorded in *A True Relation of the Victory* (Thomason Tracts E59 19) are all described as having *red* crosses on white besides any other distinguishing marks. This might suggest that on Newcastle's colours the St George's cross normally displayed in the canton was either omitted, or perhaps even replaced by a white cross.

15. *Official Account*
16. Quoted in Firth p29
17. Sir Philip Warwick quoted in Firth *op. cit.* Sir Thomas Fairfax also claimed 'his orders (which I have seen) were to go into Essex, and block up London on that side.' On the face of it these orders would appear to support Brigadier Young's theory of a Royalist plan for a converging or 'triple-pronged' offensive against London. On the other hand it was very much a secondary plan adopted (and swiftly abandoned) after Newcastle proved reluctant to bring his troops to Oxford. In any case clearing the Eastern Association would have cost at least one campaigning season and it is unlikely that Newcastle could have been established in Essex before late 1644 or 1645. And the Scots invasion was only months away.
18. In return Lord Fairfax received a reinforcement of 400 foot. Although some secondary sources state that they were sent by Manchester, they actually appear to have been Meldrum's Midlanders.
19. Elements of the following regiments can be identified, or their presence at least inferred. As Parliamentarian accounts refer to them being drawn up in four bodies it may reasonably be inferred that Saville was commanding a brigade comprising units from Newcastle's army and that the centre and reserve were made up of Cavendish's old brigade and an ad hoc one made up of the garrison horse from Newark and Lincoln:
Right Wing:
Sir John Henderson's Horse
Lieutenant General James King's Horse
Centre:
Colonel Maurice Baud's Horse
Sir Peregrine Bertie's Horse
Sir Charles Dallison's Horse
Sir Gervase Eyre's Horse
Lord Henry Cavendish's Horse
Sir William Pelham's Horse
Colonel Samuel Tuke's Horse
Left Wing:
Colonel Robert Brandling's Horse
Sir William Saville's Horse
Sir William Widdrington's Horse
20. His attacker, Sir Ingram Hopton, is often referred to as a colonel, but no trace can be found of his regiment. He himself was killed in the *melee* but although Cromwell was soon remounted there is no evidence that he played any meaningful part in the battle.

CHAPTER VIII

Holding the Gates:
Nantwich, Newark and Selby

After the capture of Gainsborough on 20 December 1643 Sir Thomas Fairfax was assigned a new and urgent task – the relief of Nantwich in Cheshire. There had been continuous fighting in Cheshire and the Welsh border area since the early days of the war. The Parliamentarian Sir William Brereton, based on Nantwich, was faced first by Sir Thomas Aston and afterwards by Arthur, Lord Capel. Until the end of 1643 Brereton was successful in containing the Royalists and indeed made considerable headway against them, but in the late summer of that year two related events led to the struggle assuming something more than regional significance.

Both King and Parliament, stalemated on the central front, were actively seeking outside assistance. It soon became apparent that the Scots were willing to enter the war on the side of Parliament, and indeed they began mobilising their army on 28 July. In the face of this threat the King authorised the signing of a Cessation or cease-fire between the Dublin government and the Irish rebels on 15 September.

The cease-fire was far from universally observed, particularly in the north where the war continued with unabated fury, but its immediate effect was to release thousands of troops from the King's Leinster and Munster armies for service in England.[1] There is no doubt that the King would have preferred to see this mighty reinforcement landed in a body at a single port. Unfortunately for a variety of reasons the Royalist commander in Ireland, the Earl of Ormonde was only ever able to ship across a few regiments at a time. A number of units from Munster were landed at Bristol[2] and at least one Leinster regiment, Sir Philip Byron's Foot, landed at Whitehaven, but the obvious landing place for the bulk of the Leinster regiments was Chester.

Unfortunately it was clear that Lord Capel was incapable of opening a military corridor linking the city with the south. On the contrary, by late 1643 he was very much on the defensive and Brereton was actually moving into north Wales in order to isolate Chester as a prelude to besieging the city. Accordingly, as soon as the fighting died down on the central front, Sir John Byron was ennobled as Lord Byron and sent north with the King's commission as 'Field Marshall Generall of all His Mat^ies forces in ye Countyes of Worcester, Salop: Chester, Flint, Denbigh, Montgomery, Merioneth, Anglesey & Carn'von'. Rather more practically he also took with him thirty barrels of powder,[3] and 1,000 horse and 300 foot from the Oxford Army[4] since it was correctly assumed that Capel's army was too small and too demoralised to accomplish anything. By 30 November he was at Shrewsbury.

Then the Irish arrived. Seven ships had been despatched from Bristol to pick up the Leinster Army, and on 16 November four regiments of foot and a small cavalry regiment[5] were landed at Mostyn on the Welsh side of the Dee estuary under the command of Major General Sir Michael Earnley. Estimates of their strength in secondary sources vary between 1,500 and 4,000 men, but as the local Commissioners of Array were instructed to supply them with 1,300 suits of clothes[6] the lower figure is certainly correct. Had he been able to move swiftly it might just have been possible for Brereton to defeat Earnley before Byron arrived, but at this critical juncture he was abandoned by his Lancashire allies. Fearing that a similar landing might be effected at Liverpool they promptly marched off home and left him to his fate.

After making an attempt to persuade Earnley to change sides, he left a garrison at Hawarden (which surrendered after a twelve-day siege), flung another under Sir George Booth into Nantwich and then scoured the countryside for recruits. Naturally enough he made the most of the fact that the bloody 'Irish' were coming, while at the same time continuing to persuade them to change sides!

Earnley meanwhile joined Byron at Chester in early December where they were reinforced by a further 1,300 foot from Ireland[7] . This enabled them to take the field on the 13th. Just before dawn that morning one of the 'Irish' officers, Captain Thomas Sandford[8], scaled the cliff at Beeston Castle and possibly with the connivance of the governor got into the upper ward. The garrison of the supposedly impregnable castle then surrendered with indecent haste. A week later a Royalist raid on Nantwich itself was beaten off, although Colonel Booth's second-in-command, Major James Lothian, managed to get himself captured. In the days which followed Byron steadily surrounded the town and picked off its outposts. At one of them, Barthomley, the defenders of the church were murdered after surrendering on Christmas Eve.[9] Brereton meanwhile was trying to assemble a relief force, but on Christmas Day Byron concentrated his army and routed the Parliamentarians in a brisk little action at Middlewich on the 26th. Having lost 500 men Brereton had little option but to haul off and sit tight until help arrived.

Theses were the circumstances in which Sir Thomas Fairfax was ordered to march westwards. At first lacking clear directions, let alone sufficient arms, clothing and pay, he set off in the early days of January 1644 with 1,800 horse and 500 dragoons. Marching through the north

Midlands he successfully avoided interception by the Marquis of Newcastle's men who were then quartered in Derbyshire. Unfortunately, while he was waiting at Stafford for Brereton to join him, a detachment of Byron's horse led by Colonel John Marrow beat up an outlying quarter at Newcastle-under-Lyme. Predictably enough this dampened any enthusiasm on the part of the Staffords to join in the relief expedition, but moving north to Manchester Fairfax was joined there by 3,000 infantry including some of his old Yorkshire foot under Colonel John Bright. He is said to have burst into tears on seeing the ragged condition of these veterans of Adwalton Moor, but a more serious problem was the continuing reluctance of the Lancashire regiments to leave their home territory. They were eventually persuaded to accompany him, but it was not until 21 January that he was able to march.[10]

In the meantime the Royalists, who had summoned the town on 10 January, appear to have been running short of ammunition. A convoy being brought up from Shrewsbury by Sir Nicholas Byron was ambushed and captured by a detachment from Wem on 14 January.[11] Notwithstanding this setback his nephew made a brisk attempt to storm the town on 18 January. Swarming forward at dawn the Royalists attacked the five forts covering the entrances to the town. On the west side Gibson's brigade, comprising his own regiment and Captain Sandford's Firelocks, actually broke into the defences before being tumbled out again by a desperate counter-attack. Byron eventually broke off the assault, but the town was so closely blockaded that it was clear the garrison would not be able to hold out for much longer. It was realisation of this fact rather than any rumours of the Scots invasion which finally persuaded the Lancashire regiments to march with Fairfax.

Advancing through the snow Fairfax's advance guard bumped a Royalist cavalry picket in Delamere Forest on the morning of the 24th. Although the skirmish was easily won, it alerted a previously ignorant Byron to his approach. That night the Parliamentarians halted at Tilstone Heath, eight miles short of the town, knowing that they had a battle on their hands.

Unbeknown to Fairfax, Byron was having trouble concentrating his army. Nantwich straddles the River Weaver, and as a result the besieging army was split into two unequal parts, with most of them lying on the east bank of the river. Naturally enough the principal crossing point in the area was within the town itself, and another at Beambridge, just to the north, had been broken down before the siege began. Instead Byron was relying on a temporary wooden replacement for this bridge and a third crossing point at Shrewbridge, two miles to the south of the town. Before the light failed on the afternoon of the 24th Byron evidently succeeded in passing a part of his army across the river, but during the night a thaw set in with disastrous results. The river rose rapidly, and not only swept away the crossing at Beambridge but flooded the water-meadows around Shrewbridge as well.

This left Byron's acting second-in-command, Colonel Richard Gibson (Sir Michael Earnley was sick) in an extremely awkward position. At dawn on the 25th he only appears to have had his own brigade and a part of Sir Fulk Huncke's Regiment facing Fairfax. Consequently he left only 100 musketeers covering the Welsh Row end of Nantwich while he deployed the rest across the Chester Road beside Acton Church, with an outpost at Barbridge, two miles farther up the road.

Fairfax quickly overran the post at Barbridge and by early afternoon he had come in sight of Gibson's position at Acton. At this point he and his officers suddenly had second thoughts. Although they were on higher ground it is questionable whether they could actually see very much of the Royalists since the area was criss-crossed with hedges. It was immediately obvious to them that an infantry brigade was deployed around the church, and by counting the colours they ought to have been able to work out its strength. What they were less certain about was what was behind that brigade. Reinforcements could be seen marching up but naturally it was difficult if not impossible accurately to assess their strength. Assuming the worst Fairfax wrongly concluded that he had insufficient men to fight Byron's army on his own. Instead he decided to by-pass the Acton position and try to effect a junction with George Booth's garrison in Nantwich.

He was obviously taking a considerable risk in doing so, particularly as his progress was slowed by the need to hack gaps in the numerous hedges which lay in his path. Sure enough the Royalists very quickly went on to the offensive. The problem was that none of the attacks were properly coordinated. Although Byron was afterwards at some pains to give the impression that his army was properly deployed before the fighting began, the whole affair actually appears to have been a confused encounter battle in which units were hurried into action piecemeal as they came up from Shrewbridge. Some units, including most of Byron's cavalry, may never have been engaged at all for he claimed that he was unable to deploy them amongst the hedgerows.

Nevertheless it is possible broadly to reconstruct what happened. By the time Fairfax began his 'dash' for the town, Gibson had been joined by the rest of the 'Irish' foot[12]. It is likely that initially they were drawn up along the Chester Road. Robert Byron's Regiment was on the left wing and Gibson's on the right, with the rest of the Royalist foot standing between them. Even if this was a proper battle-line it broke up as soon as the fighting began.

Robert Byron was first into action, swinging around into the rear of Fairfax's column. Sir Thomas thereupon dropped off Richard Holland's and John Booth's foot and his own regiment of horse to face them. With the rest of his army he kept marching until the head of the column ran into Gibson's regiments. This forced him to deploy Assheton's and Brereton's regiments to support his Forlorn. Initially both Royalist attacks met with some success, but Fairfax's cavalry managed to slow them down and the hedgerows hampered coordination. Suddenly Warren's and Earnley's gave way in circumstances which afterwards gave rise to accusations of treachery. Then, to complete the Royalists' discomfiture, the garrison of Nantwich decided to join in.

A force of some 700 musketeers burst out of the town, scattered Huncke's little detachment and moved up the Chester Road until they arrived in the Royalist rear. Not surprisingly this quickly led to the total collapse of Gibson's command. The compartmentalisation of the battle-field saw the regiments destroyed piecemeal and he managed to fight his way back to Acton Church. Whether he halted there deliberately or because he could go no farther is unclear, but by that time Robert Byron's Regiment was retreating towards Chester. Lord Byron himself claimed to have remained on the field with his cavalry until darkness fell but they had played no significant part in the battle and he made no attempt to rescue Gibson. He, poor man, held out in the churchyard until dawn the next morning. Then, finding themselves abandoned, he and his remaining men came out and surrendered.

Typically neither side admitted to losing very many killed or wounded, but Fairfax took seventy-two officers and 1,500 men prisoners. Of these about 600 displayed their professionalism by immediately changing sides. For the most part they were distributed amongst the various regiments present, but the Firelock companies remained intact and simply transferred their services under their own officers.

In the wake of this disaster Byron held on to Chester and some of its outlying garrisons. Most of his Irish troops were sent down to Shrewsbury to recruit and recuperate while further reinforcements were sought. He himself began raising a regiment of foot and obtained five companies for it from Ireland. Colonel Henry Tillier brought a strong regiment across in February[13], and was followed shortly afterwards by another regiment led by Colonel Robert Broughton. Both units were immediately sent down to join the others at Shrewsbury.

Initially this garrison was chosen as the headquarters for the 'Irish' army simply to ease the supply situation in and around Chester. Nevertheless the concentration was very convenient for Prince Rupert, who was ordered north to retrieve the situation. Few troops could be spared from Oxford and Rupert moved north up the Severn valley by way of Worcester and Bridgenorth accompanied only by 700 cavalry belonging to his own and Sir John Hurry's regiments. On Tuesday 19 February he opened his headquarters at Shrewsbury and a few days later was joined there by Tillier's brigade. Tillier, possibly a French Huguenot, was not merely a professional soldier but a noted tactician and Rupert immediately appointed him Quartermaster-General.[14] No doubt his first task was to take the rest of the Irish in hand, but by 1 March Rupert was ready. That day he sent some horse up to Wem, and when they returned to report that all was quiet, he set in train one of his raids.

On the 4th Colonel Tillier took 500 musketeers up the road towards Market Drayton and at nightfall the Prince followed after with his horse. Sir Thomas Mytton and the Earl of Denbigh were quartered in the town with their forces and they had been joined by a small cavalry brigade under Sir William Fairfax. The Royalists' target was this concentration and Rupert was no doubt hoping to surprise them in their beds. If so he was disappointed, for when he arrived outside Market Drayton next day (Shrove Tuesday), he found the Parliamentarians drawn up and waiting for him in a close, or hedged, field. They may indeed have been hoping to ambush the raiders, but Rupert, impetuous as ever, promptly attacked the gate at the head of his Lifeguard and succeeded in keeping them penned within until the rest of his men came up. They were then routed and he claimed afterwards to have taken forty prisoners and one of Fairfax's cornets without loss.

Having thus announced himself as it were in no uncertain terms, he rode north to a conference with Byron at Chester on the 11th. Despite a chilly reception from the local authorities he ordered the destruction of some of the suburbs and set in train various other improvements to the city's defences. Then on the 12th he received news that Newark was in danger and that he must at once march to its relief. This can hardly have come as a surprise for the fortress had to some extent been living on borrowed time ever since the disaster at Winceby in the previous October. Henderson had been replaced as governor by Sir Richard Byron[15] but otherwise little or nothing had been done to secure this vital garrison. It was of course part of Newcastle's fiefdom, but while Sir John Meldrum steadily mopped up the Lincolnshire garrisons and a Scots invasion grew daily more imminent, Newcastle ignored both major threats in favour of a lackadaisical campaign in Derbyshire. Directed against a largely imaginary 'rebellion' this diversion might just conceivably have been a way of avoiding any substantial commitment of his forces until it became apparent whether Meldrum or his countrymen posed the greater threat to the King's Peace. In reality it looks rather more like some singularly futile 'displacement activity' undertaken by a commander unable or unwilling to seize the initiative.

At any rate, left to their own devices the Newarkers carried out a last (unsuccessful) raid on Nottingham on 16 January before Meldrum finally closed in. He had at his disposal some 5,000 foot and 2,000 horse. Some of them were his own Midlanders, but most of his infantry regiments came from the Eastern Association.[16] Where Ballard had rather too hastily rushed into an unsuccessful escalade, Meldrum resolved on a slower, more methodical siege.

For that he first needed to surround the town. This was easily accomplished on the south side, but on the north lay two branches of the river Trent, and lying between them was a broad flat expanse of land known as the Island. Capturing this 'island' would not only considerably shorten the line of circumvallation, but it would also deprive the garrison's remaining cavalry of a valuable source of forage.[17] While the Island was clearly too large to be properly defended by anything short of an army, the only viable access to it was at the northern end, over a wooden drawbridge at Muskham. This bridge was covered by a substantial earthwork fort or sconce, defended by Colonel Gervase Holles' Regiment. On 6 March Colonel Edward King and his regiment stormed this fort, killing Holles in the process. This then allowed Meldrum to throw a bridge of boats across the southern branch of the river linking his headquarters at the Spital, the shell of a large stone house just north of the town, with his forces on the Island. A more general probing attack on 8 March was repulsed, but unlike Ballard, Meldrum simply shrugged his shoulders and carried on with the siege.

By this time Newcastle was fully occupied in containing the Scots on Tyneside, and an attempt by Sir Gervase Lucas to raise the siege with the Newark Horse was unsuccessful. There was no alternative but to call upon Prince Rupert. The problem was of course that as yet he had no army with which to accomplish this. One would have to be pulled together on the march. On the 14th he returned to Shrewsbury. Some fast marching was clearly called for so 1,200 musketeers were commanded out of the three strongest Irish regiments, Henry Tillier's, Robert Broughton's and Sir Fulk Huncke's, and shipped down the Severn as far as Bridgenorth. On the 16th Rupert marched with the Irish and his cavalry to Wolverhampton, picking up another 100 horse and 200 musketeers under the terrifying Colonel Thomas Leveson. At Ashby de la Zouch on the 18th, Blind Harry Hastings and George Porter brought in another 1,800 foot and perhaps as many as 2,500 horse. It was an odd little army totalling 3,300 horse and 3,120 foot. All of the latter were musketeers and the horse, although experienced, were mainly garrison troopers.[18] Their expertise lay in raiding and skirmishing, rather than standing in the battle-line, and this meant that they were liable to prove brittle. When Rupert fought his battle he was going to have to win it quickly.

Next day the Royalists moved on to Rempstone, and on the Wednesday night quartered in a field outside Bingham. They were now just ten miles short of their objective, and in the early hours of the 21st Prince Rupert commenced his advance to contact. Meldrum was well aware that he was coming. A substantial body of his cavalry, led by Sir Edward Hartop, had already made an unsuccessful attempt to prevent the union with Hastings. Another spoiling attack was in contemplation but aborted on the 20th when it was realised that the Royalists were getting dangerously close. Instead Sir Miles Hobart, the senior Eastern Association colonel, advocated breaking up the siege and falling back on Lincoln. Meldrum quite properly rejected this proposal. It was certainly time to break up the siege but he was not prepared to retire without a fight. Drawing his men out of their lines he concentrated his army at the Spital, with most of his remaining horse on the 100-foot high Beacon Hill just to the east.

It was intelligence of this concentration which led Rupert to set off in the moonlight at 2am. Understandably suspecting that it was the prelude to a withdrawal he intended to force a battle before they could get away. This perception was reinforced when swinging through Balderton he saw Meldrum's cavalry evacuating their position on top of Beacon Hill. Shortly afterwards he moved on to the hill himself and at last saw the Parliamentarian infantry drawn up by the Spital. The horse had not retired very far and were drawn up in four divisions on the lower slopes of the hill.

It might have been prudent at this juncture to wait for the arrival of his own foot and the greater part of his horse. Instead, still obsessed by the fear that Meldrum might escape, he decided to launch a hasty attack with the troops immediately at hand. He drew them up in two lines with his own regiment, commanded by Lieutenant Colonel Daniel O'Neale on the right and his Lifeguard led by Sir Richard Crane on the left. In his rear was Colonel George Porter's little regiment[19] and Colonel Charles Gerard's Troop. In total Rupert had only just over 800 horse, nevertheless he may not have been too badly outnumbered for, in addition to the men still absent with Hartop, Meldrum had sent the Derby Horse across to the Island. All that can be said with any certainty is that Colonel Francis Thornhaugh commanded the two divisions on the right and Colonel Edward Rossiter had the divisions on the left.

At about 9am the Royalists moved down off the hill and were immediately counter-charged by the Parliamentarians. Rossiter had doubled up his own division and the six deep formation initially proved unstoppable. He succeeded in driving the right hand division of Rupert's Regiment back up the hill against their reserves. An initial counter-attack by Colonel Gerard made no impression, and the gallant Colonel was himself unhorsed, wounded and captured. Then Captain Clement Benson managed to swing the next division of Rupert's around and, as Rossiter's men were by now a little disordered, he managed to beat them off.

On the Royalist left the fight went much better. Lord Willoughby's Horse had rarely distinguished themselves during the fighting of the previous summer – save by the speed with which they ran away. Now they did it again leaving Thornhaugh's Nottinghamshire men to stand alone. Unsurprisingly Rupert and his Lifeguard, shouting *King and Queen* rode right over them. At one point a Parliamentarian trooper is famously said to have laid his hand on the Prince's collar before having it hacked off. Notwithstanding this, the issue was never in doubt and the hapless Midlanders were pursued up to Meldrum's fortifications at the Spital.

So far so good, but Rossiter had managed to bring his men off in good order and not even Rupert was up to charging a whole army with a few hundred troopers on blown horses. The cavalry battle was then followed by a considerable lull while Rupert waited for his infantry support and the rest of his horse to come up. Meldrum now decided that the time had come to retreat after all, and took the opportunity to pass his cavalry across the bridge of boats on to the Island. But then, before he could start getting his infantry and guns away, Tillier arrived on the scene.

Rupert was still wary of launching a frontal assault, especially as Meldrum's infantry were dug in. Instead Tillier and his Irish musketeers swung around to attack from the north-east, in an attempt to get between Meldrum and the bridge. This attack was beaten off, but once Tillier was safely out of range of the Parliamentarian guns Rupert ordered him to hold his position. This ruled out any realistic chance of a breakout in the direction of Lincoln. Meldrum's only remaining escape route was across the Island and up the Great North Road. Having learned from a prisoner that the Parliamentarians only had enough provisions to last two days, Rupert scaled down his attack and resolved instead to starve them into submission. First he had to close the last exit. This agreeable task was allotted to Sir Richard Byron and the Newark garrison. Sallying out on to the Island they immediately pushed northwards to Muskham and the drawbridge. Panicking, the defenders of the fort fled straight across it. They also broke it down to prevent any pursuit and by so doing they sealed their comrades' fate. As the news that they were trapped spread, Meldrum's army collapsed. The 'Norfolk Redcoats'[20] mutinied and 'the poor old man' (he was 59) was left with no alternative but to surrender. In the circumstances the terms he was granted were reasonable enough and reflected the fact that mutinous or not his infantry still outnumbered the Royalists. When Meldrum marched out next morning he was forced to turn over 3,000 muskets, eleven brass guns and two mortars, but he was allowed to keep his drums and colours and his men had their swords and knapsacks. Once they were re-equipped they would be ready to fight again.

The surrender of Meldrum's army not only preserved Newark – it would now remain in Royalist hands until the end of the war – but also brought about a welcome improvement in Royalist fortunes throughout the region. Gainsborough appears to have been abandoned by its Parliamentarian garrison on the 22nd and Lincoln was evacuated the following day. Somehow Royalist garrisons were scraped together for both, but beyond this a shortage of troops prevented Rupert from further exploitation of his victory. Most of his army had been cobbled together from other Midland garrisons and it was time for them to return. A week after the battle he retraced his steps back through Ashby and Lichfield, dropping them off on the way. Returning to Shrewsbury on 4 April he should have been able to resume building a proper field army – thanks to Meldrum he now had a fine train of artillery – but little more than a fortnight later he was recalled to Oxford for an urgent conference. This time York was in danger.

When Newcastle rode north in January 1644 to confront the Scots he left most of his Yorkshire regiments behind. Sir Francis Mackworth was left in charge of the West Riding and, despite his poor showing at Winceby, Sir William Savile was installed as governor of York. His tenure did not last long for he died suddenly on 22 January and was replaced on the 28th by Colonel John Belasyse. Although a Yorkshireman born and bred Belasyse had until then been serving with the Oxford Army. His appointment, together with the simultaneous reassignment of Sir Charles Lucas to the Northern Army as well, almost certainly represents an attempt to reduce the independence of that army.

Once he was established at York his first priority was to reorganise the scattered garrisons into an efficient field army. This was no easy task, and it became progressively more difficult when the Parliamentarian garrison of Hull began to act aggressively. Sir William Constable was able to launch a series of steadily more dangerous forays, gradually picking off small garrisons and isolating Scarborough. At the same time Sir Thomas Fairfax's troops, still temporarily operating out of the Manchester area, started to 'liberate' the West Riding. Colonel John Lambert took Bradford and on 6 March won a useful little action against a small cavalry brigade at Hunslet. Fearing for the safety of Leeds, Belasyse ordered his forces to concentrate at Selby and recaptured Bradford on 25 March.

The respite thus gained was only temporary, for shortly afterwards Sir Thomas Fairfax returned bringing not only his old cavalry but a number of Lancashire units as well. Meeting his father at Ferrybridge they resolved to move on Selby and deal with Belasyse. As far as can be ascertained he had some 1,500 horse and 1,800 foot[21] ; the Fairfaxes outnumbered him by about two to one. On 11 April after they had been joined by Sir John Meldrum (it is unlikely he brought many troops) they attacked. Typically the initial objective was to secure three of the four entrances to the town at Brayton Lane, Gowthorpe and Ousegate. This apparently took some time and according to Sir Thomas: 'Our men at length beat them from the Line; but could not advance farther because of the Horse within.' At length Fairfax got a 'Barricado' open at or near Ousegate and, instead of trying to force his way up the street, he led his cavalry between the houses and the river. There he received two cavalry 'charges' and was at one stage unhorsed while riding ahead of his men, but both were defeated. In the second charge he took Belasyse prisoner and, although many of the Royalist cavalry got away across a bridge of boats there was no escape for the foot. In all 1,600 prisoners were taken including twenty-seven captains and field officers. A siege of York was now inevitable.

NOTES

1. These troops are for the sake of convenience invariably referred to as 'Irish'. In actual fact they fell into three not very neat categories. In the first place were those units which had been sent out from England in 1642. Secondly there were a number of regiments which had been raised in Ireland, either as part of the old Irish Army, or since the outbreak of the rebellion. Keeping these units, and particularly the 'English' ones up to strength was obviously difficult and there was a long standing custom of enlisting 'native' Irishmen into their ranks. Thirdly a number of regiments, such as Lord Byron's Foot, were recruited in Ireland specifically for service in England. It is hardly surprising therefore that Parliamentarian propaganda linking *all* of these regiments with the Catholic rebels should have been so effective.

2. The Duke of York's Regiment commanded by Sir William St Leger joined the Oxford Army, as did Sir Charles Vavasour's, Sir John Paulet's and the mysterious Colonel (John?) Talbot's. Lord Broghill's and the Earl of Inchiquin's regiments were sent to join Prince Maurice in the West Country, although both defected to Parliament in August 1644. There may well have been a seventh Irish regiment serving under Sir William Courtney, but since there were a number of officers bearing that name it is difficult to be certain whether the Sir William Courtney commanding a regiment at Lostwithiel in 1644 is the same Sir William who earlier served in Munster.

3. Roy. p311. He was actually given a warrant for forty barrels, but only thirty were issued which points to a continuing shortage of powder at Oxford.

4. In addition to his own regiment of Horse, Byron also took Lord Molyneux's Horse and Sir Thomas Tyldesley's Horse (issued with pistols and carbines on 17 November – Roy p312) and Foot. Tyldesley had fought at Edgehill as Lieutenant Colonel of Lord Molyneux's Foot and it now appears that this regiment was drafted into his own in order to replace his heavy losses at Newbury.

5. The four regiments were:Col. Robert Byron's (part only)
   Sir Michael Earnley's
   Col. Richard Gibson's
   Sir Fulk Huncke's
   Three of them were originally raised in England (Gibson's was originally Sir Simon Harcourt's) but Robert Byron's Regiment was only formed in March 1643 from detachments of musketeers drawn from the locally raised units of the Leinster Army. In addition this first lift included two companies of Firelocks commanded by Captain Francis Langley and Captain Thomas Sandford and three troops of horse commanded by Sir William Vaughan.

6. Hutton, R. *The Royalist War Effort* p122. In actual fact Byron was only able to muster 4,000 foot by combining this and the second Irish contingent, with Tyldesley's 300 foot and some local levies.

7. The second lift consisted of Colonel Henry Warren's Regiment and the remainder of Robert Byron's. The former had originally been the Lord General's Regiment (albeit the Earl of Leicester never set foot in Ireland), and

the actual commanding officer was Lieutenant Colonel George Monck. Byron initially entertained some doubts about Monck's loyalties but he was reinstated in time to lead the regiment, less than gloriously, at Nantwich.

8. Sandford was a 'character' much given to bombastic letter writing. One addressed to the garrison of Hawarden shortly before it surrendered closed with the words: 'Sirrah behold the messenger of death, Sandford and his firelocks, who neither use to give, nor take quarter' Sadly he was himself killed during the unsuccessful attack on Nantwich 18 January 1644.

9. Although much condemned the massacre seems to have taken place because the defenders of the church were not regular soldiers but armed villagers – just the sort of insurgents the 'Irish' were used to liquidating. The identity of those responsible is uncertain. Traditionally the atrocity is said to have been carried out by some of Byron's Irish troops under a Major Connought. This might be the officer of that name serving in Robert Byron's Foot, but it has also been suggested that he was in fact Major John Connock (or Cannock) of Colonel Ralph Snead's Horse – a small Staffordshire unit.

10. The following units can be identified, although this is probably an incomplete listing:

Horse:		**Foot:**	
	Sir Thomas Fairfax		Col.John Bright (Yorkshire)
	Sir William Fairfax		Col. Richard Holland (Lancs.)
	Col. John Lambert		Col Ralph Assheton (Lancs.)
	Col. Hugh Bethell		Col. John Booth (Warrington)
			Col. Alexander Rigby (Lancs.)

Col. Thomas Morgan's Dragoons

The figure of 3,000 foot and 1800 horse probably includes Brereton's own regiments of horse and foot, and Colonel Henry Mainwaring's Cheshire foot which only joined Fairfax on the 23rd.

11. As a result a fresh supply of fifty barrels of powder was despatched from Oxford in ten covered wagons on 24 January (Roy pp327-8). The Conductor, Savage Bent, was pointedly instructed that 'after wch delivery you are to retourne with all possible expedicon you are likewise to haue an especiall Care as well of ye said Waggons as of horses wth theire ffurniture.'

12. None of the accounts mention what happened to Sir Thomas Tyldesley's Foot. This may simply be an oversight, for there is no mention either of the firelocks and dragoons who were certainly with Gibson, or for that matter of the greater part of Sir Fulk Huncke's Regiment. On the other hand it is quite likely that they were left watching the east side of the town.

13. Symonds, *Diary* p75. 'Colonel Sir Charles Coote . . . Col. Sir Henry Tichbourne . . . Lord Lambert . . . Lord Burlacy . . . These four regiments were raysed about and in Dublyn . . . Some of these came over with Tilyard, 1,000 foot greencoates came with him . . .'

14. Secondary sources invariably refer to him as being Rupert's Major General but the *Rupert Diary* clearly identifies him as 'Q^{tr} Mr Gen^{ll} '(See Young, P. *Marston Moor* p212)

15. Henderson was at Oxford in early January but shortly afterwards went abroad and entered the Danish service.

16. Although no formal muster ever took place the following units can be identified from contemporary accounts (based on raw listing in RCHM *Newark* p96):

Col. Bingley's Horse	Sir Miles Hobart's Foot (Eastern Assn.)
Lord Grey's Horse	Col. Edward King's Foot(Eastern Assn.)
Sir Edward Hartop's Horse	Sir John Palgrave's Foot(Eastern Assn.)
Col. Edward Rossiter's Horse	Col. Francis Pierrepoint's Foot (3 coys.)

Col. Francis Thornhaugh's Horse   Lord Willoughby's Foot
Lord Willoughby's Horse   2-3 coys of Yorkshire foot

17. Just before the siege began Byron sent away all but six troops of horse – belonging to his own and Sir Gervase Eyre's regiments.

18. Rupert's cavalry included the following regiments (RCHM *Newark* p19):

Prince Rupert's Lifeguards   140
Prince Rupert's Regiment   500
Col. Charles Gerard's Troop   60
Col. Thomas Leveson's Regiment 100
Col. George Porter's Brigade   1,000

    Porter was Commissary General of Newcastle's horse. The composition of his brigade is unknown, but if the rather high figure of 1,000 men is not a mistake for the 100 men of his own regiment, it probably comprised the regiments sent out of Newark at the outset of the siege.

Lord Loughborough's Brigade*   1,500
Lord Loughborough's Regt.
Sir John Harpur's Regt.
Col. Rowland Eyre's Regt.
Col. John Frescheville's Regt.
* Loughborough was of course 'Blind Harry Hastings'

19. This does suggest that the figure of 1,000 men supposedly brought in by Porter is an error. If he really did command a brigade why was he now only leading his own regiment?

20. Probably all three of the Eastern Association regiments

21. Young, *Marston Moor* pp 179-80
Analysis of the prisoner lists and other contemporary accounts identifies the following regiments. Since most of the horse escaped (as usual) they may be under-represented here:
Col. John Belasyse's Horse
Sir George Middleton's Horse
Sir Philip Monckton's Horse (ex Sir William Savile's)
Sir Walter Vavasour's Horse
Col. John Belasyse's Foot
Sir Francis Fane's Foot
Sir John Ramsden's Foot
Sir William Robinson's Foot
Sir Robert Strickland's Foot

CHAPTER IX

All the Blue Bonnets: The Scots Invasion 1644

The Scots intervention in the war can hardly have come as a surprise. As early as 27 June 1643 Parliament was making formal approaches to the Scots government, or Estates. These eventually led to the signing of the

Solemn League and Covenant on 25 September, but military preparations had actually begun some time before. On 28 July, just a month after that first approach, the Estates obligingly ordered the raising of five companies of foot and three troops of horse. Ostensibly they were to serve in Scotland as a quasi-police force, but at the end of September they suddenly marched into Berwick upon Tweed. This bloodless coup infuriated the local Royalist commander, Colonel Edward Grey, but there was nothing he could do about it.[1] For the next three months his regiment patrolled the border and gloomily observed the military build-up to the north.

While he performed this lonely duty the full mobilisation of the Scots Army got under way. It was a conscript army and the first fencible[2] musters were authorised on 18 August. Little more than a week later the first regiments started to form and Alexander Leslie, Earl of Leven was appointed Lord General. Then on 29 November a definitive treaty was signed committing the Scots to provide an army of 18,000 foot, 2,000 horse, 1,000 dragoons and a competent train of artillery. This army was to have two important objectives. The first and in Parliament's eyes the most vital was to seize control of the Tyne. This would not only shut down a crucially important Royalist gun-running operation, but at the same time it would re-open the 'sea-coal' trade with London. It is not very clear how much importance Parliament attached to the destruction of Newcastle's army by the Scots, but Leven himself correctly saw this to be his primary *military* objective.

Once the greater part of the army was assembled Leven launched the invasion on 19 January 1644. A detachment came across the Tweed at Coldstream, but most of the Scots marched over Berwick Bridge and advanced as far as Haggerston that night.[3]

It is difficult to establish just how large the Scots Army actually was. Rushworth's figure of 18,000 foot, 3,000 horse and 500 or 600 dragooners is widely accepted, perhaps because it so nearly conforms to the totals contracted for. A close analysis however reveals that it is certainly too high. There were in all fifty-two troops of horse, which allowing for an average of fifty men apiece produces a total of 2,600, so Rushworth's 3,000 may not be too far adrift. Colonel Hugh Fraser's Dragoons on the other hand mustered only four companies.[4] The greatest discrepancy lies in the number of infantry. There were twenty-two regiments in all, but while most of them had the required ten companies, others had less. Most notable amongst these was the Earl Marischal's Regiment with just three companies. In total Leven seems to have had some 198 'colours' or companies, but as the surviving pay warrants only commence in November 1644 it is impossible to establish how well recruited each company actually was. If we once again assume an average of fifty men apiece then Leven may have had as few as 9,900 infantry.[5] While at first sight this might appear too low it is probably not too wide of the mark, for on 28 January Newcastle received an intelligence report putting the whole of Leven's army at 14,000 men.[6] This would also go some way to explaining what followed.

Whatever the truth of the matter they were quite unstoppable as far as the local Royalist commander was concerned. This was Sir Thomas Glenham who had been relieved of his charge as governor of York and sent north by Newcastle in November 1643. By January he was said to have mustered some 5,000 men but only half of them were armed and very few of them were infantry.[7] Unable to offer any serious resistance he called in his outposts, broke the bridge over the Aln and retired to Newcastle upon Tyne. By the 28th the Scots advance guard was at Morpeth, fifteen miles north of the city.

At this moment the Marquis of Newcastle was still in York, complaining to Prince Rupert that he could scarcely muster 5,000 foot. The next few days were to prove critical. Leven halted at Morpeth until 1 February, waiting for his army to close up, and in the meantime the Marquis was hurrying northwards. Both armies were struggling over roads flooded by the same thaw which confounded Byron's concentration at Nantwich. Conditions were so bad that Leven was forced to call another halt at Stannington on the 2nd. This proved to be his undoing for the Marquis threw himself into Newcastle that night. Given the timing it is likely that he did so with only a small escort, but his arrival came just in time to stiffen the resolve of the defenders.

The city lies on the north bank of the River Tyne, girdled by a mediaeval wall. Only the castle was properly fortified when Glenham arrived in November (excavations have revealed a stone-faced ravelin), but he had the ditch cleared and the town walls plastered to hinder scaling attempts. A number of outworks were also constructed and the northern suburbs razed. During the last ten weeks 150 barrels of powder were brought into the Tyne, two Danish ships had brought in some brass cannon, and coasters brought 500 muskets up from Scarborough. Most intriguingly of all the *Ipswich Sarah* was reported to be loading coal for Hamburg.[8] Glenham's forces and the Trained Bands should have been an adequate enough garrison – as indeed very soon proved to be the case – but encouraged by Glenham's headlong retreat Leven summoned the city at noon on the 3rd. Naturally enough he received a dusty answer but a few hours later his troops stormed an outwork at Shieldfield on the north-east side of the defences.

After clearing a smaller, unfinished work one party of musketeers was sent to assault the east side of it while another attacked on the west. The defenders held out for about six hours, and at one point some horse tried to come to their assistance. They were however operating in an industrial landscape and the ground was thickly strewn with coal-pits which according to one Scots account prevented either side from charging more than three abreast. As a result the fight ended without any casualties although the Scots took two prisoners, one of them a Lieutenant 'who cursed and railed for halfe an houre together . . .'[9]

Having lost the fort the Royalists were obliged to burn the riverside suburb of Sandgate that night. Leven on the other hand was unable to launch a more general assault on the city since his heavy guns were not landed at Blyth until the 6th. It took a further two days to drag them down to Newcastle. Nor was he any more successful in getting across the river. Colonel William Stewart's attempt on the night of the 8th to seize sufficient keel boats to build a bridge failed because there was a neap tide and they were stuck fast in the mud by the glass-works. In any case, now that he was aware that the Marquis's army was closing up to the city, Leven had no desire to immobilise his own one in siege-lines. Having failed to throw a bridge across the river below the town he now began feeling his way upstream in search of an alternative crossing point. The first and most obvious one was the broad tidal ford at Newburn, where he won a notable victory in 1640. Not surprisingly this time the Royalists forestalled him by fortifying it, and over the next two weeks both sides gradually pushed their outposts farther and farther upstream. Naturally enough this wide degree of dispersal eventually invited a Royalist counter-attack.

Initially the Marquis intended to launch a number of simultaneous raids at various points along the front, but at the last minute all but two of them were called off. The Duchess of Newcastle long afterwards darkly ascribed this to 'Treachery'. Given the number of Scots officers then serving in his army this is entirely possible, particularly as most of them 'went home' to join their country's army during the next few weeks.

At any rate the first attack was launched by Sir Marmaduke Langdale, who was then occupying Hexham, twenty miles west of the city. At dawn on 19 February he moved out of the town at the head of twenty-five troops of horse; belonging to his own, Colonel Robert Brandling's and Sir John Fenwick's regiments, and 300 musketeers. His objective was a Scots cavalry brigade quartered in nearby Corbridge and the plan was quite simple. He himself would move down the Newcastle Road with two of the regiments and the musketeers while Brandling stayed on the south bank of the river and swung around by Dilston in order to approach Corbridge from the south.

Straightforward though it should have been, the operation came apart as soon as it began. In the first place as he approached Corbridge Langdale was shocked to find the Scots waiting for him. Two regiments, the Lord General's and Lord Kirkcudbright's commanded by Lieutenant Colonel James Ballantyne and Lieutenant Colonel James Mercer, totalling fifteen troops were drawn up on the flat Red House Haugh.

Though this Effigies here does Represent
and Portray forth his faces Liniament
Yet Read his Booke and you therin will find
that he hath Pictur'd there a Soldiers minde

1 William Bariffe: as the author of *The Young Artilleryman*, Bariffe was one of the
more influential figures in shaping infantry tactics during the English Civil War.

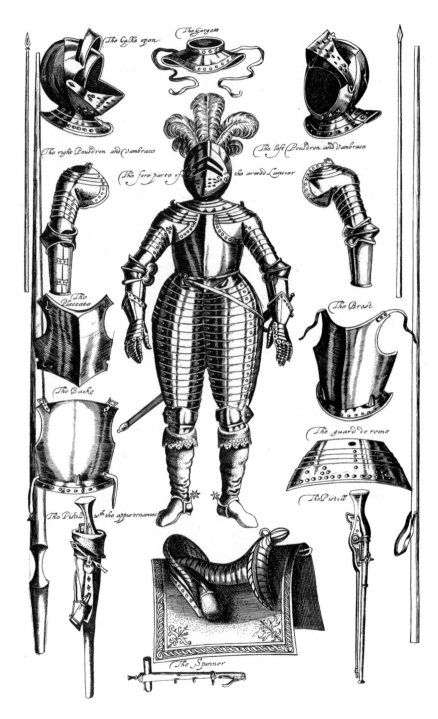

The Caske open.

The Gorgett

The right Pouldron and Vambrace

The soft Pouldron and Vambrace

The fore parte of the armed Lancier

The Placcate

The Breſt

The Backe

The guard de reine

The Piſtoll with the appurtenances

The Piſtoll

The Spanner

2 Cuirassier equipment as depicted in John Cruso's *Militarie Instructions for the Cavallrie* - and cribbed from an earlier work by Wallhausen. A number of individuals and Lifeguard units were equipped as cuirassiers.

3 Sir Thomas, afterwards Lord Fairfax, Lord General of Parliament's forces.

4 Marston Moor: the Cromwell Monument, marking the approximate area in which he defeated Goring's cavalry in the closing stages of the battle. The Allied front line was probably drawn up along the road in front of the Monument, while the Royalist front line was in the distant hedgerow.

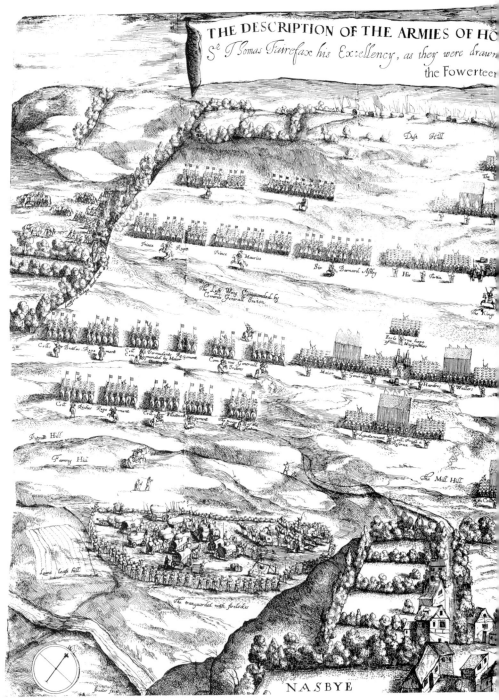

5 Streeter's famous engraving of the Battle of Naseby.

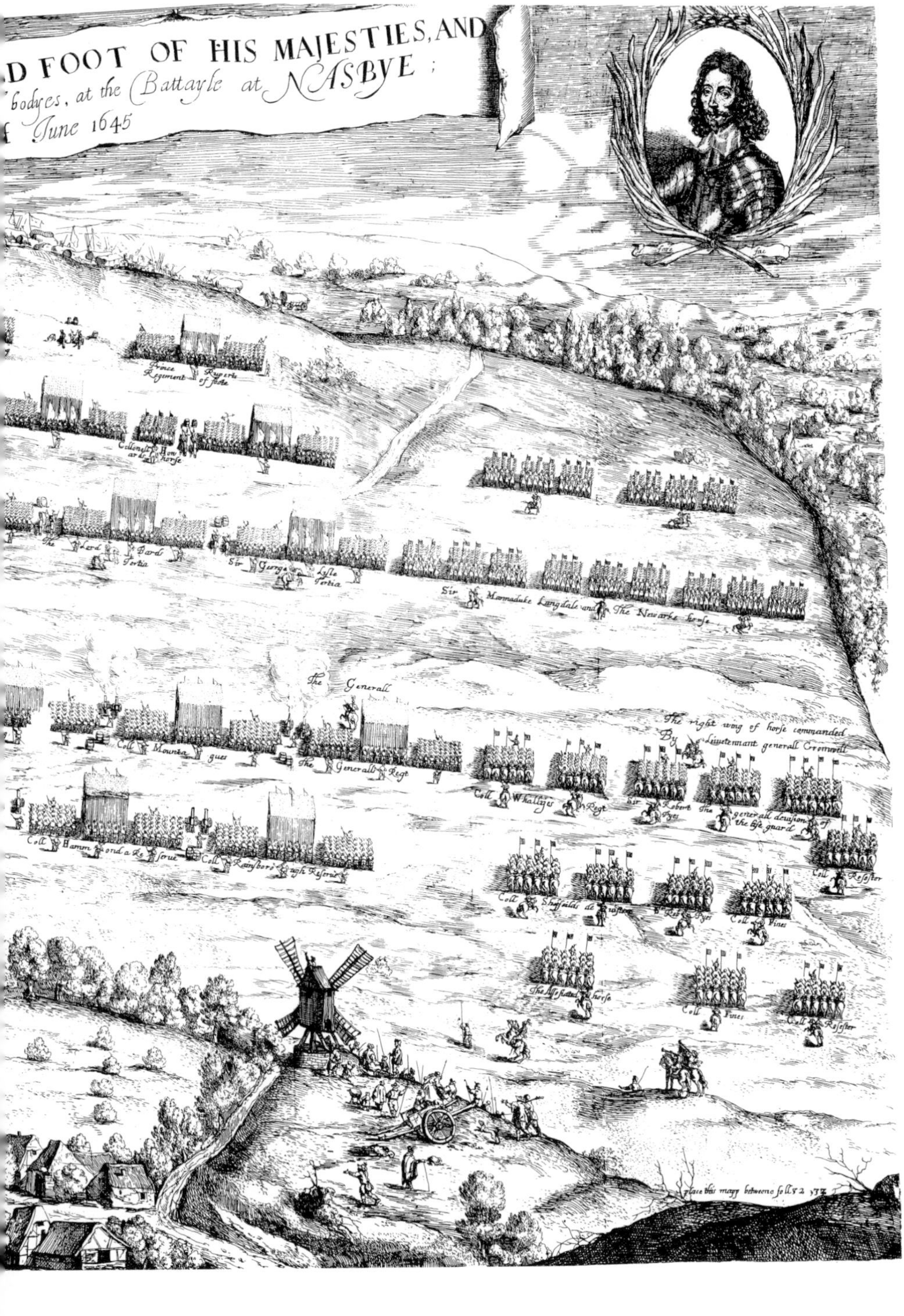

FOOT OF HIS MAJESTIES, AND
bodyes, at the Battayle at NASBYE;
June 1645

Prince
Regiment of Sir worth of foote

Willoughby Hou
ard of Horse

The Blood
Bard
Foote
Sir George Lisle
Foote

Sir Marmaduke Langdale and The Newarke horse

The Generall

The right wing of horse commanded
By Lieutenant generall Cromwell

Coll Mouns—
gues
The Generall his Rege

Coll Whalleys Regt

Sir Robert
Pye

The generall devision of
the life guard

Coll Hammo
ond a life foote

Coll Rainsborough Reserve

Coll Sheffeilds de vise

Coll Robert
Pye

Coll Rossiter

Coll Pines

The life foote horse

Coll Pines

Coll Rossiter

place this mapp betweene fo [?] 2 [?]

6 Although the musket-rest was little used in the Civil War this illustration from Jacob de Geyhn's *Exercise of Arms* (1607) provides a good picture of a musketeer's equipment.

7 The Swedish Brigade.

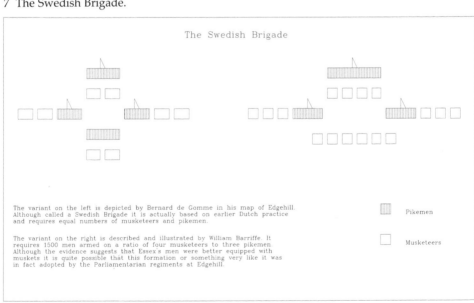

The Swedish Brigade

The variant on the left is depicted by Bernard de Gomme in his map of Edgehill. Although called a Swedish Brigade it is actually based on earlier Dutch practice and requires equal numbers of musketeers and pikemen.

The variant on the right is described and illustrated by William Barriffe. It requires 1500 men armed on a ratio of four musketeers to three pikemen. Although the evidence suggests that Essex's men were better equipped with muskets it is quite possible that this formation or something very like it was in fact adopted by the Parliamentarian regiments at Edgehill.

Pikemen

Musketeers

8 William Cavendish, Earl of Newcastle.

9 Marston Moor: the Allied position. The front line was almost certainly drawn up along the road in the foreground and the second line on the low ridge behind. The third line was hidden in the dead ground between this ridge and the higher one crowned by "Cromwell's Plump", seen in the distance.

10 Cavalry fight as depicted in Cruso's *Militarie Instructions for the Cavallrie*.

Nothing daunted he charged them at once only to be counter-charged, and in three successive engagements was thrown back on his supporting musketeers. For their part they stoutly held their ground and treated the Scots to a volley. Thrown into disorder they were in turn forced to retreat.

Langdale had been too well battered to pursue them far, but no sooner had they drawn off than an extraordinary accident occurred. As they approached Corbridge what should they find but Robert Brandling and his ten troops, who had just crossed the river. Expecting to fall on the unsuspecting rear of the Scots, Brandling's men were understandably taken aback to meet them coming head on. Not surprisingly they pulled up and in an attempt to encourage them Brandling himself spurred forward to challenge one of the Scots officers to single combat. This turned out to be a mistake for a Lieutenant Elliot of the Lord General's Regiment accepted, pulled him off his horse and took him prisoner. Dismayed, his men bolted and were chased through Corbridge and back across the Tyne.

The day was not over yet. The Scots brigade commander, Lord Balgonie (Leven's son) now decided that his position was too exposed and that it would be prudent to fall back down river. Meanwhile eight miles away Sir Gamaliel Dudley had forded the Tyne below Prudhoe Castle and beaten up the quarters of Fraser's Dragoons in Ovingham. So far so good, but he tarried too long and was still on the north side of the river when Balgonie turned up and unceremoniously chased him across it. As to casualties the usual inflated claims were put about, but the truth of the matter seems to be that about sixty men in total were killed – most of them English. In addition the Scots had Major Agnew of Kirkcudbright's badly wounded and captured, together with three other officers, while they themselves took Brandling and an unnamed Lieutenant. Both sides also claimed rather optimistically to have taken about 100 other prisoners apiece.[10]

Two days later Leven got his army moving again. Leaving six infantry regiments and a few troops of horse to cover Newcastle he then marched with the rest of his army to Heddon, four miles up the river. On the 23rd they quartered between Ovingham and Corbridge and at midnight Langdale evacuated Hexham. At this point the weather turned bad again but on the morning of the 28th the Scots Army crossed the Tyne at three different points and began marching towards Sunderland.

The Marquis was slow to respond to this threat and Leven safely entered the town on 4 March, without having been intercepted. The inhabitants immediately took the opportunity to declare for Parliament and he was able to threaten the Royalist line of communications, while at the same time drawing his own supplies through the port. Most important of all he now had dry quarters for his soldiers.

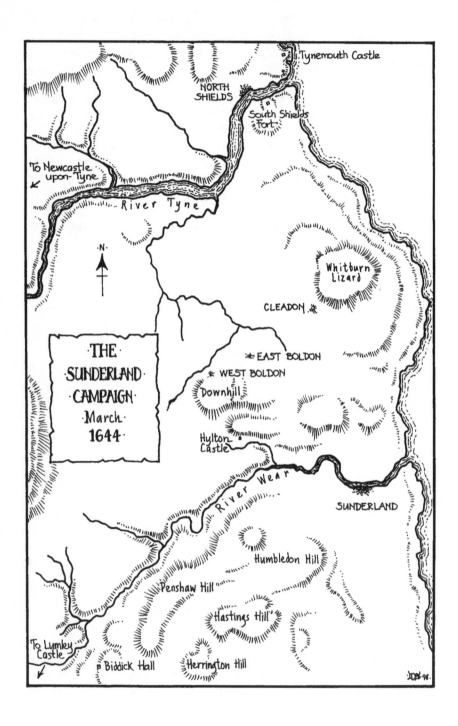

THE
SUNDERLAND
CAMPAIGN
March
1644

The natural consequence of this move was that the Marquis now had to move the Royalist field army out of Newcastle and fall back southwards. Having in the meantime been strengthened both by some Trained Bands from Durham and twelve troops of horse under Sir Charles Lucas, he was persuaded to go looking for a battle. On 6 March he crossed the River Wear by the New Bridge below Lumley Castle and came in sight of a Scots cavalry outpost on Penshaw Hill. After some skirmishing the Scots fell back and next day both armies drew up in order of battle.

By this time the Scots were established on Humbledon Hill just to the south-west of the town and Newcastle's army was probably on Hastings Hill a little to the east of Penshaw.[11] Heavy snowfalls prevented any movement during the morning, but there was some skirmishing in the afternoon as both sides tried to feel their way forward. It quickly transpired that this was no place to fight a battle, for it was heavily enclosed with banks and hedges and the Scots moreover had part of their front covered by a stream called the Barnes Burn running through a dene or narrow valley. Both armies therefore faced each other until nightfall when the Royalists retired to Penshaw. Encouraged the Scots pushed forward again on the 8th at which the Royalists set fire to their quarters and drew off, covered by some horse:

> . . . we sent off 120 horses to entertain them near their own leaguer, Sir Charles Lucas his major (Sir Simon Fanshaw) commanding them, when meeting with 200 of the enemy's, the first that charged them not passing 60 of this one regiment, notwithstanding the enemy was so placed before a hedge, where they had some dragooners as it seems, they were confident ours would not have come up unto them; but when they saw that their muskets could not prevent the courage of our men, they turned their backs and leaped over their dragooners, affording our men the execution of them to a great body of theirs, in which chase our men killed some 40 of them, and had taken near 100 men, but they advanced so suddenly we could bring off but 20 of them, of whom there were three English – one of them were hanged immediately, having formerly served in our army: their lancers did seem to follow eagerly upon our men in their retreat in great numbers, but we had not passing six men hurt, whereof one died . . .[12]

For a time the skirmishing escalated and the Scots cavalry received the support of some commanded musketeers. Then, just as they were working themselves up to an all-out attack on Newcastle's rearguard, the weather closed in again. As a result the Royalists safely retired to Durham, having accomplished nothing but the loss of a considerable number of horses to the bad weather and consequent shortage of forage. These were losses which Newcastle could ill afford.

Leven tried to follow up his advantage by advancing towards Durham on the 12th, but Newcastle failed to oblige him with a battle. As there was no forage to be found for his cavalry he in turn retired back to Sunderland on the 13th and tried to take steps to improve his supply position. Since neither food nor forage could be obtained locally he was totally dependent on the provisions being shipped in through the port. Unfortunately the same bad weather which hampered military operations was also causing havoc at sea. Of five ships sent from Scotland at the beginning of March three were lost and two driven to take shelter in the Tyne. Both of the latter were of course seized by the Royalists.

Consequently, after the abortive advance to Durham, Leven turned his eyes northwards. On the 15th an unsuccessful attempt was made to storm one of the Royalist forts covering the mouth of the Tyne, at South Shields. Undismayed, the Scots made a second and this time successful attempt on the 20th. The technical details of how it was accomplished are not without some interest:

A party not so strong as the former, was sent to storme the Fort, there being no other way of taking it; Col. [William] Stewart, Col. [William] Lyell, Lieutenant Col. [Andrew] Bruce, and Lieutenant Col. Johnson, with some inferiour Oficers, led on the party, the Fort was very strong, the Graffe without being esteemed 12 foot broad, and 11 deep, the work above ground three yards high, and within it five iron peece of Ordnance, some nine pound ball, some more, an hundred souldiers, seventy musquetiers, and thirty Pike-men: It was situated with great advantage, being defended on the one side by the Ordnance of Tinemouth Castle, and on the other by a Dunkirk Frigot with teen peeces of Ordnance; notwithstanding 140 of our souldiers, without any other Armes but their swords, carried bundles of straw and sticks, wherewith they filled the ditch, set up scaling ladders (wherof some did not reach the top of the Fort, the ditch not being well filled) and with their swords gave the first assault, then a party of Musquetiers, and after them a party of Pikes, all marching up till they entred the ditch, where they disputed the matter above an houre, in which time the Enemy discharged upon them 28 shot of Cannon, some with Musquet ball, others with cut lead and iron, besides many Musquet shot: Our soldiers did resolutely scale the ladders, and some entred at the gunports: the Defendants behaved themselves gallantly till it came to stroke of sword, and then they fled away by water in boates; sixteen of them were killed, a Lieutenant and five souldiers who stood out to the last, were taken, and so we gained the Fort, with the peeces, and some barrels of powder, and their colours.[13]

So far so good, and Royalist morale was not improved when Lieutenant

Colonel Ballentyne of Leven's Horse beat up a Royalist cavalry quarter at Chester-le-Street on the same day. Stirred into action the Marquis once again drew his army out of Durham on the 23rd and moved forward to offer battle for a second time. On this occasion he moved along the north bank of the Wear, perhaps hoping to force the Scots to relinquish the fort at South Shields.

Realising what he was about Leven very quickly got the bulk of his own army across the river, and on Sunday 24 March both took up their positions facing each other about three miles apart. The Marquis drew up his army on the imposing Boldon Hill (now known as Down Hill) facing north-eastwards to the Scots on the only slightly lower Whitburn Lizard. Between them lay a flat expanse of moorland cut across by the valley of a stream called the Don and interspersed with hedged enclosures around the villages of West Boldon, East Boldon and Cleadon. The latter played no part in the battle but the two former lie at the foot of Down Hill.[14] It was not particularly suitable ground for cavalry to operate upon and the fight which followed was very largely an infantry battle.

With the aid of some local keelmen Leven's General of Artillery, Sandie Hamilton, managed to get one of his big guns across the Wear, together with a number of smaller ones, but in the process two other large pieces were lost in the river.[15] For most of the day both sides then contented themselves with a fairly ineffectual cannonade. Neither side was keen to launch a frontal attack against the other since it appears that they were fairly well matched in size. The Marquis had come north with some 5,000 foot and, although many of those raised by Glenham were perforce left as a garrison for Newcastle, he had also been joined by some of the Durham Trained Bands. Even allowing for the inevitable heavy wastage attendant on a winter campaign, he still ought to have been able to bring about 5-6,000 men into the field. The Scots were in a similar situation. Leven had crossed the border with around 10,000 infantry in January but close on 3,000 men were left behind at Heddon to mask Newcastle. Sir James Lumsden brought some or all of the cavalry left there across on the 23rd, but nevertheless by the time smaller detachments and wastage are taken into account, his total field force cannot have outnumbered that of the Royalists.

Late in the afternoon Fraser's Dragoons opened the battle with an attack on some Royalist musketeers lining the hedges around East Boldon. The fight quickly escalated and, according to the Royalist account in *Mercurius Aulicus*, four of Newcastle's Regiments were engaged by six Scots ones.[16] Once begun the fighting continued through the night:

After the Armies had faced each other most part of that day, toward five aclock the Cannon began to play, which they bestowed freely though to little purpose, and withall the commanded Foot fell to it to drive one another from their hedges, and continued shooting till eleven at night, in which time we gained some ground, some barrels of gun-powder, and ball and match; wee lost few men, had more hurt and wounded, of whom no Officer of note hurt with danger but the Lievtenant Colonell of the Lord Lothian's Regiment; [Patrick Leslie] what their losse was is yet uncertain to us, but we know they had more slaine, as wee finde being masters of their ground.[17]

Once driven out of East Boldon, Newcastle's men retreated up the slopes of Down Hill. They were not followed in the darkness and at some point during the early hours of the following morning the Scots broke contact and fell back to their main position on Whitburn Lizard. Although the *Mercurius Aulicus* report made the most of this, it also had to admit to the loss of some 240 men. In any case the Marquis began drawing off his army on the 25th and covered once again by Sir Charles Lucas he retired to Durham on the 26th. While the battle tends to be dismissed as a minor skirmish the true scale of the affair is evident both from the 240 Cavalier dead and the thirty-seven barrels of powder which the Scots expended in killing them.

Five days later, after re-equipping his regiments, Leven broke up his camp at Sunderland and moved southwards to Easington. There he was able to find sufficient forage for his cavalry and still maintain contact with the Royalists. On 8 April the weather at last began to improve and he decided to increase the pressure. Moving south-west on to the Quarrington Hills he took up a position threatening the Royalist line of communications a mile or two south of Durham. Newcastle's position was once again untenable. Faced with the choice of fighting or falling back he opted for retreat.

On the night of 12 April the last Royalist cavalrymen evacuated Lumley Castle. A few hours later Durham was also abandoned and the Royalists marched west to Bishop Auckland. Having twice been turned out of his positions the Marquis was now hoping to hold the line of the river Tees at Piercebridge. Ironically this was the same position which his own forces had stormed in 1642, but he was destined never to occupy it. Sometime on the 13th – probably near Barnard Castle – a messenger met him on the road with news of the battle at Selby on the 11th.

In the face of this catastrophe a council of war unanimously agreed to march straight for York in order to save it from capture by Lord Fairfax. In the circumstances there was little else the Royalists could have done but now something quite remarkable happened.

Alexander Leslie, the Earl of Leven was a professional soldier who had been given the command of the Scots Army on the strength of his reputation. 'Such was the wisdom and authoritie of that old little, crooked souldier, that all, with ane incredible submission, from the beginning to the end, give themselves to be guided by him, as if he had been Great Solyman'[18] There were suggestions from some quarters that the old man was getting past it, but now he took one of the most momentous decisions of his career. Leaving the strong Royalist garrison of Newcastle in his rear and a decidedly tenuous supply line behind him, he immediately set off in pursuit of the Marquis.

For the Royalists the ensuing march must quickly have turned into a nightmare. Leven did not actually learn of their flight until mid afternoon on the 13th. Consequently he only got his army as far as Ferryhill that night. Next morning however he sent his cavalry off before dawn and the excitement of the chase is related by a quartermaster in Eglinton's Horse named John Somerville:

> . . . and upon the 14 day, being Sunday, we marcheit verrie airlie befoir the soon rais, and the hors men followit in haist and cam to Derntoun [Darlington] befoir 7, acloak in the morning and sent out a pairtie of horse to persew thair reir. Our major [James Montgomerie] commandit the pairtie; he with his pairtie tuik fourtie men and many horses and slew many of their straggillars and gat tuo thousand merkis worth of silver plait, and mikell cheis, pork and bread,[19]

At nightfall the Scots Army got on the move again, crossed the Tees and reached Northallerton by the following evening. On the 16th they pursued the Royalists as far south as Thormanby, but at this point, with Newcastle only about ten miles short of York, they gave over the pursuit. Instead they turned aside to Boroughbridge and on the 18th had a happy rendezvous with Sir Thomas Fairfax and his cavalry at Wetherby.

That same day Newcastle was sending off a frantic appeal to the King and on the 22nd, with the combined Scots and Parliamentarian armies closing in, he sent off the greater part of his cavalry. Once again Quartermaster Somerville was enjoying himself:

> . . . and in the nicht the haill trouppes that the Marquis of Newcastel had in York went out and fled and our troupes with my Lord Fairfax his troupes folled and tuik 60 prisonars and many horses; and they war so hard chaisit that they war forcit to tak the cullouris from the standaris and ryd with and live the staff behind them.[20]

Laying siege to a garrison of some 4,000[21] men esconced behind strong fortifications was not to be undertaken lightly. Next day the Scots cautiously took up a position along the west side of the city while Fairfax covered the east with their respective headquarters at Middlethorpe and Heslington. The north side of the city was presumably covered by cavalry patrols pending the arrival of the Eastern Association army led by the Earl of Manchester. Ordered northwards he cleared Lincolnshire as he marched, retaking Lincoln itself on 6 May and Gainsborough on the 24th. His forces eventually joined with those of Leven and Fairfax on 3 June.

By that time the risks Leven was running in leaving the Royalist garrison at Newcastle upon Tyne had become all too apparent. Back in March the Marquis had been persuaded to lend Sir Robert Clavering and 100 or so horse and dragoons for an ill-conceived Royalist uprising in Scotland. Its leader, the Marquis of Montrose had briefly raised the King's standard at Dumfries before being ignominiously chased back across the border by the Earl of Callendar. Afterwards Clavering quite understandably insisted on returning to Tyneside.

There were too few of them[22] to take on the main Scots encampment at Heddon since there were still elements of six infantry regiments and Colonel Michael Weldon's Horse based there. Instead they threw themselves into Newcastle. On or about the 10th of May Montrose and the Earl of Crawford moved out again and launched an unsuccessful attack on Morpeth. The town fell at once but the castle was held by two companies of Lord Sinclair's Regiment. The initial attack was beaten off by Captains Somerville and McCulloch but Montrose brought up six guns from Newcastle and commenced a proper siege of the castle. It did not surrender until the 29th, but in the meantime Clavering and another Royalist officer, Sir Philip Musgrave were loose on the south side of the Tyne. The fort at South Shields was recaptured in mysterious circumstance – the officer in charge, Captain Thomas Rutherford appears to have 'sold' it to Clavering on or about 21 May.[23]

Emboldened by this success Clavering now turned his attention to Leven's supply depot at Sunderland. There do not appear to be any extant accounts of what happened next, which is a great pity for it does not take much reading between the lines to get a feel for it. The governor of the town, Colonel Allane had no regular troops at his disposal except for the usual details and sick left behind when Leven marched south. All he did have were two local volunteer companies commanded by a Captain Lee and Captain Tobias Knowles.

On 21 May, presumably after hearing of the capture of the fort at South Shields, Knowles drew three barrels of powder and some other ammunition for his men. Next day, when it was realised that Clavering was actually on his way, all hell broke loose. First Knowles' Lieutenant, Roger Wouldhave turned up and drew another three barrels of powder, match and ball and Captain Lee signed for one as well. A fifth barrel and thirty-six rounds of 3lb ball was sent across the river to an outpost at Monkwearmouth and various people drew spades and mattocks. So far so good, but when the Royalists hove in sight there seems to have been a general rush to the magazine. Afterwards it was noted that a further seven barrels of powder, besides match and ball, over 100 pikes and other pole-arms, together with some artillery ammunition was taken 'By severall seamen upon compulsion.' To cap it all the garrison's big gun was disdainfully recorded as having been 'Broken at Sunderland by a sea gunner'.[24]

Clavering does not appear to have pressed his attack – he and Musgrave may only have had some cavalry – but he may have tried again on the 26th for more ammunition was issued to the garrison that day. In the meantime however Colonel Charles Fairfax appeared on the scene with a Parliamentarian cavalry regiment. As a result Clavering fell back on Newcastle and helped prepare it for the inevitable siege. A second Scots army, led by the Earl of Callendar, crossed the border on 25 June but Clavering did not wait for him. Instead, in response to a summons from Prince Rupert, he marched south to assist in the relief of York.

NOTES

1. The 1640 Treaty of Ripon had expressly forbidden the placing of a garrison in the town.
2. A term used to describe those men deemed to be capable of bearing 'arms defencible' and therefore liable to be balloted for military service.
3. Col. Francis Anderson to Sir Thomas Glenham 20 January 1644
4. Rushworth *Historical Collections* p604 cites only three officers, but there were evidently others and James Somerville describes them as 'four compleat companies' (*Memorie of the Somervilles* Vol.II p315)
5. While it could be argued that an average of fifty men per company might be too low, it should be noted that the three companies of the Earl Marischal's Regiment which left Aberdeen on 16 February only mustered a total of 130 officers and men. After the nine commissioned officers are deducted this equates to an average of just forty men per company. (Spalding, John *Memorialls of the Trubles in Scotland* Vol.II p320)
6. Warburton, E. *Memoirs of Prince Rupert* Vol.II p368
7. The signatories of a letter written from Alnwick on 22 January included the following officers:

Sir Francis Anderson	colonel of horse
Charles Brandling	colonel of foot
Francis Carnaby	colonel of horse
Sir Robert Clavering	colonel of horse and foot
Sir Thomas Glenham	colonel of horse and foot
Edward Grey	colonel of horse
Sir George Muschamp	colonel of foot
Ralph Mylott	colonel of horse
Sir Richard Tempest	colonel of horse

8. HMC Portland pt.I app. p167. If an Ipswich boat really was loading, this would confirm suggestions that the blockading ships were capable of being bought off. Worse still it was intended to exchange the coal for a cargo of arms and ammunition.
9. The Scots admitted to losing nine men in the storming of the fort, including

Captain-Lieutenant Patrick English of the Earl of Lindsay's Regiment. Judging by records of ammunition issues it is possible that detachments of Colonel James Rae's, Hepburn of Waughton's and Lord Gordon's regiments were also present. The cavalry covering force was commanded by David Leslie and appears to have comprised his own and the Earl of Eglinton's regiments. (Terry, C.S. *The Army of the Covenant* Vol.I var. refs.)

10. *A Faithfull Relation of the late Occurrences and Proceedings of the Scottish Army before Newcastle*, in Terry, C.S. 'The Scottish Campaign in Northumberland and Durham' *Archaeologia Aeliana* (New Series) Vol.XXI (1899) pp162-3.

11. *ibid.* and Firth, *Memoirs* pp201-2 (Newcastle's account) The location of the fighting on the 6th can be worked out, with a little application, from both the accounts above and the Duchess's reference (Firth p35) to 'Pensher Hill'. As to the position occupied by the Scots on the 7th there is an unambiguous reference in the ordnance papers to thirty axes being issued to the army while it was at 'Hamelton' Hill. Newcastle also describes the Scots as standing on a 'plain' behind the valley and oddly enough there is in fact a Plains Farm in what would have been the Scots rear area on Humbledon Hill.

For some reason, and despite the fact that it undoubtedly took place on the south side of the River Wear, historians also tend to have some difficulty in distinguishing this engagement from the later one at Boldon on the north side of the river.

12. Firth *Memoirs* p203

13. *The Taking of the Fort at South Shields*, in Terry, *loc. cit.* pp168-9. The garrison was commanded by a Captain Chapman, probably belonging to Sir Thomas Riddell's Regiment. The attackers were evidently drawn from Colonel William Stewart's, the Master of Yester's (Lyell and Johnson) and Lord Livingston's (Bruce) regiments.

14. Once again it is relatively straightforward to identify the site of this battle using the available texts. All too often historians casually refer to it as 'Bowden' Hill without troubling themselves to take the rather obvious step of looking at a map. Others prefer to call it the Battle of Hylton. This again can be misleading as Hylton Castle actually lies between the southern slopes of Down Hill and the river Wear. No fighting took place on this side of the hill, but the now vanished Jacobean mansion which stood there in 1644 was the home of one of Newcastle's officers – Colonel John Hilton – and the Marquis may well have slept there or even used it as his headquarters. One source does rather confusingly refer to the fighting taking place at West Bedwich (Biddick), but this lies on the other side of the river and it is clear from the context that West *Boldon* is intended.

15. The Scots ordnance papers record two guns (weight unspecified) 'broken' at Boldon Hill. One of them was dredged from the bottom of the river in the 19th century.

16. All six of the Scots regiments can be identified from the ammunition records in the ordnance papers. In addition, when the army's equipment deficiencies were made good on the 29th all six (uniquely) received pikes – presumably to replace those lost or broken in the fighting at Boldon – the numbers appended to each unit refer to the number of pikes issued to each.

General of the Artillery's Regt. (Hamilton's)	36
Lord Chancellor's Regt. (Loudoun's)	24
Earl of Lindsay's Regt.	25
Lord Livingston's Regt.	30
Earl of Lothian's Regt.	40
Master of Yester's Regt.	20

17. *A True Relation of the Proceedings of the Scottish Army from the* 12 *of March instant to the* 25.
18. Baillie, Robert *Letters and Journals* (Ed. Laing, D) Vol.I p218
19. HMC 10th report, app pt.I p53
20. *ibid.*
21. *City of York House Books* 29 April 1644. Quoted in Wenham, P *The Great and Close Siege of York* p164.
22. The composition of Clavering's force is unknown. Former officers of horse, foot and dragoons claimed him as their Colonel in the 1663 *List of Indigent Officers,* and Musgrave also had horse and foot. All that can be said with any certainty is that when Clavering joined Prince Rupert near Thirsk on 3 July he only had 1,300 horse and no foot (*Prince Rupert's Journal* ed. Barrett, J. p15).
23. The last delivery of ammunition to the fort was made on 20 May. Montrose usually gets the credit (or blame) for its capture, but he was at Morpeth at the time and the subsequent proceedings against Rutherford make it clear that he surrendered the fort to Clavering. Although he was court-martialled it is uncertain whether Rutherford was ever executed.
24. Terry, C.S. *Army of the Covenant* Vol.I var. refs. The gun was evidently a 24-pounder.

CHAPTER X

York March:
The Prelude to Marston Moor

While York was both well supplied and strongly garrisoned it was abundantly clear to all concerned that only outside intervention could save it from eventual capture by the grandly titled 'Army of Both Kingdoms'. Unfortunately the Marquis of Newcastle's plea for assistance arrived at a particularly bad moment. A serious defeat at Cheriton in Hampshire on 29 March had thrown the Oxford Army on to the defensive at the very outset of the campaigning season. When Prince Rupert arrived at the Royal headquarters on 25 April the most urgent question to be addressed was not how to effect the relief of York, but rather how best to hold the line around Oxford. It was currently threatened by not one but two armies, the first led by the Earl of Essex and now a second led by Sir William Waller. The Oxford Army was still a match for either one singly, but not for both of them acting in concert. The military balance could and should have been restored by committing the army which Rupert was assembling at Shrewsbury, but the bad news from the north ruled this out for the time being. Consequently Rupert recommended that the existing ring of major garrisons around Oxford, at Wallingford, Abingdon, Reading and Banbury, should be strengthened and that a strategic reserve of cavalry should be established at or near Oxford itself. This reserve could then move to support any of the fortresses which might be threatened. If followed these measures would ensure the security of the Royalist capital long enough for the Prince to relieve York and then rejoin the King before the summer was out.

Nevertheless the real problem remained that Rupert himself had as yet too few troops for the task he was now committed to undertaking. His original brief was to establish his headquarters at Shrewsbury and there assemble a new field army which could be employed on the central front or against the Scots as the situation demanded. At the same time, in order to safeguard the passage of the troops he needed from Leinster, it followed that he must secure Chester and the military corridor linking that city with Shrewsbury and Oxford. Unfortunately the sudden and quite unexpected collapse of Newcastle's forces meant that his army would have to take the field before it was ready. To make matters worse the improving weather also meant the appearance of greatly increased Parliamentarian naval patrols in the Irish Sea. As a result the flow of reinforcements from Dublin all but dried up just when they were most needed.[1]

Nor would it be possible for Rupert to attempt a repeat of the Newark operation by marching at once to York and stripping additional soldiers from every friendly garrison on the way. Although he could certainly count upon the assistance of Newcastle's own cavalry, who had escaped at the outset of the siege, the arithmetic simply did not add up. He had the guns he needed, he could probably count upon assembling sufficient cavalry from a variety of sources, but he lacked infantry. With no immediate prospect of more Irish troops before the dark nights returned at the end of the year he was going to have to raise them himself. As the Welsh Marches had already been combed out, the only place where it appeared to be possible to find volunteers in any number was Lancashire. It is frequently argued, with the benefit of hindsight, that after securing Chester, Rupert had always planned to march into Lancashire and so complete the conquest of the north-west. However this would have been a futile diversion into a military backwater and only military necessity was now about to compel him to embark upon it.

In the present circumstances it was certainly a quite beguiling prospect. The Earl of Derby had succeeded in raising a sizeable Royalist army there early in the war – before throwing it away in a dazzling display of military ineptitude. The remnants of that army, two regiments of cavalry and an infantry regiment commanded by Lord Molyneux and Sir Thomas Tyldesley were presently serving in Cheshire under Lord Byron. Derby too had returned from a self-imposed exile on the Isle of Man and could undoubtedly exert his considerable local influence in raising a fresh army around this nucleus. The plan was of course open to a number of obvious drawbacks, not the least of which was that the new levies so confidently expected would be raw and undisciplined, but in the circumstances there was probably no alternative.

On 16 May Prince Rupert marched out of Shrewsbury at the head of three regiments of cavalry, one regiment of dragoons and five regiments of infantry.[2] On the 23rd he rendezvoused with Lord Byron's army[3] at Knutsford in Cheshire, and two days later stormed Stockport. Then no more than a large village it was unfortified, and the only impediment to the Royalist assault was the fact that it stood on the far side of a single bridge over a high-banked river. In the event, after the customary bickering amongst the hedgerows, a general assault spearheaded by Washington's Dragoons cleared it at the first attempt. The defenders ran fast and escaped to Manchester under cover of darkness. Neither side suffered any casualties in this trifling affair but it was a very different matter three days later at Bolton.

The Earl of Derby's fortress home, Lathom House, had been under siege for some months. Learning that the Royalists were over the river at Stockport the Parliamentarian commander, Colonel Alexander Rigby, abandoned the siege and retired to join Colonel Shuttleworth in the supposed safety of Bolton. Unaware of this Rupert sent Tillier there on the 28th with a regiment of horse and one of foot in order to secure quarters for the army. On arriving he was surprised to find the town stuffed full of Parliamentarian soldiers, apparently in some disorder, so he very sensibly stood off and called on Rupert to come up as quickly as he could. By the time the Prince arrived it was pouring with rain but nevertheless an immediate assault was ordered.

Four regiments, Rupert's own (commanded by Lieutenant Colonel John Russell), Colonel Henry Warren's, Colonel Robert Ellis's Welshmen, and Sir Thomas Tyldesley's, went forward. The first two were beaten off with heavy casualties, Rupert's lost Colonel Russell wounded, Major Dominic Mitchell captured and no fewer than 300 killed or wounded.[4] The other two regiments got into the town but were tumbled out again by a counter-attack.

Only one other regiment, Colonel Robert Broughton's, was immediately at hand and Rupert ordered it forward at once. The Earl of Derby also put himself at the head of Tyldesley's regiment and this time both units successfully stormed the mud walls. After the failure of the first assault Colonel Shuttleworth's men had been so injudicious as to hang one of Warren's men as an Irish papist.[5] At the best of times this was inflammatory behaviour to say the least, but at Bolton it had fatal consequences. Tyldesley's men were militantly Catholic – indeed one Parliamentarian tract made a point of enumerating those few officers in the regiment who were *not* Catholics. Now the murder of an alleged Catholic was all the excuse they needed to perpetrate a bloody massacre.

Even Royalist accounts spoke of great slaughter and 1,000 dead in the streets and surrounding fields. The Parliamentarians claimed that one of Tyldesley's officers, Major Hugh Anderton, had boasted of being red to the elbows with Catholic blood, and seven years later the Earl of Derby would be executed for his part in the massacre. Eventually the killing was brought under control, and 650 officers and men who had taken refuge in the church managed to get their surrender accepted.[6]

Only two garrisons of any importance now remained in Parliamentarian hands. Manchester, held by Sir John Meldrum was ignored, presumably because the Prince could not afford to waste time besieging it. Liverpool on the other hand was a different matter. The garrison was weak and possession of the town would provide another useful entry point for future Irish reinforcements. On 5 June Rupert moved to Wigan, sending Washington ahead to observe the town. By the 7th the rest of the army had closed up and Lord Molyneux delivered a formal summons. Naturally enough the governor, a local man named Colonel John Moore, refused to surrender. Next day the Prince sent in his own summons but this time Moore underlined his refusal by shooting the trumpeter's horse.

After Bolton this was perhaps only to be expected. As the fortifications were somewhat stronger Rupert prepared the assault with care. Three of his heavy guns were brought up, and by the 10th enough of the mud and turf wall had been tumbled into the ditch to make storming it a practical proposition. At noon he launched his assault only to see it beaten off after an hour's fighting. Nevertheless Moore decided that the game was up and started evacuating his garrison by boat under cover of darkness. Unfortunately it was a slow process and daylight on 11 June found his rearguard still in place. Colonel Tillier found it too, and realising what was happening, launched an immediate assault on his own initiative and broke into the town without much difficulty.[7]

With Liverpool taken, recruiting could now begin in earnest. Two days after the storming of Bolton Lord Goring joined the Prince at Bury. He not only brought Newcastle's cavalry but some units drawn from Midlands garrisons as well, including 300 infantry. Now it was hoped even more could be raised in Lancashire. Tyldesley certainly appears to have doubled the size of his regiment for it was to stand in two battalions on Marston Moor. One of the erstwhile defenders of Lathom House, Edward Chisenall, raised a new regiment of his own, but otherwise the results fell short of expectations. The massacre at Bolton had won the Royalists few friends. Indeed the net result was probably quite negative. Another regiment was raised by Colonel Cuthbert Clifton, but it was to be employed as a garrison for Liverpool alongside Sir Robert Byron's men. Notwithstanding the importance of the town, leaving Byron's veterans there was undoubtedly a mistake. Rupert would have done much better to have kept this excellent regiment with his field army for many of the raw levies taken in its stead were to run without firing a shot.

Be that as it may, the recruiting drive was in any case cut short by a 'peremptory order' directing the Prince to march on York without delay.[8] This order was to be of such pivotal importance to the outcome of the war that it merits a complete transcription here:[9]

Nephew,

First I must congratulate with you for your good successes, assuring you that the things themselves are no more welcome to me than that you are the means. I know the importance of the supplying you with powder, for which I have taken all possible ways, having sent both to Ireland and Bristol. As from Oxford, this bearer is well satisfied that it is impossible to have at present; but if he tell you that I can spare them from hence, I leave you to judge, having but thirty-six left.[10] But what I can get from Bristol (of which there is not much certainty, it being threatened to be besieged) you shall have.

But now I must give you the true state of my affairs, which if their condition be such as enforces me to give you more peremptory commands than I would willingly do, you must not take it ill. If York be lost I shall esteem my crown little less; [ie, regard it as all but lost] unless supported by your sudden march to me; and a miraculous conquest in the South, before the effects of their Northern power can be found here. But if York be relieved, and you beat the rebels army of both kingdoms, which are before it; then (but otherwise not) I may make a shift (upon the defensive) to spin out time until you come to assist me. Wherefore I *command and conjure you*, by the duty and affection which I know you bear me, that all new enterprises laid aside, you immediately march, according to your first intention, with all your force to the relief of York. But if that be either lost, or have freed themselves from the besiegers, or that, from want of powder, you cannot undertake that work, that you immediately march with your whole strength to Worcester, to assist me and my army; without which, or you having relieved York by beating the Scots, all the successes you can afterwards have must infallibly be useless unto me. You may believe that nothing but an extreme necessity could make me write thus unto you, wherefor, in this case, I can no ways doubt of your punctual compliance with

Your loving uncle and faithful friend
CHARLES R.
P.S. – I commanded this Bearer to speak to you concerning Vavasour
Ticknell June 14th 1644

This letter was to provide Rupert with his justification for fighting the Allies on Marston Moor shortly afterwards. Historians have frequently advanced a contrary view. The late Brigadier Young for example opined that: 'A modern staff officer would be hard pressed indeed to make of this a direct order to fight a battle after York had been relieved.' Dr Peter Newman goes much further and, drawing attention to the first paragraph (while simultaneously suppressing the last sentence), declares it to be 'less a letter of instruction than one of information, news and advice.'[11] This will simply not do. The first paragraph is indeed concerned with news and information, but it serves to provide the background to the King's subsequent instructions and explains why his *commands* are more peremptory than he would like.

Although poorly drafted the message is in fact quite clear. Contrary to what was agreed at the Oxford conference in early May, Reading had been evacuated. Of itself this might not have been too serious, but on 25 May Abingdon was also abandoned. Unsurprisingly Essex and Waller soon marched their armies through the gap and threatened Oxford itself. In order to avoid a siege the King was compelled to flee at the head of a small mobile column and was now being chased for his life up and down the Midlands. In short the King was presently in serious trouble and urgently required the assistance of Prince Rupert's army. Nevertheless he was only too well aware that abandoning York to its fate could cost him the war, and if Rupert considered it possible to do so he was given permission to delay returning long enough to relieve York 'by beating the Scots'.

At this brief moment in time Rupert therefore had a choice. He could simply turn his army southwards to join the King 'in punctual compliance' with his orders, or he could first try to save York. But about one thing there could be no doubt. Once he set off across the Pennines he was irrevocably committed to fighting the Scots and their allies, and to fighting them quickly.

The King's letter must have reached Rupert at Liverpool, where he was supervising a remodelling of the defences, on or about 19 June. At any rate he set off that day marching north-east by way of Lathom House, where he took his leave of the Earl of Derby[12], Croston, Preston and Ribchester, to Clitheroe which he reached on Sunday the 24th. A small garrison was left in the castle there under a Colonel Daniel[13], and pressing on into Yorkshire the Royalists arrived at Skipton on the 26th. There Rupert halted for two days in order to let his men 'fixe our armes, and send into Yorke.'

At first sight it appears that the sole cause of his urgency was the fact that the operation was being run on borrowed time. The city's Civil War defences were a typical mixture of old and new. The primary defensive line consisted of its mediaeval walls and gates, or bars. Ordinarily such walls are considered to offer only limited protection against artillery fire, but at York most of the mediaeval masonry crowned older earthen rampart which was much less vulnerable. The castle and its Norman mound formed an integral part of the southern perimeter at the confluence of the Ouse and the Fosse, and a gap in the defences on the eastern side was covered by a stagnant expanse of water known as the King's Fishpond.

During the early part of the Civil War the rather neglected castle was renovated, a century's accumulation of household rubbish was cleared out of the ditch, barricades were constructed at the lane ends behind the walls, and large stocks of food and other supplies were laid in. All of these measures were both sensible and practical. A complete remodelling of the three-and-a-half-mile circuit of the defences in a more modern style was evidently regarded as being too expensive. Instead, an outer ring of sconces or self contained forts was thrown up partly with a view to protecting sufficient grazing land for the city's cattle and other livestock, and just as importantly to keeping any attackers at a safe distance.

Obviously this also meant that the besieging army's lines encircling the city had to be correspondingly longer and thinner. They were therefore vulnerable either to a breakout attempt by the strong Royalist garrison within, or to a relief force coming from outside. In either case any concentration to meet the danger would be hampered by the fact that the siege lines were bisected by the river Ouse both above and below the city. Accordingly the circuit was completed by the erection of two temporary bridges at Poppleton to the north of the city and near Fulford to the south. A large cavalry outpost was established at Wakefield to give timely warning of any hostile force approaching from outside, but should the Marquis take it into his head to come out and fight, there was still a very real danger that he might succeed in beating one of the Allied armies before the others could come to its assistance.

In fact throughout the siege the initiative lay squarely with the Army of Both Kingdoms. Initially it was a slow business, and in its early stages was pretty well confined to a series of inconsequential skirmishes. Many of them took place well beyond the city. On 17 May for example 160 Cavaliers of unknown origin launched an unsuccessful attack of some Scots dragoons quartered at Northallerton, while the Allies took Cawood Castle on the 19th. Nevertheless the tempo of operations picked up considerably after Manchester's arrival. The first battery was established in Fairfax's sector on 5 June, and two nights later Leven launched an attack on the three forts covering the west side of the city. Examination of the Scots ordnance papers reveals that it was a substantial affair involving elements of at least six regiments in the assault with three others in reserve.[14] Presumably, as on other occasions, each fort was simultaneously attacked from opposite sides by two assault columns while a third unit occupied a covering position.

> About midnight, a commanded Company of the couragious Scots, assaulted fiercely and bravely the three Forts on the west side of the City, and after a very hot service, for the space of two houres . . . they became possessors of two of them. The one of the Forts (which was nearest the Towne) was strengthened with a double ditch, wherein there were 120 souldiers, above 60 were slaine, and all the rest taken prisoners. The other Fort taken, had only 50 men to maintaine it, who were all either killed, or taken prisoners desiring quarter. And the 3d. Fort had been possessed by the Scots also, if that a strong party of both Horse and Foot, had not come out of the Towne for the reliefe thereof.[15]

According to this particular account, written by Manchester's chaplains, the Scots had three captains killed and a lieutenant colonel and two other captains badly wounded. However this may be a case of double counting, for Leven's chaplain, Robert Douglas, who was obviously better placed to know, related that Lieutenant Colonel (William) Carmichael was shot in the storming of the first fort and died the next day. He also records the deaths of a Captain Campbell and ten soldiers in attacking one of the forts and a Captain Panter and ten soldiers before another.[16]

The loss of the two forts severely dented the Royalists' confidence, and the following evening Newcastle opened negotiations for a surrender by genteelly reproaching Leven for his failure formally to summon the city. This was quite understandably taken as a hopeful sign by the Allies, and after a further preliminary exchange of correspondence, a cease-fire was agreed for 14 June. That day commissioners from both sides met in a tent near the captured forts and the Royalists presented their proposals. The gist of them was that Newcastle would surrender the city if not relieved within twenty days. His army would then be allowed to march out with all the usual courtesies, bag and baggage, and was to have safe convoy to join either the King or Prince Rupert.

Needless to say this was totally unacceptable. The Allies wanted York but not badly enough to stand back while the Marquis's army marched away unscathed to fight another day. Leven's hand is plain in the uncompromising counter-proposal that all the arms and ammunition in the town be handed over, and that the Royalists' Northern Army should be disbanded. The best he was prepared to offer was that its personnel would be allowed to return to their homes upon giving their parole not to fight again. Unsurprisingly Newcastle rejected the terms. Whether he had entered into the negotiations in the first place simply in order to win time is perhaps a moot point, since all he gained was about twenty-four hours. While it is often claimed that this was the case there seems no reason to doubt that it was the beginning of surrender negotiations on the 8th which triggered the King's fateful letter of the 15th.[17] While Newcastle's personal bravery is unquestioned he certainly seems to have lacked determination, and had Leven been prepared to offer better terms he might well have accepted them.

In the event the cease-fire quite literally ended with a bang. Recognising that the walls were too strong to be breached by artillery fire a number of mines were sunk by the Allies. On Leven's sector the high water table soon forced their abandonment, but elsewhere two were looking particularly promising. In Fairfax's sector Sir James Lumsden was in the process of sinking a mine under Walmgate Bar at the south-east corner of the defences. Near Bootham Bar, diametrically opposite, the Earl of Manchester's pioneers tunnelled through some cellars in the ruined suburbs and planted a mine beneath St Mary's Tower. This tower strengthened the northern corner of the wall enclosing the King's Manor, outside the main circuit of the mediaeval defences. Significantly it was unprotected by earthworks.

On the morning of the 16th Manchester's artillery quickly knocked a breach in the Manor wall, fronting Marygate. According to Slingsby the defenders quickly filled it up with earth and sods,[18] but at noon the adjacent mine was suddenly exploded. Afterwards it was claimed that its premature explosion was forced by the threat of flooding, but there was a general feeling that Laurence Crawford, Manchester's Major General, was too eager. Whatever the truth of the matter no attempt was made to co-ordinate the assault which followed with diversionary attacks on the other sectors. Even more surprisingly the initial assault group also appears to have been poorly supported.

Some 600 men[19] got in through the breach and into a bowling green. There they were met by Sir Philip Byron's Regiment which was providing a garrison for the Manor. Unfortunately the gallant Colonel was shot down as soon as he opened the doors into the green[20], and the attackers pressed on to take the Manor House itself. In the meantime a hasty counter-attack was being organised. As it happened, because it was Trinity Sunday, most of the garrison's senior officers were attending a service in the nearby Minster and now they rushed out, sword in hand. The principal entrance to the Manor Yard lay on Marygate, but the counter-attack would appear to have been channelled through the now vanished Lendal Postern by the river and possibly also through another hard by Bootham Bar. Newcastle himself led eighty of his own Whitecoats. In a sharp little action which cost the Royalists Lieutenant Colonel Samuel Breary and Lieutenant Colonel Ralph Huddleston[21] the breach was sealed off. Curiously Crawford had neither secured the breach nor brought up reinforcements. In the adjacent Scots sector the Earl of Lindsay's Regiment was hastily served out with ammunition, but before any help could reach them the Parliamentarian troops occupying the Manor were forced to surrender. Estimates of their casualties varied. By and large the Allies admitted to around fifty or sixty killed and wounded and as many as 200 killed, but no mention is made by either side of any officer casualties. It may well be the case therefore that, prisoners aside, the Royalists did indeed lose more men, as the Allies claimed. Losing three colonels in an affair of this size looks remarkably careless.

Afterwards the siege proceeded without major incident, except for an unsuccessful sally from Monk Bar on the 24th, but the Allies became increasingly concerned about the imminent approach of Prince Rupert's army. For some time efforts had been made to persuade the Earl of Denbigh to bring up his Midlanders. At the beginning of June he had reported his disposable forces to number only some 750 horse and 1,000 foot,[22] but the Committee of Both Kingdoms, which was now directing the Parliamentarian war effort, ordered Gell, Brereton and other commanders to join him. A rendezvous with Meldrum and the Lancashire forces at Manchester was also proposed, but Denbigh still displayed a disquieting reluctance to move.

Not so the Prince of Darkness. On 29 June he moved forward from Skipton, and by the 30th he was at Knaresborough, just fourteen miles short of the city. Indeed some of his cavalry pushed on as far as Skip Bridge on the river Nidd, only four miles away. Leven had no intention of being trapped against the city. Although this was only an advance guard he ordered the Army of Both Kingdoms to abandon their lines during the night and move westwards into a concentration area on Marston Moor. Rupert had so far failed to get into contact with the garrison and Slingsby relates that they were in some doubt of their deliverance:[23]

> . . . till we perceiv'd ye Scots had drawn off their guards, wch our Centinells gave us notice of; mistrusting it by reason their Centinells had given over talking wth ym & would not answer wh they call'd to ym as usually they had done.

Some further investigation confirmed that the Scots were indeed gone, and a party of horse commanded by Major Ralph Constable of Langdale's Regiment pushed down the road to Fulford. There they had a skirmish with some Allied horse and lost a Captain Squire, shot in the back.[24] But where was Prince Rupert?

Rupert had assembled a fair sized force with which to relieve York, but nevertheless he was still badly outnumbered by the Allies and had no desire to fight them on his own. It was essential therefore that he should avoid contact with the Army of Both Kingdoms until he had added

Newcastle's Northern Army to his own. A deception plan was necessary and worked perfectly. As we have seen in the previous chapter he sent some of his cavalry eastwards from Knaresborough on the 30th in order to give the impression that he was marching directly upon York. The Allies then obligingly lifted the siege and concentrated to block his path on Marston Moor.

In the meantime he had changed direction. Heading north from Knaresborough on the morning of the 1st he crossed the river Ure at Boroughbridge, carried on across the Swale by Thornton Bridge and then marched down the eastern bank towards York. It was a long and no doubt hot march; considerably farther than the twenty miles or so blithely bandied about by some armchair strategists. In fact the milestone at Thornton Bridge – effectively the halfway point – indicates that York is still sixteen miles away. Rupert's *Journal* states that he spent the night in the ancient Forest of Galtres. This is rather vague, but Slingsby places him 'wthin 3 or 4 miles of York, upon ye forest side' which suggests somewhere just beyond Poppleton. Rupert's cavalry certainly came this far for they surprised the regiment of dragoons left by the Allies to guard the bridge of boats there. On the other hand it is likely that the Prince's infantry and guns were stretched back along the road perhaps as far as Tollerton, for to march farther in one day would probably have been beyond their capability.[25]

At about noon Rupert's Brigade Major, William Legge, rode into the city carrying orders to Newcastle. Rupert intended to fight next day and wanted the Northern Army to rendezvous with his own. Unexpectedly this brisk summons met with some resistance. According to the Prince's own account[26] Newcastle initially agreed to bring his whole garrison out, but then was dissuaded by General King. This is frequently ascribed to personal animosity between King and the Prince, dating back to an unfortunate debacle at Lemgo in 1638. There may well be some truth in this, but a much more fundamental reason was King's understandable reluctance to fight his own countrymen, which had been evident from the start of the campaign. Newcastle is unlikely to have needed much persuading for he was a touchy individual all too conscious of his dignity. There were strong suspicions at Oxford that his failure to join the King after beating the Fairfaxes at Adwalton Moor proceeded from a reluctance to give up his independent command. Far from mustering his forces he allowed them to spend the afternoon of 1 July plundering the abandoned siege lines.

Trusting to the Marquis's initial acquiescence Rupert got his own army moving early on the morning of the 2nd. How early we do not know, but since the first of his cavalry did not begin moving on to Marston Moor until about 9am it is clear that the bulk of his men had halted well short of York. Unfortunately, although both the Marquis of Newcastle and General King turned up at about the same time, there was no sign of the Northern Army. The Duchess's version of what happened next is instructive[27]:

'[Newcastle] went himself the next day in person to wait on his Highness; where after some conferences, he declared his mind to the Prince, desiring his Highness not to attempt anything as yet upon the enemy; for he had intelligence that there was some discontent between them, and that they were resolved to divide themselves, and so to raise the siege without fighting: besides my Lord expected within two days Colonel Cleavering with above three thousand men out of the North, and two thousand drawn out of several garrisons (who also came at the same time, though it was then too late).[28] But his Highness answered my Lord, that he had a letter from his Majesty (then at Oxford), with a positive and absolute command to fight the enemy; which in obedience, and according to his duty he was bound to perform.

The 'positive and absolute command' was of course the letter of 14 June. As we have seen, it offered the Prince two alternatives; he could march at once to Worcester or he could delay long enough to relieve York 'by beating the Scots'. Although they and the rest of the Army of Both Kingdoms had temporarily lifted the siege and appeared to be in full retreat, they had not yet been beaten. Ordinarily it might well have made sense for Rupert to rest and refit his men, let reinforcements come in and properly concert his operations with the Northern Army, but the tenor of the King's letter appeared to allow no latitude. As it was unthinkable that he should now march away to Worcester without first beating the Scots, he had to beat them quickly. In any case, orders aside, he presently had them on the run and it was unlikely that he would ever have a better opportunity to smite them hip and thigh.

For their part the Allies had hoped to fight Rupert's army alone at Marston Moor sometime on 1 July. Then, finding that he had slipped past and successfully reached York, they did indeed start falling out amongst themselves. Leven, who was in overall command of the Army of Both Kingdoms, decided on a withdrawal. Sir John Meldrum and the Earl of Denbigh were expected to arrive at Wakefield on the 5th with the Midlanders and the bulk of the Lancashire forces. In the meantime the Allies planned to withdraw through Cawood to Selby:

. . . partly to possess the River intirely, so to hinder him for furnishing *Yorke* with provisions, out of the East-Riding; as also to interpose between him and his march Southwards, he having no other way to march, (the Earle of *Denbigh* and the *Lancashire* Forces interposing between him and his march West-wards, the way he came:)Accordingly early in the morning, wee began our march towards *Cawood*, with all our Armie, leaving three thousand Horse and Dragooneers to bring up the Reare of our Foote and Ordnance.[29]

It was this rearguard, occupying the high ground to the south of the moor which realised that Rupert was not merely observing their departure but coming after them with his whole army. The three officers in charge, Cromwell (now Lieutenant General of Manchester's cavalry), Major General David Leslie, and Sir Thomas Fairfax, hastily conferred and sent word to their superiors urging the necessity of making a stand. If Rupert was intending to fight it was better to hold on to their present position than run the risk of the Prince catching them upon the march.

This, according to his 'Diary' was exactly what he intended, but frustrated by the non-appearance of Newcastle's infantry, he hesitated and instead of forcing the issue began to concentrate his forces on the moor. Granted this respite the Allies, whose advance guard had already reached Tadcaster, halted, turned their men around and hurried back to fight the battle which might finally decide the outcome of the war.

NOTES

1. The Parliamentarian blockade was not entirely successful. A brigade of three regiments which sailed from Waterford that summer got through to Scotland with the most unfortunate results.

2. Prince Rupert's Horse

   Prince Rupert's Lifeguard
   Sir John Hurry's Horse
   Col. Marcus Trevor's Horse
   Col. Henry Washington's Dragoons

   Prince Rupert's Foot
     (formerly Henry Lunsford's)
   Col. Henry Tillier's Foot
   Col. Robert Broughton's Foot
   Sir Michael Earnley's Foot
   Colonel Henry Warren's Foot
   Colonel Richard Gibson's Foot

3. Lord Byron's Horse   Lord Byron's Foot
   Sir William Vaughan's Horse   Sir Robert Byron's Foot
   Lord Molyneux's Horse   Col. Robert Ellis's Foot
   Sir Thomas Tyldesley's Horse   Sir Thomas Tyldesley's Foot

4. *Prince Rupert's Diary* in Young, P. *Marston Moor* p212

5. *Mercurius Aulicus* for the week ending 15 June reported that the hanged man was an officer – which seems quite likely. As it happens *The Royal Martyrs* also records the death of a Captain William Ashton at Bolton. He may well have been killed in the assault, and in any case this particular source is far from being a complete list of Royalist casualties during the war. If however the hanged officer was indeed a Lancashire Catholic this would go some way to explaining why Tyldesley's men took such a prominent part in the massacre.

6. *ibid.* pp212-3 and another (anonymous) Royalist account p210

7. *ibid.* p211. The assault *may* have been carried out by Tillier's own greencoats, but the account of the action in *Mercurius Aulicus* (week ending 15 June) refers to the attackers as 'the *red regiment*'.

8. *ibid.* p213
9. This version is taken from Young (*op.cit.* pp86-7)
10. The seriousness of the King's powder shortage may be gauged from the fact that the Scots had just shot away thirty-seven barrels in the action at Boldon Hill, while the Oxford Army had used over twice as much at Newbury. In other words, even in his present weakened condition the King had barely enough ammunition to fight one day of battle.
11. Newman, P. *The Battle of Marston Moor* (1981) pp39-41
12. Derby was evidently regarded by the Prince as a nuisance and perhaps after Bolton as something of a liability as well. He was not entrusted with any command and shortly after this he returned to the Isle of Man.
13. He is usually identified as the Lieutenant Colonel Thomas Daniel who served in the Prince of Wales' Regiment of Horse. However this seems unlikely as the regiment was serving with the Oxford Army. Instead he was probably the otherwise unidentified Lieutenant Colonel of Tyldesley's Foot, for a soldier named Edmund Robinson who served in the regiment under Captain Cuthbert Bradkirk was in garrison at Clitheroe in 1644 (*Committee for the Advance of Money*). It is possible that the officer in question was the grandfather of a Lancashire Catholic named John Daniel, who left a valuable memoir of the 1745 rebellion.
14. Lord Coupar's, Lord Dudhope's, Douglas of Kilhead's, the Earl of Livingston's, the Master of Yester's and Hepburn of Waughton's regiments all drew ammunition on the 8th, presumably to replace what they expended the previous night. The three regiments commanded by the Earls of Buccleugh, Cassillis and Dunfermline drew only slow-match.
15. Ashe and Good in Wenham, P. *The Great and Close Siege of York 1644* (1970) p40
16. Douglas in Wenham *op.cit.* p44. His account is not particularly clear and does not actually mention the small fort in the middle. It is impossible therefore to establish whether Campbell (unidentified – but probably serving in Coupar's Regiment) was killed in attacking the first fort with Carmichael, or the last one. Panter probably died at the middle one for Douglas associates his death with the killing of eighteen 'of theirs' and the capture of thirty-three more which equates pretty well with the fifty men mentioned by Ashe and Good. Wenham tentatively identifies Panter with a captain of that name serving in Dudhope's Regiment, but if so reports of his death were exaggerated for he was still serving with the regiment a year later. Carmichael belonged to Sandie Hamilton's Regiment, but there is no record of any ammunition being served out to it. While it is possible that they advanced into the assault with muskets unloaded and match unlit, a simpler explanation might be that Carmichael was field officer of the day and as such had overall command of the operation.
17. It might also be significant that the twenty days proposed by Newcastle would have expired on 4 July – just three days after Rupert's arrival.
18. Slingsby, *Diary* p109
19. A petition from a soldier in Colonel Edward Montague's Regiment refers to his having taken part in the fight, but otherwise the composition of the assault force is unknown.
20. A Captain Hackworth also killed in the fighting was described as an Irishman so presumably belonged to Byron's Regiment.
21. Breary, the son of a York Alderman, was described by Christopher Hildyard as 'Lieutenant Coll of a Company of 250. stout Volunteer Citizens.' Although Slingsby refers to his own regiment as being the City one, his Lieutenant Colonel was Thomas Metcalf. Breary must therefore have been serving in the

City Trained Band regiment commanded by Colonel Henry Wait. Huddleston was probably serving as Lieutenant Colonel under his kinsman Sir William Huddleston. Oddly enough Dugdale's *Visitation* refers to him as a Major, so if his rank is reported correctly it must have been a recent promotion.

22. CSPD 1644 pp193-94
23. Slingsby, *Diary* pp111-12
24. *ibid.* A Captain Robert Squire appears in the *List of Indigent Officers* under Langdale's Foot. Presumably the man shot at Fulford was his brother.
25. Infantry normally marched about nine or ten miles a day. It was possible for musketeers to march farther but both contemporary testimony and modern experiment shows that it is much more difficult for pikemen. The eighteen miles from Knaresborough to Tollerton is therefore an exceptional enough feat without expecting them to stagger as far as Poppleton. The same comments obviously apply equally well to the Prince's artillery.
26. *Diary* in Young. P. *Marston Moor* p213. His informant was Colonel Sir Francis Cobbe, who commanded the castle garrison.
27. Firth. ed. *Memoirs* p38
28. In actual fact, according to Rupert's *Journal*, Clavering had only 1,300 men. The 2,000 garrison soldiers appear to be equally imaginary.
29. Scoutmaster General Lionel Watson in Young *op.cit.* p228. The Allied generals' official despatch gives their intended destination as Tadcaster, but this was only to be their first day's halting place.

CHAPTER XI

No Such Thing in the Fields:
The Battle of Marston Moor – Part 1

The Allied deployment at Marston Moor was an untidy affair with elements of all three armies mixed up pretty indiscriminately. Nevertheless they were doubtless thankful for the opportunity to deploy at all. The battlefield was broad, and for the most part uncluttered, moving Leven's Sergeant Major General, James Lumsden, to write that it was '. . . ane playn feild 3 myles in length and in breidth, the fairest ground for such use that I had seen in England.'

The Army of Both Kingdoms drew up amongst the cornfields on Marston Hill. The hill itself merely forms the north-western end of a longish ridge, and contrary to the impression given by the Ordnance Survey (and generations of historians), it does not form a continuous slope down towards the north. Instead at this point it dips quite steeply into a broad area of dead ground before rising again to form a secondary ridge running east to west. At the foot of this lower ridge is the road linking Tockwith and Long Marston. The two villages conveniently mark the western and eastern extremities of the battlefield, and the hedged enclosures surrounding Tockwith seem to have hampered the Allied deployment on the left. From the road the cornfields (sown with rye) extended up to 500 yards northwards to where a curving ditch and hedge separated the arable land from Marston Moor itself. Rupert lined this ditch with musketeers, but otherwise there is little suggestion by those who fought there that it formed a significant military obstacle.

Apart from the unavoidable intermingling of regiments the Allied deployment was broadly conventional. There are two important sources of information about this; a contemporary plan by Sir James Lumsden, and another by Captain Bernard de Gomme. While the latter is primarily concerned with the deployment of the Royalist army, he does provide some useful indicators as to the strength of the Allied front line. Lumsden shows the Allies drawn up in three lines, but as de Gomme only shows two, it may safely be inferred that the third lay in the dead ground and initially could not be seen by the Royalists – which was to be a point of some significance.

The cavalry forming the left wing, commanded by Lieutenant General Oliver Cromwell were deployed in an area known as Bilton Bream. The close proximity of Tockwith seems to have caused some problems here, for a large rabbit warren and some hedges needed to be cleared by pioneers. Lumsden quotes a figure of 3,000 men for the Eastern Association horse and 1,000 for David Leslie's Scots brigade backing them up. Cromwell's Scoutmaster General, Lionel Watson, gave no overall figure but stated that there were a total of about seventy troops on this wing.[1] This must include nine troops of dragooners, for the Eastern Association regiments are known to have mustered thirty-six troops[2] and the Scots had another twenty-two troops[3] which would produce a total of fifty-eight troops of horse and nine of dragoons to make sixty-seven in all. The Association's cavalry had a very high average strength of seventy-four men to a troop which will give a total of around 2,700 men. The Scots on the other hand are unlikely to have mustered more than forty per troop or 880 men producing a grand total of some 3,500 cavalry on this wing[4]. In addition to this the dragooners, according to Lumsden, accounted for up to 500 men.

Establishing just how they were drawn up is a touch problematic. Simeon Ashe refers to 'Brigades of Horse, consisting some of three and some of foure Troops', but some must have been stronger. Both maps depict six divisions or squadrons in the front line. Slingsby refers to only five, but Lumsden's plan shows that the outermost one of his six was composed of dragoons. These will have been the four Scots troops or companies commanded by Colonel Hugh Fraser and five Eastern Association troops under Lieutenant Colonel John Lilburne. The divisions of horse appear to have been rather uneven in size. Lionel Watson speaks of Cromwell's own division being 300 strong and de Gomme certainly depicts the right-hand division in the front line with four cornets, while the other four have only two apiece. This need not be taken literally, but it does confirm that Cromwell's division was larger than the others. It is entirely possible therefore that the remaining four divisions represented the rest of his double regiment.

According to Lumsden's plan there were six divisions in the second line, commanded by Colonel Bartholomew Vermuyden. De Gomme on the other hand shows only five, but this may simply mean that the outer-most one was hidden from his view by the end of the ridge. These divisions were probably made up of the eleven troops of Manchester's and a further eleven belonging to Vermuyden's and Charles Fleetwood's regiments.

However Lumsden also shows that the third line, commanded by Major General David Leslie, comprised four divisions. At first sight this appears odd as there were three regiments there, all pretty much the same size. It is just conceivable that he simply formed his brigade into four divisions without preserving any distinction between its regiments. On the other hand it seems much more likely that three of the divisions each represent one of his regiments and that the fourth was an Eastern Association formation.

On the right wing Sir Thomas Fairfax commanded the Northern Association Horse, also drawn up in two lines with a brigade of Scots cavalry in reserve. According to Lionel Watson, Fairfax had a total of eighty troops 'being his owne and the Scotch Horse.' Again the latter accounted for twenty-two of them[5] and at least four others, perhaps more belonged to Colonel Thomas Morgan's Dragoons. Northern units were not as strong as their Eastern Association counterparts, so if we allow an average of forty men per troop this would indicate that Fairfax and Eglinton had some 3,200 men under their command. This figure is rather less than Lumsden's estimate, especially if 200 of them were dragoons.

As to precisely how they were drawn up Lumsden's plan shows five divisions in the front line, and four each in the second and third, although the left-hand division in the front line is identified by him as dragooners. Each of the twelve divisions of horse must therefore represent a whole regiment. Fairfax's own regiment seems to have been on the right, and on the testimony of the Royalist Sir Philip Monckton so was Colonel Hugh Bethell's, but beyond that and the fact that Colonel John Lambert commanded the second line it is impossible to place individual units[6]. As to the four divisions commanded by Eglinton, three were obviously his Scottish regiments and the fourth was probably another Northern Association regiment since nine of its units can be identified but only eight appear to have been standing in the first two lines.

On both wings the horse were interlarded with detachments of musketeers, each one deployed on the right flank of a division of horse.

Lumsden notes that each detachment was fifty strong mustering some 1,300 men in total.

Between the two wings of cavalry lay a considerable body of infantry, though it may not have been quite so considerable as is generally supposed. Once again the single most important piece of evidence as to their strength and deployment is Lumsden's plan. This shows five brigades in the front line, four each in the second and third, and yet another brigade in reserve. De Gomme on the other hand, although unable to see the third line, depicted *six* brigades in the front line with *five* in the second. Although Lumsden makes no mention of such a movement, it is possible that there was some re-adjustment of the Allied dispositions during the course of the afternoon. At some point two brigades may have been brought up from the third line to prolong the right flank of the first and second.

According to Lumsden from left to right the front line comprised two brigades of Manchester's foot, one of Lord Fairfax's[7] and two brigades of Scots. As to the regiments involved, Lumsden assigns a combined strength of 2,666 men to the two brigades of Manchester's foot. This as it happens agrees pretty well with the July musters for Manchester's own regiment (1,053) and three smaller regiments which are known to have been brigaded together; Colonel Edward Montagu's (418), Colonel John Pickering's (524), and Colonel Francis Russell's (662)[8]. No such positive identification is possible when it comes to Lord Fairfax's brigade although the tenor of the references to it clearly suggests that his own regiment was present. The other may have been Sir William Constable's, for Simeon Ashe refers to its Lieutenant Colonel, Simon Needham, who 'did manfully'. The two Scots brigades according to Lumsden comprised Colonel James Rae's and Sandie Hamilton's regiments, and Viscount Maitland's and the Earl of Lindsay's regiments.[9]

The second line was entirely made up of Scots regiments paired off into brigades. From left to right these were; the Master of Yester's and Lord Livingston's, Lord Coupar's and the Earl of Dunfermline's, Colonel William Douglas of Kilhead's and the Earl of Cassillis', and finally the Earl of Buccleugh's and the Lord Chancellor's regiments.

The third line was made up of two brigades of Fairfax's foot, a brigade of Scots and a brigade of Manchester's. Fairfax's two brigades must have comprised Colonel John Bright's, Colonel Robert Overton's, Colonel Richard Thornton's and probably Colonel George Dodding's regiments.[10] The Scots are identified by Lumsden as Sir Arthur Erskine of Scotscraig's and Viscount Dudhope's regiments. As we shall see the two Eastern Association regiments were Laurence Crawford's and Sir Miles Hobart's, totalling 1,333 men. Finally, standing behind the left of the third line was one more Scots brigade comprising Sir Patrick Hepburn of Waughton's and another, unidentified regiment.[11]

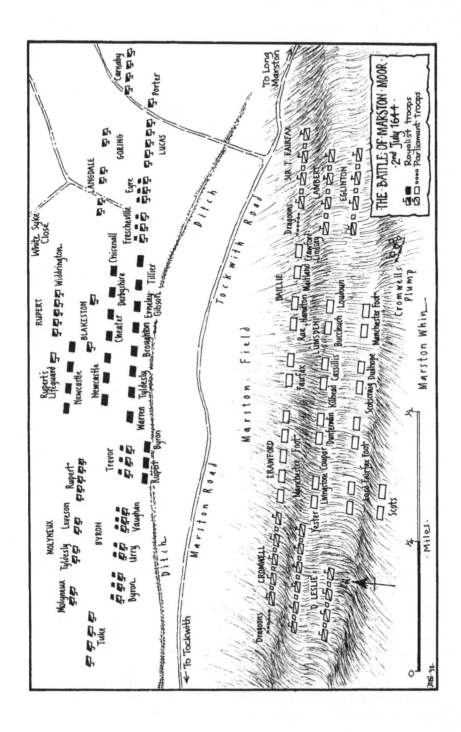

Establishing the strength of the Allied infantry is far from straightforward. Lumsden's figure of 3,999 men for Manchester's contingent is consistent with the July musters and sufficiently precise to suggest that he had sight of a morning state of some description. However he provides suspiciously rounded figures of 1,000 men apiece for Fairfax's three brigades, and an equally vague 1,500 men for each of the Scots brigades, or 3,000 men and 12,000 men respectively.

Unfortunately no muster lists appear to have survived to corroborate either figure. While the first is quoted by a number of contemporary sources, they generally refer to the strength of Fairfax's army at the commencement of the siege two months before. It would therefore be prudent to devalue it by at least ten percent, and 2,500-2,700 is probably a more realistic figure. Estimating the number of Scots is even more problematic. Lumsden's figures suggest that the Scots brigades were stronger than the English ones with an average strength of 750 men to a regiment. This is demonstrably untrue of Scotscraig's Regiment which had only five companies at Marston Moor, although it is possible that it was combined with five companies of Sinclair's Regiment. Reinforcements had caught up with the army since its arrival in England, albeit balanced by a frightening level of desertion, so an average of fifty men to a company might still be valid. If so this would produce a total of only 8,000 Scots infantry.

It was inevitable in the circumstances that the Allies would find it difficult to bring up much in the way of artillery. Nevertheless there were some. Lumsden shows a gun position in the right rear of Cromwell's cavalry wing and a number of Saker (5 or 6-pounder) balls have been recovered from the moor. In addition Robert Colquhone drew eighty-four rounds of 3-pound ball for the light *fframes*[12] attached to the Scots infantry brigades.

Turning to the other side of the Marston cornfields we have one of de Gomme's excellent plans. This is a particularly useful document since it not only depicts the Royalist dispositions but, if interpreted properly, also reveals something of their movements in the hours leading up to the battle.

Facing Cromwell across the area of the Bream was the Royalist right wing commanded by Lord Byron. Well clear of Tockwith and its associated enclosures its deployment was fairly loose and reflected the fact that its flank was very much 'in the air'. The front line proper comprised four regiments in line, Byron's own one on the right, Sir John Hurry's, Sir William Vaughan's 'Irish' Regiment and Colonel Marcus Trevor's Regiment on the left. Hurry's Regiment was drawn up in two squadrons, but the others had three apiece. According to de Gomme they totalled 1,100 men which perhaps rather too neatly equates to 100 men per squadron, and behind each of them was a detachment of forty to fifty musketeers.

Also, strictly speaking, part of the first line was Sir Samuel Tuke's Regiment. While positioned to the right of Byron's Regiment it was deployed slightly farther back in order to 'refuse' the open flank and protect it against any turning movement.[13] De Gomme shows this formation to comprise 200 horse formed in four little squadrons or perhaps even individual troops.

The second line was made up of four regiments, each covering the gaps in the first. Three units, Lord Molyneux's, Sir Thomas Tyldesley's and Colonel Thomas Leveson's, each drawn up in two squadrons and totalling some 800 men, formed what de Gomme termed a reserve under Molyneux. The fourth regiment, drawn up in five squadrons on their immediate left, was Prince Rupert's own. It is possible that it may have been 500 strong, but comparison with the frontline units and a very similar one commanded by Sir William Blakiston suggests that 400 might be nearer the mark.

In total therefore it looks as if the Royalist right wing comprised 1,300 men in the front line and 1,200 in the second, besides some 500 musketeers. Although Byron was to be scapegoated both at the time and afterwards for the disaster which followed, the truth of the matter is that he was heavily outnumbered, and this simple fact goes some way to explaining why he was to act as he did.

Forward of Trevor's Regiment and just behind the ditch and hedge separating the moor from the cornfields stood a rather lonely infantry brigade. Why Lord Byron's Regiment and the two battalions of Prince Rupert's were posted there and for how long they remained in that exposed position is something which has never been adequately explained. It has been suggested that they were so placed in order to cover some sort of gap in the ditch, but this is patently absurd since the Cavalier horse were expected to move forward through and to the west of this position.

It is just possible that their presence is connected with an odd incident which seems to have taken place early in the day:

> . . . With as great expedition as could be, our Army was called back. In the mean while, the Enemy perceiving that our Cavalry had possessed themselves of a corn hill, and having discovered neer unto that hill a place of great advantage, where they might have both Sun and Winde of us, advanced thither with a Regiment of Red Coats, and a Party of Horse; but we understanding well their intentions, and how prejudiciall it would be unto us if they should keep that ground, we sent out a party which beat them off, and planted there our left wing of Horse.[14]

If so the red-coats might be Byron's regiment, for Rupert's wore blue, but on the whole it seems unlikely as these particular infantrymen are more likely to have been musketeers assigned to support the divisions of cavalry.

Be that as it may the brigade was very unfortunately placed, for it promised to hinder any forward movement by Trevor's Regiment. In the light of this rather obvious point it may be concluded that since the Prince did not expect to have to fight until the morning of the 3rd, the brigade was deployed forward of the cavalry in order to serve as a night picquet, in accordance with best practice, and that they otherwise had no tactical function.

De Gomme also notes that the hedge and ditch were lined with musketeers. Just how many is unclear. They may have been no more than a picquet line but Allied accounts refer to a number of guns being interspersed among them.

Rupert's rather indifferently organised front line comprised eight battalions of foot. On the right of the line was Colonel Henry Warren's Regiment, represented by a single battalion. Next came two battalions of Sir Thomas Tyldesley's Regiment, two more of Colonel Robert Broughton's, a sad little composite battalion formed from the remains of Sir Michael Earnley's and Richard Gibson's regiments, and two battalions of Colonel Henry Tillier's. Initially the second line comprised just four battalions. Two of them were commanded by Colonel Henry Chaytor[15] and another by Edward Chisenall, while the fourth, unidentified by de Gomme, may have been commanded by Richard Millward.[16]

De Gomme states that Rupert had 11,000 foot at Marston Moor. If 2,500-3,000 of them are admitted to be the Marquis of Newcastle's men – of whom more in due course – and a further 1,000 musketeers are drawn off to the wings, then the fifteen battalions of the Prince's own army would have averaged 460 men apiece[17]

It is at this point that one of the peculiarities of de Gomme's map becomes apparent. Ordinarily, when two allied armies formed together on the field of battle, they would each take responsibility for one of the wings and then divide the centre in order to place all their best men in the front. Yet at Marston Moor this did not happen because the Royalists, like the Allies, arrived on the field piecemeal. Although the Prince's cavalry started to move on to the moor early in the day, the first of Newcastle's units may not have turned up until about 2pm and his infantry not until after 4pm.

In the meantime the Prince had to cover the whole of the army's projected front on his own. Simeon Ashe notes that, before the Allied infantry began moving into position at about 2pm, 'the enemy was possessed of the Moore . . . and had in many small bodies bespread themselves . . .' Consequently, although Rupert's right wing was deployed pretty much as he would have liked, *all* his veteran infantry were positioned in the front line with nothing but raw levies to back them up. Worse still his left wing was initially only covered by two rather dubious cavalry regiments led by Colonel Rowland Eyre and Colonel John Frescheville. Both of these regiments were made up of garrison troopers and the only possible justification for their presence in the front line is that no one else was available at the time.

In due time they were joined by Newcastle's cavalry and their deployment on the left now more or less mirrored that on the right. Five of Newcastle's squadrons and a little independent troop commanded by George Porter[18] joined the six commanded by Eyre and Frescheville in the front line. Once again de Gomme reckons the whole lot to have been 1,100 strong. This may however be rather too optimistic.[19] Again, as on the right, they were backed up with 500 musketeers and the flank was refused by means of another body of horse – 200 men in four squadrons – commanded by Colonel Francis Carnaby.

The second line comprised three regiments or perhaps small brigades mustering six divisions numbering 800 men and designated as a reserve. Two other little brigades were posted behind Rupert's foot in the centre, presumably to provide some support pending the arrival of Newcastle's infantry. Sir William Blakiston's brigade, comprising two regiments or divisions, was deployed well forward, while a little way behind were Sir Edward Widdrington's 400 horse, divided into five squadrons. Standing immediately to the right of Widdrington was Prince Rupert's Lifeguard of Horse, estimated to have been 140 strong[20].

There is no doubt that Lord Goring led the cavalry on the left, but otherwise the command structure on this wing has been called into question – the extreme fragmentation of Newcastle's horse certainly hindered de Gomme from recording much more than the names of the brigade commanders. At any rate what de Gomme does clearly show is that the brigade of Newcastle's horse in the front line was commanded by Sir Charles Lucas, and that the 800 horse of the reserve were (initially at least) commanded by Sir Richard Dacre. However Brigadier Young suggests that Lucas, not Dacre, would have commanded the reserve since he was Goring's second-in-command. At the same time he also suggests that Sir Marmaduke Langdale (who is otherwise unaccounted for) might have commanded the brigade assigned by de Gomme to Lucas. This hypothesis has the virtue of being neat but it is also unsustainable. In the first place there is absolutely no evidence to suggest that de Gomme was mistaken. On the contrary, it is quite clear from the account left by Sir Philip Monckton, who fought in the front line, that Langdale was *not* his brigade commander. Nevertheless Langdale still remains to be accounted for. However since Dacre seems an odd choice to command the second line, the simplest explanation is that he was merely acting up, pending the arrival of Langdale from York.[21]

Newcastle's infantry finally turned up on the moor at about 4pm and were directed into a position behind the right of the Prince's infantry. On the face of it this looks rather odd. Indeed Dr Newman goes so far as to argue that, since no regimental commanders are identified, de Gomme's map was nothing more than what is termed a headquarters plan, depicting intended rather than actual dispositions.[22] Such a plan certainly existed, for in his notes, Clarendon has a well-known story that when General King arrived:

> Prince Rupert showed the Marquis and the Earl [King] a paper, which he said was the draught of the battle as he meant to fight it, and asked them what they thought of it. King answered 'By God, sir, it is very fine in the paper, but there is no such thing in the fields.'[23]

Sir Hugh Cholmley's version of the contretemps does not actually mention a plan, but is nevertheless both consistent and instructive:

> The Prince demanded of King how he liked the marshalling of his army, who replied he did not approve of it being drawn too near the enemy, and in a place of disadvantage, then said the Prince, 'they may be drawn to a further distance.' 'No Sir' said King 'it is too late'[24]

Ordinarily these remarks might not make very much sense, but if Rupert had first shown King a headquarters plan allocating his infantry a section of the front line, then the meaning is actually quite clear. In King's opinion the Royalist army was too close to the enemy for him to safely carry out what more modern soldiers would term a relief in place, that is, for his men to change places with some of the Prince's troops who were already positioned in the front line. In fact subsequent events show that he was almost certainly correct in this belief, but the positioning of Newcastle's men does raise another equally interesting question.

It is possible that in view of General King's uncooperative attitude they were simply moved into a harbour area with a view to redeploying under cover of darkness. On the other hand the timing may be suggestive of something rather more significant. At least one Royalist account of the battle states that the arrival of Newcastle's foot was the trigger which precipitated the Allied attack:[25]

> . . . the armies faced one another upon *Hessam-Moore*, three miles from *York*, about 12 of the clock, and there continued within the play of the enemies cannon until five at night; during all which time the Prince and the Marquess of *Newcastle* were playing orators to the soldiers in *York*, (being in a raging mutiny in the town for their pay)[26] to draw them forth to join with the Prince's foot; which was at last

effected, but with much unwillingness. The enemy perceiving the advance of that addition to the Prince's army, instantly charged our horse . . .

None of the Allied accounts explicitly mention such a linkage but it seems plausible. Trevor admittedly arrived on the moor some time *after* the battle had begun, but he might still be right about the timing of the two events coinciding. Newman rightly points out that Newcastle's infantry will have marched on to the moor by way of the track running from York's Micklegate Bar through Hessay. However he then assumes that with the battle begun they then halted in the *left* rear of the Royalist position in the area of what was known as the Atterwith Enclosures. In actual fact it is clear from all the available evidence that they came much farther out on to the moor. Moreover, given the speed with which the Royalist right wing began to collapse under Allied pressure, it may be the case that the Whitecoats' deployment on the right was not pre-planned but rather an urgent response to a deteriorating situation.

Be that as it may, de Gomme shows them formed in seven battalions or divisions with three forward and four back.[27] Although Brigadier Young suggested they were commanded by Sir Francis Mackworth there is no reason to doubt that their actual commander was General King. As to how many of them were there, Rupert rather disdainfully claims that only 2,500 appeared 'and those all drunk'.[28] As we have seen at the commencement of the siege Newcastle had some 4,000 men. This included some cavalry and the total will in any case have been reduced over the next couple of months. It would be reasonable nevertheless to assume that there were still some 3,500 infantry in York at the time of Rupert's arrival. Not all of them were marched on to the moor. Sir Henry Slingsby specifically mentions three units; 'Coll. Bellasyse Regiment, Sr. Tho. Glenhams Regiment, & my own, wch was ye Citty Regiment.' which were left behind.[29] If 300 men apiece are allowed for these regiments then Newcastle's marching infantry may well have numbered not much more than 2,500.

All in all de Gomme's figures of 11,000 infantry and 6,500 cavalry may be just about right. On the other side the Army of Both Kingdoms had up to 14,500 infantry, 6,500 cavalry and 700 dragoons. In theory the additional 3,500 infantry could have given them a slight advantage, but since so many men on both sides were to run away there is little point in reading too much into this. At first sight there appears to be a surprising equality in cavalry but the Royalists may only have achieved this by keeping their dragooners mounted. Whether this actually made any difference is perhaps a moot point but, however the figures are interpreted, it is plain that the Royalists did *not* enter the battle significantly outnumbered.

NOTES

1. <u>In</u> Young, P *Marston Moor 1644* p230
2. Earl of Manchester's Horse   11 troops
   Lt.Gen. Oliver Cromwell's Horse   14 troops
   Col. Bartholomew Vermuyden's Horse   5 troops
   Col. Charles Fleetwood's Horse   6 troops
3. Maj.Gen. David Leslie's Horse   8 troops
   Earl of Balcarres' Horse   7 troops
   Lord Kirkcudbright's Horse   7 troops
4. See Holmes, C. *The Eastern Association in the English Civil War* app 7 & 9 The Eastern Association troops mustered in April 1644 contained an average of eighty-two men. By September the average had risen to just over ninety but this reflects recruiting after the battle. As to the Scots; on 28 June Lord Balgonie signed for 150 lances for the Lord General's regiment. As contemporary accounts refer to it being deployed in two squadrons, one of which was armed with lances this would suggest a total strength of around 300, which broadly agrees with the estimated average of forty men to a troop. As all or most of the Scots cavalry regiments drew the same quantity of ammunition – 50lb of powder and 100lb of ball for the battle – this suggests that they were all pretty much of a size.
5. Earl of Dalhousie's Horse   7 troops
   Earl of Eglinton's Horse   8 troops
   Lord General's Horse   7 troops
6. The following regiments appear to have taken part in the battle. Some of them were very weak: Lord Fairfax
                   Sir Thomas Fairfax
                   Sir William Fairfax
                   Col. Charles Fairfax
                   Col. Hugh Bethell
                   Col. Francis Boynton
                   Col. John Lambert
                   Sir Thomas Norcliffe
7. Watson refers to all three of Manchester's brigades being deployed together in the front line. On the other hand a number of other sources confirm the presence of Fairfax's men. It is possible that Watson simply assumed the third brigade was Manchester's since it was not a Scots one – the latter being readily identifiable by their blue bonnets and distinctive colours.
8. Holmes *op.cit.* app 8
9. This is perhaps a convenient moment to remark that other than Rae's 'Edinburgh Regiment' and Home's 'Merse Regiment' there is no contemporary evidence for the use of the entirely bogus territorial titles invented by Professor C.S. Terry at the end of the last century.
10. Brigadier Young tentatively adds Colonel Ralph Assheton's and Colonel Alexander Rigby's Lancashire regiments on the strength of their presence at a conference with Sir Henry Vane outside York on 10 June. However they were only there to plead for assistance. Assheton's Regiment was with Meldrum in Manchester and Rigby's had been destroyed at Bolton.
11. There are some suggestions that the second battalion was Colonel William Stewart's Regiment, although he himself was governor of Sunderland at the time. Brigadier Young on the other hand identifies the battalion as five companies of Lord Sinclair's Regiment. The source cited is ambiguous and unreliable, but if they were indeed present they are more likely to have

formed a composite battalion with the five companies of Scotscraig's Regiment.

12. These were light guns with short stubby barrels mounted on frames designed to be carried on pack-horses. Designed by Sandie Hamilton they should not be confused with the leather guns introduced by James Wemyss in the 1650s.

13. The reconstructed plan of the battlefield in Brigadier Young's *Marston Moor 1644* is in many respects wildly inaccurate. Some of the problems with his interpretation of Lumsden's plan have already been noted. Here he quite inexplicably treats Trevor's regiment as an independent formation (thus adding another 400 men to the front line) and depicts Tuke's Regiment deployed immediately *behind* Byron's Regiment. Similarly Carnaby's Regiment is crammed in behind the front line on the left. As no explanation is given it has to be assumed that both this and the depiction of both armies in a crescent formation unjustified by any contemporary source has been done in order to cram everyone on to a single sheet of paper. Unfortunately subsequent studies of the battle tend to follow this flawed plan without question.

14. *A Full Relation of the Victory obtained . . .* In Terry, C.S. *The Life and Campaigns of Alexander Leslie.* p275. This important narrative is sometimes referred to as Captain William Stewart's narrative.

15. Chaytor had recently been serving in Ireland and may have brought his regiment from there by way of Whitehaven.

16. By a process of elimination this battalion must be the Midland foot which came in with Goring. According to an intelligence report from Sir John Gell they comprised 220 foot under Rowland Eyre and Richard Millward, and a few more under John Frescheville. As both Eyre and Frescheville commanded cavalry regiments on the moor it would be reasonable to suppose the composite infantry battalion was led by Millward.

17. It has to be stressed that this is just an average. Millward's for example cannot have been more than 300 strong – unless Leveson had also contributed some infantrymen to it.

18. Guessing rather hopefully, Young places Porter's troop beside Rupert's Lifeguard in the reserve, however the figure 1 by which de Gomme designates it actually appears on the left of the front line. This is also consistent with what is known of his movements during the battle. It will of course be noted that a regiment alleged by some misprint to be 1,000 strong at Newark has now shrunk to a tiny independent troop.

19. This figure again implies an average strength of 100 men per squadron and gives Eyre and Frescheville 300 men apiece, yet Gell's intelligence report of 1 June (CSPD 1644 pp191-2) credited them and Millward with having only 260 horse and thirty dragoons in total.

20. As Brigadier Young points out there seems to be something wrong with de Gomme's arithmetic. If we assume 400 men for Prince Rupert's own regiment, then the total comes to just 5,000 men rather than the 6,500 quoted by de Gomme. No figures are given for Blakiston's brigade, but even if we allow 250 men for Rupert's and Porter's own troops, it cannot cover the shortfall. At the most Blakiston may have had 500 men – Newcastle certainly had no more than 3,000 cavalry by this time – the remainder may therefore have been dragooners, who do not appear at all on de Gomme's plan. While it is true that he did not depict any on his Edgehill plan either, there is plenty of written evidence as to where they were and what they did there. On the other hand there is no such evidence in regard to the dragoons known to have been at Marston Moor. One is therefore forced to conclude that, finding himself

outnumbered, Rupert kept his dragooners on horseback and, instead of employing them as mounted infantry, he used them to fill out the ranks of his cavalry regiments. As to which of Newcastle's regiments were represented and where they stood nothing can be said with any certainty except that the following units can be positively identified by various means as having been present somewhere on the battlefield. Most of them were very small and may have amounted to little more than a troop or two:

Sir Francis Anderson's Horse		
Sir William Blakiston's Horse		
Sir William Bradshaw's Horse	:	Major Vavasour killed
Colonel Robert Brandling's Horse?		
Colonel Francis Carnaby's Horse		
Sir Richard Dacre's Horse	:	killed
Sir Gamaliel Dudley's Horse		
Col. William Eure's Horse	:	killed
Colonel John Fenwick's Horse	:	killed
Sir John Girlington's Horse		
Sir Thomas Glenham's Horse		
General James King's Horse		
Sir Marmaduke Langdale's Horse		
Sir Philip Monckton's Horse	:	formerly Sir William Saville's?
Col. Francis Stuart's (Scots?) Horse	:	killed
Sir Richard Tempest's Horse	:	Lt.Col. Salvin killed
Sir Edward Widdrington's Horse		
Lord Widdrington's Horse		

21. Young *Marston Moor 1644* p98. Newman *The Battle of Marston Moor* p91 follows Young and with even less justification he also assigns Sir John Mayney to command what he assumes to be a brigade comprising Eyre's and Frescheville's regiments. Monckton (Young *op.cit.* pp222-3), who was certainly commanding a division in the front line, tells how 'Sir Marmaduke Langdale having had those bodies he commanded broken, came to me . . .' – obviously 'those bodies' did not include Monckton's men.

22. Newman, P. *The Battle of Marston Moor* pp43-44 Against this view is the fact that Prince Rupert evidently considered de Gomme's map to have sufficient validity for him to refer to it in his *Diary* (Young, *op.cit.* p214)

23. *Clarendon State Papers* no.1805 but quoted in Firth, *Memoirs* p39

24. Young, *op.cit.* p116

25. Arthur Trevor to Marquis of Ormonde 10 July 1644 <u>In</u> Young *op.cit.* p224

26. Both Rupert and Newcastle were on the moor, so it must have been King who suppressed the mutiny. Cholmley recounts a rumour that it was in fact King who had instigated it. Whatever the truth of the matter, such mutinies were common on the continent particularly when the soldiers suspected that their general might be delaying their pay until after a battle in order to reduce the bill.

27. One of the battalions must have been Newcastle's own regiment of foot commanded by Sir Thomas Basset and Colonel Posthumous Kirton. As to the others they must have been composite units each formed from two or more of the following regiments which can all be identified from casualty lists and the various York registers (see Wenham). Those marked with an asterisk are dubious. While Langdale for example was certainly present, there is no evidence that he still had a regiment of foot:

Sir Philip Byron	:	killed in the fight for the King's Manor
Colonel Cuthbert Conyers		

Sir Timothy Featherstonhaugh*
Colonel Godfrey Floyd
Colonel Thomas Forster*
Colonel John Hilton
Sir Richard Hutton
General King
Colonel Richard Kirkbride
Sir William Lambton   :   killed at Marston Moor
Sir Marmaduke Langdale*
Colonel John Lamplugh   :   wounded and captured at Marston Moor
Lord Mansfield*
Colonel Charles Slingsby   :   killed at Marston Moor
Sir Richard Tempest*
Lord Widdrington*

28. Young. *op.cit.* p213
29. Young. *op.cit.* p215 In addition to these units there will also have been Sir Francis Cobbe's men in the castle and as Dr Newman points out, probably the local Trained Band regiment commanded by Colonel Henry Waite as well. Neither regiment is likely to have been included in the original figure of 4,000 men so their absence from the moor should not alter the projected total for Newcastle's contingent.

CHAPTER XII

The Kingdom is Ours:
The Battle of Marston Moor – Part 2

When Rupert rode across the bridge at Poppleton that morning he knew that the Allies were retreating. Once joined by Newcastle's army he intended to fall upon their rear, but despite repeated messages to hurry them forward it was 2pm before the first of the Northern Horse arrived. By then the first of the Allied infantry units were also coming back. At some point in the afternoon there was a brief exchange of artillery fire, and he essayed a half-hearted probing attack in the Bilton Bream area, but this was shut down as soon as Allied resistance stiffened. Consequently his frustration by the time General King finally arrived with the Northern infantry was palpable in their acrimonious exchange. As King returned to his men, Newcastle asked the Prince:

> ... what service he would be pleased to command him; who returned this answer, that he would begin no action upon the enemy till early in the morning; desiring my Lord to repose himself till then. Which my Lord did, and went to rest in his own coach that was close by the field,

until the time appointed. Not long had my Lord been there, but he heard a great noise and thunder of shooting, which gave him notice of the armies being engaged.[1]

It is a famous scene and it may be wondered why, with a long summer evening in front of him, the Prince had decided that there would be no battle until the following day. The answer almost certainly lies in the dead ground on the forward slope of Marston Hill. From his position on the moor Rupert could see the first two lines of Allied troops but not the third which was forming up in the dead ground.[2] As a result he evidently failed to appreciate that the Allied concentration was complete before Leven announced the fact by suddenly launching the attack.

The Royalists' surprise was compounded by the very speed of that assault. At the western end of the battlefield Lieutenant General Cromwell moved down out of the Bream and was immediately counter-charged by Lord Byron. There is a cryptic remark in the Rupert *Diary* to 'ye improper charge of ye Ld Byron'[3] and this was subsequently empha-sised or rather embroidered in the *Life* of James II where it is related that:

> Prince Rupert had posted him very advantageously behind a warren and a slough, with a positive command not to quit his ground, but in that posture only to expect and receive the charge of the enemy.[4]

As the Prince did not anticipate fighting that evening it may be questioned whether Byron's orders were quite as explicit or so positive. At any rate this slender foundation has been interpreted to mean that Rupert intended Byron's cavalry to stand still and rely upon the ditch and his supporting musketeers to break up any attack. Instead he charged forward and forfeited both supposed 'advantages'.

While this view has gained considerable currency it is neither supported by the evidence from the other side, nor by a proper appreci-ation of the situation. At this end of the battlefield the ditch was a useful landmark, but it did not constitute a significant obstacle. None of the Allied accounts refer to any difficulty in crossing the ditch, although a number of witnesses do mention the existence of a feature variously described as a morass, slough or sleeke. This may have been a particu-larly muddy area of moorland around the confluence of the east-west ditch and the Sike Beck. Standing water probably made it look a lot worse than it actually was – a point which Byron, as the local commander, may have appreciated better than Rupert. However the fact of the matter is that Lionel Watson unambiguously states that Cromwell's men got over the ditch *before* encountering Byron, and so he cannot be accused of contravening his orders on that point.

Another factor also needs to be considered – the infantry brigade which Rupert had posted out by the ditch as a picquet or perhaps as a Forlorn Hope. Whatever its true purpose it is unlikely that it was intended to help break up a cavalry charge for de Gomme shows it posted opposite Manchester's infantry. Unfortunately it also stood directly in front of Trevor's Royalist cavalry regiment on Byron's left. Consequently Byron initially went up against Cromwell with only 800 men in his front line. It may well be this rather than any supposed breach of his orders which Rupert commented upon.

At any rate, in the circumstances he did surprisingly well. His first charge bounced off, but he then fell back on his supports and brought Cromwell to a stand. This phase of the fight evidently lasted much longer than the first. Although most of the front line had disintegrated, Byron still had some 1,400 men in his second line, including Rupert's and Tuke's regiments. He was therefore able to hold on long enough for Trevor, earlier blocked by that infantry brigade, to swing his regiment around and come in on Cromwell's flank with a further 300 men. Rupert himself also came up with reinforcements. These must have included his own Lifeguard, and it is inconceivable that he would not have brought up Sir Edward Widdrington's little brigade as well, thus throwing over 500 more men into the rapidly escalating fight. By this time Cromwell's own second line must also have been committed so that there were in the region of 2,600 Eastern Association cavalry banging it out bravely with 2,200 Cavaliers. Cromwell's slight numerical advantage will have been counter-balanced by the fact that the Royalists were fresher, still had their pistols loaded, and were flanking him. Indeed Cromwell himself was wounded and temporarily left the field.[5] Consequently, as Watson admits:

> *Cromwells* own division had a hard pull of it: for they were charged by *Ruperts* bravest men, both in Front and Flank: they stood at the swords point a pretty while, hacking at one another: but at last (it so pleased God) he brake through them, scattering them before him like a little dust.[6]

This was a touch ungenerous, for it was actually the intervention of David Leslie with close on 900 Scots cavalry which eventually decided the day. This intervention was rather tardier than it might have been, for Leslie first got involved in fighting with some Royalist infantry and by the time he eventually came up, the cavalry fight was fairly static.

On both sides heavy cavalrymen routinely 'locked' their ranks by wedging themselves knee to knee. The purpose of this was to prevent the enemy forcing his way between and breaking up the formation. In this particular case neither side was showing any immediate sign of giving way. After the first exchange of pistol fire the hacking may have been noisy, but otherwise would have been fairly harmless. So long as they maintained their tightly locked ranks, it was physically difficult for cavalrymen to reach far enough over their horses' ears to strike their opponents. Instead both parties had to rely upon 'pushing', as Byron himself described at Roundway, that is both sides tried to spur their horses forward in order to force their opponents back and so, in time, burst their formation apart. The principle was exactly the same as that employed by pikemen at push of pike.

Leslie therefore had two alternatives. The first was simply to throw his men in behind the Eastern Association troopers and quite literally add their weight to the fight. This he rejected because his men were not well enough mounted and so he instead fell upon the Royalist flanks with decisive effect.[7] The Cavaliers broke and fled back past Wilstrop Wood, most of them running towards York. Rupert was also caught up in the rout, and as his enemies gleefully recounted, was forced to hide for a time in a bean field or 'land'.[8] There must then have been a pause at this point. Regiments were scattered, some units were pursuing the Royalists and at the very least pistols needed to be reloaded.

By dint of hard fighting and sheer weight of numbers the Allies had triumphed on the left, but over on the right Sir Thomas Fairfax's cavalry suffered a near catastrophic defeat. While the ditch separating the cornfields from the moor had not impeded Cromwell's men, the going at the eastern end of the battlefield was much more difficult. It seems possible that the arable land was higher than the adjacent moorland and that a substantial bank separated the two. Moreover, while Cromwell had time to employ pioneers to clear away the obstacles to his front, Fairfax seems to have come upon his ground fairly late in the day. At any rate no corresponding attempt seems to have been made to prepare the way for his advance.

> Our Right Wing had not, all, so good success, by reason of the whins and ditches which we were to pass over before we could get to the Enemy, which put us in great disorder; notwithstanding, I drew up a body of 400 Horse. But because the intervals of [the Royalist] Horse, in this Wing only, were lined with Musketeers; which did us much hurt with their shot; I was necessitated to charge them. We were a long time engaged one with another; but at last we routed that part of their Wing. We charged, and pursued them a good way towards York . . . myself only returned presently, to get the men I left behind me. But that part of the Enemy which stood, perceiving the disorder they were in, had charged and routed them, before I could get to them.[9]

A quite different version appears to be related by the unknown author of the *Full Relation*. According to him, Fairfax made the mistake of trying to move forward down a narrow lane. This was presumably either Atterwith Lane or more likely Moor Lane, both of which run northwards from the Long Marston to Tockwith Road:

> The right wing of our Foot [sic] had severall misfortunes, for betwixt them and the enemy there was no passage but at a narrow Lane, where they could not march above 3 or 4 in front, upon one side of the Lane was a Ditch, and on the other ane Hedge, both whereof were lined with Musketiers, notwithstanding Sir Thomas Fairfax charged gallantly, but the enemy keeping themselves in a body, and receiving them by threes and foures as they marched out of the Lane, and (by what mistake I know not) Sir Thomas Fairfax his new leavied regiment being in the Van, they wheeled about, and being hotly pursued by the enemy came back upon the L. Fairfax Foot, and the reserve of the Scottish Foot, broke them wholly, and trod the most part of them under foot.[10]

The two accounts at first sight appear quite incompatible, but upon closer examination it is apparent that in fact they actually relate to two quite separate actions.

In the first one, Sir Thomas led his cavalry forward through what sounds like a broad belt of broom cut up by drainage ditches. By the time they struggled out on to the open moor they were in considerable disorder, but his own veterans quickly fell back into line. Given the opportunity he might then have waited for the other regiments to sort themselves out before resuming the advance. Instead, coming under fire from the Royalist musketeers opposite, he lost his patience (not a virtue he was overly endowed with) and charged forward. Judging by the absence of any interference in the fight or the subsequent pursuit, he must have attacked Colonel Francis Carnaby's 200 men on the extreme left of the Royalist army. Despite being outnumbered Carnaby's men gave a good account of themselves for Fairfax afterwards admitted:

> . . . many of my Officers and soldiers were hurt and slain. The Captain of my own Troop was shot in the arm. My Cornet had both his hands cut, that rendered him ever after unserviceable. Captain MICKLETH- WAITE, an honest stout man, was slain. And scarce any Officer which was in this charge, which did not receive a hurt.[11]

Meanwhile Goring and Lucas had countercharged and destroyed the rest of his command. Fairfax also mentions in his account that his brother, Colonel Charles Fairfax, was 'sore wounded' after being deserted by his men. If battlefield rumour had confused the two regiments commanded by the Fairfax brothers this would fit in quite neatly with the action described in the *Full Relation*. Unlike Sir Thomas's regiment Charles Fairfax's men were indeed newly levied. Faced with the choice of forcing his way over a hedge stuffed with Royalist musketeers (and perhaps overly eager to follow his brother into the fight) it was Charles, not Sir Thomas, who made the fatal mistake of trying to move his men down the lane. There he was attacked by either Eyre's or Frescheville's regiments, whereupon his men 'wheeled about' and left him to be cut down.

The other regiments in the front line fared equally badly. Sir Philip Monckton, leading a division in Lucas's Brigade, tells how he had his horse shot from under him at the outset of the charge, but ran forward on foot. Reaching the scene of the action he found that his men had already beaten Hugh Bethell's Regiment. His servant then brought up Bethell's horse, but by the time he mounted it the fighting had completely passed him by.

Lambert was unable to bring the Allied second line forward to Fairfax's assistance but 'charged in another place.' Of Lambert's battle we know little save that he lost a number of officers and his Major (another of the Fairfax family) managed to collect at least thirty wounds! Eglinton's Scots initially did rather better[12]:

> . . . the two squadrons of Balgonies regiment being divided by the enemy each from the other, one of them being Lanciers charged a regiment of the enemies foot, and put them wholly to the rout, and after joyned with the left wing; the Earle of Eglingtons regiment maintained their ground (most of the enemies going on in the pursuit of the Horse and Foote that fled) but with the losse of four Lieutenants, the Lieut. Colonell[13], Major[14] and Eglingtons Sonne being deadly wounded.

Meanwhile the Allied infantry had initially gone forward with the cavalry at what Watson called a 'running march' and quickly stormed the Royalist-held ditch. There is an unfortunate shortage of source material on what most of the Royalist infantry actually did at Marston Moor. Nevertheless, by careful use of Allied sources and by reference to de Gomme's invaluable map, it is possible to get a reasonably comprehensive idea of what happened.

The first problem to be faced is the matter of the ditch. Apart from the fact that a small infantry brigade comprising two battalions of Rupert's Foot and one of Byron's[15] was posted at the western end, we simply do not know just how strongly it was held. Although de Gomme merely notes that it was lined with musketeers, some Allied accounts seem to suggest that it formed a fairly substantial defensive line.

At any rate, as soon as Cromwell's cavalry went forward, Colonel Hugh Fraser took his little brigade of dragooners across behind them in order to flank Rupert's Foot. At the same time Manchester's Foot were attacking head on. Consequently they and the other troops lining the ditch put up very little resistance.

> Orders being given to advance, the Battell was led on by Generall Hamilton[16], Lieutenant Generall Baylie[17], and Major Generall Crawford; the Reserve being comitted to the trust of Generall Major Lumsdaine; there was a great Ditch between the Enemy and us, which ran along the front of the Battell, only between the Earl of Manchester's foot and the enemy there was a plain; in this Ditch the enemy had placed foure Brigades of their best Foot, which upon the advance of our Battell were forced to give ground, being gallantly assaulted by the E. of Lindsie's regiment, the Lord Maitland's, Cassilis, and Kelheads. Generall Major Crawford having overwinged the enemy set upon their flank, and did very good execution upon the enemy, which gave occasion to the Scottish Foote to advance and passe the Ditch.[18]

Apart from the three battalions 'overwinged' by Fraser and Crawford, it seems doubtful that the Royalists tried to hold the ditch with four complete brigades. Nevertheless this particular account does make some sense of this phase of the infantry battle. The Allied front line went forward against the ditch and became engaged in a firefight with the Royalist musketeers and gunners. Thanks to the fact that Fraser was coming in on their flank, Rupert's and Byron's regiments quickly retreated. As they went back the rest of the Royalist musketeers peeled away with them, allowing the Allies to get over the ditch. In the process Manchester's men took two drakes (a catch-all term for light artillery pieces), and Fairfax's Brigade in the centre of the front line claimed to have captured two drakes and a demi-culverin.[19] Most of the Royalist musketeers simply ran back towards their parent units but Rupert's and Byron's regiments were less fortunate.

> L. Generall Cromwell charged Prince Rupert's horse with exceeding great resolution, and maintained his charge with no lesse valour. Generall-Major Lesley charged the Earle of Newcastle's brigade of Whitecoats, and cut them wholly off, some few excepted who were taken prisoners, and after them charged a brigade of Green-coats, whereoff they cut off a great number, and put the rest to the rout, which service being performed, he charged the enemies horse (with whom L.Generall Cromwell was engaged) upon the flanke, and in a very short space the enemies whole cavalry was routed . . .[20]

The writer was obviously mistaken in describing the Royalists as belonging to Newcastle's foot. It was far too early in the day for that. However he was evidently *not* interpolating an incident which occurred later in the battle. The obvious interpretation is that as Leslie moved forward he first mopped up the scattered detachments of Royalist musketeers who had been supporting Byron's first line, then charged Rupert's and Byron's foot as they tried to retreat. An Eastern Association cavalryman named Robert Grifen also refers to just 'one Regiment or body of their foot'[21] being routed at this time which would seem to confirm this. It is a point of some importance, for when the Allied foot crossed the ditch, the main Royalist front line was still intact and they had some hard fighting in front of them.

De Gomme shows that in accordance with best practice there were substantial intervals between each brigade in the front line. Now, General King launched the Northern Foot through those intervals in a furious counter-attack. According to Ashe it was Lord Fairfax's brigade, in the very centre of the Allied line, which took the brunt of the assault:

> . . . the Lord Fairfax his Briggade on our right hand did also beat off the Enemy from the hedges before them, driving them from their Canon being two drakes and one Demi-culvering, but being afterwards received by Marquesse New-castles Regiment of Foot, and by them furiously assaulted, did make a retreat in some disorder.[22]

Worse was to follow. Next to them Sandie Hamilton's Brigade, comprising his own and Colonel Rae's Edinburgh Regiment, also broke and ran. They at least had some excuse, for before the counter-attack came in, they must have been heavily engaged in a firefight with Tillier's Greencoats, but much to Lumsden's disgust the panic also spread into the second line[23]:

> These that ran away shew themselves most baselie. I commanding the battel was on the heid of your Lordship's regiment[24] and Buccleuche's but they carryed not themselffs as I wold have wissed, nather could I prevaill with them. For these that fled never came to chairge with the enemies, but were so possessed with ane pannik fear that they ran for example to others and no enemie following, which gave the enemie occasioun to chairge them, they intendit not, they had only the loss.

Sir Charles Lucas, meanwhile, had kept at least a part of his Royalist cavalry brigade in hand and now, attracted by the glorious sight of enemy infantrymen running away, he swung them in against the Earl of Lindsay's brigade. Lucas was to gain considerable credit from later historians for this action, but in fact it was launched too hastily to have much chance of success.

Sir Charles Lucas and Generall Major Porter having thus divided all our Horse on that wing, assaulted the Scottish Foot upon their Flanks, so that they had the Foot upon their front, and the whole Cavalry of the enemies left wing to fight with, whom they encountered with so much courage and resolution, that having enterlined their Musquetiers with Pikemen they made the enemies Horse, notwithstanding for all the assistance they had of their foot, at two severall assaults to give ground; and in this hot dispute with both they continued almost an houre, still maintaining their ground; Lieut. Generall Baily, and Generall Major Lumsdain (who both gave good evidence of their courage and skill) perceiving the greatest weight of the battell to lye sore upon the Earl of Linsies, and Lord Maitland's regiment, sent up a reserve for their assistance, after which the enemies Horse having made a third assault upon them, had almost put them in some disorder; but the E. of Lindsey, and Lieut. Colonell Pitscotti, Lieut. Col. to the Lord Maitland's Regiment, behaved themselves so gallantly, that they quickly made the enemies Horse to retreat, killed Sir Charles Lucas his Horse, tooke him Prisoner, and gained ground upon the foote.[25]

While Lucas was futilely throwing his brigade against Lindsay's men, Sir Marmaduke Langdale led the second line of Northern Horse forward in a much more destructive charge. It seems quite likely that it was in fact Langdale's men who gave Eglinton's cavalry brigade its quietus, but at any rate they now swept up the side of Marston Hill, penetrating as far as the Allied baggage train.[26] Douglas confirms the sudden departure of Sandie Hamilton's Brigade and the Chancellor's and Buccleuch's regiments and adds that two other regiments in the third line were ridden over. Both commanding officers went down. Viscount Dudhope was wounded and captured, and Lieutenant Colonel James Bryson of Scotscraig's Regiment was killed outright.

The brigade of Manchester's foot on the right of the third line was also hard hit. While there is virtually no difference between the figures quoted by Lumsden for the two front-line brigades at Marston Moor and the musters later in July, the total for Crawford's and Hobart's regiments went down by some 130 men. Moreover a Royalist cavalry officer named Lewins stated afterwards that 'most of Manchester's blew coats wch fought under the bloody colors are cutt off.'[27]

Leven too was carried away in the rout as indeed were both his colleagues, Lord Fairfax and the Earl of Manchester. The latter however had sufficient presence of mind to place himself at the head of a body of about 500 runaways and return to the field.[28] Although it is unlikely that he contributed much more than encouragement to its management, this was the crisis point of the battle.

Just an hour into the battle the left wings of both armies had triumphed, scattering their immediate opponents. In the centre the initial Allied advance had cleared the Royalist outpost line only to be thrown back by a counter-attack. On the left the situation was stabilised, according to Ashe when one of Manchester's regiments; '. . . did wheele on the right hand, upon their Flanck, and gave them so hot a charge, that they were forced to flie back disbanded into the Moore'[29] However on the right there had been a serious reverse, vigorously exploited by the Royalist cavalry. Only Lindsay's brigade was still holding firm, but Lumsden was bringing up two more Scots brigades to plug the gap left by the flight of Fairfax's and Hamilton's.[30] Opposite them the Royalist infantry were still pretty well intact. The battle could still be won by either side.

However, with all the commanding generals having fled, the responsibility for seizing the initiative lay with their subordinates. Cromwell by this time was somewhere in the region of Wilstrop Wood, gathering his command together and no doubt giving thanks to God for a glorious victory. Then a dishevelled and wounded Sir Thomas Fairfax appeared. Returning from the pursuit of Carnaby's Regiment he found the rest of his command scattered, so taking the Allies' white field-sign from his hat he made his way westwards to find Cromwell. His news of the disaster on the right came as a shock, but nevertheless the Eastern Association horse were put into a good order and turned southwards for a second charge.

As they advanced through the Royalist rear area it was inevitable that their passage would be punctuated by petty skirmishes with scattered bodies of Cavaliers. Somewhere too they seem to have joined up with Lord Balgonie's Regiment, but by the time they came up to the front the Cavaliers were waiting for them. Goring and Langdale had managed to rally enough of their men to form a battle-line and face Cromwell.

> The enemy seeing us to come in such a gallant posture to charge them, left all thoughts of pursuit, and began to thinke that they must fight again for that victory which they thought had already been got. They marching down the Hill upon us from our Carriages, so that they fought upon the same ground, and with the same Front that our right wing had before stood to receive their charge; and wee stood in the same ground, and with the same Front which they had when they began the charge.[31]

The issue of the fight can scarcely have been in doubt. Not only were the Cavaliers drawn up 'at the same place of disadvantage where they had routed our Horse formerly'[32] but they were probably outnumbered and disorganised. One charge sufficed to scatter them, but it is unlikely that they were pursued very far since large numbers of fugitives remained scattered over the moor behind the original Royalist position.

Sir Philip Monckton relates that after he lost contact with his men he retired 'over the glen' where he encountered Sir John Hurry and a substantial body of horse, perhaps as many as 2,000 strong.[33] Hurry reckoned nothing could be done with them and galloped off to York. Monckton however stayed on the moor. Langdale turned up shortly afterwards and at about midnight Hurry re-appeared with orders for them to retire to York.

In the meantime the Allies had turned on the Royalist infantry. As this final phase of the action followed the destruction of Goring's command, Cromwell must have first rejoined Manchester's infantry, still stalled by the hedge and ditch, for according to Lionel Watson's lively account, the Eastern Association cavalry and infantry worked closely together: 'Our three Brigades [sic] of Foot of the Earle of Manchesters being on our right hand, we went on with great resolution . . .'[34]

General King was in an impossible situation. Thanks to his earlier counter-attack the Royalist infantry had so far held their own. Now assailed on all sides by Allied horse and foot, and running short of ammunition, his battle-line began to collapse. According to Watson the Eastern Association regiments turned the Royalists' right flank and then proceeded to roll it up, destroying one regiment after another. However there are some clues which suggest that the destruction of the Royalist infantry was neither as smooth nor as complete as the various Allied writers suggest.

In a frequently overlooked passage of the *Diary* Prince Rupert states that:

After ye Enemy having broken o^r horse the foot stood till night and in ye night some of em came off after ye P and Gen^ll King had drawn up as many as he could.[35]

At the same time it was agreed on all hands that the Northern foot did not escape, but here we find the reason. The last stand of the Whitecoats is one of the most famous episodes in the whole Civil War. Yet it is one of the least explicable. Why did the Whitecoats fight so long and so hard on an open field when they might so easily have escaped or surrendered. Various explanations have been offered over the years, but yet the most obvious and straightforward has been overlooked. The Whitecoats died on Marston Moor not through irrational bravado, or for the sake of 'honour', but because they were ordered by General King to take on the grimmest of all military roles – that of the sacrificial rearguard.

As Rupert's veterans in the front line crumbled under Allied pressure the Whitecoats stood fast to cover their retreat. Until recently the location of the fight (and the subsequent burials) was traditionally asserted to be the White Sike Close, behind the Royalist centre. The fact that the Close itself was not actually laid out until after 1766 has led to a rather eccentric proposal that the real location lay farther east in an area then known as the Atterwith Enclosures.[36] However none of the contemporary accounts actually refer to the Royalists taking up a position in an enclosure – Camby's dubious story only mentions ditches – and in any case local traditions, stemming as in this instance from knowing where the bodies were buried, tend to be surprisingly reliable. Moreover the traditional site, whether enclosed or not at the time, accords both with the regiment's known whereabouts during the battle and the likely line of retreat followed by Rupert's regiments.

Oddly enough only two accounts deal with the Whitecoats' last stand in any detail, and only one of them, Somerville's, can be regarded as contemporary. While he was not an eyewitness he was well placed to hear the story from those involved[37]:

> . . . neither met they with any great resistance, until they came to the Marquis of Newcastle his battalion of white coats, who first peppering them soundly with their shot, when they came to charge stoutly bore them up with their pikes, that they could not enter to break them . . . until at length a Scots regiment of dragoons, commanded by Colonel Frizeall, with other two[38], was brought to open them upon some hand, which at length they did; when all their ammunition was spent, having refused quarters, every man fell in the same order and rank wherein he had fought.

Yet more famous perhaps is the account told many years later to William Lilly by a soldier turned actor named Camby[39]:

> This sole regiment, after the day was lost, having got into a small parcel of ground ditched in, and not of easy access of horse, would take no quarter, and by mere valour for one whole hour kept the troops of horse from entering amongst them at near push of pike; but when the horse did enter they would have no quarter, but fought it out till there was not thirty of them living; those whose hap it was to be beaten down upon the ground, as the troopers came near them, though they could not rise for their wounds, yet were so desperate as to get either a pike or sword a piece of them, and to gore the troopers' horses as they came over them or passed them by . . .

NOTES

1. Firth, ed. *Memoirs of the Duke of Newcastle* p39
2. It is one of the curiosities of the battle's historiography that Newman is the only writer to have noted the existence of this feature (albeit only in passing) although he apparently fails to appreciate its significance.

3. Young, P. *Marston Moor 1644* p214
   > Ld Biron then made a Charge upon Cromwell's forces
   > Rep^{r}sent here ye Posture
   > the P. put ye forces in
   > and how by ye improper
   > charge of ye Ld Byron
   > much harm was done

4. Clark, J.S. ed. *Life of James II* Vol.I p22

5. Parliamentarian accounts – some of them hostile – refer to his being slightly hurt by the negligent discharge of a trooper's pistol. On the other side there is a tradition that he was wounded by Colonel Trevor, which is at least feasible given that Cromwell was leading the division on the right of the line where his flank attack came in.

6. Young, *op.cit.* p230

7. Although Lord Saye and Sele was not an eyewitness, his remarks in a letter written in 1647 (Terry, C.S. *Life and Campaigns of Alexander Leslie* p260) have considerable relevance: '. . . the Enemies Horse, being many of them, if not the greatest part, Gentlemen, stood very firm a long time, coming to a close fight with the Sword, and standing like an Iron Wall, so that they were not easily broken; if the Scots light, but weak Nags had undertaken that work, they had never been able to stand a charge, or indure the shock of the Enemies Horse, both Horse and men being very good, and fighting desperately enough.'

8. Simeon Ashe in Terry, *op.cit.* p270. Newman's statement that the story originated in a London propaganda sheet is untrue.

9. Fairfax in Young *op.cit.* p243

10. Firth *op.cit.* p276

11. Fairfax *op.cit.* p276

12. *Full Relation* Firth, *op.cit.* p277

13. Robert Montgomerie (he survived to become Colonel of the regiment in 1645).

14. John Montgomerie.

15. Peter Young suggests that the brigade would have been commanded by Thomas Napier, who appears in the *List of Indigent Officers* as a Colonel of Foot under Lord Byron. Unfortunately there is no evidence that he actually served at Marston Moor and little enough to connect him with an active command in Byron's Regiment. Rupert's Lieutenant Colonel, John Russell had been wounded at Bolton a month before, but this may not have been sufficient to incapacitate him from commanding on 2 July.

16. Sir Alexander (Sandie) Hamilton. His *official* appointment was General of the Artillery but he served as a brigade commander at Marston Moor.

17. Lieutenant General William Baillie

18. *Full Relation*

19. Simeon Ashe in Terry *op.cit.* p269

20. *Full Relation*

21. Young *op.cit.* p233

22. Ashe *op.cit.* Newcastle's own regiment must have been familiar enough to Fairfax's men for us to consider this as a positive sighting.

23. Young *op.cit.* p268

24. Lumsden's letter was written to John Campbell, Earl of Loudon and Lord Chancellor of Scotland.

25. *Full Relation*

26. Modern accounts of the battle give the credit for this second charge to Blakiston, but while there is little doubt he took part in the charge there is no

evidence he led it. The hypothesis appears to rest on the erroneous assumption that Lucas was leading the whole second line against Lindsay, and that the only unengaged Royalist cavalrymen belonged to Blakiston's little brigade.

27. Young *op.cit*. pp217-218 The statement actually appears in a letter written from Richmond on 6 July by a Mr Ogden. He in turn read it in a letter of 'Dʳ Lewins to his wife.' Lewins was evidently a cavalryman in the Northern Horse and can most probably be identified with Captain Thomas Lewins of Brandling's Regiment. As to the 'blew coats'; they must be Lawrence Crawford's Regiment since the other regiment in the brigade was Sir Miles Hobart's 'Norfolk Redcoats'. According to Lumsden, the two regiments had a combined total of 1333 men at Marston Moor, but a few weeks later Crawford's and Hobart's could only muster 608 and 593 men respectively.

28. Douglas in Firth p282 '. . . my Lord Manchester was fleeing with a number of Scots officers. God used me as ane instrument to move him to come back againe; for I was gathering men a mile from the place and having some there he drew that way . . . I exhorted him before many witnesses to goe back to the field, and he was induced; we came back about 5 or 600 horse;' Ashe, who was one of Manchester's chaplains, also confirms this.

29. Ashe, in Firth *op.cit*. p269

30. Lumsden in Young *op.cit*. p268

31. Lionel Watson in Young *op.cit*. p231

32. *Full Relation* It will be noted that after Charles Fairfax's debacle no one else who fought in this area found it necessary to file down the Atterwith Lane.

33. *ibid*. pp222-23. Newman identifies 'the glen' as the area of dead ground on Marston Hill, but both the context and Monckton's reference to retiring over it, clearly point to it being *north* of the battlefield, perhaps in the region of Wilstrop Wood.

34. Young. *op.cit* p231

35. *ibid*. p214

36. The traditional site is challenged by Dr Peter Newman in his *The Battle of Marston Moor* and an earlier monograph on the battlefield published by the Borthwick Institute. His suggestion that the fight took place in the Atterwith or Hatterwith Enclosures appears to be primarily based on the happy conjunction of what he suggests are the only verifiable enclosures on the moor at the time of the battle, and the road from York via Hessay by which the Whitecoats must have reached the battlefield. However this identification can be challenged on three grounds. First, although the 'White Sike Close' legend has associated the action with an enclosed area of some kind, only Camby hints that it did not take place on the open moor. Secondly, if we admit the possibility that the stand *did* take place within a ditched and cultivated area, this still does not conclusively point to the Atterwith enclosures for the 'Rupert and the Beanfield' story (wrongly dismissed by Newman) shows that there *were* other cultivated patches on the moor in 1644. Thirdly, we have a positive sighting of Newcastle's own regiment in the centre of the battlefield, rather than behind the left wing where Newman leaves them standing throughout the battle.

37. Young, *op.cit*. p261

38. This suggests that Fraser's Dragoons were supported not only by Manchester's under Lieutenant Colonel John Lilburne, but by Colonel Thomas Morgan's northern regiment as well. What the latter had been doing during the preceding alarums and excursions does not appear.

39. Young, *op.cit.* p137 While one hesitates to spoil such an excellent story the strong *caveat* must be made that none of the other Eastern Association chroniclers even mention this action, far less record the involvement of Cromwell's cavalry. On the other hand the *Full Relation* suggests that it was Leslie's Scots who finished off the Whitecoats. While Camby may well have fought at Marston Moor as he claimed, his tale probably improved over the years.

CHAPTER XIII

A Miraculous Conquest in the South: Cheriton Wood and Cropredy Bridge

The Prince yᵉ next morning march'd out wᵗʰ yᵉ remaining horse, & as many of his footmen as he could force, leaving yᵉ rest in York,[1]

Thus Slingsby described Rupert's departure from York, which surrendered to the Allies on 16 July. To all intents and purposes the Northern Army had been destroyed. Its commander, the Marquis of Newcastle, had fought at Marston Moor simply as a volunteer and afterwards, pressed to regroup his forces on Tyneside, he took the extraordinary decision to go into exile.[2] In an unsuccessful attempt to persuade him to continue the fight Rupert even offered to stay in the area and help him to 'recruite in ye West Riding and form an Army;'[3] This was in direct contradiction to his orders but no one at York yet knew that those orders were out of date. The 'miraculous conquest in the South' had begun at Cropredy Bridge on 29 June.

It was a remarkable turnabout, for the year had begun very badly indeed. The Newbury campaign left the Oxford Army exhausted. In the coming year it was to act on the defensive until reinforcements arrived. Lord Byron was sent northwards to establish a military corridor for the expected reinforcements from Leinster, while in the west, Exeter was taken by Prince Maurice on 4 September and Dartmouth on 6 October. Plymouth and Lyme were still held by Parliament, but only the Royal Navy hindered the passage of troops from Munster. However, in order to cover Maurice, and to maintain pressure on London, it was decided to form a new Southern Army.

The man selected to command it was Sir Ralph (now Lord) Hopton. The choice turned out to be a less than happy one. Hopton had still not recovered from the injuries he received at Lansdown when he was summoned to a Council of War at Oriel College, Oxford on 29 September 1643. There he was informed that:

... being reasonably well recovered of his hurts, he should draw into the feild for the cleering of Dorsettshire, Wiltshire and Hamshire, and so point forward as farr as he could go towards London.[4]

In order to accomplish this he was assigned only 1,580 horse and 2,000 foot. Even then it soon became apparent that rather too many of them existed only on paper.[5] In mid-October he moved into Wiltshire, and some of his troops were engaged in besieging Wardour Castle when fresh orders arrived from Oxford. Sir William Ogle had surprised Winchester and it was considered imperative that he be supported. Hopton accordingly despatched some of his own dragoons under Major Philip Day and 600 foot under Sir Allen Apsley[6]. Then on 4 November he received an intelligence report that Sir William Waller had just moved out of Windsor with a new army of his own.

The formation of this new army had been delayed by political infighting and the Earl of Essex's dislike of Waller, but during September it began to come together. Like Hopton he was rather scraping the barrel and it comprised three distinct elements. The first was built up around a cadre of officers and men who had survived his earlier Western campaign. The second was regiments raised by the Southern Association, Kent, Sussex, Surrey, and Hampshire; and the third was a brigade of London regiments[7]. Waller was never particularly happy with this army. There were obvious difficulties in recruiting his own Western Association regiments in competition with Essex and Manchester, the Southern Association was extremely reluctant to acknowledge his authority and produce their quota of troops, while the London regiments simply wanted to go home.

Consequently he limited his initial objective to the capture of the great Royalist fortress of Basing House, rather than seeking out Hopton with an untried army. Even this proved too much for them. Advancing from Farnham on 7 November he had scarcely arrived before Basing than the Westminster Liberty Regiment mutinied. Two days later an attempted escalade foundered when the whole London Brigade followed suit. He had no alternative but to retreat without having accomplished anything.

Hopton meanwhile had received further reinforcements from both Reading and Bristol. On the 27th he moved forward with 5,000 men and the intention of fighting Waller. However, finding him unwilling to come out from under the protection of the guns of Farnham Castle, Hopton incontinently gave up, turned around again and sent his army into winter quarters. This lack of enterprise was then compounded by the decision to disperse the greater part of the army between Alresford, Alton and Petersfield.

Then Sir Edward Ford, who happened to be High Sheriff of Sussex as well as a Colonel of horse, suddenly decided to emulate Ogle by taking

Arundel. Accordingly he and Colonel Joseph Bampfield[8] moved forward from Petersfield, took the town but failed to capture the castle as well, until Hopton himself brought up reinforcements on the 2nd. It was a useful little victory, but it left the Royalists even more over-extended and was only inviting trouble.

The first setback occurred a few days later when Richard Norton's Horse beat up a Royalist outpost at Romsey, scattering Sir Humphrey Bennet's Horse and Sir William Courtney's Foot. Matters were not helped by the fact that both commanding officers were absent[9], but worse was to follow.

Waller had designs on Alton, held by a weak brigade of cavalry under the Earl of Crawford and a small infantry brigade led by Colonel Richard Bolle.[10] Hopton claimed afterwards to have been particularly concerned about the safety of this post, and to have repeatedly warned Crawford and Bolle to evacuate the town if Waller advanced from Farnham. In the event Waller managed to surprise them both. On the evening of the 12th he moved out of Farnham with 5,000 men. Crawford had vedettes out on the roads, but he avoided them by marching his men across country and attacked the town next day. At the last minute the Royalists realised what was happening and Crawford managed to break out with the cavalry.

Bolle was in an unenviable position for the town was unfortified, but he was determined to make a fight of it. At first he tried to fight Waller's men in the streets but, finding his barricades and stop positions successively outflanked, he retired uphill to the churchyard. Bolle's one hope was to hold on to it long enough for the raiders to run out of time. Waller on the other hand was quite rightly determined to destroy him, as Lieutenant Elias Archer recounts[11]:

> Now was the Enemy constrained to betake himselfe and all his forces to the Church, Churchyard, and one great work on the *North* side of the Church; all which they kept nere upon two houres very stoutly and (having made scaffolds in the Church to fire out at the windowes) fired very thick from every place till divers souldiers of our Regiment and the Red Regiment[12] who were gotten into the Towne, fired very thick upon the *South-east* of the Churchyard, and so forced them to forsake that part of the wall, leaving their musquets standing upright, the muzzels whereof appeared above the wall as if some of the men had still lyn there in Ambush and our men seeing no-body appeare to use those Musquets, concluded that the men were gone, and consulted among themselves to enter two or three files of Musquetiers, promising *Richard Guy*, one of my Captaines Serjeants (who was the first man that entred the Church-yard) to follow him if he would lead them: whereupon he advanced, and comming within the Church-yard doore, and seeing most of the Cavaliers firing at our

men, from the South and West part of the Church-yard, looked behind him for the men which promised to follow him, and there was only one Musquetier with him. Neverthelesse he flourishing his Sword, told them if they would come, the Church-yard was our owne; then *Symon Hutchinson*, one of Lieutenant Colonell *Willoughbies* Serjeants, forced the Musqueteers, and brought them up himselfe. Immediately upon this, one of the Serjeants of the Red Regiment (whose name I know not, and therefore cannot nominate him as his worth deserves) brought in another division of Musqueteers, who together with those which were there before, caused the Enemies Forces to betake themselves towards the Church for safeguard, but our men followed them so close with their Halberts, Swords, and Musquet-stocks that they drove them beyond the Church doore, and slew about 10, or 12, of them, and forced the rest to a very distracted retreat, which when the others saw who were in the greate worke on the North side of the Church-yard, they left the worke and came thinking to helpe their fellows, and comming in a disorderly manner to the South-west corner of the Church, with their Pikes in the Reare, (who furiously charged on, in as disorderly a manner as the rest led them) their front was forced backe upon their owne Pikes, which hurt and wounded many of the men, and brake the pikes in peeces. By this time the Church-yard was full of our men, laying about them stoutly, with Halberts, Swords, and Musquet-stocks, while some threw hand-granadoes in the Church windowes, others attempting to enter the Church being led on by Sergeant Major *Shambrooke*, (a man whose worth and valour Envy cannot staine) who in the entrance received a shot in the thigh (whereof he is very ill) Neverthelesse our men vigorously entred, and slew Colonel *Bowles* their chiefe Commander at the present, who not long before swore, *God damne his Soule* if he did not run his Sword through the heart of him, which first called for quarter.[13]

By the time it was all over Waller's army had killed about forty Royalists and taken 875 prisoners, including fifty officers for a reported loss of about ten of his own men killed. To make matters worse many of the prisoners promptly enlisted under Waller, as did about half of those captured at the retaking of Arundel which surrendered on 6 January. All in all Hopton lost close on 2,000 men through his failure to keep his army reasonably well concentrated and under control. It was probably just as well that the weather closed in at that point forcing operations to shut down for the winter.

During this period there were a number of changes in the respective orders of battle. Waller released his mutinous Londoners but in their place secured another brigade comprising the Yellow and White regiments, commanded by Sir John Wollston and Isaac Pennington respectively.[14] The small regiments commanded by Colonel James Carr and Edward Cooke were disbanded[15] but a strong Southern Association regiment turned up under Colonel Ralph Weldon. The greatest increase was in the cavalry. Cooke raised himself a regiment and the Southern Association grudgingly provided another from Kent under Sir Michael Livesey. The London Horse, temporarily re-assigned to Essex's army also returned under the command of George Thompson along with a very strong brigade of some 2,300 horse and 250 dragooners commanded by Sir William Balfour[16].

Hopton too was reinforced by a strong cavalry brigade and two more infantry 'brigades'[17], although it was a mark of the King's declining confidence in him that the contingent was commanded by the Lord General himself, Patrick Ruthven. This could have led to an awkward situation but Ruthven rather too tactfully used his gout as an excuse to leave Hopton in operational command, while he confined himself to giving advice as and when it was asked for.

As soon as the weather improved Waller began moving west in order to threaten Hopton. Accordingly he moved on Alresford, just five miles from Winchester. Realising he was about to be outflanked Hopton turned around and only just succeeded in reaching the town first. While he concentrated his army on Tichborne Down, between Alresford and Cheriton, the Parliamentarians closed up to a position in Lamborough Fields, a shallow valley to the east of Cheriton. The 28th saw only some desultory skirmishing, but once again the Royalist concentration may not have been quite as efficient as it should have been. Lisle's Brigade occupied some high ground by East Down, overlooking Waller's position, but the rest of the Royalists remained well back. On the morning of the 29th Hopton rode forward and discovered that Waller had moved forward during the night on to the ridge lying between the Down and his bivouac area in the Lambrough Fields. His right was already infiltrating Cheriton Wood and threatening Lisle, so Hopton pulled him back and brought the rest of the army forward to occupy the ridge on the north side of the Down. His own troops were deployed on the left with Ruthven's men on the right. The battlefield thus resembled a horseshoe placed upon its side with Cheriton Wood at the toe. Between the two ridges lay a broad depression traversed by three lanes running from north to south and one running east to west towards Cheriton. The latter at least was lined with hedgerows which were to have a significant effect on the conduct of the battle.[18]

Waller had thrown 1,000 musketeers and some horse into the wood and Hopton decided that his first priority was to throw them out again. Colonel Matthew Appleyard was therefore ordered to carry out that service with 1,000 commanded musketeers, divided into four battalions.

This was accomplished in fine style but then according to Hopton, Ruthven advised him to consolidate his position and stand on the defensive. Hopton, who had just proposed trying to roll up Waller's flank readily agreed with this advice instead. Unfortunately, or so his account claims, no sooner had he given the appropriate orders to the regiments on the left than he found Sir Henry Bard moving forward on the right.[19]

Hopton himself simply says that: 'the engagement was by the forwardness of some particular officers, without order'. While this was certainly a contributory factor there may also have been an element of confusion. From what followed it appears that the Royalists on this wing had already advanced to the hedges lining the Cheriton Lane. Presumably they had been conforming to the advance on the left and as Sir Walter Slingsby afterwards remarked Bard had simply led 'on his Regiment further than hee had orders for.'[20] Be that as it may his little brigade was on its own and Sir Arthur Hesilrige, commanding the Parliamentarian horse on that wing, came down upon them like the proverbial wolf on the fold. Within a very short period the brigade was completely destroyed.

After this the battle became more general. Balfour attacked the Royalist left with both infantry and cavalry. Colonel Walter Slingsby was here, commanding a regiment of foot[21]:

> . . . there the Enemy horse was repulssed with losse. They immediatly try'd the second charge in which Captain Herbert of my Lord Hoptons Regiment was slaine, with a fresh body and were againe repulssed, and soe againe the third time, the foote keeping theire ground in a close body, not firing till within two pikes length, and then three rankes att a time, after turning up the butt end of theire musketts, charging theire pikes, and standing close, preserv'd themselues, and slew many of the enemy.

In an effort to relieve the pressure Ruthven then ordered Hopton to attack with his cavalry on the left. The ground here was more suitable for a cavalry action than the right, where the Queen's Regiment of Horse had retreated after just one 'unhandsome charge'. Sir Edward Stawell's Brigade therefore moved forward at about 2pm.[22] Unfortunately, according to Slingsby, the Cavaliers had to deploy one regiment at a time by way of a lane's end. This was presumably the point at which Dark Lane, the most westerly of the three, crossed Cheriton Lane.[23] Nevertheless both Smyth's and Stuart's brigades were committed shortly afterwards. Casualties were high, particularly amongst the officers, and by mid-afternoon it was becoming all too plain that the Royalists were losing the fight. In the centre the battle degenerated into a sustained firefight amongst the hedgerows on either side of Cheriton Lane. The Royalist infantry were still holding their own, but once the horse gave way there would be nothing to prevent the Parliamentarians from rolling up the line.

Ruthven therefore took the decision to concede defeat and stage a phased withdrawal. Sending away his guns he drew the infantry back to Tichborne Down, while Hopton held the lane end with 300 troopers to cover the retirement of the cavalry. Waller's men had been sufficiently well battered to let them go, and at a conference outside Alresford, Ruthven and Hopton agreed to withdraw northwards, rather than fall back on Winchester.

In the early hours of the following morning they reached Basing House, rested there for a day and then retreated to Reading. Encouraged by this success the Committee of Both Kingdoms ordered Essex and Manchester to rendezvous at Aylesbury on 19 April with a view to mounting an offensive against Oxford. Waller in the meantime was to retain his independent command and move westwards against Prince Maurice. To the Committee's chagrin none of this came to pass. Essex petulantly refused to cooperate with anyone. Manchester was then too preoccupied with events in Lincolnshire and the awful prospect of Rupert advancing eastwards from Shrewsbury, and Waller, weakened by the departure of his Londoners, simply retired to Farnham. Only Balfour showed any enterprise by raiding Salisbury.

In marked contrast it quickly became apparent that the defeat at Cheriton had concentrated the Cavaliers' minds wonderfully. On 10 April the King assembled his forces on Aldbourne Chase, and next day a Council of War was held at Marlborough in order to decide what to do with them. The fifteen infantry regiments present only mustered some 5,000 foot and, as most of them had come from Reading, Ruthven urged that it should be abandoned. Although all of the officers present supported Ruthven the King deferred a decision until after Rupert had been consulted. He in turn advocated holding on to Reading and the other outer ring fortresses and relying on a central cavalry reserve to sustain them.

Unfortunately it soon became clear that the required number of cavalry could not be found and the King agreed to abandon Reading after all. This was undoubtedly the right decision for, as the events of the previous year had shown, the town was actually quite untenable. Since it lay on the south side of the Thames and was some distance away from the river itself, it was difficult for any force based on Oxford to relieve it. As it was, the decision came none too soon.

Reading was abandoned on 18 May. In the meantime Essex had shifted forward to Henley-on-Thames on the 17th, while Waller moved up to Bagshot and exchanged his Londoners for a fresh brigade led by Sir James Harrington[24]. A week later Abingdon too was abandoned by the

Royalists, and on the 24th Sir Edward Massey took Malmesbury. With the King's Road again under threat Hopton was sent back to Bristol, and on the 27th a Council of War took the first tentative steps towards abandoning Oxford itself. Recognising that the King's army was too weak to take on Essex and Waller at the same time, Ruthven recommended that the Cavaliers should take up a position to the north of the city. There it was optimistically hoped they would be in a good position to fall upon one or other of the Parliamentarian armies should they separate. If the worst came to the worst they still had a line of retreat open to Worcester.

Suddenly it became necessary to do just that. For a time the Royalists managed to hold the river crossings around Oxford, but then on the 3rd, with Essex and Waller closing in, the King took the decision to split his forces. Taking 5,000 horse and just 2,500 musketeers he abandoned the rest of his foot and all of his heavy guns in Oxford. By the night of 4 June he was in the Cotswolds at Bourton-on-the-Water, and two days later threw himself into Worcester. He was by no means out of danger there. Massey surprised Tewksbury on the 5th, while Essex and Waller had ignored Oxford and were on his trail. Then on the 6th Essex to all appearances took leave of his senses. In a meeting at Chipping Norton he ordered Waller to deal with the King while he himself marched off into the West Country, in order to relieve Lyme.

The decision was quite extraordinary. Essex's primary and indeed only objective should have been the pursuit, defeat and capture of the King. Once that was accomplished any success which Prince Maurice might have against Lyme would be meaningless. Nevertheless, the situation remained critical. On the 10th Waller marched into Evesham. This was getting too close for comfort, and on the 12th the King left Worcester and retired up the west bank of the Severn to Bewdley. There he took up his headquarters at Tickenhill Manor but quartered his horse up river towards Bridgenorth in order to create the impression that a further retreat was determined upon to Shrewsbury. Waller, at Stourbridge, congratulated himself that he was nearer to the town and could throw himself across the King's path, but the Royalists were about to outmanoeuvre him spectacularly.

Notwithstanding Essex's departure the King was still in no condition to fight a battle. In essence he needed to add Prince Rupert's forces to his own in order to be able to form a viable field army. The obvious way to accomplish this was to appoint a rendezvous at Shrewsbury. However to do so would mean abandoning York to its fate, something which he was very reluctant to do. Instead, although he sent a 'peremptory' summons to Rupert on the 14th, he also allowed him the discretion to relieve York first. In so doing the King was only too well aware that in the meantime he might be brought to battle, or at the very least forced so far northwards as to place Oxford out of his reach. The Council of War debated the question for two days before recommending a radical course of action. There were still a fair number of troops left in Oxford, so no doubt at Ruthven's urging it was resolved to double back there, pick them up and then meet with Rupert not at Shrewsbury but at Worcester.

Boats were summoned from Bridgenorth and Worcester to carry the infantry downstream, and by the evening of the 15th the Royalists were safely back in Worcester. On the 16th they passed through Evesham, picking up 1,000 pairs of stockings *en route*, and by the morning of the 17th were outside Chipping Camden. Waller took some time to react to this unexpected development and was trailing a day's march behind. By the night of the 18th the King was at Witney, and next morning there was a happy rendezvous with the infantry who had been left behind in Oxford. These included all the pikemen and the colours. According to Symonds this gave the King a total of 3,910 foot 'besides officers'[25] Just as importantly a train of artillery also arrived comprising ten brass guns of various calibres.[26] After a second muster near Woodstock on the 21st the King moved on to Buckingham.

The Committee of Both Kingdoms meanwhile was trying desperately to re-assert some control over its wayward armies. Essex was already out of reach, and to their horror they discovered that Waller was planning to follow him.[27] Instead, fearing that the move to Buckingham presaged a descent on the undefended Eastern Association, they ordered him to resume his pursuit of the King. By the 28th he was at Hanwell near Banbury.

Meanwhile the King was making his way back to the Severn valley in the hope of a rendezvous with Rupert. At Brackley he learned Waller was close at hand. Both armies were heading for Banbury at this point, but by mid-morning Waller was established in a strong defensive position at the foot of Crouch Hill, a mile to the south-west of it. The King's forces had a look at it, decided that it was too strong to attack, and early next morning began moving northwards to Daventry. It was given out that they were looking for a better spot at which to bring Waller to battle. In reality it is more likely that their real priority was once again to clear their line of communication to Worcester and Rupert's forces.

Waller soon set off after him, marching up the west bank of the Cherwell along the road to Southam. On the high ground of Bourton Hill, just three miles north of Banbury, he halted to observe the King's army. It was immediately apparent that he had an opportunity to catch the Royalists at a disadvantage. In order to reach Daventry it was necessary for them to cross the Cherwell by Hays Bridge, about a mile north-east of the village of Cropredy. However a party of Royalist dragoons sent to secure the bridge sent back word that some Parliamentarian cavalry were approaching from the north.

Consequently there was something of a hurry to get across it, first the advance guard, commanded by Ruthven, then the main body under the King himself. Unfortunately in the confusion the rearguard, comprising three cavalry brigades commanded by Lord Wilmot, and 1,000 muske-teers under Colonel Anthony Thelwall, was left behind. Waller saw his opportunity. His Lieutenant General, John Middleton, was sent to seize Cropredy Bridge with nine companies of foot and two regiments of horse[28] while he himself moved across a ford at Slat Mill, a mile to the south. Initially all went well. Middleton crossed the bridge, brushing aside the Royalist dragoons posted to guard it and immediately pushed north-eastwards to Hays Bridge. He might have captured it too if the Cavaliers had not barricaded it with an overturned wagon. Waller however was less fortunate.

No sooner had be crossed the ford than he was charged by Northampton's Brigade[29] and tumbled straight back again. At pretty much the same time the Earl of Cleveland drove Middleton away from Hays Bridge[30]:

> . . . hee presently drew vp his Bragade (Consisting of his owne, his sonne the Lord Wentworths, Colonell Richard Neuills, S[r] William Botelers, & S[r] William Clerkes Regiments of Horse) to a riseing ground faceing that passe, where vnderstanding by Colonel Neuill that he steed too neere a Hedge where the Rebells might place some ffoote hee wheeled towards the right hand & tooke more ground, there hee perceived a great Body of the Rebells Horse drawen vp ready to have fallen on his Reare Wherevpon (not havinge tyme to expect either word or Orders from the Lord Willmot Lieutenant Generall of the Horse) hee gave his owne word (Hand & Sword) & presently advan-ceing that Body of the Rebells rann . . .

He then fell back to a position near Wardington, just to the south of Hays Bridge. Middleton turned upon him there, but with the pressure on the bridge lifted Lord Bernard Stuart led the Lifeguard of Horse across to Cleveland's assistance. A running battle then developed as Middleton fell back on Cropredy. Cleveland put in a second charge and this time Wilmot came up from the south to complete the Parliamentarians' discomfiture. Wilmot himself was wounded and briefly captured in the confusion, but the Royalists pushed on as far as Cropredy Bridge. There they quite liter-ally stumbled on part of Waller's artillery train which had already been pushed across. Some fourteen guns and their commander, Colonel James Wemyss, were captured.

Dismayed, Waller fell back on the Bourton Hill position, leaving some foot and dragoons to hold the crossings. It was only 3pm on a summer's day and the Royalists tried to press their advantage by keeping up the pressure. The bridge at Cropredy was stoutly held by the Tower Hamlets

Regiment[31] and no progress was made there. However towards the south at what Symonds calls the 'farthest pass' one of the Royalist infantry brigades captured Slat Mill and got across the ford. In the process a soldier of Sir James Pennyman's Foot took a colour[32], but Waller's heavier guns emplaced on the hill prevented any further exploitation of this success.

Next day both armies remained in position, facing each other across the river, but on the evening of the 30th the King received word that another London Brigade was at Buckingham. Moreover he was running short of provisions.[33] Next morning the Royalists marched off and surprised Waller by heading west and reaching Evesham by the night of 3 July. There was still no sign of Prince Rupert, but although Waller had linked up with Browne at Towcester on the 2nd his army was on the point of mutiny. Fondly imagining that the King still intended to retire northwards, he and Hesilrige set off for Northampton on the 4th, but as soon as they reached the town their army fell apart. His London Brigade simply packed up and went home. Browne's men followed suit, wounding their commander in a scuffle when he had the temerity to order them against Greenland House, near Henley. It was the end too for Waller. Cropredy had been an indecisive affair, an action rather than a full scale battle but as Clarendon afterwards wrote 'it even broke the heart of his army.'

NOTES

1. Young, P. *Marston Moor 1644* p216
2. The Duchess states: 'That night my Lord remained in York; and having nothing left in his power to do his Majesty any further service in that kind; for he had neither ammunition, nor money to raise more forces, to keep either York, or any other towns that were yet in his Majesty's devotion, well knowing that those which were left could not hold out long, and being also loath to have aspersions cast upon him, that he did sell them to the enemy, in case he could not keep them, he took a resolution, and that justly and honourably, to forsake the kingdom:'
3. *Rupert Diary* in Young *op.cit.* p214
4. Hopton, *Bellum Civile* p61
5. The army assigned to Hopton is set out in a memorandum: BM Harl.MS.6804,f.224 item 171 summarised in Adair, J. *Cheriton 1644* pp28-29 :

Horse		Foot	
Lord Hopton's (inc dragoons)	250	Lord Hopton's Regt.	300
E. of Crawford's (inc dragoons)	250	Prince Maurice's Regt.	250
Sir Geo. Vaughan's Regt.	60	Col. Bernard Astley}	
Sir Nicholas Crisp's Regt.	100	Col. Conyers Griffin} (total)	400
Sir Edward Dering's Regt.	120	Sir Allen Apsley's Regt.	300
Sir Edward Ford's Regt.	260	Dorset & Somerset Coys.*	300
Sir James Hamilton's Regt.	50	* evidently new recruits – and	
Sir Horatio Carey's Regt.	100	presumably conscripts as yet	
Col. Richard Spencer's Regt.	60	unassigned to regiments.	
Col. Thomas Covert's Regt.	80		

Marquess of Hertford's Regt.   100
Sir Edward Stawell's Regt.   150

In addition Hopton was also assigned the regiment of foot which Colonel Henry Washington had just been commissioned to raise, and fifty foot raised by Sir James Hamilton. In the event neither unit materialised. On the other hand he was shortly joined by two regiments from Munster commanded by Sir Charles Vavasour and Sir John Paulet which added another 800-900 veterans.

6. Presumably his own regiment and the 300 men of the Dorset and Somerset companies.

7. Waller's Army can be reconstructed from a variety of sources. Those units listed below are the ones originally assigned to him although some of them took their time in arriving and some substantial alterations took place during the campaign.

Western Association

Sir Arthur Hesilrige's Horse	Col. James Carr's Foot
Col. Jonas Van Druschke's Horse	Col. Edward Cooke's Foot
Sir William Waller's Horse	Col. Edward Harley's Foot
	Sir Arthur Hesilrige's Foot
Sir William Waller's Dragoons	Col. Alexander Popham's Foot
	Col. Andrew Potley's Foot
	Sir William Waller's Foot

Commissions to raise regiments of horse were also issued to William Carr and Francis Dowett, but neither unit was completed. James Carr's Foot was poorly recruited and disbanded in March 1644, and Edward Cooke's shortly afterwards.

Southern Association

Col. Richard Norton's Horse	Col. Samuel Jones' Foot
Major Anthony Weldon's Horse	Sir William Springate's Foot

London Regiments

Sir Richard Turner's Horse*	Westminster Liberty Regt. (Harrington)
	Green Auxiliaries (Whichcott)
	Yellow Auxiliaries (Tichborne)

* re-assigned to Essex's army, but returned in January under Colonel George Thompson.

8. According to Bampfield (in Adair *op.cit.* p56) he had brought three troops of horse and an infantry brigade from Exeter comprising his own, Sir John Berkeley's, Sir John Ackland's, Col. James Strangeways' and Sir William Courtney's regiments. Not all of these units took part in the Arundel expedition.

9. Bennet's duties as High Sheriff of Hampshire had called him away from his military ones. Courtney ('not he of Devonshire but another of the same name' according to Bampfield) then followed him to Winchester to complain of his regiment's indiscipline.

10. This brigade was composed of detachments drawn out of the various Oxford Army regiments quartered at Reading. Originally it had been commanded by Sir Jacob Astley but he returned to Oxford early in December.

11. *A True Relation of the trained bands of Westminster . . .* BM 101 b.64 in Adair *op.cit.*p68-69

12. The Westminster Liberty Regiment.

13. The story that Bolle was shot in the pulpit is probably apocryphal.

14. The London 'Militia' comprised six regiments of City Trained Bands, each distinguished by its colours, viz: the Red, White, Yellow, Blue, Green and

Orange ; three Suburban Trained Bands, viz: the (Red) Westminster Liberty, Southwark and Tower Hamlets regiments. All of these were manned on a part-time basis, but in addition a number of so-called Auxiliary Regiments were raised. These were to all intents and purposes regulars, although they could not be employed outside London without the express consent of the London Militia Committee. Confusingly they were also identified as the Red, White, Yellow, Blue, Green (Cripplegate) and Orange Regiments. There also three Suburban Auxiliary Regiments: the (Blue) Westminster, Southwark and (Yellow) Tower Hamlets. The best guide to the London Militia is *London and Liberty* by Dr Keith Roberts (Partizan 1987).

15. L. Spring *Officers & Regiments of Waller's Army* (Partizan 1989)
16. This comprised: Sir William Balfour's Horse

Col. John Dalbier's Horse
Col. John Meldrum's* Horse
Col. John Middleton's Horse

* not to be confused with *Sir* John Meldrum

The dragooners were found by mounting Colonel Adam Cunningham's Regiment of Foot. This was 233 strong in April 1644.

17. Lisle's Brigade came from Reading and was made up of detachments drawn from the regiments quartered there. Symonds *Notebook* lists the following units at Reading in April 1644. All of them were then very weak so it is unlikely that they contributed more than fifty men apiece to Lisle's Brigade – Blackwell's and Eure's may not have been represented at all. This would produce a total of about 450-500 men for this brigade.

Sir Jacob Astley	(155)
Sir Thomas Blackwell	(61)
Col. William Eure	(64)
Sir Theophilus Gilby	(282)
Col. George Lisle	(203)
Col. Charles Lloyd	(324)
Col. John Owen	(111)
Sir James Pennyman	(393)
Col. John Stradling	(264)
Col. Anthony Thelwell	(134)
Sir Henry Vaughan	(207)

Bard's Brigade came from Oxford and comprised just two, or possibly three regiments: his own Greycoats (formerly Thomas Pinchbeck's) and Colonel Charles Gerard's Bluecoats. This is borne out by a Parliamentarian scout report of 13 March (Samuel Luke *Journal* p264) which stated that 'the blew and grey regiments marcht forth . . . as some say to Basing House' It is just possible however that Lord Percy's Regiment may also have gone since it and Pinchbeck's/Bard's had always been brigaded together.

18. Dr John Adair proposes another site, farther to the south (*Cheriton 1644*) but as Young and Holmes point out (*The English Civil War* p167) this would involve both armies deploying *across* the ridges rather than standing on top of them.
19. Hopton, *Bellum Civile* p82
20. Slingsby in Hopton *op.cit.* pp101-2. Bard presumably took the rest of his brigade with him. The fact that Gerard's could only muster 150 officers and men on 10 April and that Bard's and Percy's formed a single battalion (Symonds Journal) would certainly bear this out.
21. *ibid.* This was the method which Richard Elton describes being taught to the *Society of the Artillery Garden* – see chap. I

22. The Royalist cavalry comprised four brigades. The figures in brackets refer to the number of cornets:

Sir John Smyth's Brigade	Sir Humphrey Bennet	(2)
	Col. Andrew Lindsay*	(2)
	Sir John Smyth	(1)
	Sir George Vaughan	(2)
	Sir Edward Waldgrave	(3)
	* Formerly the Earl of Crawford's	
Sir Edward Stawell's Brigade	Sir Allen Apsley	(1)
	Col. George Gunter	(1)
	Marquis of Hertford	(1)
	Lord Hopton	(4)
	Col. Edmund Pierce	(2)
	Sir Edward Stawell	(2)
Lord John Stuart's Brigade	Sir William Boteler	(5)
	Sir William Clerke	(3)
	Sir Nicholas Crispe	(1)
	Col. Dutton Fleetwood	(2)
	Sir Edward Ford	(3)
	Lord John Stuart	(3)
Col. Thomas Howard's Brigade	Col. Thomas Howard	
	Lord General	
	Col. Richard Manning	
	Prince Maurice (Major Robert Legge)	
	Col. Richard Neville	
	Queen's Regiment (M. Raoul Fleury)	

23. Adair wrongly identifies the lane as Bramdean Lane, which actually lies under Cheriton Wood on the eastern side of the battlefield. The unsatisfactory nature of this can be seen in his placing of the cavalry action in the centre of the two armies rather than on the open western flank.

24. Southwark Auxiliaries (Col. James Houblon)
Tower Hamlets (Col. Francis Zachary)
Westminster Auxiliaries (Col. James Prince)

25. Symonds *Diary* p11. He reckoned the officers to account for another 1,000. This must include sergeants and perhaps drummers as well, but it is still a useful pointer to how much under strength the infantry must have been.

26. Roy, I *Royalist Ordnance Papers* pp353-4, 504

27. Waller and Hesilrige had originally proclaimed their intention of following the King wherever he went, but he evidently had discretionary instructions to follow Essex if the opportunity arose.

28. Five companies of Waller's Regiment of foot and four of Samuel Jones'. Sir Arthur Hesilrige's Horse and Jonas Van Druschke's.

29. Apart from the unbrigaded Lifeguard, those Royalist cavalrymen actually engaged at Cropredy were organised as follows (at least one other brigade remained north of Hays bridge):

Lord Wilmot's Brigade:	Col. Gerard Croker	(2)
	Col. Thomas Howard	(8)
	Lord General	
	Prince Maurice	
Earl of Northampton's Brigade:	Earl of Northampton	(4)
	Lord Percy	(7)
	Col. Thomas Weston	(2)
	Lord Wilmot	

Earl of Cleveland's Brigade: Sir William Boteler   (5)
                                    Sir William Clerke   (3)
                                    E. of Cleveland   (3)
                                    Col. Richard Neville   (5)
                                    Prince of Wales (Lord Wentworth)

30. Walker, Sir Edward *Historical Discourses* Vol.I p33
31. According to Thomas Ellis, one of the Tower Hamlets officers, they also succeeded in recovering three of the guns.
32. Symonds *Diary* p13. One of Appleyard's Ensigns also took a Dragoon guidon at the first pass, i.e. Hays Bridge.
33. Walker *op.cit* pp34-5

CHAPTER XIV

Westward Ho!:
Lostwithiel and II Newbury

While Waller was unhappily trying to hold his disintegrating army together, the King's one was resting at Evesham and debating what to do next. Although various options were considered, only two appeared viable. The King was particularly concerned about the situation in the west since the Queen, who was pregnant, had been evacuated to Exeter during the crisis in April. However, if Waller looked like following Essex into the West Country, the alternative was to move northwards and join with Prince Rupert.[1] News had been received from Newark on the 5th reporting a Royalist victory in the north, but as Walker sadly recalled: 'this good news held not consistent.' Instead it soon became clear that Waller's army need no longer be taken into consideration. On the 12th the decision was therefore taken to march into the West Country.

Essex meanwhile was behaving rather oddly. His first intention was to relieve the siege of Lyme and in this he succeeded well enough. Colonel William Ashburnham evacuated Weymouth and retired into Portland Castle on 14 June. Two days later Prince Maurice raised his siege of Lyme.[2] Not unnaturally it was then expected that the Parliamentarians would themselves lay siege to Exeter. The Queen was therefore hustled out of the way, first to Pendennis Castle and then off to France. However in a conference at Weymouth the Parliamentarians resolved on a quite different course of action, as Essex reported to his bemused political masters[3]:

I am assured by the Lord High Admiral[4] that the Western Counties will flock in from all parts to our body, in case I advance with my army further West. Plymouth men will take the field with two thousand five hundred horse and foot, and fall upon the rear of the enemy whilst we charge them in the front. Lastly it is the unanimous judgement of the joint council of war, both by sea and land (called upon this occasion by the Lord High Admiral and Myself), that it will be exceedingly prejudicial for me to retreat, or once make a stand; and that my advance will (in all human reason, by the blessing of Heaven) be effectual for the preserving of Lyme, breaking the Enemies Association and reducing the west . . .

Having taken this decision he left the Yellow Auxiliaries as a garrison for Weymouth and marched for Plymouth. Once again the Royalists abandoned their operations and retired to Crediton on 18 July. Thus far Essex had on the face of it achieved all he had set out to do in the west. Significantly however he had failed to make any effort to bring Prince Maurice's army to battle. On the contrary, he now decided to continue ignoring it and invade Cornwall instead.

This was in large part at the urging of Lord Robartes, who assured him that the population was ripe for revolt. Moreover it was known that the King was dependent upon exports of Cornish tin to pay for the guns and ammunition being shipped in through Dartmouth. Unfortunately this was hardly the time for it. On 26 July, just as Essex was crossing the Tamar at Horsebridge, the King reached Exeter. By 2 August he was at Launceston, and Essex for the first time realised his danger. He still had some 10,000 men[5] but the King, strengthened by Maurice's army, had 9,000 foot and 6,000 horse.[6] Unwilling to take on such odds Essex headed south to Lostwithiel, vainly hoping to regain contact with the fleet.

The town lies at the head of the Fowey estuary and the Earl decided to place the greater part of his forces in a defensive position anchored on Beacon Hill to the east of Lostwithiel and Restormel Castle, a mile to the north. For their part the Royalists took their time. There had been something of a contretemps on the 8th when Lord Wilmot was arrested and replaced as commander of the King's cavalry by Goring[7], but essentially by this stage in the proceedings their concentration was complete. Then, on the 11th Sir Richard Grenville drove Essex's cavalry out of Bodmin, pushed on to Respryn Bridge and thereby secured direct communication with the King.

The next step was to push a detachment down the east bank of the river. This task was allotted to Goring and Sir Jacob Astley. On the 13th Lloyd's Regiment was posted at St. Veep, covering the ferry at Golant. Next day Captain Richard Page of Pennyman's Regiment occupied Hall House and a fort at Polruan with 200 men and three guns. These modest detachments were sufficient to ensure that Essex would be unable to escape by ferrying his army across the estuary from Fowey itself. In the meantime the Earl sat tight waiting for either the navy or for Waller to turn up. He was to be disappointed in both. With the wind blowing strongly up the Channel, the Earl of Warwick was unable to beat down to his assistance. Waller on the other hand was still sitting idle at Farnham. Only John Middleton with 2,000 horse and dragoons tried to break through to Essex's assistance, but on the 14th he was defeated at Bridgewater by Sir Francis Doddington and forced to retire to Sherborne.

It was not until the 21st that the Royalists decided to advance, but now they did so in overwhelming force. Early in the morning they moved forward in three columns. First Sir Richard Grenville took Restormel Castle without any opposition after Colonel John Weare's Regiment abandoned it. By so doing he turned the Parliamentarian flank, and with Maurice and Ruthven pushing eastwards from Boconnoc, the Beacon Hill position was abandoned as well. Thereafter resistance stiffened, but although Essex still held Lostwithiel at nightfall, his position was becoming increasingly untenable. Nevertheless the Royalists continued to proceed slowly and methodically. There can be little doubt that this very professional operation was being masterminded by Ruthven and he was leaving nothing to chance. With their forces spread so widely it was essential that their movements should be properly co-ordinated and this all took time.

The next phase was scheduled to begin on the 24th. Maurice and Grenville were to attack at dawn but for 'some Reasons' it never got off the ground. Instead, by way of a diversion, it was proposed that Goring should be sent with all but 500 of the horse, and 1,500 foot under Sir Thomas Basset to St Blazey. There they would be well placed to prevent any last minute breakout to the west. The King however insisted that the main assault should go ahead first, but next morning the Parliamentarians were observed to be waiting for them. A second postponement then took place while Goring and Basset were sent off, but as it happened this was all to the good. Goring not only established himself at St Blazey and thus reduced the grazing area available for Essex's cavalry, but also occupied Par, at the head of St Austell Bay.

The Earl's position was steadily becoming more untenable. Lack of forage would soon destroy his cavalry and realisation of this at last forced him to move. A more enterprising commander might have tried to fight. The Royalist cordon was certainly becoming over-extended, and in particular the absence of any substantial body of cavalry north of Lostwithiel placed the Cavaliers at something of a disadvantage. Instead, Essex decided that he was already beaten. He decided to fall back on Fowey in the hope that his men could be evacuated by sea, if the weather permitted Warwick to bring the fleet in. Obviously it would be impossible to lift the cavalry out and so Sir William Balfour was ordered to try and make for Plymouth.

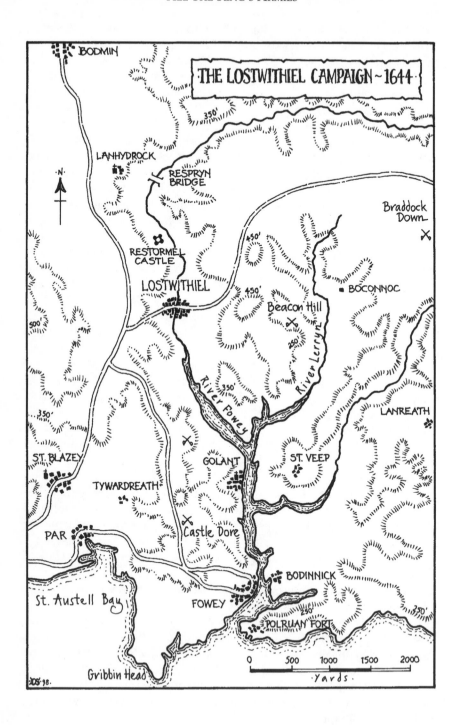

THE LOSTWITHIEL CAMPAIGN ~ 1644

BODMIN

LANHYDROCK

RESPRYN BRIDGE

Braddock Down

RESTORMEL CASTLE

LOSTWITHIEL

350'

450'

450'

Beacon Hill

BOCONNOC

250'

River Lerryn

River Fowey

LANREATH

500'

350'

ST. BLAZEY

GOLANT

ST. VEEP

TYWARDREATH

Castle Dore

PAR

BODINNICK

St. Austell Bay

FOWEY

250'

POLRUAN FORT

350'

Gribbin Head

0   500   1000   1500   2000

Yards

Despite the Royalists being alerted by two deserters, the first phase of the operation was carried out remarkably successfully. At about 3am on the morning of the 31st August Balfour led most of the cavalry[8] up the Liskeard Road. The Royalists were standing to arms in anticipation, but as luck would have it the road served as the operational boundary between Ruthven's Oxford Army and Prince Maurice's Western Army. It was therefore guarded only by fifty musketeers dug in around a cottage and they were sufficiently intimidated by the size of Balfour's force to let it pass by without firing a shot.

Consequently it was not until daylight that the Earl of Cleveland set off after them with all the available cavalry. As these at first amounted to only 250 men there was little he could do except to hang on Balfour's rear, picking up stragglers. Then 100 men of Sir Thomas Aston's Horse came up and after them 150 of Sir Richard Grenville's Cornish Horse. Thus augmented the Cavaliers became bolder and there was some wary skirmishing on Coryton Down which gradually escalated as both parties approached Saltash. Major James Dundas of Cleveland's Regiment was wounded, captured and then rescued again when elements of Sir Humphrey Bennet's little brigade came up. Finally some of Essex's Dragoons, commanded by Captain Abercrombie, barricaded themselves into a house in the village of Lee and thus brought the pursuit to a halt. Eventually an unknown lieutenant turned up with a gallant little detachment of the King's Lifeguard of Foot and stormed it, but by then Balfour had safely reached Saltash and next day was ferried across to Plymouth.[9] His breakout had been accomplished for the loss of less than 100 officers and men, but the infantry were not to be so lucky.

At daylight it became apparent that the Parliamentarians were evacuating Lostwithiel. An immediate attack was clearly called for, and while a hasty concentration took place, a party was sent down to seize the bridge. Essex had ordered its destruction but the Royalists pushed straight into the town before it could be accomplished. Sir Richard Grenville's forces then came up and a running battle followed.

The Cornish regiments initially took the lead and made good progress until they came up against some stiff resistance on some rising ground lined with hedges. This was in the region of Trebathevy Farm and Walker admits that the Cornish made a 'very hasty and unhandsome Retreat'. Grenvile's men fell back some distance before rallying on Lieutenant Colonel William Leighton's battalion[10]. The King thereupon ordered Major Brett, commanding the Queen's Troop of his Lifeguard of Horse, to put in a charge. This he did, but he was unsupported by the foot and had to fall back again. By way of a consolation Charles knighted him on the spot, but any further attempt to force the position had to await the arrival of more infantry.

Then at about 2pm Sir Thomas Basset, who had very properly been

181

marching towards the sound of the guns, fell on the Parliamentarian left flank. The rest of Ruthven's infantry had come up by this time and he appears to have launched them forward in two columns. One was headed by Leighton's battalion, belonging to the 1st (Oxford) Brigade, and the other by Colonel Matthew Appleyard of the 3rd Brigade. Presumably the 2nd (Reading) Brigade was held in reserve. Essex attempted a rather feeble counter-attack with his own regiment of foot and three troops of Plymouth Horse commanded by Captain Reynolds. At this point the Royalists' cavalry support was still limited to the King's Lifeguard, but at about 4pm Goring turned up. The King directed him to go off in pursuit of Balfour, but it took some time for him to concentrate his scattered forces. In the meantime another Parliamentarian counter-attack then came in at 6pm and drove the Royalist infantry back across two enclosures. It took an hour's heavy fighting and the intervention of the Earl of Northampton's Horse to stabilise the situation, but by the end of it the Parliamentarians were forced back to the ruins of Castle Dore. In the course of this action there was a curious incident involving Colonel John Weare's Foot. According to Walker they marched down towards the waterside; 'either resolving to have fallen on our Flank, or securing their own Passage.' If it was a breakout attempt it failed miserably, for when the main body of Essex's foot fell back to Castle Dore they were left dangerously exposed. Up came some Royalist foot and after a feeble resistance they broke and fled.

Shortly afterwards the approach of darkness led to the battle shutting down for the night, but the Royalists and indeed the King himself remained in the field and in contact. There seems to have been a feeling in the Royalist camp by this time that their victory was assured, and at a Council of War next morning it was agreed that it should not be jeopardised by any rash moves. In fact it was already all over. Essex had inexcusably compounded his miserable performance by deserting his army and fleeing in a fishing boat.

His Major General, Philip Skippon, was left behind to ask for terms and the army was extremely lucky to be allowed to march out on the 2nd after laying down its arms. The officers kept their swords – those commanding the Plymouth Horse were also allowed to keep their hatbands and pistols – and the regiments kept their colours and one carriage apiece. That was all they were allowed. Forty-two cannon, a mortar and upwards of 5,000 muskets and pikes were handed over.

Worse was to come for, as the defeated army marched through Lostwithiel in pouring rain, the locals set upon the soldiers. They claimed to be recovering their own property, which had been plundered from them earlier, but it soon degenerated into a vicious free-for-all as the victorious Royalists joined in. After this initial bout of unpleasantness a party of Royalist horse saw the defeated Parliamentarians safely to Poole and Southampton. With hindsight some Cavaliers argued that they could simply have taken the whole lot prisoner, but in fact this march destroyed the army just as effectively. Ill-provided with food, stripped of their clothing and abandoned by their officers, the soldiers fell away in their hundreds, succumbing to exposure, want and disease, or simply deserting. It seems unlikely that much more than 3,000 eventually straggled into Southampton. Of the 1,000 foot drawn out of Plymouth only 200 led by Lieutenant Colonel Martin returned.[11]

Plymouth had great need of them. On the 3rd Sir Richard Grenville was sent with his Cornish Army to join Goring outside the town. On the way he paused to seize Saltash. This was unfortunate because Balfour chose this moment to break out and Goring blamed his lack of infantry support for the failure to stop him. Thereafter Balfour's men were followed rather than harried out of the west and it is hard to escape the feeling that they would not have got off so easily had Wilmot been left in command.

The King meanwhile had halted at Tavistock for nearly a week in order to concentrate and re-equip his forces. This was certainly necessary, but on 10 September the combined Royalist armies finally sat down before Plymouth. The garrison was still badly undermanned and Walker notes that 'they were fain for want of Foot, to arm the Seamen, whom we distinguished by their Colours.'[12] Nevertheless no one felt up to storming the town. A formal summons was sent in on the 11th, but receiving a defiant answer next day the King incontinently gave up the enterprise. Leaving Sir Richard Grenville to watch the town with just 500 foot and 300 horse, he retired again to Tavistock with the rest on the 14th. From there they marched eastwards and an important Council of War was held at Exeter. There were understandable concerns in London that he might now march upon the capital, but his army was considered too weakened to undertake such a daring operation so late in the year. A number of garrisons were settled and minor forces appointed to block up Parliamentarian ones. Indeed the King's only concern at this point was to consolidate his gains and return to Oxford. On 30 September he moved out of Chard and at South Perrot met with Prince Rupert for the first time in several months. There the full extent of the disaster in the north was at last revealed to him.

Initially Rupert had succeeded in bringing away a considerable part of his army from York, but most of them had since been lost in a scrappy series of affairs. The few remaining foot were now in Chester and Shrewsbury and sufficient only to reinforce those garrisons. However Sir Marmaduke Langdale had a brigade of some 2,000 horse and it was reckoned that Charles Gerard could bring as many foot out of Wales.

Some swift marching at this point could have achieved a formidable concentration of forces, but Rupert had to return to Bristol and it was not until 8 October, that the King's forces moved eastwards from Blandford.

Even then his primary purpose was the relief of Portland Castle, which called for the diversion of 500 horse under the Earl of Cleveland and 600 foot under Sir Bernard Astley.

While this was happening Parliament had not been idle. The first of Essex's foot stumbled into Southampton on 14 September and immediate steps were taken to reclothe and re-equip them. Recognising that neither they nor Waller's equally demoralised forces were capable of stemming a Royalist offensive, Parliament also summoned the Earl of Manchester to bring his army southwards. He arrived at Reading at the beginning of October. Although he showed an understandable unwillingness to co-operate with the prickly Waller and was at odds with his own Lieutenant General, Oliver Cromwell, there can be no doubt that his appearance saved the day. Had Rupert beaten him at Marston Moor, Parliament could not have survived the winter.

As it was the Royalists took another week to reach Salisbury. Rupert sent word that he would be delayed in joining, but as the Parliamentarian armies had not yet concentrated, there was thought to be time to attempt something. Goring quite sensibly suggested attacking Waller at Andover, and a rendezvous was appointed for that purpose at Clarendon Park on the morning of 18 October. Unfortunately Maurice's men were late in coming up from Wilton, but by three in the afternoon the Royalists were within four miles of the town. Rather belatedly waking up to this danger Waller concentrated his forces, did a swift headcount and promptly retreated. There was some bickering with his rearguard but it was too late in the day to accomplish much. Instead the Royalists merely moved forward to Whitchurch on the 20th and from there to Kingsclere on the 21st. There they lay more or less halfway between Basing House and Donnington Castle, both of which were being blocked up by Parliamentarian forces. Since the ground was more open towards Basing and the Parliamentarians were reckoned to be stronger in horse, the decision was taken to make for Newbury in order to relieve Donnington, which stands just to the north of the town.

This was accomplished without difficulty next day, but less happily the Earl of Northampton was then sent off with three regiments of horse[13] to relieve Banbury Castle as well. This object was successfully accomplished, but in the meantime the King remained at Newbury, still clinging to the hope of marching on Basing once Northampton returned. Predictably enough the Parliamentarians turned up first – in some surprising strength.

When Waller was driven out of Andover on the 18th he fell back on Manchester's headquarters at Basingstoke. Suitably alarmed at what looked like the beginning of a major Royalist offensive, Manchester in turn ordered up some 2,400 men of Sir James Harrington's City Brigade from Reading.[14] Essex himself had taken to his bed at Reading, but next day Skippon also arrived at Alton with 2,500 of his foot.[15] According to the September musters of the Eastern Association foot his own marching regiments then totalled just over 3,300 men.[16] Waller on the other hand may only have been able to provide some 800[17] to make a total of just 9,000 Parliamentarian foot.

As to cavalry Manchester probably still had at the most some 2,500 Eastern Association troopers, and Essex's horse, led by the competent Balfour, numbered about the same. If the state of Waller's infantry is anything to go by he will have been extremely lucky to contribute 2,000 horse, but it is more likely that the 1,500 troopers who were to serve under Manchester during the battle represented all of Waller's cavalry. If so the Parliamentarians can have mustered no more than 6,500-7,000 troopers in total.

By the 25th this ragtag collection was at Thatcham, just three miles short of Newbury and in contact with the Royalist outposts. Against them the King will have been lucky to muster 5,000 foot[18] and 4,500 horse and dragoons. Notwithstanding the disparity in numbers the King had little option but to stand and fight, but at least he was occupying a strong position centred on the village of Shaw and covered on its right front by the river Lambourne. It might have been stronger still had the Royalists been able to hold the high ground of Clay Hill, which overlooked Shaw from the east. An attempt by the Parliamentarians to seize this feature on the 25th was beaten off, but it had to be abandoned next day and a Parliamentarian battery was promptly emplaced on it.

Notwithstanding, the Parliamentarian commanders were distinctly uneasy about the prospect of tackling the Royalists head on, especially as the King's men were busily digging in. Consequently a Council of War agreed to pin the Royalists with a holding attack while a substantial force hooked around to the north to come in on their rear. This decision may have been taken as late as the afternoon of the 26th. However Walker clearly implies that the Royalists were already taking up positions to counter such a move earlier that day.[19]

Be that as it may, by next morning Prince Maurice's army was dug in around the village of Speen to the west of the King's position. The rest of the Royalist dispositions are a touch obscure, but Sir Jacob Astley had Colonel George Lisle's tertio deployed north of the Lambourne and occupying Shaw House as a strongpoint. To the south, his son Sir Bernard Astley's weak tertio held the line between the village of Shaw and Newbury itself. Somewhere in the centre of the whole position, perhaps by the crossroads just north of Newbury, stood the greater part of Thomas Blagge's tertio as a general reserve. As to the cavalry, Walker states that most of them were deployed in 'two open fields' locally known as Speenhamland, while some of the 'Western' horse were assigned to support Prince Maurice.

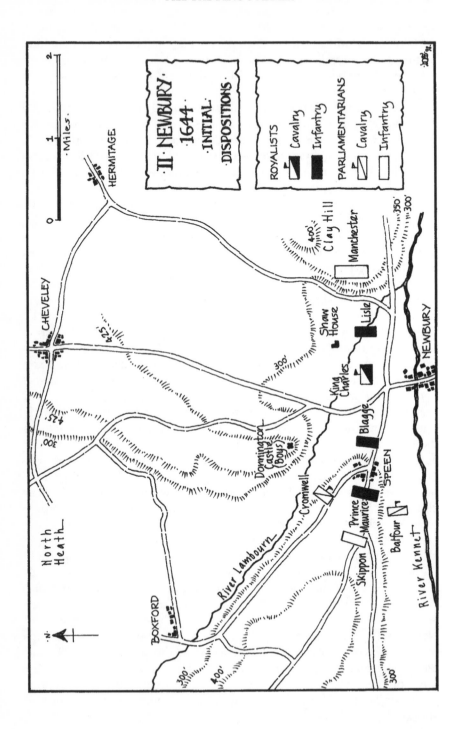

In addition Sir John Boys continued to hold Donnington Castle and a detachment of 300 horse and 200 foot, commanded by Sir John Douglas were sent to cover the Lambourne crossing at Boxford.

Sometime on the evening of the 26th the Parliamentarians divided their forces. In so doing they also sorted out their rather problematic command structure. It was agreed that Manchester should remain in front of the Shaw position with his own foot and some 1,500 horse, while the greater part of the army was to pass under Sir William Waller's command. In effect he was to have command of Essex's army – which must have afforded him some sour satisfaction – Harrington's City Brigade, and the Eastern Association Horse under Cromwell.

At daybreak on the morning of the 27th Manchester sent forward a brigade of foot which momentarily disconcerted the Royalists by crossing the Lambourne on a bridge they had secretly constructed during the night, just below Shaw. The picquet line was driven in but Sir Bernard Astley immediately counter-attacked with 400 musketeers. He must have caught Manchester's men before they had a chance to deploy properly beyond the bridge, for he succeeded in tumbling them back upon their supports. The battle on this front then degenerated into a firefight which lasted most of the day and successfully engaged the Royalists' attention.

At first sight this is surprising for the Royalist garrison in Donnington Castle had Waller's forces under observation. Setting off shortly after midnight he had marched as far as North Heath before bivouacking for a few hours. At daybreak he pressed on, brushed aside Sir John Douglas's picquet at Boxford and crossed the Lambourne. Then he swung eastwards and moved down the spine of the high ground towards Speen. However his progress was remarkably slow, and it was not until 3pm that he came into action. By this time, according to Walker, the Royalists had decided that the real battle would not take place until next morning. As a result most of the cavalry reserve had dispersed in search of forage. Consequently Waller at first made good progress. Deploying with his infantry in the centre, Balfour's horse on the right and Cromwell's on the left, he swept forward. In less than an hour's fighting he cleared the village of Speen and forced Maurice's foot back into Speenhamland. There the Royalists clung on to the hedge which formed its western boundary and Blagge's reserve tertio came up to their assistance. Waller thereupon tried to turn the position on both flanks by pushing his cavalry forward.

Balfour, preceded by some musketeers, moved through the gap between Speen and the Kennet. Coming into the field he first encountered Sir Humphrey Bennet's Brigade. After an unsuccessful spoiling attack by a small party under Major William Legge they promptly turned about and fell back. Bennet afterwards claimed this was merely in order to 'get more Ground,' but the predictable result was that many of his supports took the hint and fled towards Newbury. There they were stopped by a security cordon, turned around again and sent back to the fighting. The situation was retrieved by Sir John Cansfield who counter-attacked with the Queen's Regiment of Horse and with the assistance of the Lifeguards drove Balfour back. Bennet then came up again with his brigade and finished the business.

Much the same thing seems to have happened to Cromwell. In fact afterwards Manchester accused him of staying out of the fight entirely. The truth of the matter however is that, as he advanced into the shallow valley between Speen and the Lambourne, he was attacked by Goring at the head of Cleveland's Brigade[20] and thrown back in confusion. A second engagement was equally successful and, although Cleveland was taken prisoner, Cromwell was effectively knocked out of the fight completely.

This was just as well for Manchester now mounted his second attack of the day. This time he threw his whole weight on the Royalist left, standing north of the Lambourne. There is a certain vagueness as to the Royalist dispositions here, and all that can be said with any certainty is that Colonel George Lisle was in command of a reinforced brigade group comprising his own Reading tertio, 400 musketeers from Blagge's tertio under Lieutenant Colonel Page, some dragooners under Sir Thomas Hooper[21] and the Prince of Wales' Regiment of Horse. Page was assigned to defend Shaw House, which usefully enough was surrounded by a dry moat, while Colonel Anthony Thelwall seems to have been tasked with holding the hedges between the house and the Lambourne crossing in Shaw village. Hooper was probably covering the left flank.

Manchester sent his men forward in two divisions, one directed against Shaw House and the other trying to drive between the house and the village. At first their momentum carried them through the Royalist outpost line. There was a momentary check when Sir John Browne charged at the head of the Prince of Wales' Regiment, but the Cavaliers quickly fell back when Manchester brought up his own cavalry support. Unfortunately, once the Parliamentarians came up against the main Royalist position, the whole attack ground to a halt. Not only were the Cavaliers very strongly emplaced but the light was failing rapidly – sunset came at about 4.30pm. Consequently there was a quite under-standable unwillingness to press against dimly seen obstacles and the whole thing degenerated as usual into a protracted firefight.

That night the King concluded that the game was up. Although Lord Astley's forces were successfully holding their ground, the perimeter would collapse once Waller broke through the hedge into Speenhamland. That night, accompanied only by his Lifeguard, the King abandoned the army and fled to Bath. Prince Maurice was left with the unenviable job of extricating it from the pocket. Surprisingly enough he succeeded even though the greater part of them had to make their way across a single rather narrow bridge in Donnington. Even then the wounded, the baggage and the guns all had to be left behind in the castle.

The pursuit was half-hearted and instead the Parliamentarian commanders fell to abusing each other. Waller and Cromwell eventually headed north with some horse, but finding Maurice had crossed the Thames at Wallingford, they returned to Newbury in no very good humour. Seemingly for lack of any better ideas the Parliamentarians then agreed to try and take Donnington and the King's guns. After a failed escalade they decided to move northwards after all, only to discover that the Royalists were in the process of a dangerous concentration.

At Bath the King had been rejoined by Prince Rupert with some 3,000 horse and foot. On the 30th they marched to Burford and picked up Northampton's brigade. Shortly afterwards Langdale and Gerard came in and, by the time Charles reviewed his forces at Bullington Green on 5 November, the army was said to have numbered some 15,000 men.

It was time to fetch away the guns from Donnington. Moving south the King arrived there at about midday on the 9th. Next day the army drew up on Speenhamland to offer battle and cover the evacuation of the guns. In an ill-tempered meeting the Parliamentarian leaders declined to fight and then had to watch as the Royalists marched off with colours flying and drums beating. Although scarcely a shot had been fired, the third battle of Newbury was undoubtedly a Royalist victory. It was also the last victory for it directly led to the demise of the three old Parliamentarian armies and to the creation of a new one.

NOTES

1. Walker, Edward *Historical Works* Vol. 1 p37
2. *ibid.* p26-7. Maurice was thereby enabled to muster a marching army of 2,500 foot and 1,800 horse even after 500 foot were put into Wareham. The latter, commanded by Lt.Col. Henry O'Bryan, comprised two Irish regiments: the Earl of Inchiquin's and Lord Broghill's. Shortly afterwards both units changed sides.
3. Lords Journals 6 p603. Those who flocked in from the West Country were only sufficient to form a small regiment under Colonel John Weare.
4. The Earl of Warwick
5. The order of battle is reconstructed from documentation in Peachy & Turton *Old Robin's Foot* (figures from June 1644 musters) and from a captured list of the horse in Symonds *Diary*. Figures are exclusive of officers.

Foot:		Horse:	
Col. Edward Aldrich	(300)	Sir William Balfour	(432)
Col. Harry Barclay	(475)	Col. Hans Behre	(371)
Col. Adam Cunningham	(634)	Col. John Dalbier	(267)
Col. William Davies	(316?)	Col. Edmund Harvey	(389)
Lord General	(1292)	Sir Robert Pye	(208)
Lord Robartes	(700?)	Col. James Sheffield	(414)
Maj.Gen. Philip Skippon	(550?)	Sir Philip Stapleton	(639)*
Col. Thos. Tyrrell	(524)	* plus 65 dragooners	

Green Auxiliaries (Whichcott) (500?)
Orange Auxiliaries (Gower)   (500?)
West Country Forces:
Plymouth Foot (Col. Carre)   (1,000)   Col. Layton's Plymouth Horse
Col. John Weare   (300?)

6. The order of battle outlined below is based upon Symonds' list (*Diary* p 41): 'When the King's army was in Cornwall, the infantry was divided into three tertias, and every tertia should consist of three brigades,' Other units, including those belonging to Prince Maurice's army have been identified from the list of field officers signing a letter to Essex on 8 August (Walker pp61-2)

King's Army

First Tertio: Col. Thomas Blagge

King's Lifeguard	
Lord General	
Sir Jacob Astley	(217)
Sir Henry Bard	(176)
Duke of York	
Sir James Pennyman	(479)
Lord Percy	
Sir Lewis Dyve	(150)

Lord Wilmot's Brigade:
Lord General
Prince Maurice
Gerard Croker
Thomas Howard

Northampton's Brigade:
Earl of Northampton
Lord Wilmot
Lord Percy
Col. Thomas Weston

Second Tertio*: Col. George Lisle

Col. Charles Lloyd	(409)
Col. George Lisle	(270)
Col. Anthony Thelwell	(196)
Col. John Owen	(145)
Col. William Eure	(91)
Sir Thomas Blackwell	(86)
Sir Theophilus Gilby	(355)
Col. John Stradling	(351)
Sir Henry Vaughan	(258)

*also known as the Reading Brigade

Cleveland's Brigade:

Earl of Cleveland	(200)
Sir Nicholas Crispe	(80)
Col. Dutton Fleetwood	(160)
Col. James Hamilton	(160)
Col. Richard Thornhill	(100)
Col. Thomas Culpeper	(100)

Sir Humph. Bennet's Brigade:
Sir Humphrey Bennet
Sir George Vaughan
Sir Edward Waldgrave
Col. Andrew Lyndsay

Third Tertio: Sir Bernard Astley
Lord Hopton
Sir Allan Apsley
Col. John Talbot
Col. Francis Cooke
Sir William Courtney
Sir Bernard Astley
Col. Matthew Appleyard
Col. Henry Shelley
Sir John Paulet
Col. Walter Slingsby
Sir Edward Rodney   (200) : Somerset Trained Band unit picked up at Chard.

Lord Wentworth's Brigade:
Prince of Wales
Queen's Regt.
Col. Richard Neville

Lifeguard of Horse (unbrigaded)

Prince Maurice's Army

Foot:
Col. Joseph Bampfield
Sir Thomas Basset
Sir Henry Cary
Col. Piers Edgecumbe

Horse:
Sir Thomas Basset
Sir Henry Cary
Col. Piers Edgecumbe
Col. James Hamilton

Sir Edmund Fortescue   Col. Giles Strangeways
Col. William Godolphin
Sir John Grenville
Prince Maurice (Philip Champernon)
Col. Thomas Pigot
Col. Thomas St.Aubyn
Col. John Stocker
Col. Joseph Wagstaffe

7. The circumstances surrounding this affair are rather obscure. Wilmot was accused of treason and the arrest was engineered by Lord Digby. It is undoubtedly significant that it took place the day after Goring turned up. Another casualty was Lord Percy, forced to resign on the 14th and replaced as General of the Ordnance by Lord Hopton – less a promotion in this case than recognition that the latter was a better administrator than a field commander.

8. Essex retained two or three troops of Plymouth Horse under a Colonel Layton and Captain Reynolds.

9. Walker *op.cit.* pp70-3

10. *ibid.* p74. Leighton was Lieutenant Colonel of the King's Lifeguard of Foot, so his battalion was probably made up of that regiment and the Lord General's. Both were redcoats.

11. CSPD 1644

12. Walker *op.cit.* p84.

13. Walker (*op.cit.* p109) names them as Northampton's, Wilmot's and the Lord General's regiments. The first two certainly belonged to his brigade, but no mention is made of his other two regiments, Lord Percy's and Thomas Weston's, while the Lord General's Regiment came from what had been Wilmot's Brigade. There was evidently a considerable reorganisation of the cavalry after Wilmot's arrest, though it is intriguing that he still had his regiment.

14. Tincey, J. *London and Liberty* p26 :   Red Regiment
                                        Blue Regiment
                                        Westminster Regiment
                                        Southwark Regiment
                                        (Yellow) Tower Hamlets Auxiliaries
The five regiments totalled some 3,000 men, but the Southwark Regiment was left behind at Reading.

15. Peachy & Turton *Old Robin's Foot* p58. This total is derived from the December musters and may therefore be a little on the low side.

16. Holmes, C. *The Eastern Association in the English Civil War* p238

17. Firth, C. *Cromwell's Army* p35. Although this figure seems extremely low, Waller's army was only reckoned to be capable of contributing around 600 foot to the New Model Army. On the other hand Essex's and Manchester's armies were assessed to about 3,000 and 3,500 men respectively, which is broadly in line with *their* numbers at Newbury.

18. 6,000 suits of clothes for the foot had been extracted from the Commissioners of Array in Devon and Somerset, but the numerous futile detachments accounted for about 1,000 of them.

19. Walker *op.cit.* p112.

20. Composition as in Cornwall except that Fleetwood's had now been taken over by John Stuart.

21. Hooper commanded Prince Rupert's Dragoons

CHAPTER XV
Naseby Fight

The bitter recriminations which followed the Newbury fiasco grew into a furious debate about the conduct of the war, in which Manchester and Cromwell each accused the other of everything from cowardice to treachery, and which soon turned into a bitter power struggle between the Presbyterians and the Independents. The details of this political struggle need not detain us. It is sufficient to note that the Presbyterians represented the established social order and were prepared to reach an accommodation with the King, while the Independents represented the rising middle classes and looked to a military victory; that the quarrel rumbled on into the summer laid the seeds of the Second Civil War, and in the process spawned the New Model Army.

The three armies or rather brigades which had so signally failed to annihilate the King's forces at Newbury had too many officers and too few soldiers. It made both economic and military sense to reorganise or 'new model' the available soldiers into a single effective marching army under one commander instead of three. The consequent restoration of something like the proper ratio of officers to men clearly meant that there would be large-scale redundancies amongst the commissioned ranks and the 'new modelling' thus became inextricably intertwined with the political power struggle. In the end it was the Independents who had their way, but recognising that the appointment of their champion, Oliver Cromwell, would be unacceptable they engineered the Self Denying Ordinance which barred Members of Parliament from holding commissions in the new army. Consequently a compromise candidate, Sir Thomas Fairfax, was given the command. Essex, Waller and Manchester were to retire but Cromwell engineered his own exemption on the grounds of military necessity.

Other than the question of which faction should officer and thus control the new army, there was little to distinguish it from its predecessors. It comprised eleven regiments of horse, ten companies of dragoons, and twelve regiments of foot. There were to be 600 men besides officers in each regiment of horse, 1,200 in each regiment of foot and 100 in each company of dragooners.

The cavalry were found easily enough for it was possible to incorporate existing regiments and recruit them up to their authorised establishment, but the foot proved altogether more problematic. In March 1645 it was reckoned that the armies of Essex and Manchester could respectively contribute some 3,048 and 3,578 infantry, while Waller's could supply only 548.[1] This came to a total of only just over 7,000, so the shortfall was directed to be made up by the conscription of 8,460 men in London and the eastern counties. These recruits required to be clothed and equipped, and at the beginning of April 6,000 collars of bandiliers, 5,650 muskets and 2,000 pikes were ordered for the purpose.[2] This would imply a musket-to-pike ratio in the region of 3:1, but the regiments drafted into the New Model from the three old field armies were already equipped rather differently. When Essex's army was re-equipped after the Lostwithiel debacle, six muskets were served out for every pike[3]. Since much the same thing was happening in the Royalist armies it is likely that a similar situation prevailed amongst Manchester's and Waller's forces. Consequently it is likely that the eventual ratio of muskets to pikes in the New Model may have been four to one or even higher.

The Royalists faced similar problems, but unlike the Parliamentarians they lacked both the will properly to 'new model' their forces, and the resources to rebuild them. Although Prince Rupert was appointed Lieutenant General of the King's armies on 6 November, he found that he had very little scope to effect reforms or to direct strategy. Just as the Parliamentarians were split between two factions, so the Cavaliers were even more bitterly divided between soldiers and courtiers, and it was the latter who generally had the King's ear.

Moreover the Royalists could now draw upon just two areas for fresh recruits; the West Country and Wales. The former was potentially the more important of the two, but the continued presence of Parliamentarian garrisons, and in particular Plymouth, was a real problem. As to the latter, the King's Road was once more under threat and the year opened with a major setback.

Rupert had managed to carry many of his infantry away from Marston Moor, but the Lancashire regiments were lost at Ormskirk on 18 August and the survivors chased into Liverpool. There they were besieged by Sir John Meldrum and forced to surrender on 1 November.[4] Worse still many of the Irish veterans were lost in a disastrous battle outside Montgomery on 18 September. The victor of that fight, Sir William Brereton, then turned north to blockade Chester. Both the fortifications and the garrison were formidable, and initially it was all he could do to surround it with a chain of outposts. Unfortunately for the Royalists, although Byron initially conducted a very aggressive defence, he was badly defeated at Christleton on 18 January.

Prince Maurice was therefore despatched from Oxford to relieve the city. Unfortunately he was given very few troops with which to accomplish this feat and had to strip the garrison of Shrewsbury in order to raise the siege on 19 February. Then, while they were away, on the night of 21 February 1646 Sir Thomas Mytton surprised the town. The castle held out until noon and then its defenders too surrendered. They were allowed to march away to Ludlow, but only after they had turned over forty-nine Irishmen, thirteen of whom were summarily hanged next day.[5]

It was the worst disaster to strike the Royalists since the fall of York, and ironically it came against a background of apparent consolidation farther down the King's Road. The Royalist administration in Worcestershire had been overhauled, and the local regiments 'new modelled' with gratifying results. A similar process was underway in Monmouthshire, and in Hereford Maurice and his brother managed to overawe Parliamentarians and neutrals alike. Rupert came up from Bristol at the beginning of April to help deal with a local insurrection by 'Clubmen' resisting the demands of Royalist commissaries, and by way of a bonus he also managed to beat Massey at Ledbury on 22 April.

Similarly Colonel Charles Gerard was reasserting Royalist control over south Wales. Having quartered in Montgomeryshire over the winter, he pushed into Pembrokeshire in late April and soon had the Parliamentarians penned into just two rather lonely garrisons at Tenby and Pembroke. Successful though he was, this diversion deprived the Oxford Army of an estimated 2,000 foot and 700 horse. Gerard's experience in fact encapsulates the problem facing the Royalists generally. In order to recruit their field armies they needed to keep the King's Road open. On the whole the professional soldiers now entrusted with the task successfully maintained their garrisons, but in the process they both alienated the local population and soaked up the recruits who should have been passed down the Road to Oxford. It was against this unhappy background that the campaign which culminated in the battle of Naseby would be fought out.

Realistically there were two options open to the Royalists. They could move into the Severn valley, or into the West Country. For some reason the little Parliamentarian garrison in Taunton had mysteriously assumed a hitherto unsuspected strategic importance for both sides. The Committee of Both Kingdoms wanted it relieved and was quite prepared to commit the New Model Army to the purpose. On 28 April Fairfax was ordered to march at once to its relief.

In punctual obedience he immediately did so, was at Reading on the 30th and at Blandford in Dorset by 8 May. In the meantime Cromwell had taken a cavalry brigade on a destructive sweep around Oxford at the end of April. On the 23rd he crossed the Cherwell at Islip. Next day he routed Northampton's brigade and snapped up the garrison of Bletchingdon House in the early hours of the following morning. A little brigade of Royalist infantry under Sir Henry Vaughan and Lieutenant Colonel Littleton was then ridden over at Bampton-in-the-Bush on the 26th, and the raid ended with an unsuccessful attack on Faringdon on the 30th. In the process Cromwell had not only 'frightened them out of their wits at Oxford'[6], but he had also rounded up every draught animal he met with. The loss of these animals meant that the Royalists would employ a rather smaller train than had originally been intended, although arguably this made no real difference to their conduct of operations.

The King moved out of Oxford on 7 May, and next day his army began its concentration at Stow-in-the-Wold. At a fateful Council of War meeting that night Goring, and Lord Digby argued for moving west and fighting Fairfax. They saw this as an excellent opportunity to destroy the New Model before it had a chance to shake down. Rupert on the other hand wanted to march north, not just to consolidate further control of the King's Road, but also to relieve Chester which was once more under siege. Although Parliamentary cruisers were restricting the flow of Irish reinforcements, the city was still vital to the Royalist war effort. Moreover, having relieved Chester, he proposed to go on and try to recruit fresh troops in Yorkshire.

Walker afterwards alleged that 'the true cause was, the earnest Desire of Prince *Rupert* to be revenged of the *Scots* for the Defeat he had received the Year before;'[7] Sir Edward was undoubtedly a hostile witness but this particular accusation has the ring of truth about it, particularly in view of the pressure coming from Sir Marmaduke Langdale and his Northern Horse. This last remnant of Newcastle's army included a number of infantry officers riding in its ranks as volunteers. Their regiments had been destroyed at Marston Moor, but they argued that were the King's forces to return to Yorkshire in any strength they would be able to raise those regiments again.[8] They were encouraged in this ambition both by a remarkable raid which Langdale had just mounted, temporarily relieving Pontefract Castle on 1 March, and by the apparent success of the Royalist insurrection in Scotland. There the Marquis of Montrose had won a series of victories against the Government's forces. However his optimistic despatches glossed over the fact that his army comprised little more than a brigade, that what little popular support he had was being eroded by the excesses of his troops and that he had so far failed to gain a single foot of ground for the King.[9]

Nevertheless Rupert had his way, but Goring was to return to the west with 3,000 horse. There the condition of Colonel Blake's garrison in Taunton was now becoming critical. By the 9th the Cavaliers were in possession of the town and on the point of taking the castle as well. Nevertheless, the Committee of Both Kingdoms abruptly changed its mind. Fairfax too was to split his forces, sending a brigade on to the relief of Taunton, while he himself was to march northwards after the King's army. Fairfax therefore detached four regiments of foot and one of horse under Colonel Ralph Weldon[10], but marched the rest as far as Dorchester before turning north. Convinced by this feint that Fairfax's whole army was coming, the Royalists drew off from Taunton on the 11th.

Cromwell in the meantime, reinforced by some foot from Abingdon under 'Faggot-monger' Browne, was shadowing the King's army. He had already clashed with its rearguard near Stow-in-the-Wold but now Browne was becoming uneasy. The size of the Royalist army was increasing dramatically as troops were ruthlessly stripped from the various garrisons encountered on the march. By 14 May, while Rupert was dealing with a small Parliamentarian garrison in Hawksley House, Browne was at Southam and refusing to go farther until reinforcements arrived. There was little Cromwell could do about this since technically he lacked a commission and so had no authority over Browne. To make matters worse the Committee of Both Kingdoms ordered Cromwell to despatch a brigade under Colonel Vermuyden to the assistance of the Scots Army, and on the 17th they ordered Fairfax to besiege Oxford. In the meantime the Royalists continued moving northwards, and on the 20th Byron turned up with the happy news that Brereton had once more abandoned the siege of Chester.

Declining Byron's invitation to attack Nantwich, Rupert now decided to march for Yorkshire by way of Newark. Not surprisingly this move was interpreted by the Committee of Both Kingdoms as a possible advance into the Eastern Association counties. Vermuyden had already been ordered to halt at Nottingham on the 24th, and two days later he was recalled and Cromwell ordered to Ely. For the present Fairfax was to remain outside Oxford, but within a matter of days Parliament's worst fears were confirmed. Leicester was stormed and comprehensively sacked.

On 29 May Langdale's brigade had surrounded the town, and next day Rupert established his batteries on the south side of the defences. Within hours a large breach was opened. The garrison retrenched, but at midnight the assault began. Lisle's tertio got into the breach but was driven out again by a counter-attack led by a Scots mercenary, Major Christopher Innes.[11] Some bitter fighting then followed, but on the north side two assault columns led by Sir Bernard Astley and Sir Henry Bard broke in. As soon as they had gained a lodgement, they opened the gates and at about 1am Northampton took his cavalry brigade in to scour the streets.

According to Symonds the Cavaliers refused quarter to the Scots,[12] who not surprisingly fought to the last. With the battle thus carried into the streets, discipline soon broke down and fighting gradually gave way to plundering and all the other unpleasant atrocities which generally constitute the sack of a town. While it is easy to dismiss contemporary comparisons with the infamous sack of Magdeburg, they are perhaps not too wide of the mark. The town may not actually have been razed, but by the standards of the Civil War there was horror enough to justify the parallel.

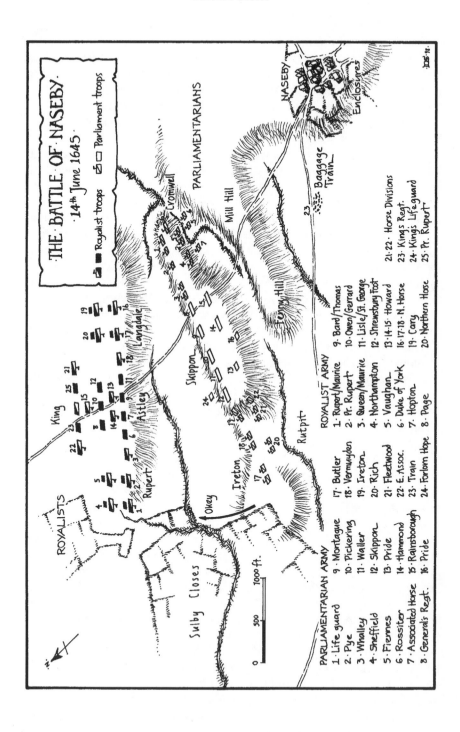

THE BATTLE OF NASEBY.
·14th June 1645·

Royalist troops Parliament troops

PARLIAMENTARIANS

ROYALISTS

NASEBY

Enclosures

Baggage Train

Mill Hill

Fenny Hill

Cromwell

Langdale

King

Astley

Skippon

Rupert

Ireton

Rutpitt

Okey

Sulby Closes

1000 ft.

500

0

PARLIAMENTARIAN ARMY
1· Life guard
2· Pye
3· Whalley
4· Sheffield
5· Fiennes
6· Rossiter
7· Associated Horse
8· General's Regt.
9· Montague
10· Pickering
11· Waller
12· Skippon
13· Pride
14· Hammond
15· Rainsborough
16· Pride
17· Butler
18· Vermuyden
19· Ireton
20· Rich
21· Fleetwood
22· E. Assoc.
23· Train
24· Forlorn Hope.

ROYALIST ARMY
1· Rupert/Maurice
2· Pr. Rupert
3· Queen/Maurice
4· Northampton
5· Vaughan
6· Duke of York
7· Hopton
8· Page
9· Bard/Thomas
10· Owen/Gerrard
11· Lisle/St. George
12· Shrewsbury foot
13·14·15· Howard
16·17·18· N. Horse
19· Cary
20· Northern Horse
21·22· Horse Divisions
23· King's Regt.
24· King's Lifeguard
25· Pr. Rupert·

197

The Committee of Both Kingdoms could delay no longer. Laying siege to Oxford had not after all drawn the King's army southwards again, so on 4 June Fairfax was ordered north. Ironically, having just learned that Oxford was not as well provisioned as had been assumed, the King marched out of Leicester on the same day with the intention of relieving the city. Unexpectedly this move immediately provoked a mutiny of the Northern Horse who marched off to Newark. With 'much ado' they were brought back, but with news of Fairfax's advance the situation changed and the Cavaliers halted for a week in a very strong position on Borough Hill outside Daventry. A large drove of sheep and cattle was then sent into Oxford and a resupply of ammunition brought out. In the meantime Fairfax was all but ignored, but on 12 June the Cavaliers learned to their consternation that he was at Kislingbury, only five miles to the east. Just why this came as such a surprise is unclear for Fairfax had sent in a trumpeter on the 10th which ought to have given them some inkling that he was in the area. Apparently the Royalists were under the impression that, having left Newport Pagnell on the 9th, he was heading for Bedford and a rendezvous with Cromwell's forces. At any rate, having stood to all night on Borough Hill, they evacuated Daventry in the early hours of 13 June with the intention of falling back on Newark.

That same morning Fairfax was rejoined by Cromwell and the combined army moved northwards in pursuit. By nightfall some of the outposts were in contact. There was a skirmish at Naseby, and in the early hours of 14 June the Royalists took the fateful decision to turn and fight. Afterwards Rupert's enemies would blame his impetuosity for bringing on an unnecessary battle, but there was no real alternative since a continued retreat would soon turn into a running battle. Even if they did succeed in breaking contact there was every prospect of meeting the Scots army head on while Fairfax came up from behind.

At about 7am the Royalists drew up in order of battle on some high ground at East Farndon.[13] They had an idea that the Parliamentarians were somewhere to the south and the Scoutmaster General, Francis Ruse, was sent to look for them. He should have gone forward until he was shot at, but instead he returned within a very short time to say that there was no sign of the enemy. Rupert thereupon went forward himself and promptly sighted Fairfax's army beginning to deploy on the ridge north-east of Naseby. The sequence of events which followed is far from clear, but Rupert seems to have formed the opinion that the Parliamentarians were on the point of pulling back. Accordingly he called forward his own main body from the East Farndon position, but the lie of the ground, which was cut up with deep ravines, forced them to fetch a compass about to the west. Fairfax and Cromwell not unnaturally interpreted this move as an attempt to outflank them and so conformed to it. By mid morning the Royalists had taken up a position on Dust Hill, between

Sibbertoft and Naseby, while across Broadmoor the New Model was deployed on a long ridge called Closter Hill.

While there is no doubt that the King's army was outnumbered, the difference may not have been as great as some modern accounts suggest. The best estimate which we have of Fairfax's army is a report in the *Scottish Dove* that it mustered 7,031 foot and 3,014 horse outside Newport Pagnell on 5 June. At this time neither Cromwell nor Vermuyden's troops had rejoined the army, but by the 14th the total must have risen to between 5,500 and 6,000 cavalry. The infantry total was probably unchanged but the *caveat* must again be entered that the effective strength of a unit was normally significantly lower than the muster figure.[14] This is a point of some importance in this particular case for it has a considerable bearing on the deployment of Fairfax's army.

According to Streeter's pictorial map, Major General Philip Skippon placed five infantry regiments in the front line, from left to right: his own, Sir Hardress Waller's, Colonel John Pickering's, Colonel Edward Montague's, and the Lord General's. Streeter depicts the regiments jammed closely together, but de Gomme evidences a much more conventional deployment with sufficient intervals to allow the supporting regiments to come forward.[15] The second or 'Reserve' line comprised three battalions: one commanded by Lieutenant Colonel Thomas Pride of Harley's covering the interval between Skippon's and Waller's, Colonel Robert Hammond's covering Pickering's and Montague's, and Colonel Thomas Rainsborough's covering the Lord General's. There was a fairly substantial gap between one of Pride's Battalions and Hammond's Regiment which looks as though it ought to have been filled by a second rather smaller battalion under Pride,[16] however this is depicted in both maps standing some distance farther back and serving as a 'rear gard'. Since the infantry were drawn up just behind the crest of the ridge, a forlorn hope of some 300 musketeers was deployed forward of the interval between Skippon's and Waller's.

The cavalry on the left wing, commanded by the Commissary General Henry Ireton probably numbered some 2,500 men.[17] It was drawn up with its left flank resting on the hedges marking the western boundary of the Sulby enclosures. There were three regiments in the front line: Colonel John Butler's, Colonel Vermuyden's[18], and Ireton's, each probably forming two divisions. In the second line were two more full regiments, Colonel Nathaniel Rich's and Colonel George Fleetwood's, and a division made up of some 'Association' horse which Cromwell had brought from Ely.[19]

On the right wing the deployment of the 3-4,000 odd horse under Lieutenant General Cromwell (who now had a proper commission) was extremely congested. In part this was because there were considerably more of them and partly because the extreme right flank was hemmed in by a substantial (man-made) rabbit warren and thick 'furze'. In the front line was Colonel Edward Whalley's Regiment, a division of Sir Robert Pye's, and the Lord General's Regiment.[20] The second line comprised Colonel Thomas Sheffield's Regiment, the second division of Pye's, and a division of Colonel John Fiennes' Regiment. Some way to the rear were two more divisions, one belonging to Gurdon's little brigade of Eastern Association horse, and the other to Fiennes'. At the last moment Colonel Edward Rossiter's Midlanders also came up and were assigned to this wing. One division was posted on the right of the third line while the other refused the extreme right of the front line.[21]

On Dust Hill there were, according to de Gomme, some 4,000 Royalist foot under Lord Astley, but this is far too low and the real total may have been closer to 5,000[22], which is not significantly lower than the likely Parliamentarian total. They were drawn up in three lines with four battalions in the front, three in the second line, and two more battalions forming a third line or reserve. The command structure was a touch odd although it was evidently based on contemporary German practice and had already been tried out at the Third battle of Newbury.

On the right was Sir Bernard Astley's tertio with two battalions in the front line: the Duke of York's and Colonel Edward Hopton's, and another commanded by Sir Richard Page in the second line. Then came Sir Henry Bard's tertio comprising just two battalions of which one stood in the front line and the other in the second line covering the interval between his own and Astley's tetras. On the left was Sir George Lisle's tertio which again had just two battalions of which one was on the left of the front line with the second, the 'Shrewsbury Foot' covering the interval. The two battalions in the third line were the King's Lifeguard of Foot and Prince Rupert's Regiment.[23]

As to the cavalry de Gomme evidences some 3,500 horse, but again this figure is certainly too low and Symonds provides a rather more convincing total of 5,420.[24]

On the right wing under the direct command of Prince Rupert himself were three divisions in the front line: both his own and Prince Maurice's Lifeguards, his Regiment, and the Queen's and Prince Maurice's Regiments. The latter division was unsupported, but the outer two each had a detachment of fifty musketeers attached,[25] and then two more divisions (also backed up with musketeers) directly behind them in the second line: the Earl of Northampton's Regiment and Sir William Vaughan's Regiment.[26] Symonds figures produce a total of 1,510 horse on this wing besides the 200 musketeers.

The deployment of the left wing, commanded by Sir Marmaduke Langdale, mirrored that of the right. There were three divisions of Northern Horse under Langdale himself in the front line, of which the outer two were backed up both by musketeers and by two more divisions of horse in the second line. Of the latter, one was made up of Northern Horse under Sir William Blakiston,[27] and the outer one was Colonel Horatio Cary's Regiment. Again working off Symonds' figures there were something like 1,700 horse and 200 musketeers on this wing.

A further 880 horse belonging to Colonel Thomas Howard's Brigade were deployed in the centre, with two divisions supporting the infantry of the front line and a third one supporting the men in the second line. This was very much a scratch formation cobbled together from a variety of small garrison units picked up along the King's Road.[28]

Finally there was a reserve standing with the Lifeguard of Foot and Prince Rupert's Foot in the third line. This comprised 130 men of the King's and Queen's Lifeguards of Horse under the Earl of Lichfield, and two divisions of Newark Horse numbering some 800 men under Colonel Anthony Eyre.

The battle began at about 10am. Despite enjoying a slight superiority in numbers, Fairfax was for once prepared to fight a defensive battle and Rupert was pleased to oblige him by attacking. At the time Colonel Okey was still in the rear, issuing ammunition to his dragoons, when Cromwell ordered him to establish an ambush position in the Sulby enclosures. This he did[29] in time to shoot up the flank of Rupert's cavalry as it came forward, and then became involved in a firefight with its supporting musketeers.

Perhaps as a result of the ambush Ireton, who came forward to meet the Royalists, may have been able to hold at least part of Rupert's first line for a time. Sprigge's extremely confusing account even goes so far as to say that he succeeded in routing most of the Cavaliers at the first onset.[30] This seems most unlikely, and at any rate Rupert's reserves were soon brought up by Sir William Vaughan and this finished the business. Most of Ireton's first line was driven back on his second and both tumbled back in considerable disorder. In the process however Ireton's own division on the right flank was left behind and would shortly make a remarkable intervention in the fight. At this point too Rupert could have done with Howard's Brigade to pursue the broken regiments while his own men rallied and reloaded their pistols. Instead the victorious Cavaliers exploited deep into the Parliamentarian rear and got into a fight with the musketeers guarding the baggage train outside Naseby.[31]

While the horse were thus engaged the Royalist foot also crossed Broad Moor, ascended Closter Hill and launched a furious assault on the Parliamentarian centre:

> . . . the first Charge being given by Prince *Rupert* with his own and Prince *Maurice's* Troops; who did so well, and were so well seconded, as that they bore down all before them, and were (as 'tis said) Masters of six Pieces of the Rebels Cannon. Presently our Forces advanced up

the Hill, the Rebels only discharging five Pieces at them, but over shot them, and so did their Musquetiers. The Foot on either side hardly saw each other until they were within Carabine Shot, and so only made one Volley; ours falling in with Sword and butt end of the Musquet did notable Execution so much as I saw their Colours fall and their Foot in great Disorder.[32]

Sir Bernard Astley's tertio drove back Skippon's and Waller's Regiments without much difficulty, but Bard and Lisle were less successful. The Royalists were simply outnumbered and the Lord General's Regiment on the Parliamentarian right was evidently able to 'outwing' Lisle's men. Consequently, although the retreat of Skippon's Regiment led to the Parliamentarian infantry swinging back, there was no general collapse. The arrival of the Royalist second line might still have precipitated one, but at this critical juncture Ireton intervened.

Sprigge merely states that: '. . . the Commissary Generall seeing one of the enemies Brigades of Foot on his right hand, pressing sore upon our Foot, commanded that Division that was with him, to charge that Body of Foot.'[33] The body in question is unnamed which has not prevented it from being identified in secondary sources as the Duke of York's Regiment, but this is unlikely for Ireton was probably still down on Broadmoor at the time. Having beaten Skippon's men it will have been necessary for Astley's front line to reorganise on the objective, and at the very least pause long enough to reload their muskets. It was now that his reserve battalions should have come up from the second line to exploit the victory either by leapfrogging on to the next objective or at least covering the reorganisation. While Ireton *may* now have attacked the Duke of York's Regiment it is much more likely that he actually fell on the flank of Sir Richard Page's Regiment in the second line. This would explain why Skippon, in spite of a nasty wound in the belly, had time to bring up his own reserves and engage the stalled Royalists in what the archaeological evidence indicates was a fierce firefight.[34]

Cromwell's battle on the other hand was never in doubt for he outnumbered Langdale by two to one. His own divisions on the extreme right were delayed in coming into the fight because they first had to negotiate the 'furze' and the rabbit warren, but Whalley's Regiment beat the Royalist divisions opposite and drove them back to shelter behind Rupert's Regiment of foot. Then Cromwell came into action and routed the rest of Langdale's command. Some of the Newarkers may have intervened unsuccessfully, but the King's Lifeguard of Horse declined to engage and instead retired in some confusion. This, as Fairfax recognised, was the crisis of the battle. His left wing had gone and his centre was under severe pressure, but now he and Cromwell fell upon the Royalist infantry reserve; Prince Rupert's Regiment and probably the King's

Lifeguard of Foot as well. The intervention of these regiments in the firefight on Closter Hill could have been decisive, but as it was, their destruction decided the battle.

Until recently it was assumed that at this point the main body of the Royalist foot surrendered, but in fact the archaeological evidence reveals a much grimmer picture. Abandoned by their horse the King's old infantry retreated back across Broadmoor and Dust Hill past their baggage train to make their last stand on Wadborough Hill nearly two miles to the north of the battlefield. In very similar circumstances Patrick Ruthven had extricated the Royalist infantry from Cheriton and, had he been present, might have done so again. Both contemporary accounts and the distribution of bullet finds show that they successfully disengaged from Skippon's battered foot, but were harried up the Sibbertoft Road by cavalry and by Okey's Dragoons. With the help of their own cavalry they might yet have won clear, but Rupert had abdicated his responsibilities as General at the outset of the battle and there was no one to coordinate a proper rearguard action.

Rupert did indeed rejoin the King before the end, but by then it was too late. When Fairfax's infantry finally came up, the Royalists surrendered, merely on condition that they should not be plundered. No fewer than 4,508 common soldiers, besides at least 161 officers, were taken prisoner, almost all of them belonging to the infantry. The cavalry as usual managed to run away, but although it was a far more complete victory than Marston Moor, neither Fairfax nor Cromwell was disposed to be magnanimous. When the Royalist baggage train was overrun, the hapless camp-followers were murdered in cold blood or merely mutilated, and in reporting his victory Fairfax added a postscript noting that there were Irish soldiers amongst the prisoners: 'I desire they may be proceeded against according to ordinance of parliament.'[35]

NOTES

1. HMC *Portland* I, p215
2. Mungeam, G.I. 'Contracts for the Supply of Equipment to the New Model Army in 1645' in *Journal of the Arms and Armour Society* Vol.VI no.3 pp53-115. Although the total of muskets (which includes fifty firelocks) comes to slightly less than 6,000, that is the number of collars of bandiliers ordered on 1 April. In addition a further 1,000 firelocks were ordered on 3 April, and 1,000 cartridge boxes on the 9th. These are plausibly argued to have been for the equipping of dragoons. However, adding the 2,000 pikes ordered between 1 and 10 April to the 7,000 or so muskets ordered between these dates, produces a total of 9,000 arms which very neatly agrees with the order for 9,000 swords and belts placed on 1 April. If all of these were indeed infantry weapons this would imply a ratio of seven muskets to two pikes. If on the other hand the 3 April order of 1,000 firelocks *was* intended for the Dragoons (only 600 saddles were ordered for Dragooners), we are still left with a 3:1

ratio of muskets to pikes rather than the two to one so often quoted. A further 300 pikes were ordered on 15 May and another 100 on the 30th, but by this time the army was in the field.

3. Peachy & Turton *Old Robin's Foot* p45

4. Learning of a Parliamentary Ordinance that Irishmen taken in arms were liable to be executed, the largely Irish garrison mutinied and handed the town over in return for safe passage back to Ireland. As a professional soldier Meldrum was well satisfied with the deal, but Brereton afterwards complained that no sooner did they arrive in Dublin than Byron's agent, Colonel Napier, shipped them straight back to Chester.

5. This was not the first instance of this sort of behaviour. Five Irish soldiers, possibly officers, were hanged in the wake of Rupert's unsuccessful attack on Abingdon on 11 January. However, after the Shrewsbury business, Rupert retaliated by hanging an equal number of Parliamentarian prisoners and this seems to have curbed the practice.

6. Sir Samuel Luke, quoted in Foard, G. *Naseby: The Decisive Campaign* (1995) p93.

7. Walker, E. *Historical Works : Brief Memorials of the Unfortunate Success of His Majesty's Army and Affairs in the Year 1645* p119.

8. The Marquis of Newcastle had brought fewer than 3,000 foot into the field at Marston Moor. Just how many of them could have been raised again in 1645 is questionable.

9. See the author's *Campaigns of Montrose* (Edinburgh 1990) for a comprehensive study of the war in Scotland.

10. **Foot:**   Col. Richard Fortescue   **Horse:**   Col. Richard Graves
Col. Richard Ingoldsby
Col. Walter Lloyd
Col. Ralph Weldon

11. Innes was an officer in Sir Samuel Luke's Dragoons who had brought reinforcements from Newport Pagnell. There are however a number of references to Scots soldiers in the garrison. No regular units can be identified, but if the reports are true it is possible that a number of mercenaries had drifted south after Marston Moor.

12. Symonds, *Diary* p52

13. The interpretation of the battle presented here is in part based on Glen Foard's *Naseby: The Decisive Campaign*, although it differs significantly from it in certain areas.

14. Detailed 18th century returns regularly show a discrepancy of around ten percent between the muster roll and those actually present and fit for duty. At Culloden, for example, the Duke of Cumberland's morning state reveals that there were only 5,521 infantrymen present out of a *mustered* strength of 6,172.

15. Foard argues that Streeter's map is to be relied upon, while elsewhere convincingly demonstrating that the topography is considerably foreshortened. On the other hand an analysis of the frontage required by the 7,000 infantry mustered on 5 June does indicate that they may have needed to bunch up in order to fit in the Closter Hill position. However if their *actual* strength was indeed some 10% lower, then allowing for those men drawn off to form the forlorn hope and to guard the baggage train, it is just possible to deploy there in the formation depicted by de Gomme.

16. The regiment was actually Colonel Edward Harley's.

17. Foard, *Naseby* p241

18. Commanded by Major Robert Huntington

19. Commanded by Lieutenant Colonel Brampton Gurdon, the MP for Sudbury. As the two divisions fought on opposite wings the command structure is problematic. Gurdon himself was probably on the right.
20. Formerly Cromwell's Regiment it now included Fairfax's own Lifeguard troop and was actually commanded by Major John Desborough.
21. Neither Gurdon's, Fiennes' nor Rossiter's men belonged to the New Model.
22. Symonds *Diary* p45 gives a total of 5,300 foot mustered at Stow-in-the-Wold at the outset of the campaign. To this needs to be added about 200 men taken out of Worcester, Colonel Richard Bagot's 300 foot from Lichfield, and 200 Newarkers under St George. This produces a total of 6,000 from which we need to deduct some 200 casualties from Leicester and perhaps another 300 left in garrison there. A further reduction of 10% to cover the usual contingencies will then produce a likely total of some 5,000 men at Naseby.
23. The actual composition of these battalions can be reconstructed from the lists of prisoners taken at Naseby and by reference to the 1644 order of battle. The figures in parentheses are taken from Symonds *Diary*:

Sir Bernard Astley's Tertio
Duke of York's Regiment   : Lt.Col. Theodore Kirton
Sir Edward Hopton's Battalion* : Col. Matthew Appleyard's Regt.
                                Sir Bernard Astley's Regt.
                                Sir Edward Hopton's Regt.
                                Sir John Paulet's Regt.
* This battalion represented what remained of the Western Tertio which Astley led in 1644.
Sir Richard Page's Battalion   : Lord Astley's Regt.?
                                Sir Richard Page's Regt. (*ex* Pennyman's)

Sir Henry Bard's Tertio
Col. Rhys Thomas' Battalion   : Sir Henry Bard's Regt.
(300)   Col. William Murray's Regt. (*ex* Percy's)
                                Col. Rhys Thomas' Regiment (Queen's)
Col. Radcliffe Gerard's Battalion : Col. Richard Bagot's Regt.*
                                Col. Radcliffe Gerard's Regt.
                                Col. Thomas Leveson's Regt.*
                                Sir John Owen's Regt.
                                Sir William Russell's Regt.
*per Young, *Naseby 1645* the attribution is uncertain but this battalion (and indeed the whole Tertio) was scraped together out of small detachments from garrisons all the way along the King's Road.

Colonel George Lisle's Tertio
Sir Theophilus Gilby's Battalion*   Sir Thomas Blackwell's Regt.?
(500)Sir Theophilus Gilby's Regt.
      Col. George Lisle's Regt.
      Col. William St.George's Regt.
      Col. Anthony Thelwall's Regt.
      Sir Henry Vaughan's Regt.
*With the exception of St George's Newark Foot, this represented the remains of the old Reading Tertio which Lisle commanded in 1644. The Newarkers probably replaced those men lost at Bampton-in-the Bush on 26 April.
Colonel (Robt?) Smith's Battalion   Col. Robert Broughton's Regt.
                                Col. Richard Gibson's Regt.
                                Sir Fulk Hunck's Regt.
                                Col. Henry Tillier's Regt.
                                Col. Henry Warren's Regt.

Reserve

King's Lifeguard of Foot (200)	:	Lt.Col. Sir William Leighton
Prince Rupert's Regiment (500)	:	Lt.Col. John Russell

24. Symonds, *Diary* p52. The actual total given by Symonds was 5,520, but this was when the army lay before Leicester and included 100 of Lord Loughborough's Horse who stayed there.

25. These musketeers may have been drawn out of the three infantry brigades, but it is perhaps more likely that on this wing at least they belonged to Prince Rupert's and Prince Maurice's Lifeguards of Foot both of which were armed with Firelocks.

26. The reason for this was that infantry turned in their own space to fall back – suddenly or otherwise. However cavalry needed to wheel off and therefore often fell foul of their own supports if drawn up in chequer – as may have happened to Ireton's men in the battle. see article by Keith Roberts in *English Civil War Times* no.51

27. Symonds (p52) refers to there being three divisions under Langdale and one under Blakiston, but otherwise it is impossible to establish their composition.

28. According to Symonds (p52) the brigade was composed as follows:

Col. Samuel Sandys	(150)	Worcester gar.
Col. Thomas Howard	(80)	
Col. Thomas Leveson	(150)	Dudley Castle
Col. Richard Bagot	(200)	Lichfield gar.
Sir Robert Byron	(100)	Chester gar.
Sir Henry Bard	(100?)	Camden House
Col. Robert Warden	(100)	Chester gar.

29. Foard suggests on archaeological evidence that Okey may have taken up a position in an enclosure on Dust Hill itself, but this is certainly too far north, and the finds which include the remains of bandiliers are more likely to relate to the last stand of an isolated infantry unit.

30. Sprigge, J. *Anglia Rediviva; England's Recovery* (1647) pp37-8.

31. The fight for the baggage train has previously been dismissed as an inconsequential affair, but Foard (pp281-2) convincingly demonstrates on the evidence of known casualties that the fight was in fact quite a serious one.

32. Walker *op.cit.* p130.

33. Sprigge p37

34. Although outnumbered the Royalists may not have been significantly disadvantaged in this fight for the garrison units naturally had a very high proportion of musketeers in their ranks and in some cases, such as Bard's, were all musketeers.

35. Official letter to William Lenthall, quoted in Young, *Naseby 1645* p335. Contemporary accounts quite clearly state that the murdered camp-followers were Irish. The late C.V. Wedgewood suggested instead that they may actually have been Welsh, but there is no reason to suppose that this was the case. There were Irish soldiers aplenty (and English ones who had served there) in the King's forces at Naseby, and no doubt they had Irish women with them. It is absurd to suggest that Parliamentarian soldiers were incapable of recognising Welsh women.

CHAPTER XVI

All the King's Horses and all the King's Men: The last year of the First Civil War

Charles and Rupert halted at Leicester just long enough to gather in the fugitives and then marched the following night for Ashby-de-la-Zouch. Three days later they were at Bewdley, but there was little hope of rebuilding an army there for the King's Road was already denuded of troops. Indeed Evesham had been so weakened by earlier drafts that Massey stormed it without difficulty on 26 May. He then went on to defeat a locally raised army under Sir Thomas Lunsford and Sir Michael Woodhouse near Ludlow on 9 June, and this was in turn followed by the fall of a number of minor garrisons throughout Shropshire.

Goring, who had ignored orders to rejoin the army before Naseby, still had a sizeable army in the West Country which the King might have joined. Instead he decided to build a new army around a nucleus of Charles Gerard's Welsh troops. The initial idea seems to have been to establish a base at Hereford as the lower Severn was still reasonably secure, but Fairfax was now marching for the West Country. In response Rupert went south, stopped at Cardiff to confer briefly with Gerard, crossed the Severn to meet the Prince of Wales at Barnstaple[1], and was in Bristol by 4 July.

In the meantime the King also left Hereford and moved into Wales. Gerard had earlier reckoned to be able to muster some 2,000 foot, but the Welsh Commissioners of Array were unenthusiastic about raising more. For some inexplicable reason the King then retired to Raglan for three weeks of what Walker sadly refers to as 'Sports and Entertainments.' While this was a shocking abdication of responsibility Rupert took advantage of his absence to draw the better part of Gerard's forces over the Severn to reinforce the garrisons of Bristol and Bridgewater.[2]

There was need enough for them. Leicester had surrendered to Fairfax without a fight on 18 June and he then turned south. Despite the arrival of Weldon's brigade, Taunton was still under threat and exercising a fatal attraction for both sides. By the 28th Fairfax was at Marlborough, and two days later he began a forced march to relieve the town. He may also have hoped thereby to confront Goring and destroy his army, but in the event the Cavaliers fell back to take up a defensive position behind the rivers Parrett and Yeo. As Fairfax closed up it soon became apparent that

207

Goring had no stomach for a fight. His forces were not only outnumbered (Fairfax had picked up Massey's men *en route*), but they were trying to cover a front of rather more than twelve miles.

Having thoroughly reconnoitred the Royalist position Fairfax success-fully turned Goring's left at Yeovil. The Royalist detachment covering the town retreated without fighting, possibly because Goring had already decided to concentrate his forces at Langport in preparation for a retreat to Bridgewater. By way of a diversion George Porter took some cavalry off towards Taunton. This worked in as much as Fairfax sent Massey's cavalry brigade and some dragoons after him on the 8th and then 2,000 commanded musketeers the next day. Unfortunately the effect was rather spoilt when Porter contrived to get surprised at Ilminster and lost most of his command.

Nevertheless Goring could delay no longer. Early on the morning of 10 July he sent away his baggage and all but two of his guns while the army took up a strong covering position on some rising ground behind a stream called the Wagg Rhyne. It was ideal for the purpose since it was enclosed by hedgerows, particularly around the road, while the far side of the stream was much more open. Goring therefore posted his muske-teers amongst the hedgerows, planted his two remaining guns to cover the ford (the 'pass') and deployed his horse on the ridge above.

Fairfax was thus faced with an awkward decision. The Royalist position was a strong one, but if he attempted to outflank it Goring would have ample time in which to draw off. There was no alternative therefore but to launch a frontal assault. First however he ordered his artillery to silence the two Royalist guns covering the ford. By noon this had been accomplished, and 1,500 commanded musketeers were sent forward under Colonel Rainsborough to clear the hedges:

> Our foot advanced down the hill to the pass, and with admirable resolution charged the enemy from hedge to hedge, till they got the pass; the enemy's horse upon this drew downe towards us, where-upon our horse advanced over the passe up the hill to the enemy; the Forlorne-hope of horse commanded by Major *Bethell*, gave a valiant and brave charge indeed, broke that body that charged him, and the next reserve: our reserve of horse that was commanded by Major *Desborough*, very resolutely charged the next standing bodies of the enemy so home, that instantly they put them to a disorderly retreat, & our musquetiers came close up to our horse, firing upon the enemy, whereupon their Regiments of white Colours, and black Colours of foot, before ever they engaged, marched away apace.[3]

Rather to the disappointment of Bethell and Desborough, Fairfax checked the pursuit until he could bring the rest of his army up, but it made little difference in the end. Goring tried to make a sight of it in a field two miles farther back, but his men refused to stand and were pursued for eight miles, having lost 1,400 prisoners, thirty colours and the two guns.

Leaving a garrison in Bridgewater under Sir Hugh Wyndham, Goring retreated westwards next day. For the moment Fairfax was content to let him go. Rightly judging that there was no danger of any interference from the Cavaliers, he unhurriedly set about the systematic elimination of the local garrisons. Bridgewater was besieged and then successfully stormed on 23 July. Colonel Okey took Bath in a surprise attack on the 31st, and Sherborne Castle surrendered after a ten-day siege on 14 August. In the meantime he also made his peace with the local Clubmen – armed bands who were prepared to defend their homes, crops and cattle against all comers. Goring had supplied them with arms in the hope that they would take his part against Fairfax, but as the Cavaliers were more inclined than the Parliamentarians to plunder, only a little bloodshed was required to lead the countrymen into the path of right-eousness. The real prize however was Bristol, which by this stage in the war was probably of far more importance to the King than Oxford.

There was in fact a suggestion that the King himself should go there since the position in south Wales was also deteriorating. A Parliamentarian force under Colonel Rowland Laugharne had won a useful little victory over Stradling at Colby Moor in Pembroke, and the Glamorgan authorities were proving uncooperative. As a result it was proposed to leave what remained of the Welsh foot in garrisons, while the horse commanded by Gerard and Langdale marched the long way round. On the evening of 21 July Rupert, having carried out a brief tour of inspection, crossed the Severn to confer with the King and his Council at Crick House, just outside Chepstow. There the arrangements were finalised, but when Charles was preparing to embark at Black Rock on the 24th, he heard that Bridgewater had just been lost. This, according to Symonds, 'rather stayed him', but worse news was to come. On the 23rd the Scots had stormed Canon Frome[4] and were closing in on Hereford!

Thus far little had been heard of the Scots since Marston Moor. This can largely be attributed to the fact that, in order to pursue Newcastle's army to its destruction outside York, Leven had been forced to by-pass a number of Royalist garrisons. Chief amongst these was the city of Newcastle upon Tyne, and in an astonishing display of ineptitude Leven besieged its mediaeval walls for three months. During this time he skirmished with the garrison, intermittently bombarded the city and steadily drove mines under the walls.[5] At last, faced by worsening weather and the unthinkable prospect of lifting the siege, he stormed it on 19 October. The fall of Newcastle was followed on the 27th by the surrender of Tynemouth Castle, and with the river reopened at last Londoners could once more warm themselves through the winter with sea coal. Unfortunately typhus, not military action, was responsible for the castle's surrender, and over the winter it not only spread through the Scots army but was carried back to Scotland as well. Leven's army was further weakened by the detachment of a reinforced brigade to besiege and afterwards garrison Carlisle, and by the urgent recall of troops to deal with the Royalist insurrection north of the border. He was also hampered by lack of money, food and transport. Now that the northern war was over, Parliament was proving less than punctilious in fulfilling its obligations to its Allies.

Nevertheless at the beginning of June 1645 Leven moved south with a sadly reduced army[6] of about 6,500, men and by the 12th was at Doncaster. Shortly afterwards having heard the happy news of Naseby, he shifted to Nottingham. Fairfax's move into the West Country was attended with some misgivings by the Committee of Both Kingdoms, since there was an obvious danger that in his absence the King might break out into the Midlands again. To guard against this Leven was therefore requested to move into the Severn valley in order to cover his rear. Initially he was far from happy about the idea, but the surrender of Carlisle on 28 June meant that he could recall David Leslie. On 2 July therefore the Scots marched out of Nottingham, crossed the Severn at Bewdley, stormed Canon Frome and sat down before Hereford on the 30th.

The King meanwhile was at Cardiff desperately trying to raise an army and discovering that the Glamorgan gentry were only prepared to raise men who would be commanded by themselves and would not march beyond the county boundary. Worse still they began referring to themselves as 'Neutrals'. In effect the gentry were setting up for Clubmen. Recognising that nothing could be done with them, he marched north with his horse and just 200 infantry brought from Carlisle by Sir Thomas Glenham. Sticking to the high ground in order to avoid the Scots outposts, he passed along the Welsh border and was at Bridgenorth by 8 August. From there he struck north-eastwards and had got the length of Doncaster by the 17th. This remarkable march had been under-taken in the hopes of raising an army in Yorkshire instead. There were still chimerical claims that 3,000 men could be raised there within a matter of days, but the reality was very different. When the army was mustered, Symonds enumerated it at just 2,200 horse, 400 foot and a rather pathetic little train comprising a string of pack horses carrying ammunition and three or four cartloads of pikes.[7]

The better part of the foot had been taken out of Welbeck and were what remained of the garrisons of Pontefract and Scarborough, now under the command of Colonel John Frescheville. There were great promises that more could soon be raised, but then almost at once word was brought that David Leslie was approaching with most of the Scots horse. Learning that he was as close as Rotherham, the Cavaliers hastily evacuated Doncaster on 20 August and retired southwards to Newark.

It seems likely that the foot were left behind in Newark, but the horse continued their march and at Stamford it was decided to turn aside and surprise some newly raised Eastern Association horse lying at Huntingdon. On the way they beat up two or three troops at Stilton and then pressed on to storm the town on the 24th. It was surrounded by a new ditch, but 'little disputed'. An unnamed Scottish major and about 100 men were taken prisoner and the rest fled to Cambridge. Afterwards the town was thoroughly plundered and well pleased with this paltry little success, the King returned to Oxford on 28 August.

To all appearances the situation had scarcely improved in his absence. Hereford was still under siege. That same night two sergeants, Thomas Innes and William Brown, were paid thirty shillings apiece for plumbing the ditch – and doubtless earned every penny of it. Subsequently the ditch was drained by the Scots and two breaches blown with mines in preparation for storming. By then the King was on his way, still without any infantry and rather unrealistically hoping that the absence of all but 800 of the Scots cavalry might afford him a chance of relieving the city. After resting up at Worcester for two days, the Royalists marched towards Hereford on 3 September and to their astonishment found the Scots in full retreat towards Gloucester.

Naturally enough they assumed that Leven was unwilling to fight, but in fact he had just received word of a disaster in Scotland. The rebels there, led by the Marquis of Montrose, had met and completely destroyed the Government's only field army at Kilsyth near Glasgow on 15 August. David Leslie's cavalry brigade was promptly turned around and sent north at once while Leven followed with the foot.[8]

Glad enough to see them gone whatever the cause, the King then passed back into south Wales. There he tried once again to raise an army, for although the threat to Hereford had been lifted for the present, Fairfax was closing in on Bristol. Having taken Sherborne the Parliamentarian commander was faced with the choice of pursuing Goring and ultimately relieving Plymouth or else besieging Bristol. No one needed reminding what had happened to Essex's army the year before, and so rather than risk a Royalist army appearing in his rear, Fairfax left Plymouth to its own devices and turned northwards to deal with Prince Rupert.

Once again his approach was slow and deliberate. Care was taken to eliminate any outposts which might hinder the siege operations. On 21 August Fairfax and Cromwell reconnoitred the defences and the army closed up two days later. Although much had been done to strengthen the city's fortifications, Prince Rupert faced pretty much the same problems in defending it as Nathaniel Fiennes had done in 1643. Geography still compelled him to defend a perimeter some five miles long. If anything his condition was worse, for he had slightly fewer men – perhaps 1,500 besides the 'townesmen'[9] – and plague to contend with as well as a generally disaffected civilian population.

Despite these disadvantages Rupert was determined to put up a fight, but from the beginning he suffered a series of setbacks. On the 23rd Sir Richard Crane, the commander of his Lifeguard, was killed in a sally from the Prior's Hill fort. Another sally the following day may have been more successful as was one against Colonel Weldon's quarter on the morning of the 26th. That afternoon however Sir Bernard Astley was fatally wounded and captured in an accidental encounter with Captain Lieutenant Joseph Molyneux of Butler's Regiment.[10] Yet another sally on 1 September was beaten back by Colonel Rainsborough, but on the 4th Fairfax at last formally summoned the city. Thus far, although he had taken some pains to pick off the various outposts, he had made no real attempt to dig in. There were some doubts as to whether the army was strong enough to undertake the task. Not only was Rupert credited with nearly double his actual numbers, but there were real fears that a relief attempt would shortly be made. An intercepted letter written by Goring on 25 August spoke of his hoping to march within three weeks, and the King was also thought certain to come. To make matters worse, just as a council of war was considering the question, news arrived of the Scots' retreat from Hereford.

It was clear therefore that if Bristol was to be taken it must be by escalade. Although the prospect filled no one with any enthusiasm, the most careful preparations were made. It was agreed that Weldon's Brigade was to attack on the Somerset side – where Maurice's men had failed two years before – the General's Brigade was to attack the sector between the rivers Frome and Avon on either side of Lawford's Gate, and Rainsborough's Brigade was to attack the sector between the Frome and the Prior's Hill fort.[11] In addition there was a contingency plan to employ 200 men from this brigade in an amphibious assault on the Waterfort at the southern end of the line, and diversions were to be mounted between that fort and Priors Hill.

Before committing himself to an escalade Fairfax sent in a formal summons to Rupert on 4 September. At the same time, by way of further intimidating the garrison, he summoned all the countrymen he could lay his hands on, gave them colours and posted them around the city. To his surprise Rupert, who probably had a pretty good idea that no relief would come, proved receptive. After a preliminary exchange of correspondence he offered to surrender on terms. Fairfax looked them over, agreed to the military clauses which entailed the Royalists marching out with the honours of war, but seems to have balked at the suggestion that the defences should be levelled. Despite some further discussion Fairfax lost patience and stormed at 2am on the morning of the 10th. Although the operation is frequently compared to the earlier one, the only point of similarity was the failure to gain a lodgement on the Somerset side. Otherwise Fairfax's men got over the defences at every point they attacked, and took the Prior's Hill fort, all for the loss of some 200 men. Rupert surrendered before daylight and then marched out on the 11th.[12]

King Charles was at Raglan when news came of the surrender. With the Scots temporarily out of the frame there was a plan to draw 3,000 foot out of the local garrisons and join with Goring's forces in an attack on Fairfax's quarters. However as even Walker admitted:

> This was a very plausible design in paper; and I fear had *Fairfax* given us time, or Prince *Rupert* not been forced to render, it would have been a longer time than we fancied to our selves before we could have made all ends to meet.[13]

Instead the King moved at once to Hereford, recalled his cavalry from South Wales and sent orders to Oxford that Rupert and his officers were to be dismissed.[14] However this exhausted his inspiration and he then remained at Hereford for a week until a fresh threat appeared. Parliament was again reaping the fruits of the previous year's victory on Marston Moor. There is no doubting that the creation of the New Model Army was a key factor in winning the war. Nevertheless an equally important one was the degree of coordination which the Committee of Both Kingdoms was now exercising both over that army and the remaining provincial ones. When Fairfax moved into the west, the Scots Army was ordered south to cover his rear. Unfortunately events in Scotland had brought about their withdrawal, but although the timing was unfortunate, the consequences were not. The Committee of Both Kingdoms merely replaced them with some of the other forces at their disposal; in this case some 2,000 Northern Association horse and dragoons commanded by Colonel General Sydenham Poyntz.[15]

With the West Country effectively closed to him and south Wales militantly neutral, the desperate resolution was taken to strike north-wards and join Montrose in Scotland. At first the Royalists succeeded in breaking contact with Poyntz by moving through the hill country along the Welsh border. Unfortunately on 22 September they arrived at Chirk to learn that not only was Chester once again under siege, but that the suburbs had fallen to a surprise attack and surrender was imminent. For once the King acted decisively. A message was sent into Byron, ordering him to hold on for another twenty-four hours while urgent preparations were made to mount a relief operation.

The situation was in fact extremely fluid, and if the Royalists moved quickly they might not only raise the siege but win a famous victory in the process. The situation was that the city stood on the north bank of the river Dee. The area enclosed by the mediaeval walls and castle was fairly compact, but there was a much larger area of suburbs to the north and east. The northern ones had been progressively razed and abandoned over the years, but the eastern ones were still enclosed within earthworks. It was this area which was taken by the parliamentarian Colonels Jones and Lothian in a surprise attack on the 20th. Since then they had been engaged in a very determined attempt to carry the inner perimeter as well. On the 23rd the King got into the city across the bridge over the Dee, which still remained under Royalist control. All he had with him were the three troops of his own Lifeguards, Gerard's Lifeguard and the Carlisle troopers under Sir Henry Stradling.[16] The rest of the Royalist cavalry, commanded by Sir Marmaduke Langdale, crossed the Dee much farther up at Holt Bridge and bivouacked on Miller's Heath to the southeast of the city.

The intention was to cut off the expected Parliamentarian retreat and if possible trap them in the suburbs. Had the Royalists been left to their own devices it might have worked, but Poyntz was closing in fast. Jones and Lothian got off a messenger who found him at Whitchurch late on the 23rd, and he very properly marched through the night to come up in time. Langdale meanwhile learned of his approach, and at dawn there was an indecisive little fight on Miller's Heath. Afterwards Langdale and Poyntz both drew off and waited for some infantry support.

Not surprisingly it was the Parliamentarians who appeared first, for not only had they a much shorter distance to cover, but they could march directly from the suburb. Realising this was likely to be the case, Langdale fell back on to Rowton Moor in order to avoid being attacked from two sides at once. He may have been successful in this since it appears that Jones and Poyntz joined before attacking him. However it did him little good for he was outnumbered by about three to two in horse and the Parliamentarians had about 300 musketeers besides. Moreover it has to be said that the Royalists were getting into the habit of being beaten and after a short fight they broke. Then Gerard appeared on the scene having marched out of the north gate and fetched a compass around the Parliamentarian-held eastern suburbs. He had with him the 300 odd horse of the Lifeguard, his own, Stradling's troops, and another 200 foot drawn out of the garrison.[16] Too late to save Langdale he ran into trouble at once. The head of his column became mixed up with retreating elements of Langdale's command, and his rear was ambushed by more Parliamentarians sallying out of the suburbs. To make matters worse he was also fired upon by Parliamentarian infantry lining the captured earthworks. With all cohesion lost the fighting spread over Rowton Moor and Hoole Heath and by nightfall the King's army was destroyed. The number of dead is unknown, but 900 prisoners were taken off to Nantwich and next day the King fled to Denbigh with just 500 horse.

There he learned that Montrose had been badly beaten by David Leslie at Philiphaugh, just outside Selkirk, on 13 September. This, according to Walker, left him with just two options; either to retire into Anglesey or try to retire to Worcester and scrape an army together from the local garrisons. While the first was not without its attractions it was the second which was pitched upon. The seemingly indestructible Sir William Vaughan was left behind at Denbigh with what remained of the army and orders to relieve Chester if he could. Byron had been given permission to surrender if he did not receive help within eight days, but although Vaughan was badly beaten at Denbigh Green on 1 November,[17] Byron clung on until 3 February 1646.

This can have come as little comfort to the King, for the news everywhere else was bad. He never made it to Worcester. After taking Bristol Fairfax correctly apprehended that he had nothing to fear either from the King or from Goring, so he detached Cromwell to clear the London Road. Political and commercial considerations as well as military ones demanded the urgent capture of the various Royalist garrisons dotted about southern England. The Devizes fell on 23 September and Winchester was stormed five days later. The castle surrendered on 5 October and, having very evidently acquired a taste for knocking places about a bit, Cromwell then summoned Basing House on 11 October and just as promptly stormed it on the 14th. Although the fall of these fortresses, and in particular the Catholic stronghold of Basing, were serious blows to the King, a more immediate problem was the loss of Berkeley Castle on 26 September. Originally it had been a part of the outer ring protecting Bristol, but its capture also meant that Worcester could no longer be regarded as secure. Accordingly the King's intention to establish his headquarters there was abandoned and the Royal party made its way instead to Newark.

Some unpleasant scenes then occurred. Digby and Langdale set off for the north in a vain attempt to reach Montrose[18], and in their absence Rupert arrived from Oxford. He was intent on clearing his name, but although a council of war duly exonerated him for his rather too hasty surrender of Bristol, it failed to heal the rift. If anything the situation grew worse. The King replaced Sir Richard Willys, one of Rupert's circle, with John, Lord Belayse, and this inspired something of a mutiny amongst the 'Swordsmen'. Dramatic though the falling out may have seemed, it was in reality of little consequence, for they were all of them officers without an army. The King's last armies were in the West Country and their destruction by Fairfax was now little more than a matter of time.

While Cromwell was clearing the London Road with such dramatic success Fairfax was slowly advancing into Devon. By the end of December he had got the length of Crediton. Goring had thrown up his command and gone overseas and his successor, the Prince of Wales' man

Lord Wentworth, contrived to get surprised and badly beaten at Bovey Tracy on 9 January 1646. A hasty retreat to Tavistock then uncovered Exeter, but relying on precedent Fairfax pressed on far enough to scare off the Royalists besieging Plymouth on the 12th. Then he stormed Dartmouth on the 19th and turned back to deal with Exeter.

In the meantime the Cavaliers had made a last attempt to pull themselves together. Lord Hopton was appointed General with Wentworth and Sir Richard Grenville under him to command the horse and foot respectively. This arrangement fell apart at once when Grenville refused to acknowledge Hopton's authority and was arrested on the spot. From a disciplinary point of view Hopton had no alternative, but it meant that he moved forward to Torrington with demoralised cavalry and discontented infantry.

Learning of the Royalist concentration Fairfax left a covering force under Sir Hardress Waller before Exeter and marched to meet it. On the 16th he found Hopton still at Torrington and apparently preparing to fight a defensive battle. The day was spent in skirmishing along the muddy lanes leading to the town, but by about 5pm the Parliamentarians were drawn up in front of it. Initially there was no thought of assaulting Torrington that night for the approaches were barricaded and the hedges stuffed full of Royalist musketeers. However that evening Fairfax and Cromwell went out to reconnoitre the Royalist positions and:

> ... hearing a noyse in the Towne, as if the Enemy were retreating, and being loath they should goe away without an affront, to that purpose, and that we might get certaine knowledge whether they were going off or not, a small Party of Dragoons were sent to fire on the Enemy neer the Barricadoes and Hedges; the Enemy answered us with a round Volley of shot, thereupon the Forlorn Hope of Foot went and engaged themselves to bring off the Dragoons, and the reserve fell on to bring off the Forlorn-Hope: And being thus far engaged, the General being on the Field, and seeing the generall resolution of the Souldiery, held fit, that the whole Regiments in order, after them should fall on . . .[19]

After two hours of heavy fighting the Parliamentarians forced their way into the town and the Cavaliers fled in confusion, blowing up their magazine in the process. This was the end for the Western army and Hopton surrendered less than a month later on 12 March.

A week later Lord Astley surrendered at Stow in the Wold. Over the winter the King had pulled together some 1,200-1,500 horse at Oxford, but they could do nothing to retrieve the rapidly deteriorating situation. With Montrose defeated Leven had moved south again to besiege Newark on 28 November, and matters were even worse in the Severn valley. Hereford finally fell to a surprise attack in mid-December and Astley failed to stabilise the situation. Instead the best he could do was concentrate some 2,000 men at Bridgenorth and try to fight his way through to Oxford. The first leg of the journey to Worcester was accomplished without too much difficulty. There however he found that Brereton was coming down from the north, and that Colonels Morgan and Birch were doing their best to throw themselves across his path. Feinting towards Evesham, he suddenly turned north by way of Droitwich and got across the Avon. Morgan however soon got on his track, and after a running battle with his rearguard, brought him to a stand at Donnington, near Stow. In the early hours of the morning of 21 March Brereton came up and the Parliamentarians then encircled him. It took a few hours of sometimes bitter fighting, but in the end some of the Cavalier horse broke out and the foot then laid down their arms. King Charles now had just a few garrisons, and as Fairfax approached Oxford, he fled from his wartime capital on 27 April and surrendered to the Scots.

If he hoped thereby to enlist their assistance he was disappointed, for they compelled him to order the surrender of Newark before marching northwards to Newcastle upon Tyne. This was a shrewd move on their part aimed at securing a satisfactory adjustment of accounts. This turned out to be a tedious business, and it was not until 3 February 1647 that the King – and the city – was handed over to the Parliamentarian authorities. By then all the Royalist garrisons save Harlech had surrendered, but a second Civil War was little more than a year away.

NOTES

1. Earlier in the year the Prince of Wales had been given a Court of his own and sent into the West Country. The intention seems to have been to provide a central figure of authority for the squabbling commanders in that theatre. Unsurprisingly his presence made no difference at all save to provide Goring with an excuse to ignore orders emanating from Prince Rupert.
2. Walker, E. *Brief Memorials . . .1645* p116
3. Sprigge, *Anglia Rediviva* p65. Major Christopher Bethell belonged to Whalley's Regiment while Desborough commanded the Lord General's. The Royalist regiments of foot with white colours and black colours were probably those commanded by Colonel William Slaughter and Colonel Matthew Wise, for Goring's Adjutant General, Sir Richard Bulstrode, complained of their behaviour and even claimed that they fired on other Royalist troops (Young & Holmes *The English Civil War* pp255-6). Both units were apparently newly raised, and as the officers still alive in 1663 all came from Brecon, Carmarthen and Glamorgan, it may fairly be inferred that they were some of the men shipped across from Charles Gerard's command.
4. Laurence Crawford, who had joined Leven after declining a command in the New Model, was killed in the assault. The garrison, commanded by Colonel John Barnard were massacred, but it is unclear whether matters simply got out of hand or whether this was a deliberate retaliation for the Royalists' earlier refusal of quarter to the Scots in Leicester.

5. The reliance upon the time-consuming process of mining is quite inexplicable for Leven had a substantial train of artillery and the town wall was unprotected by earthworks. As it transpired a few hours' bombardment was sufficient to open practicable breaches. Had he chosen to rely upon his guns there was no reason why he should not have taken the city in mid-August.

6. The following list is based on a muster outside Newark on 17 January 1646 (RCHM *Newark* p97). In addition to those units named below there were a number of independent troops of horse. At some point the army was joined by a mercenary band of Germans, Dutchmen, former Royalists (and a few Scots) commanded by Colonel Jonas Van Druschke. He and some of his officers had previously served under Waller but found themselves unemployed after the creation of the New Model. In January the army mustered 4,136 horse and 2,836 foot, but while these figures were probably down on the June 1645 totals they do include Van Druschke's Horse, and another cavalry regiment commanded by the Earl of Balcarres which was serving in Scotland in the summer of 1645. Nevertheless something like 3,500 horse and 3,000 foot would probably be not too far from the mark.

Foot:

Sir Arthur Erskine of Scotscraig
Sir David Hume of Wedderburn
Lord Livingston
Earl Marischal
Sir Thos. Ruthven of Freeland
Col. Walter Scott
Lord Sinclair
Earl of Tullibardine

Horse:

Sir John Browne
Sir Frederick Hamilton
Lt.Gen. David Leslie
Lord General
Major Gen. John Middleton
Sir James Ramsay
Colonel Michael Weldon

7. Symonds *Diary* p64.
'Munday, August 19, 1645
His Majesties army consisted of these:-
His lifeguard of horse commanded by Lord Bernard Stuart, Earl of Lichfield, consisted of the King's troope, the Queenes troope, Lord Lichfield's troope, Sir Thomas Glenham's horse commanded by Sir Henry Stradling.

Toto effectually	300
Generall Gerard (Lord Brandon)	800
Sir Marmaduke Langdale's Brigade	700
Sir William Vaughan's Brigade, with	
Prince Maurice's regiment*	400
Effectually fighting horse	2,200

* the brigade comprised his own, the Queen's, Prince Maurice's and Col. Samuel Sandys' regiments.

Foot

Welbeck	250
Lichfield, drawne out when the King came thence	150
400	

Some ammunition carried upon horses, three or four carts full of pikes, which the King had from Tedbury [sic], which were Colonel Nevill's of Holt'. Not included in this list are the 200 foot from Carlisle 'who were made into dragoons in Brecknockshire'. In actual fact they had apparently become Sir Thomas Glenham's *Horse* (Symonds p71).

8. Walker (*op.cit.* p136) claims that the Scots were initially refused leave to pass through Gloucester and that they had declared that 'if they could not pass there, they knew they should be welcome to pass through *Worcester*'. It is

218

entirely possible that harsh words were spoken but quite inconceivable that the Scots should have seriously threatened to change sides at this juncture.

9. It is difficult to establish just what the garrison comprised at this time. The Parliamentarians consistently put it at upwards of 3,000 men, but only 1,000 foot and 500 horse marched out at the surrender. The following units can be positively identified:

Prince Rupert's Lifeguard of Horse	Prince Rupert's Lifeguard of Foot
Prince Rupert's Horse	Col. John Taylor's Foot
Lord Hawley's Horse	Lord Hawley's Foot
Col. John Stuart's Horse?	Col. William Pretty's Foot
	Col. Edward Rodney's Foot?
	Col. Walter Slingsby's Foot

Prince Rupert's Lifeguard of Foot was one of the few Royalist infantry units to escape from Naseby, presumably because after fighting Okey's Dragoons it was able to get away through the Sulby enclosures. It was originally recruited on the Continent under a contract between Rupert and a Dutch gun-runner named Van Haesdonck (CSPD 1641-43 pp500-2) There are a number of Irish officers in the 1663 *List* who are more likely to have served with this unit rather than his regiment of foot. Colonel John Taylor's regiment on the other hand was described by Symonds on the 24th of July (*Diary* p61) as 'townesmen; six colours:' Hawley was the deputy governor and appears to have formed his regiment from drafts of men from Ireland. At any rate a surprisingly high proportion of his surviving officers in 1663 were Irish. Pretty's Regiment was Welsh and Slingsby's originally part of the old Western Army. Stuart and Rodney were in the city when it surrendered but it is by no means certain that they had their regiments.

10. Sprigge p91
11. *ibid.* pp94-5

Weldon's Brigade	General's Brigade
Col. Ralph Weldon	Col. Edward Montague
Col. Richard Fortescue	Col. John Pickering
Col. William Herbert	Sir Hardress Waller
Col. Richard Ingoldsby	
Rainsborough's Brigade	
Col. Thomas Rainsborough	
Col. John Birch	
Col. Robert Hammond	
Lt.Col. Thomas Pride	
Major Gen. Philip Skippon	

12. Apart from his Lifeguard of Foot, who were permitted their arms and a pound of powder apiece, Rupert's infantry marched out with swords and pikes only which explains the following quotation – origin unknown – in Fortescue's *History of the British Army* Vol.I p282 'In the works at Bristol was a company of footmen with knapsacks and halfpikes, like so many tinkers with budgets at their backs, and some musketeers with bandoliers about their necks like a company of sow-gelders'. The infantry with half-pikes were presumably garrison soldiers who had no need of long pikes.
13. Walker *op.cit.* p129
14. Rupert's dismissal was in large part inspired by the courtier Lord Digby, who successfully convinced the King that Rupert had betrayed him. While charges of disloyalty were patently absurd, there is on the other hand no doubt that Rupert recognised the war was lost and was becoming increasingly sick of prolonging the bloodshed. It is hard to escape the impression that the storm

of Bristol was undertaken only because Fairfax recognised that Rupert could not surrender the city without at least a token fight.

15. Poyntz was a professional soldier of no discernible politics who had returned from the Continent at just the right moment to replace Lord Fairfax when he retired in accordance with the Self-Denying Ordinance.

16. Symonds *Diary* p71.

17. Symonds *Diary* p76. According to Symonds, who seems to have been riding as a volunteer under Vaughan, the Royalist army comprised the following:
Prince Maurice's Lifeguard (part)
Sir William Vaughan's (Irish) Regiment*
Col. John Hurter – garrison horse from Monmouth
Col. Robert Werden's Horse
Col. Samuel Sandys' Horse

	Total	300
Col. Randal Egerton's Horse		200
Col. Roger Whitley's Horse		200
Col. Henry Grady's Horse		
General Gerard's Horse		
Col. John Davalier's Horse		
	Total	200
Lord Byron's Regiment		100

* Vaughan's Regiment apparently included garrison troopers drawn out of Ercall, Bridgenorth and Chirk.

Foot

Prince Maurice's Firelocks (part)	150
Ludlow Foot	90
Ercall Dragoons	20
Chirk Firelocks	20

18. They were defeated at Sherburn-in-Elmet on 15 October, but got as far as Burgh-on-Sands in Cumbria before giving up and fleeing to the Isle of Man.

19. Sprigge p186. This account makes it abundantly clear that it was Fairfax and not Cromwell who authorised the general assault once the action escalated. Fairfax's own account (Sprigge pp187-94) confirms this and states that the first regiments ordered forward belonged to Hammond's Brigade and comprised his own, Hammond's and Harley's regiments.

CHAPTER XVII

Darkness at Preston: The Second Civil War

The untidy end of the Civil War precluded an immediate and orderly disbandment of the victorious armies. Some of the provincial forces, maintained by local money were disbanded as soon as it appeared expedient, but Sir Thomas Fairfax's regulars were a different matter. It was not until the Scots handed over the King and marched north in early

1647 that the mechanics of the process were given serious consideration by Parliament.

There was still a need for the traditional guards and garrisons at certain strategic locations around England, and an absolutely crying need for a proper expeditionary force to go to Ireland. Otherwise there was no requirement for a standing army and those soldiers who did not volunteer for Ireland – or were not required for that service – were to be disbanded. This effectively entailed a fresh 'new-modelling' and re-opened the issue of which party would end up controlling the proposed 'Irish' army.

The Presbyterians still accounted for the majority in Parliament and might this time have succeeded in ousting the Independents had the government not been all but bankrupt. The infantry's pay was eighteen weeks in arrears, and the cavalry were owed no less than forty-three weeks. Faced with the dismal choice of volunteering for Ireland or being turned off without a penny of those arrears, they not surprisingly proved uncooperative. A petition protesting about the injustice was presented to Parliament on 30 March and was immediately denounced as seditious. Some of the more prominent signatories, who included Thomas Pride and John Lilburne were arrested, but this only served to exacerbate the situation. Leadership of what was looking increasingly like a mutiny was assumed by elected *Agitators* – in effect shop stewards – and Fairfax solemnly warned Parliament that in the circumstances it would be impossible to disband any of the regiments.

Instead he organised a general muster at Newmarket on 3 June and set up a 'General Council of the army'. This comprised all the general officers, and two officers and two agitators from each regiment. By this means he retained a measure of control over his increasingly mutinous forces. Nevertheless the *Declaration of the Army* issued on the 14th went as far as to claim that the army was more representative of the people than Parliament, and that it was therefore justified in opposing Parliament in defence of its rights. Both statements were probably true enough and, suitably alarmed by the threat, Parliament mobilised the City Trained Bands and appointed Sir William Waller to command them.

Unlucky as ever Waller found few militia men willing to turn out. Instead he tried to organise some kind of defence force out of a sorry collection of disbanded soldiers and idle apprentices. Had Parliament kept its nerve the crisis could have turned nasty, but instead the Independents succeeded in pushing through a number of concessions to the Army. Intentionally or otherwise this provoked Waller's mob into invading the House of Commons, whereupon the Speakers of both Houses, and the Independents, fled to the Army for protection.

This in turn gave Fairfax and Cromwell the excuse they needed to occupy London and present their *Heads of Proposals* (which principally

called for a limited monarchy, biennial Parliaments and religious tolera-
tion) to those Members of Parliament who had not yet run away. So far
so good, but having encouraged a spirit of insubordination in the army,
they discovered that the rank and file were becoming increasingly
radical. In order to bring the matter to a head the General Council called
a series of debates at Putney in late October. If Fairfax and Cromwell
hoped they could thereby browbeat the dissidents they were sadly
mistaken. Finding control slipping away they disbanded the General
Council on 11 November and ordered the agitators back to their
regiments. This came dangerously close to provoking a mutiny. The
agitators called for another general rendezvous of the army, but Fairfax
would only agree to three partial ones. The first of these was appointed
for 15 November at Corkbush Field, near Ware. Two regiments, Colonel
Harrison's Horse and Colonel Lilburne's Foot, turned up uninvited with
copies of a seditious pamphlet, *The Agreement of the People*, stuck into their
hats. Lilburne's Regiment was certainly in a state of mutiny and came to
the rendezvous commanded by Captain Lieutenant William Bray. For a
time it looked ugly, especially as Lilburne's drew up in order of battle.
However first Harrison's troopers were persuaded to take the pamphlets
out of their hats and then Lilburne's infantry were coerced into doing the
same. A dozen men were tried on the spot for mutiny and one of them,
Corporal Bartholomew Symonds, was shot. This firm action had a
salutary effect on the dissidents and shortly afterwards events took a
curious turn.

On 3 June, at the outset of the Army Crisis, Cromwell had seized the
King, presumably to serve as a bargaining counter. Since then he had
remained in the army's custody, latterly at Hampton Court, but on the
very night the General Council was disbanded, he escaped. The extent to
which his escape was engineered, or merely facilitated, cannot be known,
but the timing was too convenient for the Generals to be a coincidence,
and so too perhaps was what followed.

Having got safely away from Hampton Court the King turned up for
some reason at Carisbroke on the Isle of Wight. There the Governor,
Colonel Hammond, had him locked up again but served as more of a host
than a jailer. Charles resumed negotiations with his English Parliament,
and with the newly emergent Royalist party in the Scottish one.

The Duke of Hamilton had not had a good war. Appointed to be the
King's Scottish Commissioner he had failed to avert the political crisis in
1638, and then even more signally failed to land an expeditionary force to
fight the 'rebels' in the following year. In 1643 he and his brother, the Earl
of Lanark, had gone to Oxford to mediate between the King and what
was effectively by then the Scots Republic. Unfortunately he was
denounced as a traitor by his rival Montrose and bundled off to
Pendennis Castle for the duration. Now he was free and at the head of the

Royalist faction which had for the present gained the ascendancy in the Scots parliament or Estates. On 26 December 1647 the King secretly signed an 'Engagement' with Hamilton's party, in which he agreed to establish Presbyterianism in England and suppress the Independents, in return for the assistance of the Scots army.

The plan was straightforward enough. Hamilton was to lead an army across the border and this was to be the signal for a general Royalist uprising. In the event it went very badly wrong from the beginning. Like the English Presbyterians Hamilton's party represented the established social order and were prepared to reach an accommodation with the King in order to preserve it. Although for the present they enjoyed a certain ascendancy over the more radical 'Kirk' party or 'Covenanters', they found widespread opposition to the raising of an army. The Engagement was ratified by the Estates on 2 March 1648, but the shire Committees of War were only appointed on 18 April, and a general levy was not ordered until 4 May. By that time the English risings had already begun.

Ironically the first of the regional revolts was led by a Parliamentarian, Colonel John Poyer. Laugharne's Pembroke army was to be disbanded, but one of his officers, Colonel Poyer, refused to hand over Pembroke Castle to his successor on the entirely understandable grounds that neither he nor his troops had been paid. Unsurprisingly a dim view was taken of this, and largely in self defence Poyer, and Laugharne as well, declared for the King on 23 March. At first it was all Parliament could do to contain the revolt. The only 'loyal' troops in the area were under the command of Colonel Thomas Horton and he could muster only his own regiment of horse, part of another, eight companies of foot and 200 dragooners.[1] However the fact that most of them were mounted was of crucial importance for Laugharne and Poyer were desperately short of cavalry. Sustained by the news that Cromwell was marching to his assistance with another regiment of cavalry and three of infantry[2], Horton succeeded in routing Laugharne at St Fagans on 8 May. Thereafter the Welsh campaign was little more than a series of sieges.

However the Welsh revolt was followed by unrest elsewhere. There was sporadic rioting in London throughout April and May. On 8 April a riot in Norwich required three troops of Colonel Fleetwood's Horse to restore order. There was to be similar trouble at Bury St Edmunds a month later, when 600 men seized the county magazine, crying 'For God and King Charles'. That particular incident was dealt with by three more troops of Fleetwood's and two troops of the Lord General's Regiment under Major Desborough, but in the meantime there was worse news from the north.

On 28 April Sir Marmaduke Langdale seized Berwick, and next day Sir Philip Musgrave's men took Carlisle. This placed the local Parliamentarian commander, Colonel John Lambert, in a difficult position, as he had four regiments of horse and three of foot[3], and also had to deal with the distraction of a Royalist capture of Pontefract Castle. In the event he sent Colonel Robert Lilburne to deal with the Northumberland Royalists while he moved to confront Langdale and Musgrave. In the early hours of the morning of 1 July Lilburne quite literally caught Sir Richard Tempest and Colonel Edward Grey napping at Cartington, took 400 prisoners and 600 horses as well. It was a notable success but all now depended on how quickly Hamilton could raise his army in Scotland.

Recognising the seriousness of the situation Fairfax reluctantly prepared to move north, only to be diverted by yet another crisis in the south-east. On 21 May a Royalist insurrection broke out at Rochester. Five days later the rebels also took Dartford and Deptford, and the following day the fleet and its predominantly Presbyterian officers went over to them. London itself might have followed, but Fairfax was already on the move. On the 27th he concentrated his forces on Hounslow Heath[4] and marched eastwards. By the 31st he was at Gravesend, but then, learning that Rochester was strongly held, he swung south to Maidstone on 1 May.

The Royalist rebels, led by Goring's father, the Earl of Norwich, were already occupying the town with some 3,000 men,[5] while a further 7,000 stood in reserve outside. As at Torrington the battle began in a rather happy-go-lucky style. Fairfax proposed to storm Maidstone on the following day, but instead Colonel John Hewson's Regiment got into a firefight with Norwich's outpost line and the action then escalated. In the open field Fairfax's regulars might have defeated the Royalists in short order, but in the narrow barricaded streets they held out until nightfall. They might have hung on longer still had the reserve been persuaded to come in, but they remained standing outside and then scattered when Fairfax's men finally took the town.

Norwich himself however was made of sterner stuff. Not only did he get most of his own men away, but he then very enterprisingly bypassed Fairfax to launch an attack on London. On the 3rd he was at Blackheath and had seized Bow Bridge. Unfortunately the City's Royalists failed to rise and Skippon mobilised the Trained Bands against him. Undaunted the gallant old Cavalier got his men across the river and into Essex where they linked up with a north Royalist force under Sir Charles Lucas[6]. Yet another rising had taken place at Braintree on the 4th. Part of the local Trained Band, led by Colonel Henry Farr, had gone over to the rebels and Lucas had taken Colchester.

Fairfax was soon on their trail. Leaving Colonel Hewson's Regiment to deal with the remaining Kentish rebels, he crossed the river at Tilbury on the 11th. Pushing on rapidly he encountered Lucas's forces drawn up across the London Road on the 13th. Initially he tried to drive straight through, but they fought back stoutly, and it took some time to force them back within the town. Having done so Fairfax then attempted to storm the somewhat makeshift defences, but although the fighting went on until midnight, his men failed to gain a lodgement. There was no alternative but to settle down to what was to be a surprisingly lengthy siege. Scarcely disturbed by a Royalist uprising in Kingston which terminated in the battle of Surbiton on 6 July[7], Fairfax eventually starved the Royalists into submission on 28 August.[8]

Thus far the Royalists had been contained, but there was very little left in reserve to deal with the Scots when they came. In February 1647 the old Scots army which fought at Marston Moor and against Montrose had been 'new modelled' into five regiments of regular infantry, two Highland regiments and a number of independent troops of horse. This force was more than sufficient for internal security purposes but wholly inadequate for an invasion of England. The Earl of Leven declined the command on the very reasonable grounds that he was getting too old for such adventures. David Leslie would have been the next choice, but as he was an adherent of the Kirk party, he flatly declined to serve. This meant that Hamilton, whose military experience was negligible, had to take on the chief command himself. His second-in-command, the Earl of Callendar, had served under Leven without much distinction, but at least the other senior officers, William Baillie, John Middleton and James Turner, were competent professionals. The same could hardly be said for their men. Only four of the veteran regiments could be spared for the expedition, and although a fresh mobilisation was set in train, the process of conscription met with considerable obstruction. In south-west Scotland that obstruction turned into open rebellion.

Hundreds of men had fled from Lanarkshire into neighbouring Ayrshire either to avoid being conscripted, or after having deserted from the new levy. There they joined with the local opposition groups in a muster on Mauchline Moor, near Kilmarnock. Meanwhile Hamilton's second-in-command, the Earl of Callendar, was concentrating a large body of cavalry at Stewarton and despatched Major General John Middleton and the Earl of Glencairn to deal with them. Arriving at Mauchline with ten troops of horse on 12 June they found 800 foot and 1,200 horse waiting for them. However, when a deputation of ministers came forward, Middleton gave them a written assurance that if the rebels dispersed peacefully all would be well. However these terms applied only to the 'cuntrie people', not to the deserters. Unsurprisingly the latter argued in favour of fighting, and when Middleton saw no signs of the gathering breaking up, he despatched a Trumpet to demand an answer. As luck would have it he rode up to a group of deserters who roundly declared that they intended to fight.

His patience exhausted Middleton thereupon ordered his forlorn hope to charge. Falling on briskly, they drove back the Covenanters but quickly fell into disorder. Callendar afterwards claimed that some dismounted in

225

search of plunder, but at all events Middleton then had to lead in his main body to extricate them. Outnumbered he too got into difficulty, but then Callendar arrived. Increasingly concerned by the reports which were coming in, he left his infantry at Kilmarnock and hurried forward with 1,000 horse. Arriving just in time to see Middleton falling back, he paused only long enough to draw up his men before charging in and routing the Covenanters completely.

As battles go it was a pretty inconsequential affair, but it pointed up the difficulties which Hamilton faced. In the circumstances it is perhaps hardly surprising that he did not cross the border until 8 July, and that when he did he only brought an estimated 3,000 horse and 6,000 foot.

Musgrave promptly handed Carlisle over to Hamilton and he rested in the city for six days before moving against Lambert at Penrith. He for his part fought a rearguard action against Hamilton's cavalry outside the town on the 14th, but fell back to Appleby before the Scots infantry could come up. There was another skirmish there three days later, but then Hamilton halted at Kirby Thore until the end of the month, waiting for reinforcements.

From a military point of view the delay was decidedly unfortunate, but the weather was foul and had been since the beginning of the campaign. Apart from the more obvious problems which this caused – not the least of which was a frighteningly high level of desertion – it meant that the English Royalist leaders had some difficulty in persuading volunteers to leave their warm hearths. Hamilton had no alternative therefore but to await the arrival of more regiments from Scotland. When they finally arrived he may in theory have been able to muster as many as 10,000 foot and 4,000 horse, exclusive of Langdale's contingent. In actual fact it is unlikely they mustered anything like that number, and something like 7,500 foot is much nearer the mark[9]. At least at this stage there was the prospect of more to come, for a substantial part of the Ulster Army had been recalled.[10]

Lambert meanwhile, despite having been joined by a regiment of foot and some horse raised in Lancashire by Colonel Ralph Assheton, had taken the opportunity to withdraw into the Stainmore Pass. A Scottish reconnaissance in force then drove him back to Barnard Castle on 26 July. Nevertheless he was still well placed to block a descent on Yorkshire aimed at relieving Pontefract, or to threaten the flank of an advance into Lancashire. Moreover next day he was joined by the advance elements of Cromwell's army. Having pacified south Wales the Lieutenant General immediately sent his cavalry north and followed as fast as he could with his infantry.

No such energy was being displayed by Hamilton. He was admittedly in an unenviable position. The expected English support was not materialising, and his hungry army was beginning to disintegrate. Then Monro arrived at Kendal and promptly fell out with everybody else. Hamilton naturally wanted him to bring his veterans forward as soon as possible, but Monro claimed that his commission placed him on an equal footing with the other two Lieutenant Generals, the Earl of Callendar and William Baillie. As he flatly refused to take orders from either of them, Hamilton had no alternative but to give way. However, since Callendar refused to admit of any equality, Monro was then ordered to remain behind and wait for the artillery train which was expected from Scotland.

These contretemps were the least of Hamilton's worries, for it became increasingly apparent that the ramshackle invasion had been launched without any clear objectives. The Royalist uprising it was intended to support had already been crushed and it had never been envisaged that the Scots would be on their own. At Hornby on 9 August a Council of War tried to thrash out some sort of strategy. Lambert by this time had fallen back to Knaresborough, so crossing into Yorkshire was a viable option. Middleton argued in favour of this and Sir James Turner agreed with him:

> . . . for this reason only, that I understood Lancashire was a close country, full of ditches and hedges; which was a great advantage the English would have over our raw and undisciplined musketeers . . . while, on the other hand, Yorkshire was a more open country and full of heaths, where he might both make better use of our horse, and come sooner to push of pike.

Turner's argument sounds plausible enough, but Baillie disagreed and probably rightly so. Whatever the supposed shortcomings of the infantry when it came to hedge-fighting, trying to take on Cromwell's cavalry in the open would have been suicidal. Callendar for his part professed himself indifferent, but Hamilton resolved to press on through Lancashire and link up with the Royalist rebels in north Wales. Nevertheless he still displayed a conspicuous lack of urgency, and the army did not leave Hornby until 14 August. Two of Langdale's regiments, commanded by Sir Thomas Tyldesley and Sir Philip Musgrave, were dropped off at Lancaster to besiege the castle, while the rest seem to have marched along the Pennine foothills, acting as a flank guard. Other than this rather obvious precaution, Hamilton's march discipline was extremely poor. By the night of the 16th his cavalry had reached Wigan but his infantry were still straggling into Preston, sixteen miles behind them.

Thus far he was ignorant of Cromwell's whereabouts and was completely unaware that the English army was closing in fast. Having rendezvoused with Lambert at Wetherby on the 12th, Cromwell pushed westwards through Skipton and across the Pennines to Gisburn on the

15th. From there he could descend the Ribble valley to Preston. By his own account Cromwell had 2,500 horse and dragoons, 4,000 regular foot, and another 1,600 foot and 500 horse belonging to provincial units.[11]

Langdale was unaware of his approach until a party of Colonel Richard Tempest's Horse[12] was captured at Waddow near Clitheroe on the morning of the 16th. Unaccountably he either failed to pass on a warning to Hamilton or more likely did not at first attach enough importance to the incident. Cromwell on the other hand had learned from his prisoners that he was now sitting on the flank of the Scots army and a brief council of war was held three miles beyond Clitheroe. The question was whether to turn aside, cross the Ribble at Whalley (the first bridge above Preston) and try to get ahead of the Scots, or to continue along the north bank and try to catch them in Preston. The latter course was adopted, and that night Cromwell closed up his forces in the grounds of Stonyhurst Hall.

Langdale's outpost line was just three miles away, and by now he was aware of the danger. Hamilton's only chance was to concentrate his forces at once. His horse was equal in numbers if not in quality, and with Langdale's men he would be able to muster some 9,000 foot against Cromwell's 5,600. Unfortunately Langdale failed to convince Hamilton of the seriousness of the situation. Callendar, who had just ridden back from Wigan, seems to have assumed that the enemy force was only Lambert's brigade. Consequently he argued that the infantry should instead move forward to join the cavalry at Wigan. As a result Langdale and his 2,000 men were effectively left to face Cromwell on their own throughout most of the battle on the 17th.

Early that morning he got his men under arms and started falling back on Preston, but his rearguard was caught at Longridge by the Parliamentarian advance guard: a party of horse under Major Smithson of Lilburne's and foot under Major Henry Pownell of Bright's. This in turn forced Langdale to halt his main body two miles short of Preston, astride the sunken lane which linked Longridge and Preston. It was a strong position with hedged and ditched enclosures on either side of the lane. After weeks of heavy rain, the going within the enclosures was extremely soft which further inhibited Cromwell from exploiting his cavalry superiority. Accordingly Langdale deployed his musketeers in the hedges and planted his stand of pikes with 'a great body of colours' in the lane.

Having deployed his men he then galloped off to the Scottish concentration area on Preston Moor in a vain attempt to get some support. Hamilton had already ordered his infantry to begin crossing the bridge, and Callendar argued that the move should go ahead. The reasoning behind this is unclear, but there may still have been some doubt as to whether Cromwell was indeed present. At any rate Hamilton gave way to him as usual and Langdale returned to his position, accompanied only by some Scots lancers[13].

By this time his outpost line on Ribbleton Moor was coming under pressure from Cromwell's advance guard:

> The General comes to us, and commands us to march; we not having half our men come up, desired a little patience. He gives out the word 'march!' And so we drew over a little common, and came to a ditch, and the enemy let fly at us (a company of Langdale's men that was newly raised). They shot at the skies, which did so encourage our men that they were willing to adventure upon any attempt; and the major orders me to march to the next hedge, and I bid him order the men to follow me, and then drew out a small party, and we came to the hedge end, and the enemy, many of them, threw down their arms, and run to their party where was their stand of pikes.[14]

Major Smithson then tried to probe down the lane towards this stand of pikes but was charged and driven back by the lancers. As the situation did not allow for any subtlety Cromwell deployed his regular infantry on either side of the lane. Overton's, Deane's and Pride's regiments were on the right, while Bright's and the Lord General's were on the left. A detachment of provincials had been left behind to cover the bridge at Whalley, but the remainder formed a reserve under Colonel Assheton. Two cavalry regiments, Cromwell's and Harrison's, were assigned the job of clearing the lane. As it was obviously going to be a difficult task a third regiment, probably Lilburne's, was designated as a reserve. Two other cavalry regiments, Twisleton's and Thornhaugh's, were posted in support of the right flank, while the remainder stood on the left. Thanks to the nature of the ground this deployment took some considerable time, and it was not until around 4pm that Cromwell was able to resume the attack.

At first he made little progress. His right wing overlapped Langdale's left to the extent that both Pride's and Deane's regiments found nobody in front of them. However the thickly hedged enclosures initially prevented him from exploiting this advantage, and in the centre the offensive soon ground to a halt. Eventually he was forced to commit Colonel Assheton's provincials. Then by sheer weight of numbers he at last forced Langdale back hedge by hedge and out on to the open road towards Preston.

By now Hamilton had become convinced of the seriousness of the situation. Now, when it was too late, he started deploying his infantry on Preston Moor. Turner was sent forward with some foot and a resupply of ammunition, and the cavalry summoned back from Wigan. No sooner was this done than Callendar rode up from the bridge and angrily pointed out the dangers. Standing on the open moor without cavalry support was asking for trouble at the best of times, and with a river at their backs it was nothing short of suicidal. He argued instead that the infantry should be sent across the bridge as quickly as possible. They could then take up a good defensive position on the other side and wait for Middleton to bring the cavalry up.

As usual Hamilton gave way to him and has been roundly condemned ever after since this meant that Langdale was abandoned to his fate. In reality he had no choice, for the time to fight had long since passed. Cromwell's men were already driving Langdale's men into the streets of Preston. South of the town Baillie had successfully pushed most of his infantry across the river but was still holding the bridgehead with two brigades.[15] Hamilton had remained up on Preston Moor waiting for Langdale, but by the time the surviving Royalists had disengaged, it was too late. Baillie's bridgehead was already under attack. Whatever his failings as a general there was no doubting Hamilton's personal courage. Ordering their men to head northwards and find Monro, he and Langdale managed to fight their way down to the river and swim across.[16]

Meanwhile a furious battle was raging on the low ground to the south. While the two brigades held on to the bridge over the Ribble, Baillie began deploying the rest of the Scots infantry farther back behind the rather smaller river Darwen. Once they were in position Callendar sent forward 600 musketeers to extricate the men on the bridge. Unfortunately as they tried to cross the flat ground between the two rivers they came under heavy fire and were driven back. Despite being left unsupported, the bridge-guard held on against the Lord General's Regiment and some of the Lancashire provincials for two hours. Eventually the position was carried 'at push of pike' and the momentum served to carry the Darwen Bridge as well.

By this time it was getting dark. Many of Cromwell's men were dropping away to find dry quarters in Preston, and others had got in amongst the Scots baggage train, abandoned by the Darwen Bridge. As the fighting died down both sides convened councils of war.

Cromwell reckoned that he had won a useful victory, but was concerned by two possibilities. One was that Hamilton would march his infantry upstream and try to recross the river by the bridge at Whalley. This was considered unlikely, but he countered it by sending seven troops of horse to reinforce the existing garrison. The second and much more serious prospect was finding Monro coming in on his rear. Accordingly the remainder of Assheton's provincials were posted astride the Lancaster Road, and then he proposed to attack Hamilton next morning with all his regulars.

At the top of the hill Baillie and Turner were arguing that they should stand fast and meet that attack, but Callendar successfully convinced Hamilton to fall back towards Middleton and the cavalry. At this point the operation degenerated into farce. There were two roads between Preston and Wigan; one went by way of Chorley and the other by way of Standish. In response to his earlier orders Middleton was already marching northwards. As it happened he was moving up the Chorley Road while the infantry set off down the Standish Road. Inevitably they passed each other in the night, and in the early hours of the morning Middleton rode straight into Cromwell's men at Darwen.

Recovering quickly he swung around and conducted a textbook fighting retreat down the Standish Road, killing Colonel Francis Thornhaugh in the process. Reunited on Wigan Moor the Scots drew up in order of battle, but although they still outnumbered Cromwell's men, thanks to the detachments he had left behind, they were in no condition to fight. Much of the powder they carried was soaked and useless, and their reserve supply had been abandoned at Darwen. They were exhausted and morale was low. A further retreat or rather this time a flight was decided upon. Covered by Middleton's cavalry the foot marched off through Wigan, making for Warrington and the bridge over the Mersey.

Under cover of darkness most of them got away successfully, but the rearguard was still in Wigan when Middleton's cavalry were driven in by Cromwell's advance guard. At least one of his little regiments was routed, and as the troopers galloped into Wigan, the cry went up that the English were coming. Colonel Turner immediately drew up his brigade in the market-place ready to receive them. In the event it was some of Middleton's men who turned up first and Turner ordered his men to let them through:

> But now my pikemen, being demented (as I think we were all), would not hear me; and two of them ran full tilt at me. One of their pikes, which was intended for my belly, I gripped with my left hand; the other ran me nearly two inches in the inner side of my right thigh; all of them crying of me and the Horse 'They are Cromwell's men . . .' I rode to the Horse and desired them to charge through these Foot. They, fearing the hazard of the pikes, stood. I then made a cry come up from behind them, that the enemy was upon them. This encouraged them to charge my Foot so fiercely that the pikemen threw down their pikes, and got into the houses. All the horse galloped away, and as I was afterwards told, rode not through but over, our whole Foot treading them down.[17]

This was the beginning of the end. Cromwell halted just outside Wigan for a few hours but he knew that the Scots were on the point of collapse, and at daybreak he resumed his pursuit. At Winwick, three miles north of Warrington, they made a stand. Somehow they had found some dry powder, for they blocked the road with pikemen and stuffed the hedges on either side with musketeers. The engagement which followed is poorly documented, but even Cromwell afterwards admitted to being held up 'for many hours'. They were commanded by an unknown officer identified only as 'a little spark in a blue bonnet'[18], but Cromwell eventually found local guides who brought some of his infantry on to the Scots flank. They were then driven back on to the green by the church and there finally routed.

With that it was all over. Recognising his infantry could go no farther Hamilton sent a message to Baillie ordering him to surrender, while he and the horse tried to escape. Baillie, who may have been wounded in the fight at Winnington, was so shocked by this betrayal that he at first begged his officers to shoot him, but eventually he surrendered on the promise of quarter and civil usage. Hamilton and his party were no more fortunate. Narrowly escaping being murdered by his own men he surrendered at Uttoxeter on the 25th and was eventually executed.[19]

The campaign however was by no means over:

> ... when the nues of it came unto Sir Thomas Tildesley (who was then with a part of the English forces before Lancaster Castle) he drue off, and joyning with those English that were gott off from Preston, and others that were left behind in Westmorland, they went to Major Generall Monro (who was then upon the confines of Lancashire) and moved that his forces, the Scotch that were about Kendale, and the English might martch together to Preston,* but he would not consent to it but retreated to the other end of Westmorland.
> (*These forces conjoined would have made a body of above 7000 horse and foot.[20])

Had he indeed been able to muster that number Monro might have been justified in making the attempt. As he could only depend on his own 1,200 men his decision to retreat was the most sensible one taken by any Scots officer throughout the whole sorry affair. What the English Royalists also failed to appreciate was that the Scots government itself was in a very shaky position, and that it was Monro's responsibility to preserve its only effective army.

Consequently they split up. The Royalist foot led by Musgrave retired into Cumberland and embarked on a rather pointless siege of Cockermouth Castle while the horse, led by Tyldesley, made for Berwick by way of the Stainmore Pass. Monro was glad enough of their company until they reached the border, but there he cast them adrift and refused to let them cross. Meanwhile Colonel Assheton had come north and Musgrave too tried to retreat into Scotland. This time it was the Scots governor of Carlisle, Lieutenant Colonel Sir William Livingston, who refused them entry and rejoining Tyldesley at Appleby they surrendered to Assheton on 9 October.[21]

In the meantime the crisis which Monro feared had arisen. In late August the Kirk party's supporters had raised a substantial body of men in the south-west. In what later became known as the 'Whiggamore Raid', the Earl of Eglinton seized Edinburgh Castle on 5 September.[22] Monro arrived too late to save the capital but having rendezvoused with another 2,000 men under the Earl of Lanark, he stormed Stirling on 12 September. The town had been occupied by the Marquis of Argyll's men only the day before, but Monro personally kicked down a small postern door and chased them out again.

The Whigs then regrouped under David Leslie at nearby Falkirk. After a series of truces the Engagers agreed to surrender Stirling and Carlisle by 1 October and to disband by the 10th. Leslie for his part agreed to disband all but 1,500 men on the 1st, and the rest on the 10th.[23] It seems a curious arrangement but Cromwell had come north with a brigade and there was a clear threat of English intervention in any civil war. As it was he stayed in Edinburgh from 2 to 7 October as the guest of the Kirk party. It was a curious alliance, but one that was soon to be broken.

NOTES

1. Horton's forces comprised his own regiment of Horse, three troops of Colonel Adrian Scroope's Regiment under Major Nathaniel Barton, six troops of Okey's Dragoons and eight companies of Colonel Robert Overton's Foot.
2. Cromwell had his own regiment of horse, Colonel Richard Deane's, Colonel Isaac Ewer's and Colonel Thomas Pride's regiments of foot.

3. **Horse:**
   Col. Thomas Harrison
   Col. John Lambert
   Col. Robert Lilburne
   Col. Philip Twisleton

   Foot:
   Col. John Bright
   Col. Charles Fairfax*
   Lord General

   *not to be confused with his nephew slain at Marston Moor.

4. **Horse:**
   Lord General
   Col. Charles Fleetwood
   Col. Henry Ireton
   Col. Nathaniel Rich
   Col. Edward Whalley

   Foot:
   Col. John Barkstead
   Col. John Hewson
   Col. Richard Ingoldsby (5 coys.)

   After Maidstone Hewson's regiment remained in Kent to mop up the Royalist garrisons, but in its place Colonel Simon Needham's Tower Regiment joined Fairfax at Tilbury. After the siege of Colchester began, the Trained Bands were also called out and employed in covering the approaches to the town in case of further trouble in Suffolk.
5. The following Royalist infantry units can all be identified as having been raised in Kent in 1648. Those marked with an asterisk went on to fight at Colchester and so presumably took an active part in the fight at Maidstone.

Norwich also had a small regiment of Horse:
Sir Francis Clerke
Sir William Compton
Col. Edward Hammond*
Earl of Norwich*
Col. James Till*

6. Lucas appears to have had the following regiments:
   Col. William Ayliffe's Foot   (garrison of Colchester Castle)
   Colonel Henry Farr's Foot
   Sir George Lisle's Horse
   Sir Charles Lucas' Foot

7. The rebels were about 500 strong, and were led by the Earl of Holland and Lord Francis Villiers. The winners, led by Sir Michael Livesay, comprised two troops of Ireton's Horse, led by Major Robert Gibbon, two troops of Rich's Horse and some local volunteers.

8. The terms of surrender were harsh. Only the common soldiers and those officers below the rank of captain were promised their lives. Sir Charles Lucas and Sir George Lisle were at once put up against a wall and shot. Farr would certainly have been shot too had he not found a hiding place in the town. Norwich was also sentenced to death but reprieved.

9. The organisation of Hamilton's Foot was straightforward enough with most regiments having a theoretical establishment of some 800 men. Most of them were lucky to muster half that number. The first figures appended refer to the number of soldiers (exclusive of commissioned officers) who surrendered at Warrington (source: *THREE LETTERS CONCERNING THE SURRENDER OF MANY Scottish Lords . . . Read in both Houses of Parliament the 25 of August 1648*). By that point the army had all but disintegrated and the second figure, indicating the number of colours (BM Harl.1460) which can be identified as taken might be a better indicator of strength. If an average ratio of 100 is allowed for each of the seventy-five colours this would suggest some 7,500 foot, but even this may be too high. Those units marked with an asterisk had formed part of the 1647 New Model Army and might be considered as veterans, but the rest were appallingly raw. In addition to those units listed below the Earl of Callendar's Regiment of Foot was left behind as a garrison for Carlisle. The listing for the cavalry is incomplete, but it should be noted that in 1648 regiments comprised just three troops, each commanded by a field officer.

Horse:	Foot:	
Lord Cranstoun	Marquis of Argyll* (det.)	(0/1)
Earl of Dalhousie	Earl of Atholl	(160/7)
Duke of Hamilton's Lifeguard*	Lieut. Gen. William Baillie*	(124/3)
Col. William Hurry	Lord Bargany	(84/2)
Col. William Lockhart	Lord Carnegie	(148/5)
Earl Marischal	Lord Cochrane (?)	(0/0)
Major General John Middleton*	Col. Richard Douglas	(131/10)
Earl of Traquair	Sir James Drummond	(92/5)
	Earl of Dumfries	(48/1)
	Sir Alexander Fraser's Firelocks	(154/2)
	Sir John Grey	(34/1)
	Duke of Hamilton	(379/8)
	Sir Alexander Hamilton*	(51/0)
	Earl of Home	(264/5)
	Col. George Keith	(134/5)

Earl of Kellie	(105/3)
Col. Harry Maule	(122/4)
Earl of Roxburgh	(33/1)
Earl of Tullibardine	(127/2)
Col. James Turner*	(127/3)
Lord Yester	(62/8)

10. This was a decidedly hard-bitten collection of mercenaries. One of the regiments, Robert Monro's, was formed as a penal battalion in 1640. The others were recruited for service in Ulster in 1642 by beat of drum rather than conscription. They had no objection in principle to serving the 'Engagers', but they were very insistent on receiving their arrears of pay first. As it was still necessary to maintain some kind of a force in Ireland it was agreed to send a detachment of 300 men from each of the regiments listed below. This should have produced 1,500 foot, but as many as 300 may have been intercepted at sea and turned back, while others may have deserted after reaching Scotland. The horse may have mustered 400 men and were organised in single troops – once again the listing here is defective.

Horse:	Foot:
Lt.Col. William Cunningham	Col. John Hamilton
Lt.Col. George Monro	Col. Robert Home
Capt. Daniel Monro	Major Gen. George Monro
	Major Gen. Robert Monro
	(Major Thos Dalyell)
	Col. James Montgomerie

11. Cromwell's regulars comprised the following regiments, and there were in addition a number of provincial units such as Colonel George Fenwick's Horse from Northumberland, Colonel Ralph Assheton's Lancashire Foot, and Colonel Charles Fairfax's Yorkshire Foot.

Horse:	Foot:
Lieut.Gen. Cromwell	Lord General
Col. Thomas Harrison	Col. John Bright
Maj.Gen. John Lambert	Col. Richard Deane
Col. Robert Lilburne	Col. Robert Overton
Col. Adrian Scroope (3 troops)	Col. Thomas Pride
Col. Francis Thornhaugh	
Col. Philip Twisleton	Col. John Okey's Dragoons (2 troops)

12. Not to be confused with Sir Richard Tempest, captured in his bed at Cartington Castle.

13. As most of the Scots cavalry were at Wigan these lancers probably belonged to Hamilton's Lifeguard.

14. Hodgson, J. *Autobiography of Capt.John Hodgson* (1822) p32. Although almost invariably referred to as *Captain* Hodgson in secondary sources, he was at this date still only the Lieutenant of Major Pownall's company.

15. The brigades are not identified, but given the fact that all of the Scots regiments were very badly understrength, they can only have been composite battalions. One of those taken prisoner when the bridge was captured was Colonel George Keith.

16. They were not quite alone. Turner was in this fight too and so was at least one troop of Hamilton's Lifeguard – they lost their cornet; a blue one with a heavy gold fringe, bearing a crown and the letters *Date Caesari* (BM Harl. 1460)

17. Turner *Memoirs* pp66-7 As his rearguard was at least holding together, his decision to encourage the fugitives to ride it down is decidedly questionable. He was indeed 'demented'.

18. It is all but impossible to identify this officer. He is said to have been slain, but so far as can be ascertained none of the Scots army's general or field officers were killed that day. The most likely candidate therefore is Baillie himself.
19. As to the other senior officers; Callendar escaped to Holland, Turner was captured but ransomed himself, while Middleton and Langdale were both taken prisoner but subsequently escaped. It is uncertain when Baillie was released, but he was back in Scotland by 1651 and still alive twenty years later although he never again accepted a command.
20. Sir Philip Musgrave's *Relation* in Scottish History Society Miscellany Vol.II p309
21. Chetham Soc. *Civil War Tracts* p255. The terms were remarkably lenient. The senior officers were banished from the kingdom, but everybody else was simply allowed to go home. Ordinarily any horses surrendered would have become the property of the state, but by a mutually convenient arrangement the Royalists sold them to the besiegers before the surrender officially took effect!
22. The name is said to derive from the traditional cry of 'Whiggam!' used by cattle drovers in the south-west. At any rate it was subsequently shortened to 'Whig'.
23. Monro's own forces were supposed to return to Ireland, but in the event they too disbanded rather than embark.

CHAPTER XVIII

The Scots War: Dunbar and Worcester 1650–1651

The most prominent casualty of the Second Civil War was the King himself, beheaded in Whitehall on 30 January 1649 and having cut off the present incumbent Parliament then briskly proceeded to abolish the monarchy itself. However the Scots now proclaimed his son as King Charles II. Nevertheless this was as far as the Scots government was then prepared to go, and a Royalist uprising was very promptly suppressed. The Estates were willing to allow the young King to assume the throne, but only upon certain conditions. The chief of these was that he should embrace Presbyterianism and 'take the Covenant'.

At first he was understandably reluctant and delayed committing himself long enough for the Marquis of Montrose to attempt yet another Royalist uprising. In the event Montrose walked straight into an ambush at Carbisdale in Sutherland on 27 April 1650, and was hanged in Edinburgh a month later.

Philosophically Charles signed the Covenant on 23 June and landed at Speymouth the next day. In the meantime the English army had gone through another messy round of political unrest and a successful campaign in Ireland. Both events had left just twelve regiments of horse and eleven of foot serving in England, but notwithstanding Parliament resolved on a new war with the Scots and the 'Scottish King'. Cromwell was recalled from Ireland, beating orders issued for new regiments, and on 12 June he and Fairfax were nominated once again as Lieutenant General and General respectively.

Fairfax however refused the command, and so Cromwell was appointed General instead on 26 June. Fleetwood got the Lieutenant General's place, Major General Lambert was to have the horse, and Colonel George Monck became Major General of the Foot. The expeditionary force itself comprised seven regiments of horse, nine of foot and some dragoons.[1] If all of them were fully recruited to establishment they ought to have mustered something in the region of 15,000 men all told.

At first events moved quickly. Cromwell concentrated his forces at Berwick on 19 July and crossed the border three days later. His preparations had not gone unnoticed in Scotland. A small standing army had been in existence since Pluscardine's Rising in August of the previous year, and on 25 June fresh levies were ordered. The Earl of Leven was once more appointed to serve as Lord General, and while some thought him too old for the job, he soon showed what he was capable of. At first there was no resistance to Cromwell's advance, and instead the intervening countryside was swept clean. All the corn and cattle was carried off, and in consequence Cromwell quickly realised that all his supplies would either have to be passed up a single road, or carried by sea. His first objective therefore was to occupy Dunbar, the only halfway decent port between Berwick and Edinburgh. From there he pushed on to Haddington on the 26th, and Lambert was sent forward to Musselburgh with a cavalry brigade. They duly hustled Leven's outposts back towards Leith and discovered that the Scots army was busily engaged in digging in. There was already a long line of entrenchments linking Leith and Edinburgh more or less along the alignment of the present-day Leith Walk.

Cromwell brought the rest of the army up to have a look for himself and quickly concluded that the position was too strong for a frontal attack. Instead he tried to probe around its southern end while the fleet bombarded Leith. Neither attempt accomplished anything and to make matters worse it started raining. There was no alternative but to fall back, and predictably enough no sooner did the retreat begin than the Scots cavalry came out and began beating up his rearguard.

One Scots brigade sallied out of Edinburgh's Canongate Port and another from Leith. The English rearguard, comprising just 200 horse under Captain William Evanson of Whalley's Regiment, was quickly driven in. Then the Lord General's Regiment put in a charge temporarily

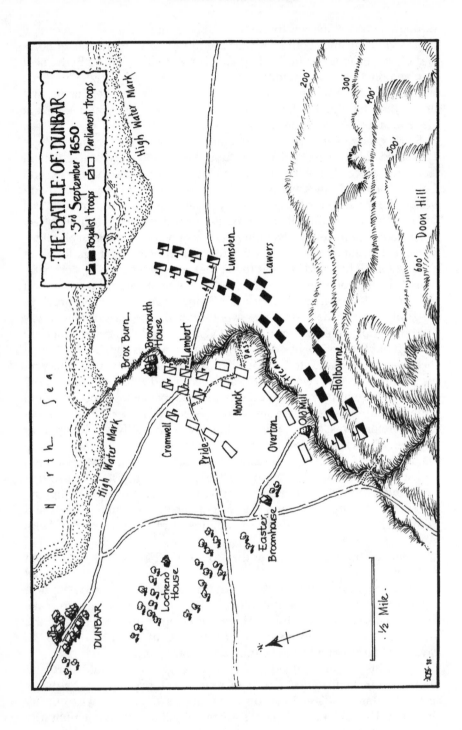

THE·BATTLE·OF·DUNBAR·
·3rd September 1650·
▪ Royalist troops ▱ Parliament troops

Doon Hill

600'

500'

400'

300'

200'

High Water Mark

Lumsden

Lawers

Holbourn

North Sea

Brox Burn

Broxmouth House

Lambert

High Water Mark

Monck

Cromwell

Pride

Overton

Old Mill

stream

PASS

Easter Broomhouse

Lochend House

DUNBAR

½ Mile.

N

238

checking the pursuit, but it didn't last long and they too found themselves in the unusual situation of running away. Next came Lambert's and Hacker's regiments and the remaining four troops of Whalley's. By this time the Scots had become disordered and were tumbled back towards their own lines. Neither side suffered many casualties although the English claimed to have captured two cornets. Lambert himself was wounded three times by lance thrusts and was captured for a short time.

Encouraged by their success the Scots tried it on again the following day with a brigade commanded by Major General Robert Montgomerie[2]. At about 3am they overran the outer picket line but then Lilburne's Regiment counter-attacked and they were driven off, losing about 100 prisoners.

Despite the failure of this raid Cromwell recognised that Musselburgh was too exposed to serve as a forward base, and temporarily pulled back to Dunbar. There he remained until 12 August before making a second attempt to feel his way around the right flank of the Scottish position. This time he pushed farther south than before and successfully established himself on the lower slopes of the Braid Hills, due south of Edinburgh. He was now well placed to move against Leven's line of communications out to the west. So far so good, but Leven thrust a garrison into a house called Redhall, and occupied a strong position on Corstorphine Hill with the better part of his army. The outpost was successfully stormed on 26 August, but not liking the look of the Corstorphine position, Cromwell edged farther to the west on the 27th. This move gained him no advantage for Leven simply drew up in an even stronger position at Gogar. At first it looked as if there might be a battle, but then it was discovered that the Scots flanks were covered by bogs. An artillery exchange followed but that was the extent of the hostilities. By now the English army was running short of food. Moreover the numerically superior Scots looked like being able to counter the turning movements indefinitely. Cromwell therefore gave up again. On the 28th he fell back, first to Musselburgh and then all the way back to Dunbar.

This time the Scots army followed him. Thus far they had comfortably held their own, and it was obvious that the withdrawal was not a tactical move but a full-scale retreat. Furthermore Leven saw and quite rightly seized an opportunity to inflict a decisive defeat.

From Dunbar the coastline and the coastal road to which Cromwell was effectively confined turns down in a jagged arc from the north point of a compass to somewhere about east-nor'east. The road then runs due south through a defile at Cockburnspath. If Cromwell was to extricate his army safely he needed to secure this defile as quickly as possible, but Leven forestalled him. The English army reached Dunbar on the evening of 31 August. Unfortunately later that night Leven succeeded in throwing a brigade across the road at the point where it entered the defile. Of itself this might not have been sufficient to stop a determined effort to force a passage, but on 1 September Leven followed with the rest of his army. Marching straight across country he cut along the chord of the coastal arc to take up an extremely strong position on the commanding eminence of Doon Hill. Cromwell was now comprehensively trapped. An evacuation by sea was beginning to look like a real possibility, but then the Scots at last made a serious blunder.

Historians have generally discounted the part played in this campaign by the Earl of Leven, and it is argued that the effective commander of the Scots army was his Lieutenant General, David Leslie. Leven was certainly getting too old for active campaigning, but he was still the Lord General and his sureness of touch is evident in the conduct of the Scots army up to this point. David Leslie on the other hand was a competent enough brigade commander but invariably demonstrated that he was sadly out of his depth when called upon to handle larger formations. However on 2 September Leslie effectively supplanted Leven as operational commander of the army on Doon Hill.

Having penned Cromwell into a position where he must either surrender or undertake a potentially hazardous evacuation by sea, Leven can have been in no hurry to move off the hill. Unfortunately he had to contend with a rather noisy collection of Presbyterian ministers and lay members of the ruling Kirk party dignified by the title of the Committee of Estates. These were his political masters, and their presence was not eased by the fact that both his Lieutenant General and Major General James Holburne were strong adherents of that party. Afflicted by a mindset firmly rooted in the Old Testament[3] they cried out for a great smiting of the foe. Thus far Leven had been successful in restraining these fanatical impulses, but now he had to contend with the weather as well. It was raining heavily and with a strong wind behind it this made the exposed slopes of Doon Hill a very uncomfortable place on which to exercise the required patience. It would be reasonable to suppose that the foul weather increased the pressure upon Leven to move down off the hill while simultaneously undermining his resistance to such folly.

He must however have made his feelings upon the matter very plain, for Lieutenant General David Leslie assumed operational command of the army and Leven afterwards escaped all blame for the debacle which followed. At any rate, early on the morning of 2 September, Leslie began moving the army down off the hill. By the time he was finished it was occupying a front just over a mile long, aligned on a stream called the Broxburn. This might have made an admirable start line for the proposed attack were it not for the fact that the upper reaches run through a deep ravine.

Naturally enough Cromwell and Lambert then spent much of the day in redeploying the army to face the Scots across the Broxburn. At first they may have anticipated fighting a defensive battle but a certain uneasiness at the situation is evident in the *Brief Relation*:

> There was between the two Armies a great ditch, of fortie or fiftie foot wide, and near as deep, with a rill of water in the bottom, which would be a verie great disadvantage to that party who should first attempt to pass it. Upon the brink of this ditch there was a little house, and by it a shelving path where the Enemie might with greater facilitie than anie where els com over. About five of the clock that Monday morning there was twentie four Foot and six Hors sent to that house to secure that passage. The Enemie sent down two troops of Lanciers, who caused our six Hors to return. Those Lanciers killed three of our Foot, took three prisoners, and wounded most part of the rest; so the Enemie remained master of the Pass, which yet they presently acquitted.[4]

About four o'clock Leslie brought his artillery train down off the hill, and Cromwell then ordered his forces to close right up to the Broxburn. There had been a considerable wastage over the last month, particularly amongst infantry, and he could muster only 7,500 foot and 3,500 horse[5]. On the other hand he estimated the Scots to number 16,000 foot and 6,000 horse. In reality the Scots were only half as strong and both sides were in fact pretty evenly matched.

The *Brief Relation* states that there were eighteen regiments of foot and an intelligence summary identifies fifteen of them.[6] If a hypothetical total of 1,000 men was to be allowed for each of the fifteen to eighteen battalions estimated to have been present this would explain Cromwell's estimate of 16,000 foot. If on the other hand a much more realistic average of 500 men per battalion is allowed – as indicated by surviving muster figures which reveal some of the older units down to about 3-400 men – then the true figure must have been nearer 8-9,000 foot, although even this may still be too high.

No fewer than nineteen cavalry units are listed in the intelligence summary, although this may be incomplete. Most units had only three troops and a few were represented by only a single troop. If a total of around fifty troops were present each with an average of fifty men this would produce a total only 2,500 Scots cavalry at Dunbar. This is probably too low and some units may have had more than three troops, but it is very hard to find any justification for increasing the number to any significant extent.

The train of artillery was afterwards captured in its entirety and the highest estimate was '32 pieces of ordnance, small, great, and leather guns', although another refers to just nine. The lower figure presumably only refers to field pieces, with the remainder being leather guns. The latter were made by the General of the Artillery, and were usually mounted in pairs or sometimes in fours. Some of them were very small, firing a 12lb ball and were 'handled like a musket.'[7]

Nevertheless Cromwell was now intending to launch a preemptive attack and with Lambert's assistance convinced a council of war to back him. The plan of attack was simple enough. Since the Broxburn represented a significant obstacle Cromwell decided to attack across it by way of the Berwick Road and try to roll up the Scots right flank.

His plan succeeded admirably. The initial attack was launched by three regiments of horse commanded by Fleetwood, Lambert and Whalley, with three more, Lilburne's, Hacker's and Twisleton's, in reserve[8]. They successfully secured the crossing, but were then checked by a series of counter-attacks led by Colonel Archibald Strachan. Next Monck came up with a brigade of infantry. He is usually credited with having three and a half regiments, but a number of accounts speak of only two – or perhaps two and a half.[9] He too made some progress against the Scots infantry. This would appear to have been Sir James Lumsden's Brigade. As the senior Scots infantry officer his place was certainly on the right, and at some point during the battle he was taken prisoner. It was very evidently destroyed in Monck's attack, for one of his Colonels was killed and a particularly large bag of colours were taken from all three of his regiments.[10] However a further advance was checked by the next brigade in line, and it then became necessary for Cromwell personally to commit Pride's Brigade[11]:

> . . . our first foot after they had discharged their duty (being overpowered with the enemy), received some repulse, which they soon recovered. But my own regiment, under the command of Lieutenant-Colonel Goffe, and my major, White, did come seasonably in; and, at the push of pike, did repel the stoutest regiment the enemy had there . . .[12]

Other accounts refer to a whole brigade, and an anonymous Scottish chronicler describes how: 'Two regiments of foot fought it out manfully, for they were all killed as they stood (as the enemy confessed)'. Another states that resistance was only broken after a troop of English horse took them in flank and charged 'from end to end'.[13] Two of the regiments involved may well have been Colonel Alexander Stewart's and Sir John Haldane of Gleneagles'. Both of them were killed, as were the latter's Lieutenant Colonel and Major. Another was certainly Sir James Campbell of Lawers', for it is specifically referred to both in a Scottish account and in Gumble's *Life of Monk*:

> Onely Lawers his regiment of Highlanders made a good defence, and

the chief officer, a lieutenant-colonell, being slain by one of the general's sergeants (the colonel was absent), of the name of the Campbells, they stood to the push of pike and were all cut in pieces.[14]

Unfortunately the three other Scots brigades were incapable of using this brief respite to retrieve the situation. Many officers had absented themselves to go in search of shelter during the night, but the real problem seems to have been the difficulty of deploying in the relatively confined space between the Broxburn and the foot of the hill. Horribly outnumbered, the horse on the right wing soon gave way, and according to Walker carried a substantial part of the foot away with them in their flight. The horse on the Scottish left wing never seem to have come into the fight at all. Some of the fugitives made for the defile at Cockburnspath, but the greater part of the Scots army fell back to Haddington. The English pursued as far as the town and claimed to have killed and captured Biblical numbers of them. In reality, although there is no doubting the severity of the defeat, very few of the Scots regiments disappeared, and Walker commented that 'not many of them in proportion were either slain or made prisoners.'[15]

With his own army to all intents and purposes undamaged Cromwell was quick to follow up his victory. Next day Lambert was sent forward to Edinburgh with an infantry regiment and all the cavalry except Hacker's Regiment. Nevertheless despite Cromwell's self-congratulatory despatches the Scots army was far from destroyed. David Leslie had already pulled together an estimated 4-5,000 men and was falling back to Stirling. Fresh levies were ordered on 5 September, and three of the more prominent Covenanters, Colonels Gibby Ker, Archibald Strachan, and Robert Halkett, were sent to Glasgow to raise a new army from amongst the western Whigs.

Dropping off Overton's brigade to hold Leith and blockade Edinburgh Castle Cromwell moved westwards on 14 September. Once again the weather had turned foul, and although he arrived before Stirling on the 17th, nobody had the stomach for an assault. The defences were too strong for a frontal attack and the position could not be outflanked. Next day the English army fell back to Linlithgow and, having established a garrison of five troops of horse and six companies of foot there, Cromwell then retired to establish a proper base in Edinburgh.

For the next ten months Linlithgow Bridge and the river Avon formed the frontier of English-occupied Scotland, but neither the frontier nor Cromwell's communications were secure. There was still a Scots garrison in Edinburgh Castle, but the governor, Walter Dundas, was far from happy, and the castle's defiance was more symbolic than real. Much more potent were the threats posed by Ker's Western Army and by the rise of the Moss Troopers.

The former was soon dealt with. In late November Cromwell and Lambert went after them with the cavalry. At 4am on the morning of 1 December Ker launched a surprise attack on Lambert's quarters at Hamilton. In a brisk little action Lambert was initially driven out of the town. In the process the Scots naturally became disordered, but when Ker tried to pull them back to reorganise, his raw levies took this as a signal for a full-scale retreat. As they scattered and ran Lambert rallied his own men and counter-attacked, completely routed the Westerners, and captured Ker himself. Later that same day Cromwell moved on to Glasgow. Strachan fled without fighting, disbanded what remained of the Western Army on the 2nd, and shortly afterwards defected to the English.[16] It was less easy however to deal with the growing bands of Moss Troopers or 'Mossers'.

After the rout at Dunbar many of the fugitives formed marauding bands instead of rejoining the army. Initially the Mossers were simply involved in highway robbery and the capture or murder of stragglers and unescorted messengers. As time went on however the sole practitioners were either killed off or forced into the larger bands. The most famous was led by Captain Augustine 'a heigh Germane.'[17]

On the night of 13 December he carried out his most famous exploit by crossing the Forth at Blackness with 120 men and making his way to Edinburgh. Getting in through the Canongate Port the Mossers galloped straight up the High Street and into the castle. Then, having dropped off the bags of powder and spices tied to their saddle-bags, they burst out again half an hour later and got clean away.

The castle still surrendered ten days later, but the raid was a clear sign that the Scots were recovering their confidence. This was further under-lined by the coronation of Charles II at Scone on 1 January, and this in turn led to a renewed English push against Stirling in early February. Although Leslie was forced to evacuate an outpost at Callendar House, Cromwell soon fell back once again to Edinburgh in appalling weather. This time he too joined the ranks of the sick and was effectively laid up at Edinburgh until June.

In the meantime the Scots recovery continued. There was a particu-larly heavy raid by 700 horse and dragoons on Linlithgow on 14 April. Under cover of thick fog a small party of Scots penetrated the outposts, killed a man and then ran away. As they hoped, the Governor, Major John Sydenham of Hesilrige's Horse, immediately set off after them with his quick reaction force. Blinded by the fog he rode straight into an ambush and was mortally wounded in the rout which followed. Further minor successes followed. The English were forced to evacuate Hamilton, and in May the Scots won a series of skirmishes at Paisley, Carnwath and Linlithgow. All this time Leslie's army was growing in strength, and on 28 June it moved forward to the Torwood, near Falkirk.

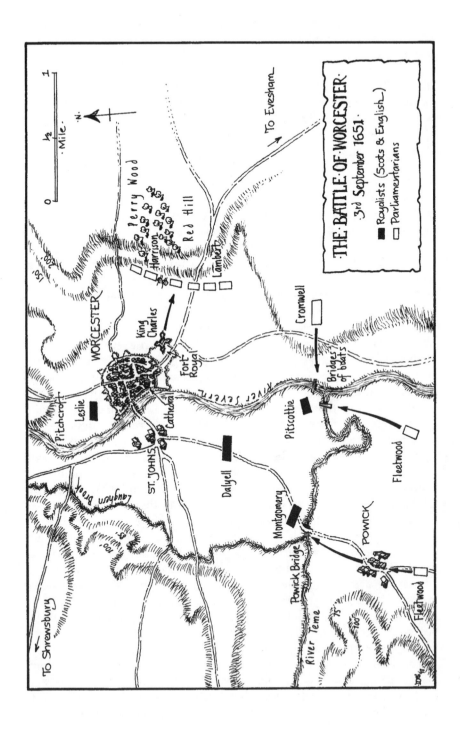

THE·BATTLE·OF·WORCESTER·
3rd September 1651·

■ Royalists (Scots & English)
□ Parliamentarians

This brought Cromwell forward again. Since Dunbar he too had been reinforced and now had some thirteen regiments of horse, twelve of foot and a newly raised regiment of dragoons. Most of them however were understrength by now, and although Leslie offered battle near Callendar House, Cromwell felt compelled to decline. The Scots General was only too well aware of his own limitations, and having taken up a strong position behind a stream, he refused to come out and fight either. Nevertheless since Leslie had at least been drawn out of the Stirling lines, Cromwell decided to attempt an ambitious turning movement.

Early on the morning of 17 July Lambert crossed the Forth with four troops of Colonel Leonard Lytcott's Horse, Daniel's Foot 'and as many forth of Leith as made them 1600'[18]. Landing safely at North Queensferry he immediately began digging in across the peninsula. Leslie reacted promptly by sending off Major General James Holburne with some infantry, and a reinforced cavalry brigade under Sir John Browne[19], but Cromwell had no intention of losing the bridgehead. Two days later Lambert began shipping across two more regiments of horse, his own and Colonel Okey's[20], and two regiments of foot, Colonel Francis West's and Edmund Syler's. By midday on Sunday 20th they were all across, and Holburne prudently decided to withdraw.

Lambert however followed up and Holburne turned to fight. Deploying two Highland regiments on the right and his regulars on the left, he halted and waited for Lambert to attack. After some time he did so and became engaged in what turned out to be a surprisingly volatile little action. On the left Balcarres and Augustine routed the English cavalry opposite them – probably Lytcott's newly raised troopers – but were then charged and routed in their turn. The rest of the Scots cavalry were also driven off and the regular infantry executed an equally swift retreat. The Highlanders on the other hand made several attempts to charge, but the English foot failed to be intimidated. When the Highlanders then tried to withdraw they found themselves surrounded by cavalry and got 'ill quarter'.[21]

Once again Cromwell was quick to reinforce success and began pushing troops across the Forth as fast as he could find shipping for them. By 26 July he reported that he had 13-14,000 horse and foot in Fife, and on the 31st he marched north to threaten Perth. This was a shrewd move for it placed him firmly astride Leslie's lines of communication and ought to have forced him to fight. Instead something quite extraordinary occurred. Rather than fight Cromwell outside Perth, Leslie set off on a crack-brained invasion of England.

The reasoning behind this move is obscure, for unlike Hamilton's invasion in 1648 there was no attempt to coordinate it with Royalist uprisings. It is argued that the King ordered the move in opposition to Leslie's views, but as the Lieutenant General had been shy of fighting in the open ever since Dunbar, he cannot have been a very passionate advocate of fighting Cromwell.

Be that as it may Cromwell learned of it on 1 August, but waited until Perth surrendered next day before responding. Leaving Colonel Daniel's Regiment as a garrison and dropping off Monck with a reinforced brigade to besiege Stirling, he headed south in pursuit. As usual Lambert was sent on ahead with the cavalry and orders to sweep up every man he could lay his hands on.

Unlike Hamilton, the King was moving swiftly. He crossed the border near Carlisle on 6 August, and little more than a week later he was at Warrington. The Earl of Derby and Sir Thomas Tyldesley had been ordered to join the King in Lancashire, but only made the crossing from the Isle of Man on the 15th. Although Derby caught up with the King at Warrington, he and Tyldesley had perforce to be left behind to raise their forces. On 25 August Colonel Robert Lilburne caught up with them at Wigan, and in a brisk little action in Wigan Lane he killed Tyldesley and scattered the last English Royalist army.

By that time the Scots army was quartered in Worcester. The King seems to have contemplated turning it into a base for a more general Royalist uprising, for steps were taken to repair the defences. On the 24th he also tried to mobilise the *Posse Comitatus*, requiring all men aged between 16 and 60 to muster on Pitchcroft Green two days later. Needless to say most of them had a great deal more sense, but 1,000 or so were rounded up by Lord Talbot and Sir John Packington. Further proclamations were equally ineffective, and in any case Cromwell was closing in fast.

Having rendezvoused with Lambert at Warwick on the 24th, the Lord General was at Evesham three days later. On the 28th Lambert seized Upton Bridge and in the process routed Major General Edward Massey's brigade. This gave Cromwell the ability to operate on either side of the Severn, and on 29 August he held a council of war to consider how best to proceed. He had a comfortable superiority in numbers. His army, including militia units, may have been as much as 25,000 strong,[22] and while the Scots were occupying a strong position they only had about 9-10,000 infantry and an unknown number of cavalry.[23] In order to make the best use of this superiority it was decided that Fleetwood would advance up the west bank and get across the Teme at or near Powick, while the greater part of the army launched a direct assault on the city from the east.

That assault was fixed for 3 September and at dawn Fleetwood went forward in two columns, but for some reason he did not actually come into action until mid-afternoon. One column launched a direct assault on Powick Bridge, which was defended by Montgomerie's 2nd Cavalry Brigade and an infantry brigade under Colonel George Keith. This successfully diverted attention away from the second column which was accompanied by a bridging train. In concert with Cromwell's men on the east bank they first threw a bridge across the Severn just below its junction with the Teme, and then threw a second bridge across the Teme itself.

This enabled Cromwell to lead four regiments of horse and two regiments of foot across to support Fleetwood. All that faced them on the north bank of the Teme was a single brigade, largely composed of Highlanders, led by Colonel Colin Pitscottie. Outnumbered he was soon forced back, and this in turn rendered Montgomerie's position at Powick Bridge untenable. Fleetwood put in a heavy attack which carried the bridge, captured Colonel Keith and wounded Montgomerie. While the three Scots brigades fell back on a fourth, commanded by Colonel Dalyell, at St Johns, the King mounted an enterprising counter-attack on the east bank.

Rather than simply feed more men into the hedge-fighting north of the Teme he assembled all the uncommitted infantry and sallied out the Sidbury Gate. Attacking up the London Road he was only facing militia and at first made some progress. Lambert and Harrison were pushed back from their positions on Red Hill, but as the fighting escalated, more and more regular units were committed. Unfortunately the greater part of the Scots cavalry, commanded by Leslie himself, remained standing on Pitchcroft Green to the north of the city. Had they been led through the city and fed into the battle on Red Hill the battle might have ended differently. Instead Cromwell had time to recross the Severn, and after three hours' hard fighting the Scots were driven back to the city. Fort Royal was stormed by the Essex Trained Bands, and about much the same time Fleetwood forced his way into St Johns. A general collapse followed. Dalyell's brigade surrendered, and although most of the cavalry broke out to the north, the bulk of the Scots foot were trapped in the streets of Worcester. Desultory fighting went on all night but by morning all or most of them had surrendered.

The King eventually managed to escape to France, but the greater part of the fugitives surrendered over the next few days. A surprising number made it back to Scotland, where Monck was engaged in mopping up the last garrisons, but to all intents and purposes the English Civil War ended where it had begun, at Worcester on 3 September 1651.

NOTES

1. **Horse:**
   Lieut.Gen. Charles Fleetwood
   Col. Francis Hacker
   Major General John Lambert
   Col. Robert Lilburne

   Foot:
   Col. Alban Coxe
   Col. William Daniel
   Col. Charles Fairfax
   Col. George Fenwick (5 coys?)**

Lord General*
Col. Philip Twisleton
Col. Edward Whalley

Major General John Lambert
Lord General
Col. John Malverer
Col. George Monck
Col. Thomas Pride

* Oddly enough this was the same regiment which Cromwell raised in 1643. It passed to Fairfax when the army was 'new modelled' and now Cromwell took it over again on becoming Lord General in Fairfax's place.

** Monck's Regiment was formed by taking five companies apiece from Fenwick's and Sir Arthur Hesilrige's. Fenwick was then ordered to raise five more to replace them but in the meantime his remaining five went off with the army and fought at Dunbar.

2. The brigade appears to have included the following units:
Lord Brechin's Horse
Sir James Halkett's Horse
Earl of Leven's Lifeguard
Major Gen. Robert Montgomerie's Horse
Col. Archibald Strachan's Horse

3. So convinced were they of the need to field an army of the righteous, that a series of purges took place that summer. Experienced officers were turned out and replaced by men whose religious credentials were, by and large, more impressive than their military ones. This may not necessarily have been quite such a destructive process as hostile witnesses such as Sir Edward Walker claimed. Religious fanaticism and military ability are not mutually exclusive - often the contrary is true. However there is no doubting the disruption which it must have caused.

4. *Brief Relation* in Terry, C.S. *Life and Campaigns of Alexander Leslie* p476

5. Cromwell to Speaker Lenthall 4 September 1650 quoted in Young & Holmes *The English Civil War* p304

6. BM Harl.6844 fol.123 This list was evidently collated after the battle and is incomplete. However other regiments can be identified by the heraldic devices on several of the colours captured at Dunbar (BM Harl.1460) and Sir James Balfour's list of the principal casualties. According to BM Harl.6844 the following infantry regiments took part in the battle:

Lieutenant Gen Lumsdale (Sir James Lumsden)
Maj Gen. Hoburn (James Holburne)
Maj Gen. Pettscobbie (Colin Pitscottie)
Coll. Lawnes (Sir James Campbell of Lawers)
Coll. Innis (John Innes)
    These commanded Brigades
Coll. Glanagis (Sir John Haldane of Gleneagles)
Coll. Tallifield (Sir George Preston of Valleyfield)
Lord Kilcowberry (Lord Kirkcudbright)
Lord of Egell (Col. John Lindsay of Edzell)
Mr Loveit (Master of Lovat)
Lord of Buchannan (Sir George Buchannan of Buchannan)
Sir Elex Stuart (Col. Alexander Stewart)
Gen: of the Artillery's Regi: Weams (James Wemyss)
Coll Hume (Sir David Hume of Wedderburn)
Coll ffreeland (Sir Thomas Ruthven of Freeland)
    Reg of ffoot 15

Three regiments not named in the list, commanded by Sir William Douglas of Kirkness and Sir Andrew Ker of Greenhead, were certainly present for the first was killed, the second lost its Lieutenant Colonel, James Ker, and both units lost several colours, as did a third regiment, Lord Balfour of Burleigh's. The colours of up to four other units are also recorded, but there is reason to believe that they may in fact have been taken in Lambert's victory at Inverkeithing in the following July.

The following cavalry units were listed in BM.Harl.6844:-

The Earl of Leaven's Rg	(Earl of Leven)
Leu: Gen Lashlie	(David Leslie)
Maior Gen Mongonny	(Robert Montgomerie)
Ma: Gen Browne	(Sir John Browne)
Coll Crag	(Thomas Craig of Riccarton)
Coll Arnott	(Sir Charles Arnott)
Coll Strathen	(Archibald Strachan)
Master of fforbes	(Master of Forbes)
Coll Scott	(Walter Scott)
Sir James Hackett	(Sir James Halkett)
Lord Mackline	(Lord Mauchline)
Lord Brichen	(Lord Brechin)
Coll Scotts Cragg	(Sir Arthur Erskine of Scotscraig)
Sir Robert Adaer	(Sir Robert Adair)
Coll Steward	(William Stewart)
Earl of Casseals	(Earl of Cassillis)
Robert Harkhert	(Col. Robert Halkett)
Coll Gibby Car	(Gilbert Ker)
Adiutant Gen Bickerton	(Thos. Craig of Riccarton – above)

7. Stevenson, D & Caldwell, D. *Leather Guns and other Light Artillery in mid-17th-century Scotland* in Proceedings of the Society of Antiquaries of Scotland Vol.108 pp300-17

8. Firth, C. *The Battle of Dunbar* (Transactions Royal Historical Soc. 1900) p38

9. Identification of the units making up Monck's brigade is not entirely straight-forward, but a process of elimination suggests they were Monck's, Malverer's and the five companies of Fenwick's. At any rate shortly after the battle Overton's Brigade comprised Coxe's, Daniel's and Fairfax's regiments (Hodgson *Memoirs* p315).

10. It comprised his own, Balfour of Burleigh's, and Douglas of Kirkness' regiments. All three of them were newly raised in Fife and at the outset of the campaign may have totalled some 2,700 men.

11. This included the Lord General's and Lambert's regiments as well as Pride's.

12. Cromwell, quoted in Firth & Davies *Regimental History of Cromwell's Army* p330.

13. *Collections by a Private Hand* quoted in Firth *Dunbar* p45.

14. Firth *op.cit.* Lawers' men in fact managed to fight their way out of the debacle. None of the colours taken at Dunbar can be identified with any certainty as belonging to the regiment, and it was still over 400 strong in July 1651. Although Gumble refers to them as Highlanders, this was no longer the case, and most of the men serving in the ranks at this time appear to have been levied in the Linlithgow area.

15. Walker p181. Cromwell claimed to have taken an astounding 10,000 prisoners, but only 5,000 were marched south. Walker on the other hand says that 6,000 prisoners were taken, of which 1,000 wounded were released. This sounds altogether more convincing and would in turn indicate something like 300 rather than 3,000 killed. Cromwell's total of killed and prisoners equals or exceeds the total number of Scots present at the battle.

16. Strachan in common with many of the more extreme Covenanters was bitterly opposed to the accommodation reached with the young King. He died in 1652 in what was described as a fit of 'religious mania'.

17. He is most likely the Captain Augustine Hoffman who served in David Leslie's Horse during the 1640s.

18. The additional troops from Leith included two companies of Colonel George Fenwick's Regiment. Lytcott's was newly raised and disbanded shortly afterwards.

19. Most of the cavalry belonged to the 3rd Brigade, assigned to Browne on 7 May:
Col. Charles Arnott's Horse
Earl of Balcarres' Horse
Sir John Browne's Horse
Sir Walter Scott's Horse.
In addition Lord Brechin's Horse (1st Brigade) and Augustine's Mossers were also present. It may well be significant that at least six of the fifteen cornets recorded in BM Harl.1460 can be attributed to regiments which fought at Inverkeithing.
A least four infantry regiments can be identified and the figures relate to the July musters:

Col. George Buchannan of Buchannan	(896)
Master of Grey	(610)
Major Gen. James Holburne	(646)
Sir Hector MacLean of Duart	(800? – tradition)

Other units which may have been present include Lord Balmerino's, Lord Coupar's and Colonel John Forbes of Leslie's Foot. Colours belonging to these units are recorded in BM Harl.1460 but there is no evidence that they were at Dunbar.

20. Okey's had been converted from dragoons to horse a few months earlier.

21. Lambert claimed a rather Biblical total of 2,000 Scots dead. This would account for between half and two thirds of all the Scots infantry on the field. In point of fact Duart's Highlanders are known to have lost some 140 men besides officers. As all sources agree that they were the hardest hit, this provides a good indication of the unreliability of Lambert's estimate.

22.
Foot:	**Horse:**
Col. Ralph Cobbet (det. only)	Lord General
Col. Thomas Cooper	Col. John Desbrowe
Col. Richard Deane	Lt. Gen. Charles Fleetwood
Col. Charles Fairfax	Col. Francis Hacker
Col. Robert Gibbon	Col. Thomas Harrison
Col. William Goffe (ex Lord General's)	Maj.Gen. John Lambert
Col. Richard Ingoldsby	Col. Thomas Saunders
Maj.Gen. John Lambert	Col. Nathaniel Rich
Col. Thomas Pride	Col. Matthew Tomlinson
	Col. Philip Twisleton
	Col. Edward Whalley

In addition to these regular units Cromwell also had the Trained Bands of Essex (a complete brigade), Suffolk, Surrey and Staffordshire at his disposal.

23.
Foot:	**Horse:**		
Lifeguard of Foot	(236)	1st Brigade	
General of the Artillery	(391)	Lt.Gen. David Leslie	
Master of Banff	(515)	Earl of Rothes	
Master of Caithness	(637)	Col. James Craig	

Col. Thomas Dalyell (664)
Col. William Drummond (958)
Col. Walter Forbes of Tolquhon (608)
Col. John Gordon of Rothiemay (423)
Laird of Grant (322)
Col. George Keith (731)
Earl of Kellie (961)
Lord Kintail (982)
Master of Lovat (522)
Tutor of Macleod (596)
Col. Harie Maule (564)
Col. Colin Pitscottie (231)
Col. David Ross of Balnagowan (476)

Col. Harie Sinclair (635)
Lord Spynie (567)
Earl of Sutherland (375)

The figures quoted above for the infantry are the musters for 18 July 1650. There will obviously have been rather fewer of them at Worcester although the level of desertion was probably not so high as in 1648.

2nd Brigade
Maj.Gen. Robert Montgomerie
Earl of Linlithgow
Earl of Dunfermline
Lord Cranstoun
4th Brigade*
Lt.Gen. John Middleton
Earl Marischal
Lord Ogilvy
Sir Arthur Erskine of Scotscraig
Col. James Mercer
5th Brigade
Maj.Gen. Edward Massey
(ex Leven's)
Earl of Erroll
Lord Drummond
Lord Kenmure
6th Brigade
Maj.Gen. Jonas Van Druschke
Lord Maclean
Lord Erskine
Lord Forbes
7th Brigade
Duke of Hamilton
Duke of Buckingham
(English Royalists)
Earl of Home

*The 3rd Cavalry Brigade had been left behind in Scotland

252

Conclusion

The last English conquest of Scotland met with little opposition after Leslie and the King marched south, for they took with them the better part of the Scots army. The burgh of Stirling surrendered to Major General Monck on 6 August 1651, and his mortars bombarded Colonel William Cunningham and the castle into submission on the 15th. Next he turned north again to Dundee which was summoned on 26 August and stormed, amidst the customary excesses, on 1 September. Two days earlier, while the siege was still in progress, a cavalry raid on Alyth, twelve miles to the north-west snapped up the provisional government and most of its military leaders. These not only included the Earl of Leven but his designated successor, the Earl of Crawford-Lindsay[1]. This twin success effectively broke the back of Scottish resistance. Aberdeen was occupied without a fight on 7 September, and the last of the field armies commanded by the Marquis of Huntly and the Earl of Balcarres surrendered on 21 November and 3 December respectively. The mopping up obviously took a little longer. Augustine's Mossers only disbanded themselves in late January or early February 1652[2], and Dunottar Castle did not surrender to Colonel Thomas Morgan until 24 May 1652.[3]

A notional conquest of the Highlands followed and had to be repeated during Glencairn's Rising in 1653 and 1654[4], while there were English Royalist revolts in 1655 and 1659. The first of these, led by Colonel John Penruddock, was little more than a riotous assembly, while the second was smashed by Lambert at Winnington Bridge in Cheshire. Otherwise the eight years which separate the defeat of the Scots at Worcester from the Restoration of King Charles II in 1660 might justly be considered to lie within the realms of political rather than military history – at least so far as England is concerned.

Nevertheless, since the Protectorate of Oliver Cromwell was a military dictatorship, the army was central to events in those years, and ultimately it was also central to the Restoration. While it is popularly referred to as the New Model Army, that term properly belongs only to those regiments which marched under the direct command of Sir Thomas Fairfax in 1645-6, that is to say those units which were 'new-modelled' out of the remnants of the old armies of Essex, Waller and Manchester. Military victory in the First Civil War meant that the English government, whether it be the 'Rump' Parliament, or the Protectorate, enjoyed a proper central control over all its armed forces. The old distinctions between the 'New Model Army' and the various provincial armies raised and maintained by the County associations therefore blurred, and within a very short space of time disappeared altogether.

Instead there was a single standing army supported as and when required by the individual county militias.[5] The true nature of that army is still a matter of considerable debate. Nevertheless it would certainly be fair to say that the wilder radical elements of the original 'New Model' regiments were curbed in the Army Crises of 1647 and 1649. In any case the absorption of provincial regiments into the army, and the wholesale raising of new ones particularly for service in Scotland altered its character entirely.

It was not a Parliamentarian army (far less a Cromwellian one) which invaded Scotland in 1650, suppressed Royalist uprisings, campaigned in Ireland, Flanders and the West Indies, and even served as a rudimentary police force. It was the *English Army*, operating in the service of the state rather than on behalf of any party or faction within it.

It was also this English Army, or at least elements of it led by George Monck which effected the Restoration of King Charles II in 1660. While it might at first sight appear that this was a classic example of a military coup, it was carried out not in defiance of the proper constitutional authority, but rather in the absence of one. Cromwell's Protectorate barely outlasted his own death on 3 September 1658, and it soon became clear that the only authority capable of replacing him was the exiled King. Charles II was often accused of forgetting his old supporters although his means of rewarding them was small enough in all conscience. He did not however forget the part played by the army in his restoration. George Monck was created Earl of Albemarle and named Commander-in-Chief over the heads of many old Cavaliers, while the army survived to form the nucleus of the Royal army and ultimately the British army.

NOTES

1. This gentleman had once simply been known as the Earl of Lindsay (not to be confused with the similarly titled English nobleman), however upon the attainder of the Royalist Ludovick Lindsay, Earl of Crawford, he assumed that more senior title in addition to his own.
2. By this time they had withdrawn into Sutherland. Augustine was last heard of taking ship for Norway. Had he been captured there is little doubt that he would have been hanged.
3. Although the garrison, commanded by George Ogilvy of Barras, was very small, the 'Honours of Scotland' (the Scottish Crown jewels) and a great quantity of state papers had been sent there for safe keeping. The near impregnable castle was blockaded in early August 1651 but bad weather prevented Morgan from bringing up a siege train until the following May. By that time the Honours had been smuggled out and safely hidden elsewhere.
4. Just how notional this conquest was may be gauged by the fact that the Earl

of Atholl's Regiment, a regular formation left behind when the King marched south in 1651, was still operating in Perthshire three years later. It was finally dispersed during Glencairn's Rising.

5. The old term Trained Band seems to have begun falling out of use after the First Civil War. The dislocation caused by the war meant in any case that it was difficult to apply the old property-based assessments efficiently. Instead the term militia seems to have applied to any temporary units raised by the county authorities. How they actually raised them was seemingly something for each county to decide.

Select Bibliography

Adair, John, *Roundhead General: A Military Biography of Sir William Waller*, (1997). *Cheriton 1644* (Kineton 1973)

Atkyns, Richard, *Vindication*, in *Military Memoirs of the Civil War* (ed. Young & Tucker 1967)

Barriffe, William, *Militarie Discipline: or the Young Artilleryman* (6th Edn. 1661)

Boynton, L., *The Elizabethan Militia 1558-1638* (London 1967)

Broxap, Edward, *The Great Civil War in Lancashire* (Manchester 1910)

Bull, S. and Seed, M., *Bloody Preston* (1998)

Bund, J.W. Willis, *The Civil War in Worcestershire* (1905)

Cooke, Dave, *The Forgotten Battle: The Battle of Adwalton Moor* (Heckmondwike 1996)

Cruso, John, *Militarie Instructions for the Cavallrie* (Cambridge 1635)

Dore, R.N., *The Civil Wars in Cheshire* (Chester 1966)

Firth, Charles, *Cromwell's Army* (Oxford 1962)

Firth & Davies, *Regimental History of Cromwell's Army* 2 vols. (Oxford 1940)

Foard, Glenn, *Naseby: The Decisive Campaign* (Guilford 1995)

Furgol, Edward, *A Regimental History of the Covenanting Armies* (Edinburgh 1990)

Gaunt, Peter, *The Cromwellian Gazetteer* (Gloucester 1987)

Haythornthwaite, P., *The English Civil War, 1642-1651* (Poole 1983)

Hopton, Ralph, *Bellum Civile* (Somerset Records Soc. 1902)

Hutton, Ronald, *The Royalist War Effort 1642-1646* (London 1982). *A List of Officers Claiming to the Sixty Thousand Pounds &c Granted by His Sacred Majesty for the Relief of his Truly-Loyal and Indigent Party* (London 1663 – 'Indigent Officers')

Newark on Trent: The Civil War Siegeworks (RCHM 1964)

Newcastle, Margaret, Duchess of, *The Life of . . . William Cavendish, Duke of Newcastle* (ed. Firth, C. 1886)

Newman, Dr Peter, *Royalist Officers in England and Wales 1642-1660* (London 1981). *The Battle of Marston Moor 1644* (Chichester 1981)

Parker, Geoffrey, *The Army of Flanders and the Spanish Road 1567-1659* (Cambridge 1972)

Peachy, S & Prince, L.ECW *Flags & Colours (1) English Foot* (Leigh on Sea 1991)

Peachy & Turton, *Old Robin's Foot: the equipping and campaigns of Essex's Infantry* (Leigh on Sea 1987)

Journal of Prince Rupert's Marches ed. Barrett, J. (Birkenhead 1996)

Reid, Stuart, *The Campaigns of Montrose* (Edinburgh 1990). *Scots Armies of the Civil War* (Leigh on Sea 1990). *Scots Colours*, (Leigh on Sea 1990)

Roberts, Keith, *Soldiers of the English Civil War(1):Infantry* (London 1989). *London & Liberty; Ensigns of the London Trained Bands* (1987)

Roy, Ian, *The Royalist Ordnance Papers* 2 vols (Oxford 1964 & 1975)

Smith & Toynbee, *Leaders of the Civil Wars 1642-1648* (Kineton 1977)

Sprigge, Joshua, *Anglia Rediviva* (1647)

Stevenson, David, *Scottish Covenanters and Irish Confederates* (Belfast 1981)

Symonds, Richard, *Diary* (Leigh on Sea 1989)

Terry, C.S., *The Army of the Covenant* 2 vols. (Scottish History Society 1917). *The Life and Campaigns of Alexander Leslie* (London 1899)

Tincey, John *Soldiers of the English Civil War (2) Cavalry* (London 1990)

Toynbee & Young, *Cropredy Bridge 1644* (Kineton 1970)

Turton, Alan, *The Chief Strength of the Army: Essex's Horse* (Leigh on Sea n.d.)

Vernon, John, *The Young Horseman or the Honest Plain Dealing CAVALIER* (1644)

Walker, Sir Edward, *Historical Discourses upon Several Occasions . . .* (1705)

Wenham, Peter, *The Great and Close Siege of York* 1644 (Kineton 1970)

Woolrych, Austin, *Battles of the English Civil War* (London 1991)

Young, Peter, *Edgehill 1642* (Kineton 1967). *Marston Moor 1644* (Kineton 1970). *Naseby 1645* (London 1985)

Young & Adair, *Hastings to Culloden* (Kineton 1979)

Young & Embleton, *Sieges of the Great Civil War* (London 1978). *The Cavalier Army* (London)

Young & Holmes, *The English Civil War: A Military History of the Three Civil Wars* (London 1974)

Index